Key Issues

LIBERTY

Contemporary Responses to John Stuart Mill

Key Issues

LIBERTY

Contemporary Responses to JOHN STUART MILL

Series Editor

ANDREW PYLE

University of Bristol

THOEMMES PRESS

© Thoemmes Press 1994

Published in 1994 by
Thoemmes Press
85 Park Street
Bristol BS1 5PJ
England

ISBN
Paper : 1 85506 245 3
Cloth : 1 85506 244 5

Liberty: Contemporary Responses to John Stuart Mill
Key Issues No. 1

British Library Cataloguing-in-Publication Data

A catalogue record of this title is available
from the British Library

Printed in Great Britain by Antony Rowe Ltd., Chippenham

CONTENTS

INTRODUCTION
by Andrew Pyle vii

1. THE ATHENÆUM
No. 1635, February 26, 1859, pp. 281–282.
Anonymous 1

2. THE SATURDAY REVIEW
Vol. 7, February 12 and 19, 1859,
pp. 186–187, 213–214.
Anonymous 6

3. FRASER'S MAGAZINE
Vol. 59, 1859, pp. 509–542.
by H. T. Buckle 25

4. THE NATIONAL REVIEW
Vol. 8, 1859, pp. 393–425.
by R. H. Hutton 81

5. THE WESTMINSTER REVIEW
Vol. 73 os (Vol. 17 ns), 1859, pp. 392–426.
by R. Bell 118

6. THE RAMBLER
Vol. 25 os (Vol. 2 3rd series), 1859–1860,
pp. 62–75, 376–385.
by T. Arnold 159

7. BRITISH QUARTERLY REVIEW
Vol. 31, 1860, pp. 173–195.
Anonymous 184

8. BENTLEY'S QUARTERLY REVIEW
Vol. 2, 1860, pp. 434–473.
by R. W. Church 210

9. THE DUBLIN REVIEW
Vol. 13 NS (Vol. 65 OS), July 1869, pp. 62–75.
by E. Lucas 255

10. THE FORTNIGHTLY REVIEW
Vol. 20, 1873, pp. 234–256.
by J. Morley 271

11. BLACKWOOD'S EDINBURGH MAGAZINE
Vol. 114, 1873, pp. 347–362.
by H. Cowell 298

12. THE QUARTERLY REVIEW
Vol. 135, 1873, pp. 178–201.
by J. Wilson 321

13. THE CONTEMPORARY REVIEW
Vol. 36, 1879, pp. 369–397.
by M. Müller 349

14. THE CONTEMPORARY REVIEW
Vol. 37, 1880, pp. 548–564.
by J. T. Mackenzie 386

15. THE NINETEENTH CENTURY
Vol. 13, 1883, pp. 493–508, 653–666.
by L. Stephen 409

The reviews reprinted in this book have been taken from original copies and the different grammatical and stylistic arrangement of each has been preserved.

INTRODUCTION

'The *Liberty* is likely to survive longer than anything else that I have written (with the possible exception of the *Logic*), because the conjunction of her mind with mine has rendered it a kind of philosophic text-book of a single truth, which the changes progressively taking place in modern society tend to bring out in ever greater relief: the importance, to man and society, of a large variety in types of character, and of giving full freedom to human nature to expand itself in innumerable and conflicting directions.'[1]

Mill's *On Liberty* has indeed, as he predicted, outlived most of his other writings, and is still read by every serious student of politics and philosophy.[2] It is studied, however, not as a 'text-book of a single truth', but as a marvellous source-book for the problems facing any attempt to construct a coherent liberal political philosophy. Wherever questions are raised concerning the relation between a society and the individuals that constitute it — eg questions about censorship, marital law, or religious toleration — Mill's name, and his 'simple principle', are certain to be invoked.

Mill claimed, famously, that the only legitimate justification for curtailing the freedom of action of any mature adult was to prevent that person doing harm to others. But what exactly constitutes harm? Can a principled distinction be drawn between acts that are purely 'self-regarding', and acts for which the individual is answerable to Society at large? Must even the opinions of the intolerant be tolerated? What if the majority, in a democratic state, vote for repressive legislation? Wherever one looks in *On Liberty*, one finds problems rather than solutions. All that can be said in Mill's defence is that he faces the real problems, and faces them with courage and integrity.

1 J. S. Mill, *Autobiography*, (London, Penguin Classics, 1989), p. 189. The woman referred to is of course Mill's wife Harriet.

2 For a new edition of *On Liberty*, with a selection of the modern critical literature, see J. Gray and G. W. Smith, editors, *On Liberty in Focus* (London, Routledge, 1991).

In this volume we examine the reactions and responses of Mill's contemporaries to *On Liberty*, from its initial publication in 1859 to the appearance of Leslie Stephen's article, 'On the Suppression of Poisonous Opinions' in 1883. No attempt has been made to include *all* of this literature: a number of minor reviews have simply been excluded without comment.[3] Attention is also confined to Britain, although the reception of Mill's works in Continental Europe and in America would make a fascinating study. What we offer in this volume is the great bulk of the serious literature, from the quality magazines and reviews of Victorian Britain, on a classic work.

Some of Mill's critics focus on issues of perennial philosophical importance: the nature of liberty; individualistic versus organic theories of Society; the vagueness of the harm principle; and the compatibility between liberalism and utilitarianism. Others are more concerned with the affairs of the moment: the position of the established church; the right to publicly teach atheism; the alleged perils of conformism; and the implications of Mill's views for education. It is precisely in this mixture of high philosophy and practical politics that the interest and value of this debate reside. Let us turn first to those critics who are concerned primarily with topical issues, who regard *On Liberty* as, first and foremost, a 'Tract for the Times'.

Political Issues in Victorian Britain.

(a) *The Perils of Conformism.*
Several of the reviewers respond to Mill's warning that the pressures of public opinion could turn Victorian Britain into a nation of dull conformists. For the most part, the critics respond with incredulity and outright denial. The anonymous writer in the *Saturday Review* clearly has considerable respect for Mill, but explicitly dissents from this particular opinion. The *British Quarterly* reviewer goes further: Victorian Britain, he insists, has such a Babel of conflicting opinions that the real danger is anarchy, not conformism.

---

[3]   Omissions include 'Christian Ethics and J. S. Mill', *Dublin University Magazine*, Vol 54, 1859, pp. 387–410, and 'Religious Liberty', *London Quarterly Review*, Vol 16, 1861, pp. 115–145. The former is essentially a defence of Christian ethics against Mill's criticisms in *On Liberty*; the latter is a defence of the right of a Christian state to prohibit atheism.

Writing in *Bentley's Quarterly*, the ecclesiastical historian Richard Church adopts a more considered tone. He gives Mill credit for noticing a danger implicit in the increasing democratization of society: the danger of a sort of uniform 'levelling down'.[4] Nevertheless, Church feels, Victorian Britain is not currently faced with that sort of peril. In a society which derives its history from such diverse sources as Carlyle, Froude, and Buckle, and receives spiritual advice from John Henry Newman, on one side, and his unorthodox brother Frederick, on the other, there is no present reason to fear the paralysing inertia of uniformity. Mill's warnings are, Church insists, mere exaggerations and half-truths.

Even Buckle, although he defends Mill on most points, thinks that his hero has exaggerated the threat of conformism. Only Robert Bell, in his *Westminster* article, seems to share Mill's sense of danger, Mill's feeling that Britain may be lapsing into 'Byzantine' or 'Chinese' inertia. It is striking that Bell associates this danger with the bibliolatry of the Protestant churches. There is, he insists, such a thing as mental slavery: once the values and attitudes of a repressive culture have been internalized, there is no longer any need for the Inquisition or the secret police.

Clearly, Mill's portrait of Victorian Britain was unrecognizable to many of his contemporaries. He takes notice of this fact in his *Autobiography*. Our fears, he remarks, 'might easily have appeared chimerical to those who looked more at present facts than at tendencies . . .'[5] The Victorian period, in his view, was one of instability and transition — hence the multitude of conflicting opinions. But after this transitional period, he predicts, a new orthodoxy will emerge and come to dominate society. The lessons of *On Liberty* will have to be learned over and over again.

(b) *Are Mill's Principles mere Commonplaces?*
Two of the critics enquire, in effect, what all the fuss is about. Mill's liberal principles, they suggest, are mere commonplaces,

---

4   This concern can be traced to de Tocqueville's classic, *De la démocratie en Amerique* (4 vols, Paris, 1835–1840), for which Mill had considerable respect. For an English translation, see *Democracy in America* (2 vols, New York, Vintage Books, 1945).

5   *Autobiography*, (reference 1) p. 190.

already fully acknowledged and honoured in Victorian Britain. The *British Quarterly* reviewer argues that Britain already enjoys complete freedom of speech and civil liberties, at least as far as the criminal law is concerned. That public opinion will 'punish' the holders of offensive opinions — eg by excluding them from polite society — is inevitable and perfectly proper.

Twenty years later, the same objection was raised by the great linguist and orientalist Max Müller. Why, Müller asks, did *On Liberty* appear in Britain, where it was not needed, rather than in Spain or Russia, where it might have done some good? Haven't Mill's goals already been achieved?

Müller's article prompted an immediate reply, in the same journal, the *Contemporary Review*, by James MacKenzie. Müller is advised to get his head out of his Sanskrit tomes and take a look at the newspapers. How can anyone speak of civil liberties where publishers and booksellers can still be prosecuted for producing and selling atheistical books? Worse still, MacKenzie insists, are the 'infamous' Contagious Diseases Acts of the 1860s. Intended to check the spread of sexually transmitted diseases, the acts gave the police the authority to detain women on the street and subject them to compulsory medical examination. They aroused fierce opposition until they were eventually repealed in 1883.[6]

Müller has completely failed, MacKenzie explains, to see some of the radical implications of Mill's principles. To take a crucial example, Mill's claim that no one is entitled to sell him or herself into slavery was *intended* to be applicable to the institution of marriage. Mill's views about marriage and divorce were *far* from having been incorporated into English law in 1880.

(c) *Liberty, Equality, Fraternity.*

While some of Mill's critics sought to portray him as a mere purveyor of platitudes, two other attacks, published in Tory journals in the year of Mill's death (1873), paint a very different picture. Far from harmless platitudes, Mill's principles are, we are told, radical and subversive, posing a threat to the very foundations of social order. Both Cowell (*Blackwood's*) and Wilson (*Quarterly*) regard Mill as a sort of

---

6   For the 'C.D. Acts', see any biography of Gladstone, eg Richard Deacon, *The Private Life of Mr Gladstone*, (London, Muller, 1965), especially Chapter 7.

latter-day Jacobin, intent on tearing up the existing social fabric in the name of wild Utopian dreams.

The barrister Herbert Cowell contrasts Mill unfavourably with his greatest critic James Fitzjames Stephen.[7] While Mill was filing reports in the India office, Cowell reminds us, Stephen was actually working in India, trying to frame a code of laws for that vast, populous, and incredibly diverse country. Stephen's authoritarian views are thus based on first-hand knowledge of men; Mill's ideas are simply derived from books.

Mill's principles, Cowell argues, would justify not only Mormon polygamy but also the excesses of the Hell-Fire Club. (So long as all the members are consenting adults, and there is no pubic nuisance, this conclusion will indeed follow.) But this, Cowell claims, is to open the doors to mere anarchy and license.

John Wilson, in the *Quarterly*, raises similar objections. Mill, he writes, is still tainted by the Benthamite dogma, 'whatever is, is wrong'. He is thus deliberately trying to subvert the established institutions of Victorian Britain, especially of course the family.

Both Cowell and Wilson are particularly scathing about Mill's feminism: both see *The Subjection of Women* as the natural sequel of *On Liberty*. The key idea linking the two books, in the eyes of these Tory critics, is Mill's sustained attempt to overturn all legitimate *authority*, to undermine the hierarchic principle on which Society rests. Subordination to her husband, both men insist, is not slavery for a woman: it is both her natural role, and her best protection against male exploitation. If marriage becomes a sort of contract terminable by either party at will, won't that make women more vulnerable to exploitation rather than less?

(d) *The Right to teach Atheism.*

Were people free, in Victorian Britain, to write, publish, and sell atheistical books and pamphlets? Certainly works such as those of G. J. Holyoake (1817–1906) and Charles Bradlaugh

---

7   James Fitzjames Stephen, *Liberty, Equality, Fraternity*, (2nd edition, London, Smith, Elder & Co, 1874, reprinted Cambridge University Press, 1967). For a modern defence of a similarly conservative position, see Patrick Devlin, *The Enforcement of Morals* (Oxford, Oxford University Press, 1968).

(1833-1891) appeared in print, and were widely read.[8] On the other hand, there was a long history of prosecution, not for atheism as such but usually for *blasphemy*. Opinions, it seems, were free, but some opinions were so offensive to the sensibilities of a Christian nation that they could not be expressed without being regarded as blasphemous, and prosecuted as such.

It was in this context that Mill referred, in *On Liberty*, to the case of Thomas Pooley, convicted at Bodmin Assizes in 1857 on a charge of blasphemy. Had Pooley been imprisoned for atheism — that is, for merely holding or expressing atheistical opinions? Buckle takes up Pooley's case with great vigour, and heaps abuse on the judge, one Justice Coleridge, who had convicted him. Others leap to Coleridge's defence. Pooley's crime, according to the *British Quarterly* reviewer, was not atheism but blasphemy: he deliberately expressed his views in a manner designed to give offence to his Christian neighbours, and was therefore a public nuisance. Wilson, in the *Quarterly*, repeats the same point. But this issue raises a serious problem of interpretation. What is the *proper* place, time, and manner for the expression of atheistical opinions? Is there a form and medium of expression that will *not* count as blasphemy?

Church is very clear on this point. His attitude can be summed up in the classic phrase, 'not in front of the servants'. If an educated man holds atheistic views, and expresses them in private — perhaps over the port, after dinner, to a few friends — that is perfectly proper. But the fabric of Society itself rests on the maintenance of Christian belief among the lower classes: to teach atheism in public is therefore shocking and dangerous.

Church even attempts to defend the administration of religious oaths in the law courts. Mill had claimed that this essentially leaves the atheist with no enforceable legal rights, unless he is prepared to lie! Church struggles to justify the existing practice, but finds it hard to meet Mill's main point: that an atheist who is also a liar may obtain legal redress that an honest atheist cannot obtain.

Edward Lucas, writing in the Roman Catholic *Dublin Review*, goes one step further than the High Anglican Richard Church. If the State rests on divine authority, he argues, then

---

[8]   For British atheism in this period, see David Berman, *History of Atheism in Britain* (Routledge, London, 1988), chapter 10.

an atheist is — and must be treated as — a rebel. On such a view, the State not only may but *must* prosecute atheistic publications, suppress atheists' schools, and so on. This conclusion follows, Lucas argues, from Mill's own utilitarian assumptions, and is perfectly compatible with the harm principle. Who is more harmful to his fellow-citizens than a rebel, whether open or unavowed?

Perennial Philosophical Issues.

(a) *What is Liberty?*

The most fundamental objection, under this heading, comes from Edward Lucas. Mill, he protests, has written a whole book on the subject of liberty, without once stopping to define the term! And this from a man with such a great reputation as a logician!

Is liberty essentially a negative concept — the absence of external constraints of various kinds — or is it something more positive? This question, extensively discussed in our own century,[9] was raised by one of the most perceptive and sympathetic of Mill's critics, John Morley. Mill's thesis seems to be that *positive* liberty (autonomy, self-mastery) is something inherently desirable, and that this autonomy is likely to be fostered by allowing people to develop their own talents and invent their own lifestyles, i.e. by a great measure of *negative* liberty. But this alleged connection can easily be denied.

Mere negative liberty, Cowell insists in *Blackwood's*, is 'a despicable thing', unless an individual is guided by a sense of duty. But how is this sense of duty to be developed and reinforced, if not by means of social pressure? How can the mere absence of external constraints produce anything worthwhile? Mill's Chapter Three emphasises the values of individuality, but will the vigorous, self-willed, autonomous individuals Mill cherishes be produced in the sort of tolerant, even lax, society that he advocates? Is negative liberty either necessary or sufficient for positive liberty? Hutton, Cowell, and Müller all perceive a weakness in Mill's argument at precisely this point.

Only Bell, in his *Westminster* article, actually attempts to meet the fundamental objection of Lucas. Liberty is, he

---

[9] I. Berlin, 'Two Concepts of Liberty', in *Four Essays on Liberty*, (London, Oxford University Press, 1969).

explains, the absence of external obstacles to an organism's *natural* growth and development.[10] To clip the wings of a bird, or to confine the roots of a tree to a small pot, are thus infringements of liberty. But if man is by nature a social animal, as Aristotle taught us long ago, it may be *natural* to us to be educated into a culture — a culture largely shaped and determined by its shared values. In that case, to deprive a child of that background of tradition might count as a violation of his or her liberty! Letting alone might be a terrible injury to a social animal. How we seek to resolve this issue is clearly going to have momentous consequences for our views on education. Of all the critics, only Max Müller sees the fundamental importance of this point.

(b) *Does Society require shared Values?*
The fundamental objection, on this score, is made by Richard Hutton in the unitarian *National Review*. As a unitarian, we might expect Hutton to have some sympathy with Mill's views, but in fact he takes a quite different line. A nation needs, he insists, a shared system of values, extending to such supposedly 'private' matters as gambling and fornication. One can't just say, eg to one's children, 'well, I don't do such things myself, but I don't condemn those who do'. Mill thus presents us with a model of Society that is much too *individualistic* for Hutton's tastes; he seeks to replace it with a more *organic* model.[11] Mill emphasises the freedom of the individual, Hutton objects, but denies the freedom of the nation to develop and grow as a nation. The 'social conscience' must be enlightened, not eliminated, and questions of toleration must be dealt with piecemeal by the enlightened social conscience of the nation.

Several of the critics question the coherence of Mill's views about the rights of the orthodox majority, in a given state, to express their revulsion and outrage at the views or lifestyles of a heterodox minority. The reviewer in the *British Quarterly*, and Wilson in the *Quarterly*, both think that Mill falls into a paradox here: that to protect the freedom of expression of the minority group, he will have to deny the same freedom to the

---

10   To make sense of Mill's position in *On Liberty*, according to Gray, we need to attribute to him a doctrine of individual essences. See *On Liberty in Focus* (reference 2), pp. 190–211.

11   For modern discussions of similar issues, see Stephen Mulhall and Adam Swift, eds. *Liberals and Communitarians* (Blackwell, Oxford, 1992).

majority. Similar objections are raised by Church and Müller.
If each individual believer in a Christian community is allowed
to express his or her abhorrence of atheistical opinions, or
Mormon polygamy, how does this differ from organized
persecution?

In fact, of course, Mill had given considerable attention to
just these difficult questions. No one, he wrote, can compel me
to frequent the society of a man whose lifestyle I abhor, or to
do business with a man whose principles I distrust. The natural
and inevitable expressions of like and dislike, approval and
disapproval, are perfectly unrestricted. All that is excluded is
punishing a person for his or her views. But if all the
inhabitants of a village boycott its atheistical grocer, will he not
feel persecuted? Does it matter whether they do so individually
or collectively? (The effect will be the same: the grocer will go
bankrupt.) Sympathetic critics like Morley and MacKenzie
take up Mill's defence against this line of objection, but it
cannot be claimed that either he or they — or, for that matter,
their twentieth century liberal successors — have resolved all
the problems of principle and application that arise here.

(c) *Self-Regarding Acts and the Harm Principle.*
We may only interfere with an individual's freedom of action,
says Mill, to prevent harm to others. In all purely self-regarding
acts, the individual is sovereign. But what exactly constitutes
harm, as opposed to mere offence? Are there any purely self-
regarding acts? If all my actions affect my fellow citizens, might
it not turn out that my sphere of absolute individual
sovereignty is vanishingly small?

The crucial objection to Mill's harm principle is its apparent
vagueness. The *British Quarterly* reviewer insists that the
distinction between self-regarding and other-regarding actions
is just too vague to do any useful work. The *Athenaeum*
reviewer accepts Mill's principle, but argues that it could be
used to justify repressive legislation, eg laws prohibiting the
sale and consumption of alcohol. Mill clearly thought that an
individual citizen should be at liberty — at least if he has no
overriding duties to others — to squander his wealth and
destroy his health by drinking himself into a stupor every night;
but is it true that such an individual does no harm to others?

Church takes up the same point, but presses it still further.
Since even the opinions of one person have effects on others,

Mill's principle could, he argues, justify censorship. If, for example, religious beliefs are the necessary foundation for moral conduct and political obedience, the militant atheist may be harming his fellow-citizens merely by expressing his views.

This has clearly gone too far. To defend Mill, we need to articulate and defend two crucial distinctions. The first is the distinction between harm and offence. The drunkard reeling back from the pub may be an offensive sight to his teetotal neighbour, but need not actually do him any harm. (The drunkard must, of course, come home quietly!) Likewise the man who wants to eat pork in a Moslem country, a right Mill explicitly defends. As Morley sees, Mill needs a concept of harm that *excludes* what are called, in the modern literature, 'morality-dependent' harms, ie cases where Smith is pained by Jones' violation of Smith's moral code.[12] Problems arise here for many versions of utilitarianism.

The other crucial distinction that Mill needs was pointed out by MacKenzie. The conservative social theorist insists that the drunkard and the fornicator set bad examples, and that the atheist preacher may corrupt the morals of his audience. But, MacKenzie retorts, I may not be blamed for the effects of my teaching or of my example, if those effects are mediated by the free and informed consent of the individuals affected. Such effects, labelled 'dialogue effects' in the recent literature, do not constitute harms.[13]

Clearly, if Mill's distinction between 'self-regarding' and 'other-regarding' acts is to do any work; and if the individual's domain of absolute sovereignty is to have non-zero extension, these two crucial distinctions must be maintained. All my acts affect others, directly or indirectly, but not all such effects on others, however disagreeable or regrettable, count as my *harming* them.

(d) Liberalism and Utilitarianism.

In his review of *On Liberty*, Buckle states bluntly that liberty is something of intrinsic value, something that should not be regarded as a mere means to some further end. Mill would

---

[12]   On the difficult issues that arise here, see Ted Honderich, ' "On Liberty" and Morality-Dependent Harms', *Political Studies*, Vol 30, 1982, pp. 504–514.

[13]   See John Skorupski, *John Stuart Mill*, (London, Routledge, 1989), pp. 369–376.

probably not have agreed. The ultimate justification for the social and political theses of *On Liberty*, he insisted, must be a utilitarian one, with one crucial proviso. In Mill's own words,

> 'I regard utility as the ultimate appeal on all ethical questions; but it must be utility in the largest sense, grounded on the permanent interests of man as a progressive being.'[14]

In other words, the justification of liberal principles must ultimately be a utilitarian one, but may take into account not only immediate pleasures and pains but also long-term effects such as those stemming from the progress of education and the spread of enlightenment.[15] This provides Mill with at least the beginnings of a reply to the obvious objection that utilitarian principles could justify all manner of illiberal measures.

The most forceful and vehement of Mill's contemporary critics, James Fitzjames Stephen, pressed precisely this line of objection. Influenced by Carlyle's pessimistic views of human nature, and drawing on his own experience of a career in the law, Stephen urged — on utilitarian principles — the necessity for authoritarian measures such as censorship. Some of our critics raise similar objections. If the dissemination of an opinion has harmful social consequences, asks Hutton, cannot a utilitarian justify censorship? Lucas, as usual, goes further still. Mill, he notes, explicitly admits the legitimacy of paternalist measures in dealing with children, idiots, and savages. But who is to say that the working classes in Victorian Britain don't fall into the same category? Could we not provide a justification for a sort of benevolent despotism — justified, of course, by the 'improvement' of the subjects, or even of their descendants? Mill's 'permanent interests of man as a progressive being' might seem to license just such measures.

Much of Morley's article in the liberal *Fortnightly*, of which he was then editor, consists in a reply to Fitzjames Stephen. Many of Stephen's criticisms, he shows, rest on misunderstandings of Mill, and fall by the wayside once those misunderstandings are exposed and corrected. More fundamentally, Stephen has failed to realize that *progress* is Mill's creed, and that

14 *On Liberty*, (reference 2) p. 31.

15 For critical discussion of the incompatibility objection, see C. L. Ten, *Mill on Liberty* (Oxford, Clarendon, 1980), and John Gray, *Mill on Liberty: A Defence* (R.K.P., London, 1983).

liberty is to be justified as the best means of furthering the cause of progress. Since Fitzjames Stephen starts with Carlyle's assumption that men are pigs, and has no faith that things will ever be otherwise, it is no wonder that he arrives a political conclusions so diametrically opposed to those of Mill.

The best treatment of the compatibility problem, as applied to the domain of free speech, is that of Fitzjames' brother Leslie Stephen. In his article on 'The Suppression of Poisonous Opinions', he admits that there might be a *prima facie* utilitarian case for suppressing an opinion that is clearly both false and socially harmful. (One might think today of National Front propaganda.) Opinions, however, do not exist in isolation, and cannot be treated as if they were separable atoms. To suppress one opinion (eg Darwin's theory of evolution) might involve suppressing a whole field of enquiry, and this would have overwhelmingly negative long-term consequences. So long as one believes that people are *educable*, one can always oppose a long-term argument against censorship to the superficially appealing short-term arguments for it.

Leslie Stephen goes on, in the second part of his article, to show that, on utilitarian principles, freedom of speech is not always and necessarily a good thing. Only under certain historical circumstances, he argues, will utilitarian principles yield liberal conclusions. *On Liberty* should thus be read, not as a defence of some absolute moral principle, but as a *historical* thesis, to the effect that Victorian Britain is ready for liberalism.

There is a curious coincidence of opinions here between the agnostic Leslie Stephen and the Catholic Thomas Arnold. Convinced that the truth (ie Catholic dogma) is known, Arnold is not prepared to take seriously the sort of mitigated scepticism employed by Mill. When, Arnold asks, are coercive measures justified in our attempts to convert unbelievers or to bring schismatics back to the faith? His answer is extremely simple: such measures are justified when, and only when, they are likely to be effective. So Augustine was right to justify the forcible conversion of the Donatists; the persecution of the Huguenots by Louis XIV counts as a borderline case; but in nineteenth-century Europe such measures would be counterproductive and therefore wrong.

(e) *Politics and Epistemology: The Ethics of Belief.*

Mills' treatment of the freedom of speech, in chapter two of *On Liberty*, often takes on a strongly sceptical tone. To many readers, it seemed as if Mill's defence of toleration and his objections to censorship rested on sceptical views concerning human knowledge.

Lucas, as might be expected, takes issue with Mill at precisely this point. Mill's whole political theory, he objects, rests on 'the old exploded Pyrrhonism'; but attempts to build any sort of superstructure on such insecure foundations are bound to fail.

Others take issue with Mill's apparent views concerning the ethics of belief. On Mill's view, says Arnold, one *should* listen to arguments on all sides in any dispute, and should in particular seek out the arguments of those who disagree with one's own firmest convictions. But this is both impossible and undesirable. The *British Quarterly* reviewer agrees. It may be tyranny to burn an atheistical book, he argues, but it would be worse tyranny to compel Christians to read it.

The crucial objection is that Mill treats human beings as disinterested reasoning machines, with no vital emotional interests at stake in the subject under dispute. But only a Pyrrhonist, argues the *British Quarterly* reviewer, could hear all opinions propounded and attacked with equal equanimity. Mill's creed, says Church, leaves no room for faith, for an emotional commitment to a proposition that goes far beyond its evidential support. But human life, as opposed to mere theorizing, would be impossible without faith.

On this topic, as on others, Morley and Leslie Stephen give a fairer and more sympathetic account of Mill's position. Mill's arguments, Morley insists, do not lead to Pyrrhonism. I may on occasion be entitled to a firm (albeit provisional) confidence that some belief is true, but only if I have impartially studied the arguments and the evidence on both sides. Mill's own presentation of his case, Leslie Stephen explains, is misleading at this point. He makes it look as if toleration is the fruit of scepticism, but that cannot be his considered view. On the contrary: Mill argues for free speech as the best means of discovering the truth. If truth were undiscoverable in principle (that is, if Pyrrhonism were true) this argument would collapse. There would be no reason to assume that an opinion arrived at by a long progress of vigorous and open debate was any more likely to be true than one imposed by an arbitrary authority, or settled on by mere chance.

4. *Notes on the Contributors.*

Only a few of these articles were signed by their authors. Buckle nailed his colours firmly to the mast with his review in *Fraser's Magazine*, but the majority of the earlier reviewers were anonymous — a perfectly normal procedure at the time. As the Victorian era progressed, however, the conventions gradually changed, and it became increasingly common for reviews to be signed. Morley thus signs his *Fortnightly* article, 'The Editor', while the articles by Max Müller, MacKenzie, and Leslie Stephen all bear the authors' names.

With the aid of the *Wellesley Index to Victorian Periodicals*[16] it is possible to identify most of the other contributors to this debate. The names of R. H. Hutton, R. Bell, T. Arnold, R. Church, E. Lucas, H. Cowell, and J. Wilson were all identified by the compilers of the *Wellesley*. Of the longer reviews included in this volume, only the authorship of the *British Quarterly* review remains uncertain.

So who were these men? Some were extremely well-known; others were much more obscure and shadowy figures. In order of their appearance in this volume they were as follows:

Henry Thomas Buckle (1821–1862) was a historian of free-thinking and anti-clerical opinions, whose *History of Civilization* (1857) was widely read in Victorian Britain, although its reputation has suffered since.

Richard Holt Hutton (1826–1897) was a prominent unitarian, educated at University College London and then in Germany. He was a critic, theologian, and editor of the unitarian journals *National Review* and *Prospective Review*.

Robert Bell was educated for the Church of Scotland, but was unable to sign the standards. (This may explain the tone of his attack on Protestant bibliolatry.)

Thomas Arnold (1823–1900), younger brother of Matthew, was a literary historian and a professor of English literature. He was converted to the Roman Catholic church in 1856. (*The Rambler* was of course a Catholic magazine.)

---

[16] *The Wellesley Index to Victorian Periodicals*, 5 volumes, 1966–1989, (University of Toronto Press and Routledge Kegan Paul).

Richard William Church (1815–1890) was a clergyman and a prominent ecclesiastical historian. He was educated at Bristol, then at Oxford, where he came under the influence of J. H. Newman. In 1871 he succeeded Mansel as Dean of St Paul's.

Edward Lucas (1822–1899) was the brother of Frederick Lucas, founder the *The Tablet*, and author, in 1886, of a *Life* of his more celebrated brother.

John Morley (1838–1923) was born in Blackburn, Lancashire, and educated at University College London, then at Oxford. During the 1860s and 1870s he worked as a freelance journalist in London, becoming prominent in liberal political circles as editor of *MacMillans* and the *Fortnightly*. He became M.P. for Newcastle in 1883, and entered the House of Lords as Viscount Morley in 1908.

Herbert Cowell (b 1837) was a barrister and a prolific contributor to the periodical literature, especially on topics connected with Indian legislation.

John Wilson was author of a book entitled *Studies of Modern Mind and Character* (1881). His article in the *Quarterly* reflects the solidly conservative views of that magazine.

Friedrich Max Müller (1823–1900), the famous orientalist and philologist, was born in Dessau, gained his Ph.D. from the University of Leipzig in 1843, and settled in Oxford in 1848, becoming a full professor there in 1854. His many interests included Sanskrit, Comparative Religion, and the complex relations between Language and Thought.

J. T. MacKenzie was perhaps James Thompson MacKenzie (1818–1890), who had a special interest in India and its affairs.

Leslie Stephen (1832–1904) was one of the great men of letters of the Victorian age: critic, philosopher, historian of ideas, editor of *Cornhills Magazine*, and founder of the *Dictionary of National Biography*.

Andrew Pyle
University of Bristol
1993

THE ATHENÆUM
No. 1635, February 26, 1859

On Liberty. By John Stuart Mill. (Parker & Son.)

Mr. Mill appears once more before the world after a period of anxiety followed by sorrow. This work is dedicated to the memory of the wife whom he has lost: to her he attributes all the inspiration, and *part of the authorship*, of all that is best in his writings of many years past.

The subject of the work is *Liberty*: not in the philosophical sense, not in the political sense, but in the social sense. Mr. Mill treats of the conduct of society, the whole, towards its individual parts. He lays down his principle; he enters upon the question of the liberty of thought and discussion; he treats of the value of that individuality which can only exist when the forest allows room for its trees to grow; and he then endeavours to fix the limits of the authority of society over the individual. Nothing more definite than the subject or than the partitions: but the details are rather too much of the essay cast to suit the neatness of the title and the sharpness of the divisions. It would be a great improvement if little side-notes were attached to the paragraphs.

Of the style and the matter, we need only say that it is John Mill all over: and those who do not read large works on logic and political economy, and those — no small number — who cannot realize the individual character of the writer of a review article, even when they know his name, are here presented with a small work, on a subject of universal interest, with the author's characteristics very strongly impressed.

Mr. Mill makes it his principle that the sole end for which mankind are warranted, individually or collectively, in interfering with the liberty of action of any of their number, is *self-protection*. We doubt if any one, in modern times, will venture to dispute the principle. Some will take it as their guiding rule *on principle*: others will aver that, whatever other principles they may also allow to act, there is no proper case of

1

application in which this principle does not *also* apply. Thus those who still think that the honour of God is to be upheld, meaning that their own religious opinions are to be enforced by the State, also maintain that such upholding is necessary to the protection of society.

Of what use then is a principle which everybody grants, and which anybody can turn as he pleases. Of very great use indeed: because it is a true principle and all truths are useful; because it is a sufficient principle, and will do all that is wanted when properly used. That it may be nullified by any one who pleases is no more than must be said of every principle which is to act by conscience, and is to be the rule of the community only so far as it is the sum total of the convictions of the units which make up that community. Nothing is more common than confusion between a rule of law, the penalties of which are to be enforced upon external evidence, and a rule of morals, which is to have its application settled, as it is aptly said, *in foro conscientiæ*. So then, a person will exclaim, I have only to say I believe it to be for the protection of society, and I may do anything that law will let me do. Not a doubt about it — because you may do all that law will let you do without saying anything to anybody: but to whom are you to *say* it? To your own inner self, to which every rule must appeal that cannot be heard before the Queen at Westminster. If you like to say to yourself, Now, my dear fellow, let you and I lie to each other, you can do it. But the truth is, we believe, that people in general stand more in awe of themselves than they know of: they seldom cheat themselves wilfully. Nor need they attempt such fraud, while there are so many easy ways of putting on an inner mask.

Mr. Mill's book is all the more likely to be useful, from the very vagueness of the rule which he is obliged to lay down. Either this or something as vague must be the rule: and nothing but calm discussion, such as ranges opinions against each other without displeasing any prejudice short of rabid feeling, can fix the rule in the minds of men. And Mr. Mill's mode of arguing is pre-eminently of this character. He is always in good humour with the bodies and souls of those whose opinions be condemns: and when, as happens not seldom, he attacks established notions in a manner well calculated to shock those who cannot bear opposition to their fundamental tenets, he never makes the reader feel that himself is looked at. We are much in want, on the subject of society, of that good teaching, meaning that self-teaching, which arises from discussion of the opinions of powerfully thinking men. We are living at a time in which law is invoked on a score of matters which no law can reach. Mr. Mill handles one of the subjects as follows:—

"Under the name of preventing intemperance, the people of one English colony, and of nearly half the United States, have been interdicted by law from making any use whatever of fermented drinks, except for medical purposes: for prohibition of their sale is, in fact, as it is intended to be, prohibition of their use. And though the impracticability of executing the law has caused its repeal in several of the States which had adopted it, including the one from which it derives its name, an attempt has notwithstanding been commenced, and is prosecuted with considerable zeal by many of the professed philanthropists, to agitate for a similar law in this country. The association, or 'Alliance,' as it terms itself, which has been formed for this purpose, has acquired some notoriety through the publicity given to a correspondence between its Secretary and one of the very few English public men who hold that a politician's opinions ought to be founded on principles. Lord Stanley's share in this correspondence is calculated to strengthen the hopes already built on him, by those who know how rare such qualities as are manifested in some of his public appearances, unhappily are among those who figure in political life. The organ of the Alliance, who would 'deeply deplore the recognition of any principle which could be wrested to justify bigotry and persecution,' undertakes to point out the 'broad and impassable barrier' which divides such principles from those of the association. 'All matters relating to thought, opinion, conscience, appear to me,' he says, 'to be without the sphere of legislation; all pertaining to social act, habit, relation, subject only to a discretionary power vested in the State itself, and not in the individual, to be within it.' No mention is made of a third class, different from either of these, viz., acts and habits which are not social, but individual; although it is to this class, surely, that the act of drinking fermented liquors belongs. Selling fermented liquors, however, is trading, and trading is a social act. But the infringement complained of is not on the liberty of the seller, but on that of the buyer and consumer; since the State might just as well

forbid him to drink wine, as purposely make it impossible
for him to obtain it. The Secretary, however, says, 'I claim,
as a citizen, a right to legislate whenever my social rights are
invaded by the social act of another.' And now for the
definition of these 'social rights.' 'If anything invades my
social rights, certainly the traffic in strong drink does. It
destroys my primary right of security, by constantly creating
and stimulating social disorder. It invades my right of
equality, by deriving a profit from the creation of a misery, I
am taxed to support. It impedes my right to free moral and
intellectual development, by surrounding my path with
dangers, and by weakening and demoralizing society, from
which I have a right to claim mutual aid and intercourse.' A
theory of 'social rights,' the like of which probably never
before found its way into distinct language – being nothing
short of this – that it is the absolute social right of every
individual, that every other individual shall act in every
respect exactly as he ought; that whosoever fails thereof in
the smallest particular, violates my social right, and entitles
me to demand from the legislature the removal of the
grievance. So monstrous a principle is far more dangerous
than any single interference with liberty; there is no violation
of liberty which it would not justify; it acknowledges no
right to any freedom whatever, except, perhaps, to that of
holding opinions in secret, without ever disclosing them: for
the moment an opinion which I consider noxious passes any
one's lips it invades all the 'social rights' attributed to me by
the Alliance. The doctrine ascribes to all mankind a vested
interest in each other's moral, intellectual, and even physical
perfection, to be defined by each claimant according to his
own standard."

Here is a good instance of the attempt to do by law what can
only be done, if at all, by the role of society, acting for its own
protection by opinion. But Mr. Mill might have noticed, in
reinforcement of other arguments, that the strange doctrine
attributed to the *Alliance* takes a sanction from the arguments
brought forward in favour of suppression of opinions by law.
There is not a single reason why "dangerous" doctrines should
be prohibited which does not apply with greater force to
dangerous drinks. And the actual evils of the dram-shop,
numerically speaking, far outweigh those of the seditious or

irreligious pamphlet. The friends of the Maine Law would be benefited by Mr. Mill's book on any supposition. Its practised line of argument, and the variety of its cases, would enable them to reinforce every right and true part of their view, and to question all the rest. For, as happens in every public movement, there is a sound part in this same agitation against drunkenness. There are various things which law can do, and ought to do, to discourage the fearful vice to which society at last has opened its eyes. We say this, because we do not believe that the evil, as compared with population, is anything like what it was in the last century: the cheering truth is, that men are better able to see what is passing before them. And by judicious efforts, law being made to do all it can, and opinion and education doing the rest, we trust in the final extirpation of this great national plague. In the mean time, we recommend Mr. Mill's book on Liberty as a sound source of thought.

Mr. Mill on Political Liberty[1]

Mr. Mill is one of the few men who could venture in the present day to publish a treatise, little longer than an ordinary review article, on a subject of first-rate importance, with the certainty of commanding the deepest and most respectful attention from all who have the least title to be considered as serious. It is a significant, and in some respects a rather melancholy fact, that one of our ablest living writers should feel himself called upon, by the course of events, to vindicate doctrines which to so many persons appear to have long since passed from the sphere of discussion into that of action. That Englishmen at the present day should need to be reminded of truths which for the most part they look upon as established beyond the reach of controversy, is, no doubt, humiliating; and when we take into account the tone in which Mr. Mill writes, as well as the subject which he chooses, the impression is considerably deepened. Our agreement with the general tone of the book is so complete, and it coincides so entirely with the temper of mind in respect to political institutions and to customary social law which we have uniformly advocated, that we feel disposed rather to congratulate ourselves on being able to claim the sanction of so great a name for opinions which we have maintained in such various forms, and with reference to so many different subjects, than to praise the wisdom or the truth of the opinions themselves.

Mr. Mill begins by tracing very shortly the growth of the conception of liberty. After showing how it meant, in early times, the possession of immunities on the part of subjects which their rulers were not to be allowed to infringe — and how to this succeeded the theory of a delegation by the nation, to a certain number of agents, of powers to be exercised for the

---

[1] *On Liberty*. By John Stuart Mill. London: John W. Parker and Son, 1859.

common good — he shows how in our own day the process must be carried a step further, and how the rights of individuals must be protected against the oppression of society at large, whether that oppression operates through legal enactments or through prevailing sentiments and general customs:—

> Protection against the tyranny of the magistrate is not enough; there needs protection also against the tyranny of the prevailing opinion and feeling; against the tendency of society to impose, by other means than civil penalties, its own ideas and practices as rules of conduct on those who dissent from them; to fetter the development, and, if possible, prevent the formation of any individuality not in harmony with its ways, and to compel all characters to fashion themselves upon the model of its own.

Hitherto, he proceeds, men have, with scarcely an exception, regulated their legal and social codes by their likings and dislikings. They have made no attempt to lay down principles by which it should be decided what particular acts or classes of acts should be visited with legal or social penalties, but have been actuated on the one side by a dislike of law, and on the other by a contempt for freedom. Mr. Mill's object is to supply such a principle, and he accordingly enunciates it as follows:-

> The sole end for which mankind are warranted individually or collectively in interfering with the liberty of action of any of their number, is self-protection. The only purpose for which power can be rightfully exercised over any member of a civilized community against his will, is to prevent harm to others. His own good, either physical or moral, is not a sufficient warrant. He cannot rightfully be compelled to do or forbear because it will be better for him to do so, because it will make him happier, because in the opinion of others to do so would be wise, or even right.

The appropriate region of human liberty is thus described:—

> It comprises first, the inward domain of consciousness, demanding liberty of conscience in the most comprehensive sense, liberty of thought and feeling, absolute freedom of opinion and sentiment on all subjects, practical or speculative, scientific, moral, or theological. The liberty of expressing and publishing opinions may seem to fall under a

different principle, since it belongs to that part of the conduct of an individual which concerns other people; but being almost of as much importance as the liberty of thought itself, and resting in great part on the same reasons, is practically inseparable from it. Secondly, the principle requires liberty of tastes and pursuits, of framing the plan of our life to suit our own character, of doing as we like, subject to such consequences as may follow without impediment from our fellow-creatures, so long as what we do does not harm them, even though they should think our conduct foolish, perverse, or wrong. Thirdly, from this liberty of each individual, follows the liberty within the same limits of combination among individuals, freedom to unite for any purpose not involving harm to others, the persons combining being supposed to be of full age, and not forced or deceived.

Trite as this doctrine may appear to some persons, Mr. Mill is obviously prompted to assert it by a fear that it is by no means universally accepted in practice, and by a feeling — which we are afraid is but too well grounded — that, notwithstanding our political freedom, many causes are at work which tend to subject us to a tyranny far more searching, infinitely more powerful, and much more difficult to resist, than any which depends on merely material force; for it arises from the gradual destruction of all the peculiarities of individuals, and the general adoption of a sort of commonplace ideal of character, to which every one is forced to conform, by a vast variety of petty sanctions applying with a leaden invariable persistency to all the common actions of life. After pointing out (not with entire accuracy) a few instances in which the law of the land has been made an instrument of affixing not only disgrace, but inconvenience, to the profession of infidel opinions, Mr. Mill describes a symptom of our present national condition which is all the more serious because it requires some attention to detect its existence. This is that "strong permanent leaven of intolerance which at all times abides in the middle classes of this country" — an intolerance which attaches such a stigma to heretical opinions that the profession of opinion here is far less free than it is in many Continental States. In Mr. Mill's energetic language —

Though we do not inflict so much evil on those who think
differently from us as it was formerly our custom to do, it
may be that we do ourselves as much evil as ever by our
treatment of them. Socrates was put to death, but the
Socratic philosophy rose like the sun in heaven, and spread
its illumination over the whole intellectual firmament.
Christians were cast to the lions, but the Christian Church
grew up a stately and spreading tree, overtopping the older
and less vigorous growths, and stifling them by its shade.
Our merely social intolerance kills no one, roots out no
opinions, but induces men to disguise them, or to abstain
from any active effort for their diffusion. With us, heretical
opinions do not perceptibly gain or even lose ground in
each decade or generation. They never blaze out far and
wide, but continue to smoulder in the narrow circles of
thinking and studious persons, among whom they originate, without ever lighting up the general affairs of
mankind with either a true or a deceptive light. . . . A
convenient plan for having peace in the intellectual world,
and keeping all things going on therein very much as they
do already. But the price paid for this sort of intellectual
pacification is the sacrifice of the entire moral courage of
the human mind. A state of things in which a large portion
of the most active and inquiring intellects find it advisable
to keep the genuine principles and grounds of their
convictions within their own breasts, and attempt, in what
they address to the public, to fit as much as they can of
their own conclusions to premises which they have
internally renounced, cannot send forth the open, fearless
characters, and logical consistent intellects who once
adorned the thinking world.

The sort of men who can be looked for under it are
either mere conformers to common place or time-servers
for truth, whose arguments on all great subjects are meant
for their hearers, and are not those which have convinced
themselves. Those who avoid this alternative do so by
narrowing their thoughts and interest to things which can
be spoken of without venturing within the region of
principles — that is, to small practical matters which
would come right of themselves if but the minds of
mankind were strengthened and enlarged, and which will
never be made effectively right until then — while that

which would strengthen and enlarge men's minds, free and daring speculation on the highest subjects, is abandoned.

Apart from the injury which is thus inflicted not only on those who hold unpopular opinions, but on those who would hold them if they gave their minds fair play, the injury inflicted upon persons who fall in with received tenets is perhaps even more important. What is never fairly doubted and fully discussed is not more than half believed. Established opinions lose their vitality, as heretical opinions lose their distinctness; and so we stumble on — "destitute of faith, and terrified at scepticism." If the unpopular opinion is true, to silence its advocates is to stifle truth; if it is false, such conduct prevents the manifestation of its falsehood. If truth is shared, in whatever proportions, between the opinions in and out of possession, the prevention of discussion not only prevents the apportionment of their due to each, but weakens the hold of either party upon that share of truth which rightfully belongs to him.

From the consideration of freedom of thought and discussion, Mr. Mill passes to a subject of which it is impossible to over-rate the importance, especially in a time when it is so frequently overlooked. This is "individuality as one of the elements of well-being." It is, he admits, indispensable to all that men hold dear that restraints should be imposed on individual inclination. In early times, when society was in its infancy, the individual element was too strong for the legal one; but this state of things has long since gone by. Society in our days has got the upper hand, and beliefs and restraints are in all directions asserting a tyrannical superiority over desires and impulses. We are losing sight of the great maxim that "it really is of importance, not only what men do, but also what manner of men they are that do it;" and large masses of people are growing up "incapable of any strong wishes or native pleasures, and generally without either opinions or feelings of their own." It is sad that a man of genius should feel it necessary to show that this is a tremendous misfortune; but it would be impossible to discharge that duty more splendidly than in the following words:—

If there were nothing new to be done, would human intellect cease to be necessary? Would it be a reason why those who do the old things should forget why they are done, and do them like cattle, not like human beings? There is only too great a tendency in the best beliefs and practices to degenerate into the mechanical; and unless there were a succession of persons whose ever-recurring originality prevents the grounds of those beliefs and practices from becoming merely traditional, such dead matter would not resist the smallest shock from anything really alive, and there could be no reason why civilization should not die out, as in the Byzantine Empire.

The necessity for original minds was never greater than it is now, when "masses, that is to say, collective mediocrity," govern the world; for "the initiation of all wise or noble things comes, and must come, from individuals," and the dominant mass ought to wish for, as they can have, no higher glory than that of following with their eyes open that initiative. Mr. Mill does not advocate a system of hero-worship in which the strong man is to force the world to adopt his views. Such a state of things would corrupt the strong, and check the growth of the weak. All that he claims for men of genius is the freedom of asserting their position, and the special duty which he imposes upon them is that of claiming the position to which they are justly entitled, in order that the world may be shaken out of the self-satisfied mediocrity into which it is so much disposed to settle down. Mr. Mill augurs sadly — too sadly, let us hope — of the consequences of "the present low state of the human mind;" but it is right that his warnings should be carefully heeded:-

Already energetic characters on any large scale are becoming merely traditional. There is now scarcely any outlet for energy in this country except business. The energy expended in that may still be regarded as considerable. What little is left from that employment is expended on some hobby which may be a useful, even a philanthropic hobby, but is always some one thing, and generally a thing of small dimensions. The greatness of England is now all collective; individually small, we only appear capable of anything great by our habit of combining, and with this our moral and religious philanthropists are perfectly contented. But it was men of another stamp than this that made England what it has been, and men of another stamp will be needed to prevent its decline.

The Chinese have succeeded beyond all hope in what English philanthropists are so industriously working at — in making a people all alike, all governing their thoughts and conduct by the same maxims and rules — and these are the fruits. The modern *régime* of public opinion is, in an unorganised form, what the Chinese educational and political systems are in an organised; and unless individuality shall be able successfully to assert itself against this yoke, Europe, notwithstanding its noble antecedents and its professed Christianity, will tend to become another China.

We know of nothing in English literature since the Areopagetica more stirring, more noble, better worthy of the most profound and earnest meditation, than these two chapters of Mr. Mill's Essay.

Passing from the subject of Individuality, Mr. Mill attempts to lay down the limits of the authority which society may rightfully exercise over individuals. Though no one who has studied his earlier works with that degree of attention which they demand and deserve can be surprised at the great outburst of feeling which lights up every line of the chapters to which we have already referred, the logical power which is his special characteristic is perhaps better marked in this most difficult inquiry than in any other part of the book. Adopting a classification of moral virtues as social or self-regarding, which, if we are not mistaken, was invented by Bentham, Mr. Mill contends that breaches of the duties arising out of the former are the only proper subjects for punishment, either legal or social; and that breaches of self-regarding duties should, as such, entail no penal consequences whatever, though they may be, and often are, associated with breaches of social duties which do deservedly incur them.

Mr. Mill does not contend that men ought to regard one another from a selfish point of view, as purely isolated beings. No man can cut himself off from his fellows, or ought to wish to do so. Considerations to aid the judgment of another, exhortations to strengthen his will, may be offered to him or even obtruded on him by others — nay, men may go further, and may properly regulate their feelings towards each other according to the manner in which they discharge their self-regarding duties. A man may become an object of contempt; his society may become offensive to others, and he may thus incur much social inconvenience by his faults. Men may lawfully caution their friends against his example or conversation, and they may prefer others to him in optional good offices; but these and similar inconveniences, "which are strictly inseparable from the unfavourable judgment of others, are the only ones to which a person should ever be subjected for that portion of his conduct and character which concerns his own good, but which does not affect the interests of others in their relations with him." Duty to oneself means either prudence, or self-respect, or self-development; and for none of these *per se* is a man accountable to his neighbours. The illustrations given of this principle are characteristically ingenious and complete. Conscientious Mahometans have no right to prevent people from eating pork, though it may be clearly wrong and offensive in the last degree according to their consciences. Sabbatarians have no right to prevent what they call Sabbath-breaking, either by moral or legal penalties. The Maine Liquor Law is given as another instance of the transgression of this principle; and the manner in which Mormonism (of which Mr. Mill strongly disapproves) is treated, both here and in America, as another. We cannot here specify, in sufficient detail to be interesting, the various applications of the principles of the Essay which are worked out in the concluding chapter. They are as valuable and as careful as they might have been expected to be.

We do not propose on the present occasion to enter upon the points on which we are obliged to differ, or to qualify our agreement, with Mr. Mill. Our points of agreement with him are so much more important and numerous that we have preferred to confine ourselves by giving our readers, as well as we could, the substance of the work. We do not think it would have been possible to convey in the same space a greater quantity of matter which is not only valuable, but absolutely vital. This treatise stands out in noble contrast to some of the most popular and most pernicious of our modern heresies. We can imagine no more effective reproof than it conveys to that complacent optimism which takes for granted, that knowledge and civilization have a sort of inherent power of progress which is not only independent of individual efforts, but supersedes the necessity for individual greatness, as if the raiment and the meat had been definitively proved to be superior to the body and the life. Nor is it less important as a protest against that vile indifference to the truth, as compared to the fancied social importance, of a doctrine, which is creeping unperceived into the holiest places, and masquerading under the most venerable disguises, whilst it palsies all that is generous in this life, and substitutes a desperate resolution to believe in the next for any real confidence in either.

It will be some consolation for the changes which have deprived the public of Mr. Mill's official services, if the leisure which he has earned so well continues to be employed so nobly. We hope on a future occasion to recur to the subject of this work, and to state some particulars in which Mr. Mill's arguments do not command our full assent.

THE SATURDAY REVIEW
February 19, 1859

Mr. Mill on Political Liberty
(*Second Notice.*)

We attempted last week to give our readers some account of the contents of Mr. Mill's *Essay on Liberty*. We purpose, on the present occasion, to fulfil the intention which we then expressed of stating some of the points in which we either differ from him, or are obliged to qualify our assent to his opinions. It would be impossible, in the limited space at our command, to attempt even to hint at all the interesting points for discussion suggested by this remarkable book. We will confine ourselves to two points, which are in themselves of great interest, and which will serve to show the character of the difference between Mr. Mill and ourselves.

The general tone of the book is altogether melancholy. It suggests, if it does not quite express, the conviction that the writer's lot is cast in petty times, in which the people are multiplied and the joy not increased, the individual dwindles, and the world is more and more. Quoting M. de Tocqueville's remark, that the existing generation of Frenchmen resemble each other far more than the last, he observes that this is still more true of Englishmen; and he concludes by the eloquent warning, which we quoted last week, that we are in danger, notwithstanding the grandeur of European history and the professed Christianity of Europe, of becoming a second China. Mr. Mill is not likely to be charged with saying rashly that the former times were better than these; and he, if any man, is likely to consider wisely concerning this. We do not in the least deny the dangers which he points out. We think them real and pressing, nor are we prepared to suggest any cure for them; but we also think that these considerations are only a part of the truth, and that Mr. Mill's language does not do justice to the present times. We fully agree with the opinion that the free development of individual differences of character is one of the

15

greatest of all elements of well-being. We also agree that the dumb intolerance of the present day, which acts in private spheres, and is closely allied to and strongly supported by the narrowness and pettiness which are so often associated with schemes of active philanthropy, tends strongly to prevent that development. But we do not think that Mr. Mill quite perceives — he certainly does not point out — what an immense scope for the development of individual character is afforded in one direction by the very social arrangements which appear to forbid it in another; and he seems to us to be distinctly wrong in asserting that, as a matter of fact, originality of character is ceasing to exist.

It is most true that the base instinct of dislike for everything that is not commonplace, which is characteristic of certain classes of society, has erected a code which executes itself with unfailing rigour, though it is altogether disconnected from any sound principles whatever. There is a standard of dress, of manner, of conversation, and of some other things which it is very difficult to transgress without incurring social penalties unpleasant enough to amount, with many persons, to a downright prohibition; and the consequence is, that the external uniformity of all classes of society is probably greater at this moment than it ever was before, and has a constant tendency to increase. It is, however, at least equally true that this code is as narrow in its range as it is arbitrary in its decrees and rigorous in its penalties. In this age of great cities, the isolation of every single person in his own house is as complete as if he lived in the Great Desert. What hat and what coat he shall wear, how far he shall express his opinions in mixed society, and in what manner, is settled for him by an inflexible law; but what he shall read, how he shall think, how he shall educate his children, whether or not he shall have any sort of religious creed, and take part in any kind of public worship, are questions which he is left to settle — not nominally, but practically — for himself. There probably never was a time when men who have any sort of originality or independence of character had it in their power to hold the world at arm's length so cheaply. The quit-rent which they have to pay for these privileges is really not worth a thought. Thou shalt wear chimney-pot hats, thou shalt shave, thou shalt not say to stupid people things that would shock them (or, as another reading has it, though shalt not cast thy pearls before swine) —

these, and a few other observances of the same kind are the only ones which society at large either does or can enforce upon that thoughtful minority whose interests Mr. Mill has very properly so much at heart. As to the degree in which it is true that social intolerance is so powerful as to "induce men to disguise their opinions, and to abstain from any active effort for their diffusion," every one of course must speak from his own experience. We should say that there are large classes of society in which the fact is so. The least educated part of the clergy — for with the minority it is far otherwise — and what is called the religious world, are very intolerant. They are also immensely powerful, and their influence is extending itself widely and deeply amongst the mercantile classes. But we should have thought that this was by no means true of the members of lay professions, or of that part of society which possesses independent fortunes. These classes form an audience large enough to secure a fair hearing to men who maintain social and theological views from which many of them who read with interest the books in which they are promulgated, and associate on friendly terms with their authors, differ very widely indeed. We could mention several books of this character which have entailed no social penalties worth speaking of; but as we have no desire to trespass on private life, we will only refer to the great popularity of Mr. Buckle's *History of Civilization.* In many points it deviates fundamentally and irreconcilably from all the ordinary standards of orthodoxy; and we should certainly have supposed that the tone in which it is written would convey to most readers the notion that the real deviation was even greater than the apparent one.

That men who hold what would be called heretical views abstain from propagating them is a fact which, if true, may be explained on a different ground from that which Mr. Mill assigns. It appears to us to be owing, to an immense extent, to the general course which philosophical and theological controversy has taken in England for some years past. Mr. Mill refers in his Essay with regret to the neglect into which the study of the art of logical controversy has fallen; but surely this is owing, in no small degree, to the fact that a great proportion of the logical battles which once raged so fiercely have been fought out, and have resulted, as such battles always must, in bringing the combatants to antagonistic assertions, the truth of which is matter not of argument, but of evidence. On the great subjects of natural theology, for example, it is surely the case that the argument between the Theist and the Atheist has gone as far as it can be carried. It is a widely-spread opinion that upon either hypothesis an account can be given of all the phenomena of existence, and that the ultimate decision must depend, not on removing misconceptions and exposing contradictions (which is all that logic can do), but on the result of a method in which history and criticism play a very important part, though its nature and limits are ill understood. So, with regard to morals, it is impossible to carry the question between the doctrines of conscience and utility much further. All that remains to be done is to attempt to find some criterion which will decide between two systems equally symmetrical as systems, but equally ill-adapted for the regulation of conduct. No one has yet decided what is the ultimate rule to which the individual conscience must conform; or what is the ultimate sanction of the law that the greatest happiness of the greatest number is to be pursued. Assume the existence of such a rule, or of such a sanction, and the system, which is at present a mere theory, will become a living guide and authority; but the investigation of the propriety of this assumption is obviously a process in which logic plays only a secondary part.

If this is a fair view of the stage at which the great standing controversies of life have at present arrived, it will follow that the absence of distinct enunciation of formal consistent doctrines, whether heterodox or orthodox, is for the present unavoidable. The method of conducting such speculations has not yet been fully investigated, nor have the necessary preparations — historical and critical — for conducting them to any satisfactory result, been completed. This view seems to us to derive force from the consideration that the silence which prevails extends to the advocates as well as to the antagonists of established opinions. Dogmatic defences of them are as rare as dogmatic attacks upon them. If the fear of consequences alone had silenced the minority, the majority might have been expected to triumph over them, but this is not the case. There is as little firing from the walls as from the trenches, but we are strangely mistaken if the Sappers and Miners are not occupied on both sides in a manner which is perhaps all the more effective because it is so quiet. To drop all metaphor, we think that all the modern investigations into natural science, into language, into mythology, into history in all its forms, political, theological, social, legal, and philosophical, have, and are felt to have, relations of the very deepest importance to all the great subjects of human inquiry, and especially to theology and morals. What result they will ultimately bring out no one can predict, but that, when the circuit is once completed, an electric shock of extraordinary power will be communicated in some direction or other, no rational man can doubt. Let any one compare the effect which geological discoveries alone have had on the interpretation of Scripture with that which has been produced by any amount of logic, and he will be in a position to estimate the results which may follow, and that at no very distant time, from inquiries of a similar character. We are for the first time beginning to understand, or at any rate to try to understand, the processes by which society grew up, the order of succession of different views of those legal and social relations which once were grouped together indiscriminately under such phrases as the social contract and the law of nature, the real character of early mythology, the sources from which it is derived, and the tendencies of the human mind which it represents — such, for example, as the state of feeling which produces such apparently monstrous creeds as Buddhism and Brahminism. We are also receiving new information every day on physiology, on the regularity or quasi-regularity which pervades large departments of human action which appear at first sight to be capricious, and on many other kindred subjects. Mere logical controversy at such a time would be out of place. It will begin again when any one possessed of adequate power of understanding and of moral and intellectual courage attempts the gigantic task of combining into one focus the scattered rays of light emitted from these various subjects, and of directing them upon the great practical questions by which human action is guided and human character formed.

Mr. Mill would say that our existing state is such that there is no probability that such a person will arise amongst us. We do not venture to prophesy, but we have a higher opinion of the level at which intelligence and originality stand in the intellectual classes of this country. To deny that there may be now living amongst us some eight or ten men of the first order, of whom two or three may ultimately be actually what they are potentially, would surely be rash. That we cannot lay our fingers upon them at the present moment proves nothing at all. We can only argue as to the probable greatness of the exceptions from the stature of ordinary people. It is that stature which Mr. Mill (himself a sort of giant) rather unfairly looks down upon. He is not to be told that all the human faculties develope themselves *pari passu*. What is genius in one man in a million is, in the rank and file of society, vigorous, lively talent — combined with the habit of looking at things with your own eyes, and drawing your own conclusions. Is this state of mind rare amongst us? Do ordinary Englishmen resemble each other every day more and more closely? Surely, all the standing oppositions of life may still be traced in our art, in our literature, in our politics, in our theology, even though they may not be represented by men of great genius. Surely, if any one will run over in his mind the names of ten or twelve of his more immediate friends, he will arrive at the conclusion that they differ from each other as radically as the ash, the oak, the birch, and the elm, though it may be that just at present the wind is not rubbing their branches together as it does occasionally. What nobler proof could any nation have given of the qualities of its commonplace members than was given by the Indian Mutiny? Hundreds of men and women thrown on their own unassisted resources to fight for their lives at a moment's notice, displayed a degree of individual resource and energy, combined with an unflinching reliance, not on each other primarily, but on themselves, which cannot be paralleled from the history of any other time or country. People who, at any common English dinner-table, or on the platform of some local Missionary Society, would have drawled out the dreariest of all incoherent twaddle, and have impressed Mr. Mill with the notion that they were not only on their way to an intellectual China, but had absolutely reached it, and given themselves over to spiritual pigtails, started into heroes at the approach of real danger, took its measure with the clearest and most original intelligence, and met, and generally conquered it with that desperate courage which is the great constituent element of individuality.

Another point in Mr. Mill's book in which we think he does injustice to his countrymen is in his estimate of the causes of the want of originality which, as he says, is spreading amongst us. After describing, with great power, the formation of a conventional character, he asks:—

Now, is this or is it not the desirable condition of human nature?

It is so on the Calvinistic theory. According to that theory, the one great offence of man is Self-will. All the good of which humanity is capable is comprised in Obedience. You have no choice; thus you must do, and not otherwise. "Whatever is not a duty is a sin." Human nature being radically corrupt, there is no redemption for any one till human nature is killed within him. To one holding this theory of life, crushing out any of the human faculties, capacities, and susceptibilities is no evil; man needs no capacity but that of surrendering himself to the will of God; and if he uses any of his faculties for any other purpose but to do that supposed will more effectually, he is better without them. That is the theory of Calvinism, and it is held, in a mitigated form, by many who do not consider themselves Calvinists, the mitigation consisting in giving a less ascetic interpretation to the alleged will of God, asserting it to be his will that mankind should gratify some of their inclinations, of course not in a manner they themselves prefer, but in a way of obedience, that is, in a way prescribed to them by authority, and, therefore, by the necessary conditions of the case, the same for all.

No one will accuse us of an undue partiality for Calvinism, but we think Mr. Mill misapprehends its whole scope. We will not quarrel about the word, which appears to us to be used somewhat vaguely; but we say that the belief that to obey God's will in every action of life is the highest aim of human existence, far from being a slavish one, is the noblest conception of life that any mortal creature can form. So far from crushing the faculties and susceptibilities, it is the best of all means of developing them to the highest pitch of excellence and glory of which they are capable. No one will accuse Mr. Mill of believing that the desirable position for man is that of living exactly as his inclinations prompt him from time to time, without reference to any general principle whatever. A man who lives to develope his own faculties, or to benefit his race or nation, subordinates his temporary inclinations to those ends, and raises and purifies his character by doing so. Self-control is, indeed, the highest and most distinctly human function of life, and differs as widely as possible from a slavish mechanical submission to superior force. Willing obedience enforced on oneself at all risks, and in the face of any amount of dislike, is the greatest of all agents in ennobling and developing the character, whether it is rendered to a principle or to a person; for it implies action, and action of the most unremitting and various kinds. Is a dog a worse dog for obeying a good master? Is a wife the less womanly for obeying a good husband? If not, is man less manly in obeying God? The iron does not obey the blacksmith, nor does a slave under the fear of the lash, in the proper sense of the word, obey his master. He rebels against him whilst he yields to him. What all Christians understand by obeying God's will is, entering into and adopting God's plans and purposes as the rule of life, and acting up to them in every particular. "Love is the fulfilling of the law." Mere acquiescence and submission is quite another thing. Almost all Christians, at least in Western Europe, have always understood the plan of God respecting them, which they were thus to obey, to involve the diligent cultivation of various parts of their nature; and, in point of fact, the extreme vivacity and individuality of much of the history of modern Europe are derived from this very obedience which appears to Mr. Mill so slavish. The Crusaders were trying to obey God when they invaded Palestine; and so were many of the Popes when they asserted, and of the feudal kings when they denied, the right of the Church to temporal supremacy. Luther, Cromwell, Queen Elizabeth, and many others, considered obedience to God as the mainspring of their lives. How far they rightly apprehended God's will is quite another question; but it is too plain for argument that obedience to God was in them an active and not a passive, a developing, and not a crushing sentiment. Indeed, the very parts of history in which great men were greatest, and in which individual energy was most highly developed, are just those periods at which the sentiment of obeying God was most powerful. Calvinism is notoriously the creed of the most vigorous and least submissive nations in the world. A theory must be strangely wrong which proves that the Scotch in the seventeenth century ought to have been a slavish pusillanimous people, with no marked characters amongst them.

It is of the essence of Calvinism, as Mr. Mill uses the word, to recognise special talents and faculties as good and perfect gifts given by God to be used and honoured by the use accordingly. Surely such a belief supplies the most effective means for developing individuality. It is only when it is perverted that it can crush the mind. That human nature is corrupt — *i.e.*, that men have a natural tendency to do wrong, or (which is the same thing) a natural incapacity to do right — is a fact which every system of morality must recognise in some form or other. That there is any element of human nature which must be radically exterminated is no part of what Mr. Mill calls the Calvinistic doctrine. We full admit that Calvinists, as well as other people, have often entertained very wrong notions as to what God's will is, and that they have frequently depicted it in such a light as to make it almost indistinguishable from the will of the Devil. Of course, to obey such a will as that is a dreadful thing; but even in that case, the result would be to develope the character (though in a very unpleasant direction), and not to crush it. A man who tyrannizes over himself, crushes his own affections, and destroys his own sensibility because he believes it to be God's will that he should do so, has done what is very wrong and very foolish, and has experienced what may almost be called blasphemous feelings; but when all is done, he has developed himself in a certain direction. His will is strengthened and not destroyed. He has a fair chance of becoming a sort of devil, but is in very little danger of being a mere commonplace man. We have little doubt that, if it were possible to effect a detailed comparison between families in which what Mr. Mill describes as "Calvinism" does and does not prevail, it would be found that, *Cæteris paribus*, the former had a larger share of originality of character than the latter. If we are right in considering the principle of obedience to be an active and not a passive one, this might have been expected.

The real sources of the prevalence of the weak, slight, ineffectual type of character which is such a grievance to Mr. Mill, appear to us to be quite unrelated to religious principle. Small French shopkeepers are, to say the least, as feeble a folk as any class of Englishmen, and their worst enemies would not accuse them of having been degraded by Calvinism. The real cause, or at least one great cause, is undoubtedly to be found in the prevalence of small prosaic occupations, which engross the attention without developing the intellectual or moral powers of those who pursue them. How can he be wise whose talk is of oxen? And if oxen, which are at any rate living creatures, with dispositions, wills, health, and other individual peculiarities, do not afford sufficient occupation to the mind to develop its

higher powers, how can the sale of pastry, the concoction of
hair-dyes and perfumes, and a hundred other petty occupations
of the same sort, with their small vicissitudes and trifling
successes, make men and women of those who pass their life in
them? When we remember that the class occupied in these
trivial pursuits is at present one of the most numerous, most
increasing, and most influential in the country — that men who
represent its level of education and knowledge make its
inclinations, the weakly propensities which would be its
passions it if had any, and the minutiæ of its daily life, the
subjects of photographic descriptions — and that literature of
this kind, which never rises above grotesqueness, and never
touches the great interests of life in any other temper than that
of Thersites, is the principal food of what many people call
their minds — we need not wonder that herds of wretched
dwarfs are growing up amongst us who are the natural prey of
intolerant bigots, and the natural enemies of all that looks
unusual to narrow minds coddled into imbecility by every
influence which can convert the strong wine of our native
English character into a wretched mixture less unworthy of the
title of *eau sucrée* than of any other.

FRASER'S MAGAZINE
Vol. LIX, No. CCCLIII, May, 1859

Mill on Liberty[1]
by Henry Thomas Buckle

If a jury of the greatest European thinkers were to be impannelled, and were directed to declare by their verdict whom among our living writers, had done most for the advance of knowledge, they could hardly hesitate in pronouncing the name of John Stuart Mill. Nor can we doubt that posterity would ratify their decision. No other man has dealt with so many problems of equal importance, and yet of equal complexity. The questions which he has investigated concern, on the one hand, the practical interests of every member of society, and, on the other hand, the subtlest and most hidden operations of the human mind. Although he touches the surface, he also penetrates the centre. Between those extremes, lie innumerable subjects which he has explored, always with great ability, often with signal success. On these topics, whether practical or speculative, his authority is constantly evoked; and his conclusions are adopted by many who are unable to follow the arguments by which the conclusions are justified. Other men we have, remarkable for their depth of thought; and others again who are remarkable for the utility of their suggestions. But the peculiarity of Mr. Mill is, that both these qualities are more effectively combined by him than by any one else of the present day. Hence it is, that he is as skilful in tracing the operation of general causes, as in foreseeing the result of particular measures. And hence, too, his influence is far greater than would otherwise be possible; since he not only appeals to a wider range of interests than any living writer can do, but by his mastery over special and practical details he is

---

[1] *On Liberty.* By John Stuart Mill. London: John W. Parker and Son, West Strand. 1859.

able to show that principles, however refined they appear, and however far removed from ordinary apprehension, may be enforced, without so dangerous a disturbance of social arrangements, and without so great a sacrifice of existing institutions, as might at first sight be supposed. By this means he has often disarmed hostility, and has induced practical men to accept conclusions on practical grounds, to which no force of scientific argument and no amount of scientific proof would have persuaded them to yield. Securing by one process the assent of speculative thinkers, and securing by another process the assent of working politicians, he operates on the two extremes of life, and exhibits the singular spectacle of one of the most daring and original philosophers in Europe, winning the applause of not a few mere legislators and statesmen who are indifferent to his higher generalizations, and who, confining themselves to their own craft, are incapable of soaring beyond the safe and limited routine of ordinary experience.

This has increased his influence in more ways than one. For, it is extremely rare to meet with a man who excels both in practice and in speculation; and it is by no means common to meet with one who desires to do so. Between these two forms of excellence, there is not only a difference, there is also an opposition. Practice aims at what is immediate; speculation at what is remote. The first investigates small and special causes; the other investigates large and general causes. In practical life the wisest and soundest men avoid speculation, and ensure success because by limiting their range they increase the tenacity with which they grasp events; while in speculative life the course is exactly the reverse, since in that department the greater the range the greater the command, and the object of the philosopher is to have as large a generalization as possible; in other words, to rise as high as he can above the phenomena with which he is concerned. The truth I apprehend to be that the immediate effect of any act is usually determined by causes peculiar to that act, and which, as it were, lie within it; while the remote effect of the same act is governed by causes lying out of the act; that is, by the general condition of the surrounding circumstances. Special causes produce their effect quickly; but, to bring general causes into play, we require not only width of surface but also length of time. If, for instance, a man living under a cruel despotism were to inflict a fatal blow upon the despot, the immediate result — namely, the death of the tyrant

— would be caused solely by circumstances peculiar to the action, such as the sharpness of the weapon, the precision of the aim, and the part that was wounded. But the remote result — that is, the removal, not of the despot but of the despotism — would be governed by circumstances external to the particular act, and would depend upon whether or not the country was fit for liberty, since if the country were unfit, another despot would be sure to arise and another despotism be established. To a philosophic mind the actions of an individual count for little; to a practical mind they are everything. Whoever is accustomed to generalize, smiles within himself when he hears that Luther brought about the Reformation; that Bacon overthrew the ancient philosophy; that William III, saved our liberties; that Romilly humanized our penal code; that Clarkson and Wilberforce destroyed slavery; and that Grey and Brougham gave us Reform. He smiles at such assertions, because he knows full well that such men, useful as they were, are only to be regarded as tools by which that work was done which the force and accumulation of preceding circumstances had determined should be done. They were good instruments; sharp and serviceable instruments, but nothing more. Not only are individuals, in the great average of affairs, inoperative for good; they are also, happily for mankind, inoperative for evil. Nero and Domitian caused enormous mischief, but every trace of it has now disappeared. The occurrences which contemporaries think to be of the greatest importance, and which in point of fact for a short time are so, invariably turn out in the long run to be the least important of all. They are like meteors which dazzle the vulgar by their brilliancy, and then pass away, leaving no mark behind. Well, therefore, and in the highest spirit of philosophy, did Montesquieu say that the Roman Republic was overthrown, not, as is commonly supposed, by the ambition of Cæsar and Pompey, but by that state of things which made the success of their ambition possible. And so indeed it was. Events which had been long accumulating and had come from afar, pressed on and thickened until their united force was irresistible, and the Republic grew ripe for destruction. It decayed, it tottered, it was sapped to its foundation; and then, when all was ready and it was nodding to its fall, Cæsar and Pompey stepped forward, and because they dealt the last blow, we, forsooth, are expected to believe that they produced a catastrophe which the course of affairs had made inevitable before they were born.

The great majority of men will, however, always cling to Cæsar and Pompey; that is to say, they will prefer the study of proximate causes to the study of remove ones. This is connected with another and more fundamental distinction, by virtue of which, life is regarded by practical minds as an art, by speculative minds as a science. And we find every civilized nation divided into two classes corresponding with these two divisions. We find one class investigating affairs with a view to what is most special; the other investigating them with a view to what is most general. This antagonism is essential, and lies in the nature of things. Indeed, it is so clearly marked, that except in minds not only of very great power, but of a peculiar kind of power, it is impossible to reconcile the two methods; it is impossible for any but a most remarkable man to have them both. Many even of the greatest thinkers have been but too notorious for an ignorance of ordinary affairs, and for an inattention to practical every-day interests. While studying the science of life, they neglect the art of living. This is because such men, notwithstanding their genius, are essentially one-sided and narrow, being, unhappily for themselves, unable or unaccustomed to note the operation of special and proximate causes. Dealing with the remote and the universal, they omit the immediate and the contingent. They sacrifice the actual to the ideal. To their view, all phenomena are suggestive of science, that is of what may be known; while to the opposite view, the same phenomena are suggestive of art, that is of what may be done. A perfect intellect would unite both views, and assign to each its relative importance; but such a feat is of the greatest possible rarity. It may in fact be doubted if more than one instance is recorded of its being performed without a single failure. That instance, I need hardly say, is Shakspeare. No other mind has thoroughly interwoven the remote with the proximate, the general with the special, the abstract with the concrete. No other mind has so completely incorporated the speculations of the highest philosophy with the meanest details of the lowest life. Shakspeare mastered both extremes, and covered all the intermediate field. He knew both man and men. He thought as deeply as Plato or Kant. He observed as closely as Dickens or Thackeray.

Of whom else can this be said? Other philosophers have, for

the most part overlooked the surface in their haste to reach the summit. Hence the anomaly of many of the most profound thinkers having been ignorant of what it was shameful for them not to know, and having been unable to manage with success even their own affairs. The sort of advice they would give to others may be easily imagined. It is no exaggeration to say that if, in any age of the world, one half of the suggestions made by the ablest men had been adopted, that age would have been thrown into the rankest confusion. Plato was the deepest thinker of antiquity; and yet the proposals which he makes in his *Republic*, and in his *Treatise on Laws*, are so absurd that they can hardly be read without laughter. Aristotle, little inferior to Plato in depth, and much his superior in comprehensiveness, desired, on purely speculative grounds, that no one should give or receive interest for the use of money: an idea which if it had been put into execution would have produced the most mischievous results, would have stopped the accumulation of wealth, and thereby have postponed for an indefinite period the civilization of the world. In modern as well as in ancient times, systems of philosophy have been raised which involve assumptions, and seek to compel consequences, incompatible with the practical interests of society. The Germans are the most profound philosophers in Europe, and it is precisely in their country that this tendency is most apparent. Comte, the most comprehensive thinker France has produced since Descartes, did in his last work deliberately advocate, and wish to organize, a scheme of polity so monstrously and obviously impracticable, that if it were translated into English the plain men of our island would lift their eyes in astonishment, and would most likely suggest that the author should for his own sake be immediately confined. Not that we need pride ourselves too much on these matters. If a catalogue were to be drawn up of the practical suggestions made by our greatest thinkers, it would be impossible to conceive a document more damaging to the reputation of the speculative classes. Those classes are always before the age in their theories, and behind the age in their practice. It is not, therefore, strange that Frederick the Great, who perhaps had a more intimate and personal knowledge of them than any other prince equally powerful, and who moreover admired them, courted them, and, as an author, to a certain slight degree belonged to them, should have recorded his opinion of their practical incapacity in the strongest terms he could find. 'If,' he is reported to have said, 'if I wanted to ruin one of my provinces, I would make over its government to the philosophers.'

This neglect of the surface of things is, moreover, exhibited in the peculiar absence of mind for which many philosophers have been remarkable. Newton was so oblivious of what was actually passing, that he frequently overlooked or forgot the most necessary transactions, was not sure whether he had dined, and would leave his own house half naked, appearing in that state in the streets, because he fancied all the while that he was fully dressed. Many admire this as the simplicity of genius. I see nothing in it but an unhappy and calamitous principle of the construction of the human mind, which prevents nearly all men from successfully dealing both with the remote and the immediate. They who are little occupied with either, may, by virtue of the smallness of their ambition, somewhat succeed in both. This is the reward of their mediocrity, and they may well be satisfied with it. Dividing such energy as they possess, they unite a little speculation with a little business; a little science with a little art. But in the most eminent and vigorous characters, we find, with extremely rare exceptions, that excellence on one side excludes excellence on the other. Here the perfection of theory, there the perfection of practice; and between the two a gulf which few indeed can bridge. Another and still more remarkable instance of this unfortunate peculiarity of our nature is supplied by the career of Bacon, who, though he boasted that he made philosophy practical and forced her to dwell among men, was himself so unpractical that he would not deal with events as they successively arose. Yet, he had everything in his favour. To genius of the highest order he added eloquence, wit, and industry. He had good connexions, influential friends, a supple address, an obsequious and somewhat fawning disposition. He had seen life under many aspects, he had mixed with various classes, he had abundant experience, and still he was unable to turn these treasures to practical account. Putting him aside as a philosopher, and taking him merely as a man of action, his conduct was a series of blunders. Whatever he most desired, in that did he most fail. One of his darling objects was the attainment of popularity, in the pursuit of which he, on two memorable occasions, grievously offended the Court from which he sought promotion. So unskilful, however, were his combinations, that in the prosecution of Essex, which was by far the most unpopular act in the reign of Elizabeth, he played a part not only conspicuous and discreditable, but grossly impolitic. Essex, who was a high-spirited and generous man, was beloved by all classes, and nothing could be more certain than that the violence Bacon displayed against him would recoil on its author. It was also well known that Essex was the intimate friend of Bacon, had exerted himself in every way for him, and had even presented him with a valuable estate. For a man to prosecute his benefactor, to heap invectives upon him at his trial, and having hunted him to the death, publish a libel insulting his memory, was a folly as well as an outrage, and is one of many proofs that in practical matters the judgment of Bacon was unsound. Ingratitude aggravated by cruelty must, if it is generally known, always be a blunder as well as a crime, because it wounds the deepest and most universal feelings of our common nature. However vicious a man may be, he will never be guilty of such an act unless he is foolish as well as vicious. But the philosopher could not foresee those immediate consequences which a plain man would have easily discerned. The truth is, that while the speculations of Bacon were full of wisdom, his acts were full of folly. He was anxious to build up a fortune, and he did what many persons have done both before and since: he availed himself of his judicial position to take bribes from suitors in his court. But here again, his operations were so clumsy, that he committed the enormous oversight of accepting bribes from men against whom he afterwards decided. He, therefore, deliberately put himself in the power of those whom he deliberately injured. This was not only because he was greedy after wealth, but also because he was injudiciously greedy. The error was in the head as much as in the heart. Besides being a corrupt judge, he was likewise a bad calculator. The consequence was that he was detected, and being detected was ruined. When his fame was at its height, when enjoyments of every kind were thickening and clustering around him, the cup of pleasure was dashed from his lips because he quaffed it too eagerly. To say that he fell merely because he was unprincipled, is preposterous, for many men are unprincipled all their lives and never fall at all. Why it is that bad men sometimes flourish, and how such apparent injustice is remedied, is a mysterious question which this is not the place for discussing; but the fact is indubitable. In practical life men fail, partly because they aim at unwise objects, but chiefly because they have not acquired the art of adapting their means to their end. This was the case with Bacon. In ordinary matters he was triumphed over and defeated by nearly every one with whom he came into contact. His dependents cheated him with impunity; and notwithstanding the large sums he received he was constantly in debt, so that even while his peculations were going on he derived little benefit from them. Though, as a judge, he stole the property of others, he did not know how to steal so as to escape detection, and he did not know how to keep what he had stolen. The mighty thinker was, in practice, an arrant trifler. He always neglected the immediate and the pressing. This was curiously exemplified in the last scene of his life. In some of his generalizations respecting putrefaction, it occurred to him that the process might be stopped by snow. He arrived at conclusions like a cautious and large-minded philosopher: he tried them with the rashness and precipitancy of a child. With an absence of common sense which would be incredible if it were not well attested, he rushed out of his coach on a very cold day, and, neglecting every precaution, stood shivering in the air while he stuffed a fowl with snow, risking a life invaluable to mankind, for the sake of doing what any serving man could have done just as well. It did not need the intellect of a Bacon to foresee the result. Before he had finished what he was about, he felt suddenly chilled: he become so ill as to be unable to return to his own house, and his worn-out frame giving way, he gradually sank and died a week after his first seizure.

Such events are very sad, but they are also very instructive. Some, I know, class them under the head of martyrdom for science: to me, they seem the penalty of folly. It is at all events certain that in the lives of great thinkers they are painfully abundant. It is but too true that many men of the highest power have, by neglecting the study of proximate causes, shortened their career, diminished their usefulness, and, bringing themselves to a premature old age, have deprived mankind of their services just at the time when their experience was most advanced, and their intellect most matured. Others, again who have stopped short of this, have by their own imprudence become involved in embarrassments of every kind, taking no heed of the morrow, wasting their resources, squandering their substance, and incurring debts which they were unable to pay.

This is the result less of vice than of thoughtlessness. Vice is often cunning and wary; but thoughtlessness is always profuse and reckless. And so marked is the tendency, that 'Genius struggling with difficulties' has grown into a proverb. Unhappily, genius has, in an immense majority of cases, created its own difficulties. The consequence is, that not only mere men of the world, but men of sound, useful understandings, do, for the most part, look upon genius as some strange and erratic quality, beautiful indeed to see, but dangerous to possess: a sparkling fire which consumes while it lightens. They regard it with curiosity, perhaps even with interest; but they shake their heads; they regret that men who are so clever should have so little sense; and, pluming themselves on their own superior sagacity, they complacently remind each other that great wit is generally allied to madness. Who can wonder that this should be? Look at what has occurred in these islands alone, during so short a period as three generations. Look at the lives of Fielding, Goldsmith, Smollett, Savage, Shenstone, Budgell, Charnock, Churchill, Chatterton, Derrick, Parnell, Somerville, Whitehead, Coombe, Day, Gilbert Stuart, Ockley, Oldys, Boyse, Hasted, Smart, Thomson, Grose, Dawes, Barker, Harwood, Porson, Thirlby, Baron, Barry, Coleridge, Fearne, Walter Scott, Byron, Burns, Moore, and Campbell. Here you have men of every sort of ability, distinguished by every variety of imprudence. What does it all mean? Why is it what they who might have been the salt of the earth, and whom we should have been proud to take as our guides, are now pointed at by every blockhead as proofs of the inability of genius to grapple with the realities of life? Why is it that against these, and their fellows, each puny whipster can draw his sword, and dullards vent their naughty spite? That little men should jeer at great ones, is natural; that they should have reason to jeer at them is shameful. Yet, this must always be the case as long as the present standard of action exists. As long as such expressions as 'the infirmities of genius' form an essential part of our language — as long as we are constantly reminded that genius is naturally simple, guileless, and unversed in the ways of the world — as long as notions of patronizing and protecting it continue — as long as men of letters are regarded with pitying wonder, as strange creatures from whom a certain amount of imprudence must be expected, and in whom it may be tolerated — as long as among them extravagance is called generosity, and economy called meanness — as long as these things happen, so long will the evils that correspond to them endure, and so long will the highest class of minds lose much of their legitimate influence. In the same way, while it is believed that authors must, as a body, be heedless and improvident, it will likewise be believed that for them there must be pensions and subscriptions; that to them Government and society should be bountiful; and that, on their behalf, institutions should be erected to provide for necessities which it was their own business to have foreseen, but which they, engaged in the arduous employment of writing books, could not be expected to attend to. Their minds are so weak and sickly, so unfit for the rough usages of life, that they must be guarded against the consequences of their own actions. The feebleness of their understandings makes such precautions necessary. There must be hospitals for the intellect, as well as for the body; asylums where these poor, timid creatures may find refuge, and may escape from calamities which their confiding innocence prevented them from anticipating. These are the miserable delusions which still prevail. These are the wretched infatuations by which the strength and majesty of the literary character are impaired. In England there is, I rejoice to say, a more manly and sturdy feeling on these subjects, than in any other part of Europe; but even in England literary men do not sufficiently appreciate the true dignity of their profession; nor do they sufficiently understand that the foundation of all real grandeur is a spirit of proud and lofty independence. In other countries, the state of opinion is most degrading. In other countries, to have a pension is a mark of honour, and to beg for money is a proof of spirit. Eminent men are turned into hirelings, receive eleemosynary aid, and raise a clamour if the aid is not forthcoming. They snatch at every advantage, and accept even titles and decorations from the first foolish prince who is willing to bestow them. They make constant demands on the public purse, and then they wonder that the public respects them so little. In France, in particular, we have within the last year seen one of the most brilliant writers of the age, who had realized immense sums by his works, and who with common prudence ought to have amassed a large fortune, coming forward as a mendicant, avowing in the face of Europe that he had squandered what he had earned, and soliciting, not only friends, but even strangers, to make up the deficiency.

And this was done without a blush, without any sense of the ignominy of the proceeding, but rather with a parade of glorying in it. In a merchant, or a tradesman, such a confession of recklessness would have been considered disgraceful; and why are men of genius to have a lower code than merchants or tradesmen? Whence comes this confusion of the first principles of justice? By what train of reasoning, or rather, by what process of sophistry, are we to infer, that when men of industry are improvident they shall be ruined, but that when men of letters are improvident they shall be rewarded? How long will this invidious distinction be tolerated? How long will such scandals last? How long will those who profess to be the teachers of mankind behave like children, and submit to be treated as the only class who are deficient in foresight, in circumspection, in economy, and in all those sober and practical virtues which form the character of a good and useful citizen? Nearly every one who cultivates literature as a profession, can gain by it an honest livelihood; and if he cannot gain it he has mistaken his trade, and should seek another. Let it, then, be clearly understood that what such men earn by their labour, or save by their abstinence, or acquire by lawful inheritance, that they can enjoy without loss of dignity. But if they ask for more, or if they accept more, they become the recipients of charity, and between them and the beggar who walks the streets, the only difference is in the magnitude of the sum which is expected. To break stones on the highway is far more honourable than to receive such alms. Away, then, with your pensions, your subscriptions, your Literary Institutions, and your Literary Funds, by which you organize mendicancy into a system, and, under pretence of increasing public liberality, increase the amount of public imprudence.

But before this high standard can be reached, much remains to be done. As yet, and in the present early and unformed state of society, literary men are, notwithstanding a few exceptions, more prone to improvidence than the members of any other profession; and being also more deficient in practical knowledge, it too often happens that they are regarded as clever visionaries, fit to amuse the world, but unfit to guide it. The causes of this I have examined at some length, both because the results are extremely important, and because little attention has been hitherto paid to their operation. If I were not afraid of being tedious I could push the analysis still further, and could show that these very causes are themselves a part of the old spirit of Protection, and as such are intimately connected with some religious and political prejudices which obstruct the progress of society; and that in the countries where such prejudices are most powerful, the mischief is most serious and the state of literature most unhealthy. But to prosecute that inquiry would be to write a treatise rather than an essay; and I shall be satisfied if I have cleared the ground so far as I have gone, and have succeeded in tracing the relation between these evils and the general question of philosophic Method. The divergence between speculative minds and practical minds, and the different ways they have of contemplating affairs, are no doubt encouraged by the prevalence of false notions of patronage and reward, which, when they are brought to bear upon any class, inevitably tend to make that class unthrifty, and therefore unpractical. This is a law of the human mind which the political economists have best illustrated in their own department, but the operation of which is universal. Serious, however, as this evil is, it only belongs to a very imperfect state of society, and after a time it will probably disappear. But the essential, and so far as I can understand, the permanent cause of divergence is a difference of Method. In the creation of our knowledge, it appears to be a fundamental necessity that the speculative classes should search for what is distant, while the practical classes search for what is adjacent. I do not see how it is possible to get rid of this antithesis. There may be some way, which we cannot yet discern, of reconciling the two extremes, and of merging the antagonistic methods into one which, being higher than either, shall include both. At present, however, there is no prospect of such a result. We must, therefore, be satisfied if from time to time, and at long intervals, a man arises whose mind is so happily constructed as to study with equal success the surface and the summit; and who is able to show, by his single example, that views drawn from the most exalted region of thought, are applicable to the common transactions of daily life.

The only living Englishman who has achieved this is Mr. Mill. In the first place, he is our only great speculative philosopher who for many years has engaged in public life. Since Ricardo, no original thinker has taken an active part in political affairs. Not that those affairs have on that account been worse administered; nor that we have cause to repine at our lot in comparison with other nations. On the contrary, no country has been better governed than ours; and at the present moment, it would be impossible to find in any one European nation more able, zealous, and upright public men than England possesses. In such extremely rare cases as those of Brougham and Macaulay, there are also united to these qualities the most splendid and captivating accomplishments, and the far higher honour which they justly enjoy of having always been the eager and unflinching advocates of popular liberty. In cannot, however, be pretended that even these eminent men have added anything to our ideas; still less can such a claim be made on behalf of their inferiors in the political world. They have popularized the ideas and enforced them, but never created them. They have shown great skill and great courage in applying the conceptions of others; but the fresh conceptions, the higher and larger generalizations, have not been their work. They can attack old abuses; they cannot discover new principles. This incapacity for dealing with the highest problems has been curiously exemplified during the last two years, when a great number of the most active and eminent of our public men, as well as several who are active without being eminent, have formed an Association for the Promotion of Social Science. Among the papers published by that Association, will be found many curious facts and many useful suggestions. But Social Science there is none. There is not even a perception of what that science is. Not one speaker or writer attempted a scientific investigation of society, or showed that, in his opinion, such a thing ought to be attempted. Where science begins, the Association leaves off. All science is composed either of physical laws, or of mental laws; and as the actions of men are determined by both, the only way of founding Social Science is to investigate each class of laws by itself, and then, after computing their separate results, co-ordinate the whole into a single study, by verifying them. This is the only process by which highly complicated phenomena can be disentangled; but the Association did not catch a glimpse of it. Indeed, they reversed the proper order, and proceeded from the concrete to the abstract, instead of from the abstract to the concrete. The reason of this error may be easily explained. The leading members of the Association being mostly politicians, followed the habits of their profession; that is to say, they noted the events immediately surrounding them, and, taking a contemporary view, they observed the actual effects with a view of discovering the causes, and then remedying the evils. This was their plan, and it is natural to men whose occupations lead them to look at the surface of affairs. But to any mind accustomed to rise to a certain height above that surface, and thoroughly imbued with the spirit of scientific method, it is obvious that this way of investigating social phenomena must be futile. Even in the limited field of political action, its results are at best mere empirical uniformities; while in the immense range of social science it is altogether worthless. When men are collected together in society, with their passions and their interests touching each other at every point, it is clear that nothing can happen without being produced by a great variety of causes. Of these causes, some will be conflicting, and their action being neutralized they will often disappear in the product; or, at all events, will leave traces too faint to be discerned. If then, a cause is counteracted, how can you ascertain its existence by studying its effect? When only one cause produces an effect, you may infer the cause from the effect. But if several causes conspire to produce one effect, this is impossible. The most persevering study of the effect, and the most intimate acquaintance with it, will in such case never lead to a knowledge of the causes; and the only plan is to proceed deductively from cause to effect, instead of inductively from effect to cause. Suppose, for example, a ball is struck on different sides by two persons at the same time. The effect will be that the ball, after being struck, will pass from one spot to another; but that effect may be studied for thousands of years without any one being able to ascertain the causes of the direction the ball took; and even if he is told that two persons have contributed to produce the result, he could not discover how much each person contributed. But if the observer, instead of studying the effect to obtain the causes, had studied the causes themselves, he would have been able, without going further, to predict the exact resting-place of the ball. In other words, by knowing the causes he could learn the effect, but by knowing the effect he could not learn the causes.

Suppose, again, that I hear a musical instrument being played. The effect depends on a great variety of causes, among which are the power possessed by the air of conveying the sound, the power of the ear to receive its vibrations, and the power of the brain to feel them. These are vulgarly called conditions, but they are all causes; inasmuch as a cause can only be defined to be an invariable and unconditional antecedent. They are just as much causes as the hand of the musician; and the question arises, could those causes have been discovered merely by studying the effect the music produced upon me? Most assuredly not. Most assuredly would it be requisite to study each cause separately, and then, by compounding the laws of their action, predict the entire effect. In social science the plurality of causes is far more marked than in the cases I have mentioned; and therefore, in social science, the method of proceeding from effects to causes is far more absurd. And what aggravates the absurdity is, that the difficulty produced by the plurality of causes is heightened by anther difficulty — namely, the conflict of causes. To deal with such enormous complications as politicians usually deal with them, is simply a waste of time. Every science has some hypothesis which underlies it, and which must be taken for granted. The hypothesis on which social science rests, is that the actions of men are a compound result of the laws of mind and the laws of matter; and as that result is highly complex, we shall never understand it until the laws themselves have been unravelled by a previous and separate inquiry. Even if we could experiment, it would be different; because by experimenting on an effect we can artificially isolate it, and guard against the encroachment of causes which we do not wish to investigate. But in social science there can be no experiment. For, in the first place, there can be no previous isolation; since every interference lets into the framework of society a host of new phenomena which invalidate the experiment before the experiment is concluded. And, in the second place, that which is called an experiment, such as the adoption of a fresh principle in legislation, is not an experiment in the scientific sense of the word; because the results which follow, depend far more upon the general state of the surrounding society than upon the principle itself. The surrounding state of society is, in its turn, governed by a long train of antecedents, each linked to the other, and forming in their aggregate, an orderly and spontaneous march, which politicians are unable to control, and which they do for the most part utterly ignore.

This absence of speculative ability among politicians, is the natural result of the habits of their class; and as the same result is almost invariably found among practical men, I have thought the illustration just adduced might be interesting, in so far as it confirms the doctrine of an essential antagonism of Method, which, though like all speculative distinctions, infringed at various points, does undoubtedly exist, and appears to me to form the basis for a classification of society more complete than any yet proposed. Perhaps, too, it may have the effect of guarding against the rash and confident assertions of public men on matters respecting which they have no means of forming an opinion, because their conclusions are vitiated by the adoption of an illogical method. It is, accordingly, a matter of notoriety that in predicting the results of large and general innovations, even the most sagacious politicians have been oftener wrong than right, and have foreseen evil when nothing but good has come. Against this sort of error, the longest and most extensive experience affords no protection. While statesmen confine themselves to questions of detail, and to short views of immediate expediency, their judgment should be listened to with respect. But beyond this, they are rarely to be heeded. It constantly, and indeed usually happens, that statesmen and legislators who pass their whole life in public affairs, know nothing of their own age, except what lies on the surface, and are therefore unable to calculate, even approximatively, remote and general consequences. Abundant evidence of their incapacity on these points, will present itself to whoever has occasion to read much of State Papers or of parliamentary discussions in different ages, or, what is still more decisive, the private correspondence of eminent politicians. These reveal but too clearly, that they who are supposed to govern the course of affairs, are utterly ignorant of the direction affairs are really taking. What is before them they see; what is above them they overlook. While, however, this is the deficiency of political practitioners, it must be admitted that political philosophers are, on their side, equally at fault in being too prone to neglect the operation of superficial and tangible results. The difference between the two classes is analogous to that which exists between a gardener and a botanist. Both deal with plants, but each considers the plant from an opposite point of view. The gardener looks to its beauty and its flavour. These are qualities which lie on the surface; and to these the scientific botanist pays no heed. He studies the physiology; he searches for the law; he penetrates the minute structure, and rending the plant, sacrifices the individual that he may understand the species. The gardener, like the statesman, is accustomed to consider the superficial and the immediate; the botanist, like the philosopher, inquires into the hidden and the remote. Which pursuit is the more valuable, is not now the question; but it is certain that a successful combination of both pursuits is very rare. The habits of mind, the turn of thought, all the associations, are diametrically opposed. To unite them, requires a strength of resolution and a largeness of intellect rarely given to man to attain. It usually happens that they who seek to combine the opposites, fail on both sides, and become at once shallow philosophers and unsafe practitioners.

It must, therefore, be deemed a remarkable fact, that a man who is beyond dispute the deepest of our living thinkers, should, during many years, not only have held a responsible post in a very difficult department of government, but should, according to the testimony of those best able to judge, have fulfilled the duties of that post with conspicuous and unvarying success. This has been the case with Mr. Mill, and on this account his opinions are entitled to peculiar respect, because they are formed by one who has mastered both extremes of life. Such a duality of function is worthy of especial attention, and it will hardly be taken amiss if I endeavour to show how it has displayed itself in the writings of this great philosopher. To those who delight in contemplating the development of an intellect of the rarest kind, it will not appear unseemly that, before examining his latest work, I should compare those other productions by which he has been hitherto known and which have won for him a vast and permanent fame.

Those works are his *Principles of Political Economy*, and his *System of Logic*. Each of these elaborate productions is remarkable for one of the two great qualities of the author; the Political Economy being mostly valuable for the practical application of truths previously established; while the Logic contains an analysis of the process of reasoning, more subtle and exhaustive than any which has appeared since Aristotle.[2]

---

[2] I do not except even Kant; because that extraordinary thinker, who in some directions has perhaps penetrated deeper than any philosopher either before or since, did, in his views respecting logic, so anticipate the limits of all future discovery, as to take upon himself to affirm that the notion of inductively obtaining a standard of objective truth, was not only impracticable at present, but involved an essential contradiction which

Of the Political Economy it is enough to say that none of the principles in it are new. Since the publication of the *Wealth of Nations*, the science had been entirely remodelled, and it was the object of Mr. Mill not to extend its boundaries, but to turn to practical account what had been achieved by the two generations of thinkers who succeeded Adam Smith. The brilliant discovery of the true theory of rent, which though not made by Ricardo, was placed by him on a solid foundation, had given an entirely new aspect to economical science; as also had the great law, which he first pointed out, of the distribution of the precious metals, by means of the exchanges, in exact proportion to the traffic which would occur if there were no such metals, and if all trade were conducted by barter. The great work of Malthus on Population, and the discussions to which it led, had ascertained the nature and limits of the connexion which exists between the increase of labour and the rate of wages, and had thus cleared away many of the difficulties which beset the path of Adam Smith. While this threw new light on the causes of the distribution of wealth, Rae had analyzed those other causes which govern its accumulation, and had shown in what manner capital increases with different speed, in different countries, and at different times. When we, moreover, add that Bentham had demonstrated the advantages and the necessity of usury as part of the social scheme; that Babbage had with signal ability investigated the principles which govern the economy of labour, and the varying degrees of its productiveness; and that the abstract but very important step had been taken by Wakefield of proving that the supposed ultimate division of labour is in reality but a part of the still higher principle of the co-operation of labour; when we put these things together, we shall see that Mr. Mill

---

would always be irreconcilable. Whoever upon any subject thus sets up a fixed and prospective limit, gives the surest proof that he has not investigated that subject even as far as the existing resources allow; for he proves that he has not reached that point where certainty ends, and where the dim outline, gradually growing fainter, but always indefinite, teaches us that there is something beyond, and that we have no right to pledge ourselves respecting that undetermined tract. On the other hand, those who stop before they have reached this shadowy outline, see everything clearly because they have not advanced to the place where darkness begins. If I were to venture to criticise such a man as Kant, I should say, after a very careful study of his works, and with the greatest admiration of them, that the depth of his mind considerably exceeded its comprehensiveness.

found everything ready to his hand, and had only to combine and apply the generalizations of those great speculative thinkers who immediately preceded him.

The success with which he has executed this task is marvellous. His treatise on Political Economy is a manual for statesman even more than for speculators; since, though it contains no additions to scientific truths, it is full of practical applications. In it, the most recondite principles are illustrated, and brought to the surface, with a force which has convinced many persons whose minds are unable to follow long trains of abstract reasoning, and who rejected the conclusions of Ricardo, because that illustrious thinker, master though he was of the finest dialectic, lacked the capacity of clothing his arguments in circumstances, and could not adapt them to the ordinary events of political life. This deficiency is supplied by Mr. Mill, who treats political economy as an art even more than as a science.[3] Hence his book is full of suggestions on many of the most important matters which can be submitted to the legislature of a free people. The laws of bequest and of inheritance; the law of primogeniture; the laws of partnership and of limited liability; the laws of insolvency and of bankruptcy; the best method of establishing colonies; the advantages and disadvantages of the income-tax; the expediency of meeting extraordinary expenses by taxation drawn from income or by an increase of the national debt: these are among the subjects mooted by Mr. Mill, and on which he has made proposals, the majority of which are gradually working their way into the public mind. Upon these topics his influence is felt by many who do not know from whence the influence proceeds. And no one can have attended to the progress of political opinions during the last ten years, without noticing how, in the formation of practical judgments, his power is operating on politicians who are utterly heedless of his higher generalizations, and who would, indeed, in the largest departments of thought, be well content to sleep on in their dull and ancient routine, but that from time to time, and

3   Thereby becoming necessarily somewhat empirical; for directly the political economist offers practical suggestions, disturbing causes are let in, and trouble the pure science which depends far more upon reasoning than upon observation. No writer I have met with, has put this in a short compass with so much clearness as Mr. Senior. See the introduction to his *Political Economy*, 4th edit. 1858, pp. 2–5.

in their own despite, their slumbers are disturbed by a noise from afar, and they are forced to participate in the result of that prodigious movement which is now gathering on every side, unsettling the stability of affairs, and sapping the foundation of our beliefs.

In such intellectual movements, which lie at the root of social actions, the practical classes can take no original part, though, as all history decisively proves, they are eventually obliged to abide by the consequences of them. But it is the peculiar prerogative of certain minds to be able to interpret as well as to originate. To such men a double duty is entrusted. They enjoy the inestimable privilege of communicating directly with practitioners as well as with specuators, and they can both dsicover the abstract and manipulate the concrete. The concrete and practical tendency of the present age is clearly exhibited in Mr. Mill's work on Political Economy; while in his work on Logic we may see as clearly the abstract and theoretical tendency of the same period. The former work is chiefly valuable in relation to the functions of government; the latter in relation to the functions of thought. In the one, the art of doing; in the other, the science of reasoning. The revolution which he has effected in this great department of speculative knowledge, will be best understood by comparing what the science of logic was when he began to write, with what it was after his work was published.

Until Mr. Mill entered the field there were only two systems of logic. The first was the syllogistic system which was founded by Aristotle, and to which the moderns have contributed nothing of moment, except the discovery during the present century of the quantification of the predicate.[4] The other was the inductive system, as organized by Bacon, to which also it

---

4   Made by Sir William Hamilton and Mr. De Morgan about the same time and, I believe, independently of each other. Before this, nothing of moment had been added to the Aristotelian doctrine of the syllogism, unless we consider as such the fourth figure. This was unknown to Aristotle; but it may be doubted if it is essential; and, if I rightly remember, Sir William Hamilton did not attach much importance to the fourth syllogistic figure, while Archbishop Whately (*Logic*, 1857, p. 5) calls it 'insignificant.' Compare Mansel's *Aldrich*, 1856, p. 76. The hypothetical syllogism is usually said to be post-Aristotelian; but although I cannot now recover the passage, I have seen evidence which makes me suspect that it was known to Aristotle, though not formally enunciated by him.

was reserved for our generation to make the first essential addition; Sir John Herschel having the great merit of ascertaining the existence of four different methods, the boundaries of which had escaped the attention of previous philosophers.[5] That the word logic should by most writers be confined to the syllogistic, or, as it is sometimes called, Formal, method, is a striking proof of the extent to which langauge is infested by the old scholastic prejudices; for, as the science of logic is the theory of the process of inference, and as the art of logic is the practical skill of inferring rightly from given data, it is evident that any system is a system of logic which ascetains the laws of the theory, and lays down the rules of the practice. The inductive system of logic may be better or worse than the deductive; but both are systems.[6] And till nearly the middle of the present century, men were divided between the Aristotelian

[5] This is acknowledged by Mr. Mill, who has stated and analyzed these methods with great clearness. — Mill's *Logic*, 4th edit. 1856, vol. i. p. 451.

[6] Archbishop Whately, who has written what is probably the best elementary treatise existing on formal logic, adopts the old opinion that the inductive 'process of inquiry' by which premises are obtained, is 'out of the province of logic.' Whately's *Logic*, 1857, p. 151. Mr. De Morgan, whose extremely able work goes much deeper into the subject than Archbishop Whately's, is, however content with excluding induction, not from logic, but from formal logic. 'What is now called induction, meaning the discovery of laws from instances, and higher laws from lower ones, is beyond the province of formal logic.' — De Morgan's *Logic*, 1847, p. 215. As a law of nature is frequently the major premiss of a syllogism, this statement of Mr. De Morgan's seems unobjectionable. The point at issue involves much more than a mere dispute respecting words, and I therefore add, without subscribing to, the view of another eminent authority. 'To entitle any work to be classed as the logic of this or that school, it is at least necessary that it should, in common with the Aristotelian logic, adhere to the syllogistic method, whatever modifications or additions it may derive from the particular school of its author.' — Mansel's Introduction to Aldrich's *Artis Logicæ Rudimenta*, 1856, p. xlii. See also Appendix, pp. 194, 195, and Mr. Mansel's *Prolegomena Logica*, 1851, pp. 89, 169. On the other hand, Bacon, who considered the syllogism to be worse than useless, distinctly claims the title of 'logical' for his inductive system. 'Illud vero monendum, nos in hoc nostro organo tractare logicam, non philosophiam.' — *Novum Organum*, lib. ii. aphor. lii. in Bacon's *Works*, vol. iv. p. 382. This should be compared with the remarks of Sir William Hamilton on inductive logic in his *Discussions*, 1852, p. 158. What strikes one most in this controversy is, that none of the great advocates of the exclusive right of the syllogistic system to the word 'logic' appear to be well acquainted with physical science. They, therefore, cannot understand the real nature of induction in the modern sense of the term, and they naturally depreciate a method with whose triumphs they have no sympathy.

logic which infers from generals to particulars, and the Baconian logic which infers from particulars to generals.[7]

While the science of logic was in this state, there appeared in 1843 Mr. Mill's *System of Logic*; the fundamental idea of which is, that the logical process is not from generals to particulars, nor from particulars to generals, but from particulars to particulars. According to this view, which is gradually securing the adhesion of thinkers, the syllogism instead of being an act of reasoning, is an act, first of registration, and then of interpretation. The major premiss of a syllogism being the record of previous induction, the business of the syllogism is to interpret that record and bring it to light. In the syllogism we preserve our experience, and we also realize it; but the reasoning is at an end when the major premiss is enunciated. For, after that enunciation no fresh truth is propounded. As soon, therefore, as the major is stated, the argument is over; because the general proposition is but a register, or, as it were, a note-book, of inferences which involve everything at issue. While, however, the syllogism is not a process of reasoning, it is a security that the previous reasoning is good. And this, in three ways. In the first place, by insterposing a general proposition between the collection of the first particulars and the statement of the last particulars, it presents a larger object to the imagination than would be possible if we had only the particulars in our mind. In the second place, the syllogism serves as an artificial memory, and enables us to preserve order among a mass of details; being at once a formula into which we throw them, and a contrivance by which we recall them. Finally, the syllogism is a protection against negligence; since, when we infer from a number of observed cases to a case we have not yet observed, we, instead of jumping at once to that case, state a general proposition which includes it, and which must be true if our conclusion is

---

[7] To what extent Aristotle did or did not recognize an induction of particulars as the first step in our knowledge, and therefore as the base of every major premiss, has been often disputed; but I have not heard that any of the disputants have adopted the only means by which such a question can be tested — namely, bringing together the most ·decisive passages from Aristotle, and then leaving them to the judgment of the reader. As this seems to be the most impartial way of proceeding, I have gone through Aristotle's logical works with a view to it; and those who are interested in these matters will find the extracts at the end of this essay.

true, so that, by this means, if we have reasoned erroneously, the error becomes more broad and conspicuous.

This remarkable analysis of the nature and functions of the syllogism is, so far as our present knowledge goes, exhaustive; whether or not it will admit of still further resolution we cannot tell. At all events it is a contribution of the greatest importance to the science of reasoning, and involves many other speculative questions which are indirectly connected with it, but which I shall not now open up. Neither need I stop to show how it affords a basis for establishing the true distinction between induction and deduction; a distinction which Mr. Mill is one of the extremely few English writers who has thoroughly understood, since it is commonly supposed in this country that geometry is the proper type of deduction, whereas it is only one of the types, and, though an admirable pattern of the deductive investigation of coexistences, throws no light on the deductive investigation of sequences. But, passing over these matters as too large to be discussed here, I would call attention to a fundamental principle which underlies Mr. Mill's philosophy, and from which it will appear that he is as much opposed to the advocates of the Baconian methods as to those of the Aristotelian. In this respect he has been, perhaps unconsciously, greatly influenced by the spirit of the age; for it might be easily shown, and indeed will hardly be disputed, that during the last fifty years an opinion has been gaining ground, that the Baconian system has been overrated, and that its favourite idea, of proceeding from effects to causes instead of from causes to effects, will not carry us so far as was supposed by the truly great, though somewhat empirical, thinkers of the eighteenth century.

One point in which the inductive philosophy commonly received in England is very inaccurate, and which Mr. Mill has justly attacked, is, that following the authority of Bacon, it insists upon all generalizations being conducted by ascending from each generalization to the one immediately above and adjoining; and it denounces as hasty and unphilosophic any attempt to soar to a higher stage without mastering the intermediate steps.[8] This is an undue limitation of that peculiar

---

8   'Ascendendo continenter et gradatim, ut ultimo loco perveniatur ad maxime generalia; quæ via vera, sed intentata.' *Novum Organum*, lib. i. aphor. xix. in Bacon's *Works*, vol. iv. p. 268. London, 1778; 4to. And in lib. i. aphor.

property of genius which, for want of a better word, we call intuition; and that, in this respect, Bacon's philosophy was too narrow, and placed men too much on a par[9] by obliging them all to use the same method is now frequently though not generally admitted, and has been perceived by several philosophers.[10] The objections raised by Mr. Mill on this ground, though put with great ability, are, as he would be the first to confess, not original; and the same remark may be made in a smaller degree concerning another objection — namely, that Bacon did not attach sufficient weight to the plurality of causes,[11] and did not see that the great complexity they produce would often baffle his method, and would render another method necessary. But while Mr. Mill has in these parts of his work been anticipated, there is a more subtle, and, as it appears to me, a more fatal objection which he has made against the Baconian philosophy. And as this objection, besides being entirely new, lies far out of the path of ordinary speculation, it has hardly yet attracted the notice even of philosophic logicians, and the reader will probably be interested in hearing a simple and untechnical statement of it.

Logic, considered as a science, is solely concerned with induction; and the business of induction is to arrive at causes; or, to speak more strictly, to arrive at a knowledge of the laws

civ. p. 294 — 'Sed de scientiis tum demum bene sperandum est, quando per scalam veram et per gradus continuos et non intermissos, aut huilcos, a particularibus ascendetur ad axiomata minora, et deinde ad media, alia aliis superiora, et postremo demum ad generalissima.'

9   'Nostra vero inveniendi scientias ea est ratio, ut non multum ingeniorum acumini et robori relinquatur; sed quæ ingenia et intellectus fere exaequet.' — Novum Organum, lib. i. aphor. lxi.; Bacon's Works, vol. iv. p. 275. And in lib. i. aphor. cxxii. [Works, vol. iv. p. 301], 'Nostra enim via inveniendi scientias exaequat fere ingenia, et non multum excellentiae eorum relinquit; cum omnia per certissimas regulas et demonstrationes transigat.'

10   And is noticed in Whewell's Philosophy of the Inductive Sciences, 1847, vol. ii. p. 240; though this celebrated writer, so far from connecting it with Bacon's doctrine of gradual and uninterrupted ascent, considers such doctrine to be the peculiar merit of Bacon, and accuses those who hold a contrary opinion, of 'dimness of vision,' pp. 126, 232. Happily, all are not dim who are said to be so.

11   Mill's Logic, fourth edition, vol. ii. p. 321. I am almost sure this remark had been made before.

of causation.§ So far Mr. Mill agrees with Bacon; but from the operation of this rule he removes an immense body of phenomena which were brought under it by the Baconian philosophy. He asserts, and I think he proves, that though uniformities of succession may be investigated inductively, it is impossible to investigate, after that fashion, uniformities of co-existence; and that, therefore, to these last the Baconian method is inapplicable. If, for instance, we say that all negroes have woolly hair, we affirm a uniformity of co-existence between the hair and some other property or properties essential to the negro. But if we were to say that they have woolly hair in consequence of their skin being black, we should affirm an uniformity not of co-existence, but of succession. Uniformities of succession are frequently amenable to induction: uniformities of co-existence are never amenable to it, and are consequently out of the jurisdiction of the Baconian philosophy. They may, no doubt, be treated according to the simple enumeration of the ancients, which, however, was so crude an induction as hardly to be worthy the name.[12] But the powerful induction of the moderns, depending upon a separation of nature and an elimination of disturbances, is, in

§ 'The main question of the science of logic is induction, which however is almost entirely passed over by professed writers on logic.' — Mill's *Logic*, vol. i. p. 309. 'The chief object of inductive logic is to point out how the laws of causation are to be ascertained.' — Vol. i. p. 407. 'The mental process with which logic is conversant, the operation of ascertaining truths by means of evidence, is always, even when appearances point to a different theory of it, a process of induction.' — Vol. ii. p. 177.

12 The character of the Aristotelian induction is so justly portrayed by Mr. Maurice in his admirable account of the Greek philosophy, that I cannot resist the pleasure of transcribing the passage. 'What this induction is, and how entirely it differs from that process which bears the same name in the writings of Bacon, the reader will perceive the more he studies the different writings of Aristotle. He will find, first, that the sensible *phenomenon* is taken for granted as a safe starting point. That phenomena are not principles, Aristotle believed as strongly as we could. But, to suspect phenomena, to suppose that they need sifting and probing in order that we may know what the fact is which they denote, this is no part of his system.' — Maurice's *Ancient Philosophy*, 1850, p. 173. Nothing can be better than the expression that Aristotle did not *suspect* phenomena. The moderns do suspect them, and therefore test them either by crucial experiments or by averages. The latter resource was not effectively employed until the eighteenth century. It now bids fair to be of immense importance, though in some branches of inquiry the nomenclature must become more precise before the full value of the method can be seen.

reference to co-existences, absolutely impotent. The utmost that it can give is empirical laws, useful for practical guidance, but void of scientific value. That this has hitherto been the case the history of our knowledge decisively proves. That it always will be the case is, in Mr. Mill's opinion, equally certain, because while, on the one hand, the study of uniformities of succession has for its basis that absorbing and over-ruling hypothesis of the constancy of causation, on which every human being more or less relies, and to which philosophers will hear of no exception; we, on the other hand, find that the study of the uniformities of co-existence has no such support, and that therefore the whole field of inquiry is unsettled and indeterminate. Thus it is that if I see a negro suffering pain, the law of causation compels me to believe that something had previously happened of which pain was the necessary consequence. But I am not bound to believe that he possesses some property of which his woolly hair or his dark skin are the necessary accompaniments. I cling to the necessity of an uniform sequence; I reject the necessity of an uniform co-existence. This is the difference between consequences and concomitants. That the pain has a cause, I am well assured. But for aught I can tell, the blackness and the woolliness may be ultimate properties which are referrible to no cause;[13] or if they are not ultimate properties, each may be dependent on its own cause, but not be necessarily connected. The relation, therefore, may be universal in regard to the fact, and yet casual in regard to the science.

This distinction when once stated is very simple; but its consequences in relation to the science of logic had escaped all previous thinkers. When thoroughly appreciated, it will dispel the ideal dream of the universal application of the Baconian philosophy; and in the meantime it will explain how it was that even during Bacon's life, and in his own hands, his method frequently and signally failed. He evidently believed that as every phenomenon has something which must follow from it, so also it has something which must go with it, and which he

---

[13]   That is, not logically referrible by the understanding. I say nothing of causes which touch on transcendental grounds; but, barring these, Mr. Mill's assertion seems unimpeachable, that 'co-existences between the ultimate properties of things' . . . 'cannot depend on causation,' unless by 'ascending to the origin of all things.' — Mill's *Logic*, vol. ii. p. 106.

termed its Form.[14] If he could generalize the form — that is to say, if he could obtain the law of the co-existence — he rightly supposed that he would gain a scientific knowledge of the phenomenon. With this view he taxes his fertile invention to the utmost. He contrived a variety of refined and ingenious artifices, by which various instances might be successfully compared, and the conditions which are essential, distinguished from those which are non-essential. He collated negatives with affirmatives, and taught the art of separating nature by rejections and exclusions. Yet, in regard to the study of co-existences, all his caution, all his knowledge, and all his thought, were useless. His weapons, notwithstanding their power, could make no impression on that stubborn and refractory topic. The laws of co-existences are as great a mystery as ever, and all our conclusions respecting them are purely empirical. Every inductive science now existing is, in its strictly scientific part, solely a generalisation of sequences. The reason of this, though vaguely appreciated by several writers, was first clearly stated and connected with the general theory of our knowledge by Mr. Mill. He has the immense merit of striking at once to the very root of the subject, and showing that, in the science of logic, there is a fundamental distinction which forbids us to treat co-existences as we may treat sequences; that a neglect of this distinction impairs the value of the philosophy of Bacon, and has crippled his successors; and finally, that the origin of this distinction may be traced backward and upward until we reach those ultimate laws of causation which support the fabric of our knowledge, and beyond which the human mind, in the present stage of its development, is unable to penetrate.

While Mr. Mill, both by delving to the foundation and rising to the summit, has excluded the Baconian philosophy from the investigation of co-existences, he has likewise proved its incapacity for solving those vast social problems which now,

---

14 'Etenim forma naturæ alicujus talis est, ut, ea posita, natura data infallibiliter sequatur. Itaque adest perpetuo, quando natura illa adest, atque eam universaliter affirmat, atque inest omni. Eadem forma talis est, ut ea amoto, natura data infallibiliter fugiat. Itaque abest perpetua quando natura illa abest, eamque perpetua abnegat, atque inest soli.' — *Novum Organum*, lib. ii. aphor. iv.; *Works*, vol. iv. p. 307. Compare also respecting these forms, his treatise on *The Advancement of Learning*, book ii.; *Works*, vol. i. p. 57, 58, 61, 62.

for the first time in the history of the world, the most advanced thinkers are setting themselves to work at deliberately, with scientific purpose, and with something like adequate resources. As this, however, pertains to that domain to which I too, according to my measure and with whatever power I may haply possess, have devoted myself, I am unwilling to discuss here what elsewhere I shall find a fitter place for considering; and I shall be content if I have conveyed to the reader some idea of what has been effected by one whom I cannot but regard as the most profound thinker England has produced since the seventeenth century, and whose services, though recognized by innumerable persons each in his own peculiar walk, are little understood in their entirety, because we, owing partly to the constantly increasing mass of our knowledge, and partly to an excessive veneration for the principle of the division of labour, are too prone to isolate our inquiries and to narrow the range of our intellectual sympathies. The notion that a man will best succeed by adhering to one pursuit, is as true in practical life as it is false in speculative life. No one can have a firm grasp of any science if, by confining himself to it, he shuts out the light of analogy, and deprives himself of that peculiar aid which is derived from a commanding survey of the co-ordination and interdependence of things and of the relation they bear to each other. He may, no doubt, work at the details of his subject; he may be useful in adding to its facts; he will never be able to enlarge its philosophy. For, the philosophy of every department depends on its connexion with other departments, and must therefore be sought at their points of contact. It must be looked for in the place where they touch and coalesce; it lies not in the centre of each science, but on the confines and margin. This, however, is a truth which men are apt to reject, because they are naturally averse to comprehensive labour, and are too ready to believe that their own peculiar and limited science is so important that they would not be justified in striking into paths which diverge from it. Hence we see physical philosophers knowing nothing of political economy, political economists nothing of physical science, and logicians nothing of either. Hence, too, there are few indeed who are capable of measuring the enormous field which Mr. Mill has traversed, or of scanning the depth to which in that field he has sunk his shaft.

It is from such a man as this, that a work has recently issued upon a subject far more important than any which even he had previously investigated, and in fact the most important with which the human mind can grapple. For, Liberty is the one thing most essential to the right development of individuals and to the real grandeur of nations. It is a product of knowledge when knowledge advances in a healthy and regular manner; but if under certain unhappy circumstances it is opposed by what seems to be knowledge, then, in God's name, let knowledge perish and Liberty be preserved. Liberty is not a means to an end, it is an end itself. To secure it, to enlarge it, and to diffuse it, should be the main object of all social arrangements and of all political contrivances. None but a pedant or a tyrant can put science or literature in competition with it. Within certain limits, and very small limits too, it is the inalienable prerogative of man, of which no force of circumstances and no lapse of time can deprive him. He has no right to barter it away even from himself, still less from his children. It is the foundation of all self-respect, and without it the great doctrine of moral responsibility would degenerate into a lie and a juggle. It is a sacred deposit, and the love of it is a holy instinct engraven in our hearts. And if it could be shown that the tendency of advancing knowledge is to encroach upon it; if it could be proved that in the march of what we call civilization, the desire for liberty did necessarily decline, and the exercise of liberty become less frequent; if this could be made apparent, I for one should wish that the human race might halt in its career, and that we might recede step by step, so that the very trophies and memory of our glory should vanish, sooner than that men were bribed by their splendour to forget the sentiment of our own personal dignity.

But it cannot be. Surely it cannot be that we, improving in all other things, should be retrograding in the most essential. Yet, among thinkers of great depth and authority there is a fear that such is the case. With that fear I cannot agree; but the existence of the fear, and the discussions to which it has led and will lead, are extremely salutary, as calling our attention to an evil which in the eagerness of our advance we might otherwise overlook. We are stepping on at a rate of which no previous example has been seen; and it is good that, amid the pride and flush of our prosperity, we should be made to inquire what price we have paid for our success. Let us compute the cost as well as the gain. Before we announce our fortune we should balance our books. Every one, therefore, should rejoice at the appearance of a work in which for the first time the great question of Liberty is unfolded in all its dimensions, considered on every side and from every aspect, and brought to bear upon our present condition with a steadiness of hand and a clearness of purpose which they will most admire who are most accustomed to reflect on this difficult and complicated topic.

In the actual state of the world, Mr. Mill rightly considers that the least important part of the question of liberty is that which concerns the relation between subjects and rulers. On this point, notwithstanding the momentary ascendancy of despotism on the Continent, there is, I believe, nothing to dread. In France, and Germany, the bodies of men are enslaved, but not their minds. Nearly all the intellect of Europe is arrayed against tyranny, and the ultimate result of such a struggle can hardly be doubted. The immense armies which are maintained, and which some mention as a proof that the love of war is increasing instead of diminishing, are merely an evidence that the governing classes distrust and suspect the future, and know that their real danger is to be found not abroad but at home. They rear revolution far more than invasion. The state of foreign affairs is their pretence for arming; the state of public opinion is the cause. And right glad they are to find a decent pretext for protecting themselves from that punishment which many of them richly deserve. But I cannot understand how any one who has carefully studied the march of the European mind, and has seen it triumph over obstacles ten times more formidable than these, can really apprehend that the liberties of Europe will ultimately fall before those who now threaten their existence. When the spirit of freedom was far less strong and less universal, the task was tried, and tried in vain. It is hardly to be supposed that the monarchical principle, decrepit as it now is, and stripped of that dogma of divine right which long upheld it, can eventually withstand the pressure of those general causes which, for three centuries, have marked it for destruction. And, since despotism has chosen the institution of monarchy as that under which it seeks a shelter, and for which it will fight its last battle, we may fairly assume that the danger is less imminent than is commonly imagined, and that they who rely on an old and enfeebled principle, with which neither the religion nor the affections of men are associated as of yore, will find that they are leaning on the broken reed, and that the sceptre of their power will pass from them.

I cannot, therefore, participate in the feelings of those who look with apprehension at the present condition of Europe. Mr. Mill would perhaps take a less sanguine view; but it is observable that the greater part of his defence of liberty is not directed against political tyranny. There is, however, another sort of tyranny which is far more insidious, and against which he has chiefly bent his efforts. This is the despotism of custom, to which ordinary minds entirely succumb, and before which even strong minds quail. But custom being merely the product of public opinion, or rather its external manifestation, the two principles of custom and opinion must be considered together; and I will briefly state how, according to Mr. Mill, their joint action is producing serious mischief, and is threatening mischief more serious still.

The proposition which Mr. Mill undertakes to establish, is that society, whether acting by the legislature or by the influence of public opinion, has no right to interfere with the conduct of any individual for the sake of his own good. Society may interfere with him for their good, not for his. If his actions hurt them, he is, under certain circumstances, amenable to their authority; if they only hurt himself, he is never amenable. The proposition, thus stated, will be acceded to by many persons who, in practice, repudiate it every day of their lives. The ridicule which is cast upon whoever deviates from an established custom, however trifling and foolish that custom may be, shows the determination of society to exercise arbitrary away over individuals. On the most insignificant as well as on the most important matters, rules are laid down which no one dares to violate, except in those extremely rare cases in which great intellect, great wealth, or great rank enable a man rather to command society than to be commanded by it. The immense mass of mankind are, in regard to their usages, in a state of social slavery; each man being bound under heavy penalties to conform to the standard of life common to his own class. How serious those penalties are, is evident from the fact that though innumerable persons complain of prevailing customs and wish to shake them off, they dare not do so, but continue to practise them, though frequently at the expense of health, comfort, and fortune. Men, not cowards in other respects, and of a fair share of moral courage, are afraid to rebel against this grievous and exacting tyranny. The consequences of this are injurious, not only to those who desire to be freed from the thraldom, but also to those who do not desire to be freed; that is, to the whole of society. Of these results, there are two particularly mischievous, and which, in the opinion of Mr. Mill, are likely to gain ground, unless some sudden change of sentiment should occur.

The first mischief is, that a sufficient number of experiments are not made respecting the different ways of living; from which it happens that the art of life is not so well understood as it otherwise would be. If society were more lenient to eccentricity, and more inclined to examine what is unusual than to laugh at it, we should find that many courses of conduct which we call whimsical, and which according to the ordinary standards are utterly irrational, have more reason in them than we are disposed to imagine. But, while a country or an age will obstinately insist upon condemning all human conduct which is not in accordance with the manner or fashion of the day, deviations from the straight line will be rarely hazarded. We are, therefore, prevented from knowing how far such deviations would be useful. By discouraging the experiment, we retard the knowledge. On this account, if on no other, it is advisable that the widest latitude should be given to unusual actions, which ought to be valued as tests whereby we may ascertain whether or not particular things are expedient. Of course, the essentials of morals are not to be violated, nor the public peace to be disturbed. But short of this, every indulgence should be granted. For progress depends upon change; and it is only by practising uncustomary things that we can discover if they are fit to become customary.

The other evil which society inflicts on herself by her own tyranny is still more serious; and although I cannot go with Mr. Mill in considering the danger to be so imminent as he does, there can, I think, be little doubt that it is the one weak point in modern civilization; and that it is the only thing of importance in which, if we are not actually receding, we are making no perceptible advance.

This is, that most precious and inestimable quality, the quality of individuality. That the increasing authority of society, if not counteracted by other causes, tends to limit the exercise of this quality, seems indisputable. Whether or not

there are counteracting causes is a question of great complexity, and could not be discussed without entering into the
general theory of our existing civilization. With the most
unfeigned deference for every opinion enunciated by Mr. Mill,
I venture to differ from him on this matter, and to think that,
on the whole, individuality is not diminishing, and that so far
as we can estimate the future, it is not likely to diminish. But it
would ill become any man to combat the views of this great
thinker, without subjecting the point at issue to a rigid and
careful analysis; and as I have not done so, I will not weaken
my theory by advancing imperfect arguments in its favour, but
will, as before, confine myself to stating the conclusions at
which he has arrived, after what has evidently been a train of
long and anxious reflection.

According to Mr. Mill, things are tending, and have for
some time tended, to lessen the influence of original minds, and
to raise mediocrity to the foremost place. Individuals are lost in
the crowd. The world is ruled not by them, but by public
opinion; and public opinion, being the voice of the many, is the
voice of mediocrity. Affairs are now governed by average men,
who will not pay to great men the deference that was formerly
yielded. Energy and originality being less respected, are
becoming more rare; and in England in particular, real energy
has hardly any field, except in business, where a large amount
of it undoubtedly exists.[15] Our greatness is collective, and
depends not upon what we do as individuals, but upon our
power of combining. In every successive generation, men more
resemble each other in all respects. They are more alike in their
civil and political privileges, in their habits, in their tastes, in
their manners, in their dress, in what they see, in what they do,
in what they read, in what they think, and in what they say. On
all sides the process of assimilation is going on. Shades of
character are being blended, and contrasts of will are being
reconciled. As a natural consequence, the individual life, that
is, the life which distinguishes each man from his fellows, is
perishing. The consolidation of the many destroys the actions
of the few. While we amalgamate the mass, we absorb the unit.

---

[15] 'There is now scarcely any outlet for energy in this country except
business. The energy expended in that may still be regarded as
considerable.' — Mill *On Liberty*, p. 125. I suppose that, under the word
business, Mr. Mill includes political and the higher class of official
pursuits.

The authority of society is, in this way, ruining society itself. For, the human faculties can, for the most part, only be exercised and disciplined by the act of choosing; but he who does a thing merely because others do it, makes no choice at all. Constantly copying the manners and opinions of our contemporaries, we strike out nothing that is new; we follow on in a dull and monotonous uniformity. We go where others lead. The field of option is being straitened; the number of alternatives is diminishing. And the result is, a sensible decay of that vigour and raciness of character, that diversity and fulness of life, and that audacity both of conception and of execution which marked the strong men of former times, and enabled them at once to improve and to guide the human species.

Now all this is gone, perhaps never to return, unless some great convulsion should previously occur. Originality is dying away, and is being replaced by a spirit of servile and apish imitation. We are degenerating into machines who do the will of society; our impulses and desires are repressed by a galling and artificial code; our minds are dwarfed and stunted by the checks and limitations to which we are perpetually subjected.

How, then, is it possible to discover new truths of real importance? How is it possible that creative thought can flourish in so sickly and tainted an atmosphere? Genius is a form of originality; if the originality is discouraged, how can the genius remain? It is hard to see the remedy for this crying evil. Society is growing so strong as to destroy individuality; that is, to destroy the very quality to which our civilization, and therefore our social fabric, is primarily owing.

The truth is, that we must vindicate the right of each man to do what he likes, and to say what he thinks, to an extent much greater than is usually supposed to be either safe or decent. This we must do for the sake of society, quite as much as for our own sake. That society would be benefited by a greater freedom of action, has been already shown; and the same thing may be proved concerning freedom of speech and of writing. In this respect, authors, and the teachers of mankind generally, are far too timid; while the state of public opinion is far too interfering. The remarks which Mr. Mill has made on this, are so exhaustive as to be unanswerable; and though many will call in question what he has said respecting the decline of individuality, no well instructed person will dispute the accuracy of his conclusions respecting the need of an increased liberty of discussion and of publication.

In the present state of knowledge the majority of people are so ill-informed as not to be aware of the true nature of belief; they are not aware that all belief is involuntary, and is entirely governed by the circumstances which produce it. They who have paid attention to these subjects, know that what we call the will, has no power over belief, and that consequently a man is nowise responsible for his creed, except in so far as he is responsible for the events which gave him his creed. Whether, for instance, he is a Mohammedan or a Christian, will usually resolve itself into a simple question of his geographical antecedents. He who is born in Constantinople, will hold one set of opinions; he who is born in London, will hold another set. Both act according to their light and their circumstances, and if both are sincere both are guiltless. In each case, the believer is controlled by physical facts which determine his creed, and over which he can no more exercise authority than he can exercise authority over the movements of the planets or the rotation of the earth. This view, though long familiar to thinkers, can hardly be said to have been popularized before the present century;[16] and to its diffusion, as well as to other larger and more potent causes, we must ascribe the increasing spirit of toleration to which not only our literature but even our statute-book bears witness.

But, though belief is involuntary, it will be objected, with a certain degree of plausibility, that the expression of that belief, and particularly the formal and written publication, is a voluntary act, and consequently a responsible one. If I were arguing the question exhaustively, I should at the outset demur to this proposition, and should require it to be stated in more cautious and limited terms; but, to save time, let us suppose it to be true, and let us inquire whether, if a man be responsible to himself for the publication of his opinions, it is right that he should also be held responsible by those to whom he offers them? In other words, is it proper that law or public opinion should discourage an individual from publishing sentiments

---

[16] Its diffusion was greatly helped by Bailey's *Essays on the Formation of Opinions*, which were first published, I believe, in 1821, and being popularly written, as well as suitable to the age, have exercised considerable influence.

which are hostile to the prevailing notions, and are considered by the rest of society to be false and mischievous?

Upon this point, the arguments of Mr. Mill are so full and decisive that I despair of adding anything to them. It will be enough if I give a summary of the principal ones; for it would be strange, indeed, if before many months are past, this noble treatise, so full of wisdom and of thought, is not in the hands of every one who cares for the future welfare of humanity, and whose ideas rise above the immediate interests of his own time.

Those who hold that an individual ought to be discouraged from publishing a work containing heretical or irreligious opinions, must, of course, assume that such opinions are false; since, in the present day, hardly any man would be so impudent as to propose that a true opinion should be stifled because it was unusual as well as true. We are all agreed that truth is good; or, at all events, those who are not agreed must be treated as persons beyond the pale of reason, and on whose obtuse understandings it would be idle to waste an argument. He who says that truth is not always to be told, and that it is not fit for all minds, is simply a defender of falsehood; and we should take no notice of him, inasmuch as the object of discussion being to destroy error, we cannot discuss with a man who deliberately affirms that error should be spared.

We take, therefore, for granted that those who seek to prevent any opinion being laid before the world, do so for the sake of truth, and with a view to prevent the unwary from being led into error. The intention is good; it remains for us to inquire how it operates.

Now, in the first place, we can never be sure that the opinion of the majority is true. Nearly every opinion held by the majority was once confined to the minority. Every established religion was once a heresy. If the opinions of the majority had always prevailed, Christianity would have been extirpated as soon as Christ was murdered. If any age of people assume that any notion they entertain is certainly right, they assume their own infallibility, and arrogantly claim for themselves a prerogative which even the wisest of mankind never possess. To affirm that a doctrine is unquestionably revealed from above, is equally to affirm their own infallibility, since they affirm that they cannot be mistaken in believing it to be revealed. A man who is sure that his creed is true, is sure of his own infallibility, because he is sure that upon that point he has committed no error. Unless, therefore, we are prepared to claim, on our own behalf, an immunity from error, and an incapability of being mistaken, which transcend the limits of the human mind, we are bound not only to permit our opinions to be disputed, but to be grateful to those who will do so. For, as no one who is not absurdly and immodestly confident of his own powers, can be sure that what he believes to be true is true, it will be his object, if he be an honest man, to rectify the errors he may have committed. But it is a matter of history that errors have only been rectified by two means; namely, by experience and discussion. The use of discussion is to show how experience is to be interpreted. Experience alone, has never improved either mankind or individuals. Experience, before it can be available, must be sifted and tested. This is done by discussion, which brings out the meaning of experience, and enables us to apply the observations that have been made, and turn them to account. Human judgment owes its value solely to the fact that when it is wrong it is possible to set it right. Inasmuch, however, as it can only be set right by the conflict and collision of hostile opinions, it is clear that when those opinions are smothered, and when that conflict is stopped, the means of correcting our judgment are gone, and hence the value of our judgment is destroyed. The more, therefore, that the majority discourage the opinions of the minority, the smaller is the chance of the majority holding accurate views. But if, instead of discouraging the opinions, they should suppress them, even that small chance is taken away, and society can have no option but to go on from bad to worse, its blunders becoming more inveterate and more mischievous, in proportion as that liberty of discussion which might have rectified them has been the longer withheld.

Here we, as the advocates of liberty, might fairly close the argument, leaving our opponents in the dilemma of either asserting their own infallibility, or else of abandoning the idea of interfering with freedom of discussion. So complete, however, is our case, that we can actually afford to dispense with what has been just stated, and support our views on other and totally different grounds. We will concede to those who favour restriction, all the premises that they require. We will concede to them the strongest position that they can imagine, and we will take for granted that a nation has the means of knowing with absolute certainty that some of its opinions are right. We say, then, and we will prove, that, assuming those opinions to be true, it is advisable that they should be combated, and that their truth should be denied. That an opinion which is held by an immense majority, and which is moreover completely and unqualifiedly true, ought to be contested, and that those who contest it do a public service, appears at first sight to be an untenable paradox. A paradox, indeed, it is, if by a paradox we mean an assertion not generally admitted; but, so far from being untenable, it is a sound and wholesome doctrine, which, if it were adopted, would, to an extraordinary extent, facilitate the progress of society.

Supposing any well-established opinion to be certainly true, the result of its not being vigorously attacked is, that it becomes more passive and inert than it would otherwise be. This, as Mr. Mill observes, has been exemplified in the history of Christianity. In the early Church, while Christianity was struggling against innumerable opponents, it displayed a life and an energy which diminished in proportion as the opposition was withdrawn. When an enemy is at the gate, the garrison is alert. If the enemy retires, the alertness slackens; and if he disappears altogether, nothing remains but the mere forms and duty of discipline, which, unenlivened by danger, grow torpid and mechanical. This is a law of the human mind, and is of universal application. Every religion, after being established, loses much of its vitality. Its doctrines being less questioned, it naturally happens that those who hold them, scrutinize them less closely, and therefore grasp them less firmly. Their wits being no longer sharpened by controversy, what was formerly a living truth dwindles into a dead dogma. The excitement of the battle being over, the weapons are laid aside; they fall into disuse; they grow rusty; the skill and fire of the warrior are gone. It is amid the roar of the cannon, the flash of the bayonet, and the clang of the trumpet, that the forms of men dilate; they swell with emotion; their bulk increases; their stature rises, and even small natures wax into great ones, able to do all and to dare all.

So, indeed, it is. On any subject, universal acquiescence always engenders universal apathy. By a parity of reasoning, the greater the acquiescence the greater the apathy. All hail, therefore, to those who, by attacking a truth, prevent that truth from slumbering. All hail to those bold and fearless natures, the heretics and innovators of their day, who, rousing men out of their lazy sleep, sound in their ears the tocsin and the clarion, and force them to come forth that they may do battle for their creed. Of all evils, torpor is the most deadly. Give us paradox, give us error, give us what you will, so that you save us from stagnation. It is the cold spirit of routine which is the nightshade of our nature. It sets upon men like a blight, blunting their faculties, withering their powers, and making them both unable and unwilling either to struggle for the truth, or to figure to themselves what it is that they really believe.

See how this has acted in regard to the doctrines of the New Testament. When those doctrines were first propounded, they were vigorously assailed, and therefore the early Christians clung to them, realized them, and bound them up in their hearts to an extent unparalleled in any subsequent age. Every Christian professes to believe that it is good to be ill-used and buffeted; that wealth is an evil, because rich men cannot enter the kingdom of heaven; that if your cloak is taken, you must give your coat also; that if you are smitten on one cheek, you should turn round and offer the other. These, and similar doctrines, the early Christians not only professed, but acted up to and followed. The same doctrines are contained in our Bibles, read in our churches, and preached in our pulpits. Who is there that obeys them? And what reason is there for this universal defection, beyond the fact that when Christianity was constantly assailed, those who received its tenets held them with a tenacity, and saw them with a vividness, which cannot be expected in an age that sanctions them by general acquiescence? Now, indeed, they are not only acquiesced in, they are also watched over and sedulously protected. They are protected by law, and by that public opinion which is infinitely more powerful than any law. Hence it is, that to them, men yield a cold and lifeless assent; they hear them and they talk about them, but whoever was to obey them with that scrupulous fidelity which was formerly practised, would find to his cost how much he had mistaken his age, and how great is the difference, in vitality and in practical effect, between doctrines which are generally received and those which are fearlessly discussed.

In proportion as knowledge has advanced, and habits of correct thinking been diffused, men have gradually approached towards these views of liberty, though Mr. Mill has been the first to bring them together in a thoroughly comprehensive spirit, and to concentrate in a single treatise all the arguments in their behalf. How everything has long tended to this result, must be known to whoever has studied the history of the English mind. Whatever may be the case respecting the alleged decline of individuality, and the increasing tyranny of custom, there can, at all events, be no doubt that, in religious matters, public opinion is constantly becoming more liberal. The legal penalties which our ignorant and intolerant ancestors inflicted upon whoever differed from themselves, are now some of them repealed, and some of them obsolete. Not only have we ceased to murder or torture those who disagree with us, but, strange to say, we have even recognized their claim to political rights as well as to civil equality. The admission of the Jews into Parliament, that just and righteous measure, which was carried in the teeth of the most cherished and inveterate prejudice, is a striking proof of the force of the general movement; as also is the rapidly increasing disposition to abolish oaths, and to do away in public life with every species of religious tests. Partly as cause, and partly as effect of all this, there never was a period in which so many bold and able attacks were made upon the prevailing theology, and in which so many heretical doctrines were propounded, not only by laymen, but occasionally by ministers of the church, some of the most eminent of whom have, during the present generation, come forward to denounce the errors in their own system, and to point out the flaws in their own creed. The unorthodox character of physical science is equally notorious; and many of its professors do not scruple to impeach the truth of statements which are still held to be essential, and which, in other days, no one could have impugned without exposing himself to serious danger. In former times, such men would have been silenced or punished; now, they are respected and valued; their works are eagerly read, and the circle of their influence is steadily widening. According to the letter of our law-books, these, and similar publications, which fearless and inquisitive men are pouring into the public ear, are illegal, and Government has the power of prosecuting their authors. The state of opinion, however, is so improved, that such prosecutions would be fatal to any Government which instigated them. We have, therefore, every reason to congratulate ourselves on having outlived the reign of open persecution. We may fairly suppose that the cruelties which our forefathers committed in the name of religion, could not now be perpetrated, and that it would be impossible to punish a man merely because he expressed notions which the majority considered to be profane and mischievous.

Under these circumstances, and seeing that the practice of prosecuting men for uttering their sentiments on religious matters has been for many years discontinued, an attempt to revive that shameful custom would, if it were generally known, be at once scouted. It would be deemed unnatural as well as cruel: out of the ordinary course, and wholly unsuited to the humane and liberal notions of an age which seeks to relax penalties rather than to multiply them. As to the man who might be mad enough to make the attempt, we should look upon him in the light in which we should regard some noxious animal, which, being suddenly let loose, went about working harm, and undoing all the good that had been previously done. We should hold him to be a nuisance which it was our duty either to abate, or to warn people of. To us, he would be a sort of public enemy; a disturber of human happiness; a creature hostile to the human species. If he possessed authority, we should loathe him the more, as one who, instead of employing for the benefit of his country the power with which his country had entrusted him, used it to gratify his own malignant prejudices, or maybe to humour the spleen of some wretched and intolerant faction with which he was connected.

Inasmuch, therefore, as, in the present state of English society, any punishment inflicted for the use of language which did not tend to break the public peace, and which was neither seditious in reference to the State, nor libellous in reference to individuals, would be simply a wanton cruelty, alien to the genius of our time, and capable of producing no effect beyond reviving intolerance, exasperating the friends of liberty, and bringing the administration of justice into disrepute, it was with the greatest astonishment that I read in Mr. Mill's work that such a thing had occurred in this country, and at one of our assizes, less than two years ago. Notwithstanding my knowledge of Mr. Mill's accuracy, I thought that, in this instance, he must have been mistaken. I supposed that he had not heard all the circumstances, and that the person punished had been guilty of some other offence. I could not believe that in the year 1857, there was a judge on the English bench who would sentence a poor man of irreproachable character, of industrious habits, and supporting his family by the sweat of his brow, to twenty-one months' imprisonment, merely because he had uttered and written on a gate a few words respecting Christianity. Even now, when I have carefully investigated the facts to which Mr. Mill only alludes, and have the documents before me, I can hardly bring myself to realize the events which have actually occurred, and which I will relate, in order that public opinion may take cognizance of a transaction which happened in a remote part of the kingdom, but which the general welfare requires to be bruited abroad, so that men may determine whether or not such things shall be allowed.

In the summer of 1857, a poor man, named Thomas Pooley, was gaining his livelihood as a common labourer in Liskeard, in Cornwall, where he had been well known for several years, and had always borne a high character for honesty, industry, and sobriety. His habits were so eccentric, that his mind was justly reputed to be disordered; and an accident which happened to him about two years before this period, had evidently inflicted some serious injury, as since then his demeanour had become more strange and excitable. Still, he was not only perfectly harmless, but was a very useful member of society, respected by his neighbours, and loved by his family, for whom he toiled with a zeal rare in his class, or indeed in any class. Among other hallucinations, he believed that the earth was a living animal, and, in his ordinary employment of well-sinking, he avoided digging too deeply, lest he should penetrate the skin of the earth, and wound some vital part. He also imagined that if he hurt the earth, the tides would cease to flow; and that nothing being really mortal, whenever a child died it reappeared at the next birth in the same family. Holding all nature to be animated, he moreover fancied that this was in some way connected with the potato-rot, and, in the wildness of his vagaries, he did not hesitate to say that if the ashes of burnt Bibles were strewed over the fields, the rot would cease. This was associated, in his mind, with a foolish dislike of the Bible itself, and an hostility against Christianity; in reference, however, to which he could hurt no one, as not only was he very ignorant, but his neighbours, regarding him as crackbrained, were uninfluenced by him; though in the other relations of life he was valued and respected by his employers, and indeed by all who were most acquainted with his disposition.

This singular man, who was known by the additional peculiarity of wearing a long beard, wrote upon a gate a few very silly words expressive of his opinion respecting the potato-rot and the Bible, and also of his hatred of Christianity. For this, as well as for using language equally absurd, but which no one was obliged to listen to, and which certainly could influence no one, a clergyman in the neighbourhood lodged an information against him, and caused him to be summoned before a magistrate, who was likewise a clergyman. The magistrate, instead of pitying him or remonstrating with him, committed him for trial and sent him to jail. At the next assizes, he was brought before the judge. He had no counsel to defend him, but the son of the judge acted as counsel to prosecute him. The father and the son performed their parts with zeal, and were perfectly successful. Under their auspices, Pooley was found guilty. He was brought up for judgment. When addressed by the judge, his restless manner, his wild and incoherent speech, his disordered countenance and glaring eye, betokened too surely the disease of his mind. But neither this, nor the fact that he was ignorant, poor, and friendless, produced any effect upon that stony-hearted man who now held him in his grip. He was sentenced to be imprisoned for a year and nine months. The interests of religion were vindicated. Christianity was protected, and her triumph assured, by dragging a poor, harmless and demented creature from the bosom of his family, throwing him into jail, and leaving his wife and children without provision, either to starve or to beg.

Before he had been many days in prison, the insanity which was obvious at the time of his trial, ceased to lurk, and broke out into acts of violence. He grew worse; and within a fortnight after the sentence had been pronounced he went mad, and it was found necessary to remove from the jail to the County Lunatic Asylum. While he was lying there, his misfortunes attracted the attention of a few high-minded and benevolent men, who exerted themselves to procure his pardon; so that, if he recovered, he might be restored to his family. This petition was refused. It was necessary to support the judge; and the petitioners were informed that if the miserable lunatic should regain his reason, he would be sent back to prison to undergo the rest of his sentence. This, in all probability, would have caused a relapse; but little was thought of that; and it was hoped that, as he was an obscure and humble man, the efforts made in his behalf would soon subside. Those, however, who had once interested themselves in such a case, were not likely to slacken their zeal. The cry grew hotter, and preparations were made for bringing the whole question before the country. Then it was that the authorities gave way. Happily for mankind, one vice is often balanced by another, and cruelty is corrected by cowardice. The authors and abettors of this prodigious iniquity trembled at the risk they would run if the public feeling of this great country were roused. The result was, that the proceedings of the judge were rescinded, as far as possible, by a pardon being granted to Pooley less than five months after the sentence was pronounced.

By this means, general exposure was avoided; and perhaps that handful of noble-minded men who obtained the liberation of Pooley, were right in letting the matter fall into oblivion after they had carried their point. Most of them were engaged in political or other practical affairs, and they were, therefore, obliged to consider expediency as well as justice. But such is not the case with the historian of this sad event. No writer on important subjects has reason to expect that he can work real good, or that his words shall live, if he allows himself to be so trammelled by expediency as to postpone to it consideration of right, of justice, and of truth. A great crime has been committed, and the names of the criminals ought to be known. They should be in every one's mouth. They should be blazoned abroad, in order that the world may see that in a free country such things cannot be done with impunity. To discourage a repetition of the offence the offenders must be punished. And, surely, no punishment can be more severe than to preserve their names. Against them personally, I have nothing to object, for I have no knowledge of them. Individually, I can feel no animosity towards men who have done me no harm, and whom I have never seen. But they have violated principles dearer to me than any personal feeling, and in vindication of which I would set all personal feeling at nought. Fortunate, indeed, it is for humanity that our minds are constructed after such a fashion as to make it impossible for us, by any effort of abstract reasoning, to consider oppression apart from the oppressor. We may abhor a speculative principle, and yet respect him who advocates it. This distinction between the opinion and the person is, however, confined to the intellectual world, and does not extent to the practical. Such a separation cannot exist in regard to actual deeds of cruelty. In such cases, our passions instruct our understanding. The same cause which excites our sympathy for the oppressed, stirs up our hatred of the oppressor. This is an instinct of our nature, and he who struggles against it does so to his own detriment. It belongs to the higher region of the mind; it is not to be impeached by argument; it cannot even be touched by it. Therefore it is, that when we hear that a poor, a defenceless, and a half-witted man, who had hurt no one, a kind father, an affectionate husband, whose private character was unblemished, and whose integrity was behind dispute, is suddenly thrown into prison, his family left to subsist on the precarious charity of strangers, he himself by this cruel treatment deprived of the little reason he possessed, then turned into a madhouse, and finally refused such scanty redress as might have been afforded him, a spirit of vehement indignation is excited, partly, indeed, against a system under which such things can be done; but still more against those who, in the pride of their power and wickedness of their hearts, put laws into execution which had long fallen into disuse, and which they were not bound to enforce, but of which they availed themselves to crush the victim they held in their grasp.

The prosecutor who lodged the information against Pooley, and had him brought before the magistrate, was the Rev. Paul Bush. The magistrate who received the information, and committed him for trial, was the Rev. James Glencross. The judge who passed the sentence which destroyed his reason and beggared his family, was Mr. Justice Coleridge.

Of the two first, little need be said. It is to be hoped that their names will live, and that they will enjoy that sort of fame which they have amply earned. Perhaps, after all, we should rather blame the state of society which concedes power to such men, than wonder that having the power they should abuse it. But, with Mr. Justice Coleridge we have a different account to settle, and to him other language must be applied. That our judges should have great authority is unavoidable. To them, a wide and discretionary latitude is necessarily entrusted. Great confidence being reposed in them, they are bound, by every possible principle which can actuate an honest man, to respect that confidence. They are bound to avoid not only injustice, but, so far as they can, the very appearance of injustice. Seeing, as they do, all classes of society, they are well aware that, among the lower ranks, there is a deep, though on the whole a diminishing, belief that the poor are ill-treated by the rich, and that even in the courts of law equal measure is not always meted out to both. An opinion of this sort is full of danger, and it is the more dangerous because it is not unfounded. The country magistrates are too often unfair in their decisions, and this will always be the case until greater publicity is given to their proceedings. But, from our superior judges we expect another sort of conduct. We expect, and it must honestly be said we usually find, that they shall be above petty prejudices, or at all events, that whatever private opinions they may have, they shall not intrust those opinions into the sanctuary of justice. Above all do we expect, that they shall not ferret out some obsolete law for the purpose of oppressing the poor, when they know right well that the anti-Christian sentiments which that law was intended to punish are quite as common among the upper classes as among the lower, and are participated in by many persons who enjoy the confidence of the country and to whom the highest offices are entrusted.

That this is the case, was known in the year 1857 to Mr. Justice Coleridge, just as it was then known, and is now known, to every one who mixes in the world. The charge, therefore, which I bring against this unjust and unrighteous judge is, that he passed a sentence of extreme severity upon a poor and friendless man in a remote part of the kingdom, where he might reasonably expect that his sentence would escape public animadversion; that he did this by virtue of a law which had fallen into disuse and was contrary to the spirit of the age;[17] and that he would not have dared to commit such an act, in the face of a London audience, and in the full light of the London press. Neither would he, nor those who supported him, have treated in such a manner a person belonging to the upper classes. No. They select the most inaccessible county in England, where the press is least active and the people are most illiterate, and there they pounce upon a defenceless man and

---

[17]   Or rather by virtue of the cruel and persecuting maxims of our old Common Law, established at a period when it was a matter of religion to burn heretics and to drown witches. Why did not such a judge live three hundred years ago? He has fallen upon evil times and has come too late into the world.

make him the scapegoat. He is to be the victim whose vicarious sufferings may atone for the offences of more powerful unbelievers. Hardly a year goes by, without some writer of influence and ability attacking Christianity, and every such attack is punishable by law. Why did not Mr. Justice Coleridge, and those who think like him, put the law into force against those writers? Why do they not do it now? Why do they not have the learned and the eminent indicted and thrown into prison? Simply because they dare not. I defy them to it. They are afraid of the odium; they tremble at the hostility they would incur and at the scorn which would be heaped upon them, both by their contemporaries and by posterity. Happily for mankind, literature is a real power, and tyranny quakes at it. But to me it appears, that men of letters perform the least part of their duty when they defend each other. It is their proper function, and it ought to be their glory, to defend the weak against the strong, and to uphold the poor against the rich. This should be their pride and their honour. I would it were known in every cottage, that the intellectual classes sympathize, not with the upper ranks but with the lower. I would that we made the freedom of the people our first consideration. Then, indeed, would literature be the religion of liberty, and we, priests of the altar, ministering her sacred rites, might feel that we act in the purest spirit of our creed when we denounce tyranny in high places, when we chastise the insolence of office, and when we vindicate the cause of Thomas Pooley against Justice Coleridge.

For my part, I can honestly say that I have nothing exaggerated, nor set down aught in malice. What the verdict of public opinion may be, I cannot tell. I speak merely as a man of letters, and do not pretend to represent any class. I have no interest to advocate; I hold no brief; I carry no man's proxy. But unless I altogether mistake the general feeling, it will be considered that a great crime has been committed; that a knowledge of that crime has been too long hidden in a corner; and that I have done something towards dragging the criminal from his covert, and letting in on him the full light of day.

This gross iniquity is, no doubt, to be immediately ascribed to the cold heart and shallow understanding of the judge by whom it was perpetrated. If, however, public opinion had been sufficiently enlightened, those evil qualities would have been restrained and rendered unable to work the mischief. Therefore it is, that the safest and most permanent remedy would be to diffuse sound notions respecting the liberty of speech and of publication. It should be clearly understood that every man has an absolute and irrefragable right to treat any doctrine as he thinks proper; either to argue against it, or to ridicule it. If his arguments are wrong, he can be refuted; if his ridicule is foolish, he can be out-ridiculed. To this, there can be no exception. It matters not what the tenet may be, nor how dear it is to our feelings. Like all other opinions, it must take its chance; it must be roughly used; it must stand every test; it must be thoroughly discussed and sifted. And we may rest assured that if it really be a great and valuable truth, such opposition will endear it to us the more; and that we shall cling to it the closer, in proportion as it is argued against, aspersed, and attempted to be overthrown.

If I were asked for an instance of the extreme latitude to which such licence might be extended, I would take what, in my judgment, at least, is the most important of all doctrines, the doctrine of a future state. Strictly speaking, there is, in the present early condition of the human mind, no subject on which we can arrive at complete certainty; but the belief in a future state approaches that certainty nearer than any other belief, and it is one which if eradicated, would drive most of us to despair. On both these grounds, it stands alone. It is fortified by arguments far stronger than can be adduced in support of any other opinion; and it is a supreme consolation to those who suffer affliction, or smart under a sense of injustice. The attempts made to impugn it, have always seemed to me to be very weak, and to leave the real difficulties untouched. They are negative arguments directed against affirmative ones. But if, in transcendental inquiries, negative arguments are to satisfy us, how shall we escape from the reasonings of Berkeley respecting the non-existence of the material world? Those reasonings have never been answered, and our knowledge must be infinitely more advanced than it now is, before they can be answered. They are far stronger than the arguments of the atheists; and I cannot but wonder that they who reject a future state, should believe in the reality of the material world. Still, those who do reject it, are not only justified in openly denying it, but are bound to do so. Our first and paramount duty is to be true to ourselves; and no man is true to himself who fears to express his opinion. There is hardly any vice which so debases us in our own esteem, as moral cowardice. There is hardly any virtue which elevates our character, as moral courage. Therefore it is, that the more unpopular a notion, the greater the merit of him who advocates it, provided, of course, he does so in honesty and singleness of heart. On this account, although I regard the expectation of another life, as the prop and mainstay of mankind, and although I cannot help thinking that they who reject it, have taken an imperfect and uncomprehensive view, and have not covered the whole field of inquiry, I do strenuously maintain, that against it every species of attack is legitimate, and I feel assured that the more it is assailed, the more it will flourish. and the more vividly we shall realize its meaning, its depth, and its necessity.

That many of the common arguments in favour of this great doctrine are unsound, might be easily shown; but, until the entire subject is freely discussed, we shall never know how far they are unsound, and what part of them ought to be retained. If, for instance, we make our belief in it depend upon assertions contained in books regarded as sacred, it will follow that whenever those books lose their influence the doctrine will be in peril. The basis being impaired, the superstructure will tremble. It may well be that, in the march of ages, every definite and written creed now existing is destined to die out, and to be succeeded by better ones. The world has seen the beginning of them, and we have no surety that it will not see the end of them. Everything which is essential to the human mind must survive all the shocks and vicissitudes of time; but dogmas, which the mind once did without, cannot be essential to it. Perhaps, we have no right so to anticipate the judgment of our remotest posterity, as to affirm that any opinion is essential to all possible forms of civilization; but, at all events, we have more reason to believe this of the doctrine of a future state than of any other conceivable idea. Let us then beware of endangering its stability by narrowing its foundation. Let us take heed how we rest it on the testimony of inspired writings, when we know that inspiration at one epoch is often different from inspiration at another. If Christianity should ever perish, the age that loses it, will have reason to deplore the blindness of those who teach mankind to defend this glorious and consolatory tenet, not by general considerations of the fundamental properties of our common nature, but by traditions, assertions, and records, which do not bear the stamp of universality, since in one state of society they are held to be true, and in another state of society they are held to be false.

Of the same fluctuating and precarious character, is the argument drawn from the triumph of injustice in this world, and the consequent necessity of such unfairness being remedied in another life. For, it admits of historical proof that, as civilization advances, the impunity and rewards of wickedness diminish. In a barbarous state of society, virtue is invariably trampled upon, and nothing really succeeds except violence or fraud. In that stage of affairs, the worst criminals are the most prosperous men. But, in every succeeding step of the great progress, injustice becomes more hazardous; force and rapine grow more unsafe; precautions multiply; the supervision is keener; tyranny and deceit are oftener detected. Being oftener detected, it is less profitable to practise them. In the same proportion, the rewards of integrity increase, and the prospects of virtue brighten. A large part of the power, the honour, and the fame formerly possessed by evil men is transferred to good men. Acts of injustice which at an earlier period would have escaped attention, or, if known, would have excited no odium, are now chastized, not only by law, but also by public opinion. Indeed, so marked is this tendency, that many persons, by a single confusion of thought, actually persuade themselves that offences are increasing because we hear more of them, and punish them oftener; not seeing that this merely proves that we note them more and hate them more. We redouble our efforts against injustice, not on account of the spread of injustice, but on account of our better understanding how to meet it, and being more determined to coerce it. No other age has ever cried out against it so loudly; and yet, strange to say, this very proof of our superiority to all other ages is cited as evidence of our inferiority. This I shall return to elsewhere; my present object in mentioning it, is partly to check a prevailing error, but chiefly to indicate its connexion with the subject before us. Nothing is more certain than that, as society advances, the weak are better protected against the strong; the honest against the dishonest; and the just against the unjust. If, then, we adopt the popular argument in favour of another life, that injustice here, must be compensated hereafter, we are driven to the terrible conclusion that the same progress of civilization, which, in this world, heightens the penalties inflicted on injustice, would also lessen the need of future compensation, and thereby weaken the ground of our belief. The inference would be untrue, but it follows from the premises. To me it appears no only sad, but extremely pernicious, that on a topic of such surpassing interest, the understandings of men should be imposed upon by reasonings which are so shallow, that, if pushed to their legitimate consequence, they would defeat their own aim, because they would force us to assert that the more we improve in our moral conduct towards each other, the less we should care for a future and a better world.

I have brought forward these views for the sake of justifying the general proposition maintained in this essay. For, it is evident that if the state of public opinion did not discourage a fearless investigation of these matters, and did not foolishly cast a slur upon those who attack doctrines which are dear to us, the whole subject would be more thoroughly understood, and such weak arguments as are commonly advanced would have been long since exploded. If they who deny the immortality of the soul, could, without the least opprobrium, state in the boldest manner all their objections, the advocates of the doctrine would be obliged to reconsider their own position, and to abandon its untenable points. By this means, that which I revere, and which an overwhelming majority of us revere, as a glorious truth, would be immensely strengthened. It would be strengthened by being deprived of those sophistical arguments which are commonly urged in its favour, and which give to its enemies an incalculable advantage. It would, moreover, be strengthened by that feeling of security which men have in their own convictions, when they know that everything is said against them which can be said, and that their opponents have a fair and liberal hearing. This begets a magnanimity, and a rational confidence, which cannot otherwise be obtained. But, such results can never happen while we are so timid, or so dishonest, as to impute improper motives to those who assail our religious opinions. We may rely upon it that as long as we look upon an atheistical writer as a moral offender, or even as long as we glance at him with suspicion, atheism will remain a standing and a permanent danger, because, skulking in hidden corners, it will use stratagems which their secrecy will prevent us from baffling; it will practise artifices to which the persecuted are forced to resort; it will number its concealed proselytes to an extent of which only they who have studied this painful subject are aware; and, above all, by enabling them to complain of the treatment to which they are exposed, it will excite the sympathy of many high and generous natures who, in an open and manly warfare, might strive against them, but who, by a noble instinct, find themselves incapable of contending with any sect which is oppressed, maligned, or intimidated.

Though this essay has been prolonged much beyond my original intention, I am unwilling to conclude it just at this point, when I have attacked arguments which support a doctrine that I cherish above all other doctrines. It is, indeed, certain that he who destroys a feeble argument in favour of any truth, renders the greatest service to that truth, by obliging its advocates to produce a stronger one. Still, an idea will prevail among some persons that such service is insidious; and that to expose the weak side of a cause, is likely to be the work, not of a friend but of an enemy in disguise. Partly, therefore, to prevent misinterpretation from those who are always ready to misinterpret, and partly for the satisfaction of more candid readers, I will venture to state what I apprehend to be the safest and most impregnable ground on which the supporters of this great doctrine can take their stand.

That ground is the universality of the affections; the yearning of every mind to care for something out of itself. For, this is the very bond and seal of our common humanity; it is the golden link which knits together and preserves the human species. It is in the need of loving and of being loved, that the highest instincts of our nature are first revealed. Not only is it found among the good and the virtuous, but experience proves that it is compatible with almost any amount of depravity, and with almost every form of vice. No other principle is so general or so powerful. It exists in the most barbarous and ferocious states of society, and we know that even sanguinary and revolting crimes are often unable to efface it from the breast of the criminal. It warms the coldest temperament, and softens the hardest heart. However a character may be deteriorated and debased, this single passion is capable of redeeming it from utter defilement, and of rescuing it from the lowest depths. And if, from time to time, we hear of an apparently well attested case of its entire absence, we are irresistibly impelled to believe that, even in that mind, it lurks unseen; that it is stunted, not destroyed; that there is yet some nook or cranny in which it is buried; that the avenues from without are not quite closed; and that, in spite of adverse circumstances, the affections are not so dead but that it would be possible to rouse them from their torpor, and kindle them into life.

Look now at the way in which this godlike and fundamental principle of our nature acts. As long as we are with those whom we love, and as long as the sense of security is unimpaired, we rejoice, and the remote consequences of our love are usually forgotten. Its fears and its risks are unheeded. But, when the dark day approaches, and the moment of sorrow is at hand, other and yet essential parts of our affection come into play. And if, perchance, the struggle has been long and arduous; if we have been tempted to cling to hope when hope should have been abandoned, so much the more are we at the last changed and humbled. To note the slow, but inevitable march of disease, to watch the enemy stealing in at the gate, to see the strength gradually waning, the limbs tottering more and more, the noble faculties dwindling by degrees, the eye paling and losing its lustre, the tongue faltering as it vainly tries to utter its words of endearment, the very lips hardly able to smile with their wonted tenderness; — to see this, is hard indeed to bear, and many of the strongest natures have sunk under it. But when even this is gone; when the very signs of life are mute; when the last faint tie is severed, and there lies before us nought save the shell and husk of what we loved too well, then truly if we believed the separation were final, how could we stand up and live? We have staked our all upon a single cast, and lost the stake. There, where we have garnered up our hearts, and where our treasure is, thieves break in and spoil. Methinks, that in that moment of desolation, the best of us would succumb, but for the deep conviction that all is not really over; that we have as yet only seen a part; and that something remains behind. Something behind; something which the eye of reason cannot discern, but on which the eye of affection is fixed. What is that, which, passing over us like a shadow, strains the aching vision as we gaze at it? Whence comes that sense of mysterious companionship in the midst of solitude; that ineffable feeling which cheers the afflicted? Why is it that, at these times, our minds are thrown back on themselves, and, being so thrown, have a forecast of another and higher state? If this be a delusion, it is one which the affections have themselves created, and we must believe that the purest and noblest elements of our nature conspire to deceive us. So surely as we lose what we love, so surely does hope mingle with grief. That if a man stood alone, he would deem himself mortal, I can well imagine. Why not? On account of his loneliness, his moral faculties would be undeveloped, and it is solely from them that he could learn the doctrine of immortality. There is nothing, either in the mechanism of the material universe, or in the vast sweep and compass of science, which can teach it. The human intellect, glorious as it is, and in its own field almost omnipotent, knows it not. For, the province and function of the intellect is to take those steps, and to produce those improvements, whether speculative or practical, which accelerate the march of nations, and to which we owe the august and imposing fabric of modern civilization. But this intellectual movement which determines the condition of man, does not apply with the same force to the condition of men. What is most potent in the mass, loses its supremacy in the unit. One law for the separate elements; another law for the entire compound. The intellectual principle is conspicuous in regard to the race; the moral principle in regard to the individual. And of all the moral sentiments which adorn and elevate the human character, the instinct of affection is surely the most lovely, the most powerful, and the most general. Unless, therefore, we are prepared to assert that this, the fairest and choicest of our possessions, is of so delusive and fraudulent a character that its dictates are not to be trusted, we can hardly avoid the conclusion that, inasmuch as they are the same in all ages, with all degrees of knowledge, and with all varieties of religion, they bear upon their surface the impress of truth, and are at once the conditions and consequence of our being.

It is, then, to that sense of immortality with which the affections inspire us, that I would appeal for the best proof of the reality of a future life. Other proofs perhaps there are, which it may be for other men or for other times to work out. But, before this can be done, the entire subject will have to be reopened, in order that it may be discussed with boldness and yet with calmness, which however cannot happen as long as a stigma rests on those who attack the belief; because its assailants, being unfairly treated, will for the most part be either timid or passionate. How mischievous as well as how unjust such a stigma is, has, I trust, been made apparent, and to that part of the question I need not revert. One thing only I would repeat, because I honestly believe it to be of the deepeest importance. Most earnestly would I again urge upon those who cherish the doctrine of immortality, not to defend it, as they too often do, by arguments which have a basis smaller than the doctrine itself. I long to see this glorious tenet rescued from the jurisdiction of a narrow and sectarian theology, which, foolishly ascribing to a single religion the possession of all truth, proclaims other religions to be false, and debases the most magnificent topics by contracting them within the horizon of its own little vision. Every creed which has existed long and played a great part, contains a large amount of truth, or else it would not have retained its hold upon the human mind. To suppose, however, that any one of them contains the whole truth, is to suppose that as soon as that creed was enunciated the limits of inspiration were reached, and the power of inspiration exhausted. For such a supposition we have no warrant. On the contrary, the history of mankind, if compared in long periods, shows a very slow, but still a clearly marked, improvement in the character of successive creeds; so that if we reason from the analogy of the past, we have right to hope that the improvement will continue, and that subsequent creeds will surpass ours. Using the word religion in its ordinary sense, we find that the religious opinions of men depend on an immense variety of circumstances which are constantly shifting. Hence it is, that whatever rests merely upon these opinions has in it something transient and mutable. Well, therefore, may they who take a distant and comprehensive view, be filled with dismay when they see a doctrine like the immortality of the soul defended in this manner. Such advocates incur a heavy responsibility. They imperil their own cause; they make the fundamental depend upon the casual; they support what is permanent by what is ephemeral; and with their books, their dogmas, their traditions, their rituals, their records, and their other perishable contrivances, they seek to prove what was known to the world before these existed, and what, if these were to die away, would still be known, and would remain the common heritage of the human species, and the consolation of myriads yet unborn.

Note to Footnote 7

Ὅτι δὲ ἐκ τῶν πρότερον εἰρημένων οἱ λόγοι καὶ διὰ τούτων, καὶ πρὸς ταῦτα, μία μὲν πίστις ἡ διὰ τῆς ἐπαγωγῆς. Εἰ γάρ τις ἐπισκοποίη ἑκάστην τῶν προτάσεων καὶ τῶν προβλημάρων· φαίνοιτ"αν "η ἀπὸ ρὸ ὅρου, "η ἀπὸ τὸν ἴδιου, "η ἀπὸ τὸν συμβεβηκότος γεγενημένη. — *Aristotelis Topicorum*, lib,. i. cap. vi., Lipsiæ, 1832, p. 104.

Διωρισμένων δὲ ρούτων, χρὴ διελέσθαι, πόσα τῶν λόγω εἴοη τῶν διαλεκτικῶν. Ἔστι δὲ ρὸ μὲν ἐπαγωγὴ, τὴ δὲ αυλλογισμὸς. Καὶ συλλογισμὸς μὲν τι ἐστιν, εἴρται προτερον. Επαγωγὴ δὲ ἡ ἀπὸ τῶν καθέκαστα ἐπὶ τὰ καθόλου ἔφοδος· οιον, εἰ "εστι κυβερνήτης ὁ ἐπιστάμενος κράτισος, καὶ ἡνίοχος· καὶ "ολως ἐστὶν ὁ ἐπιστάμενος περὶ ἕκαστον ἄροστος. — *Aristot. Topic.*, lib. i. chap. x. p. 108.

Εαν δὲ μὴ ριθῇ δι'επαλωγῆς ληπτέοω, προτείνοντα ἐπὶ ρῶν κατὰ πέρος ἐνανρίων. Ἡ γὰρ διὰ συλλογισποῦ, ἢ δι' ἐπαγωγῆς τὰς ἀναγκαίας ληπτέον· ἢ τὰς μὲν ἐπαγωγῆ, τὰς δὲ συλλογισμῷ οσαι δὲ λίαν προφανεῖς εἰσι, καὶ αὐτὰς προτείνοντα. Ἀδηλότερόν τε γὰρ ἀεὶ ἐν τῇ ἀποστάσει και τῇ ἐπαγωγῆ τὸ συμβεσόμενον· καὶ ἅμα τὸ αὐτὰς τὰς χρησίμους προτεῖναι καὶ μὴ δυνάμενον ἐκείνως λαβεῖν, "ετοιμον. Τὰς δὲ παρὰ ταένας ληπτέον μὴν 'τούτων χάριν· ἑκάστη δὲ 'ωδε χρηστέοω. Ἐπάγοντα μὲν ἀπὸ τῶν καθέκαστα ἐπὶ τὰ καθόλου, καὶ τῶν γνωρίμων ἐπὶ τὰ "αγνωστα. — *Arist. Topic.,*, lib. viii. cap. i. pp. 253, 254

Ἐπεὶ δὲ πᾶσα πρότασις συλλογιστικὴ η τούτων τίς ἐστιν, ἐξ ων ὁ σύλλογισμὸς, "η τινος τούτων ἕνεκα δῆλον δ, ὅταν ἑτέρου χάριν λαμβάνηται τῷ πλείω τὰ ομοια ἐρωρᾶν (η γὰρ δι ἐπαγωγῆς, ἢ δι ὁμοιότητος, ὡς ἐπὶ τὸ πολὺ τὸ καθόλου λαμβάνουσι) τὰ μὲν καθέκαστα πάντα θετέον, ἀν ῇ ἀληθῆ καὶ ενδοξα — *Aristot. Topic.*, lib. viii. cap. vii. p. 276.

τῇ πὲν οὖν καθόλου θεωροῦμεν τὰ ἐν μέρει, τῇ δὲ οἰκεία οὐκ ὅσμεν. Ωστ ἐνδέχεται καὶ ἀπατᾶσθαι περὶ αὐτά πλὴν οὐκ ἐναντίως, ἀλλ ἔχειν μεν πὴν καθολου, ἀπατᾶσθαι δὲ τῇ κατὰ μέρος. — *Aristotelis Analytica Priora*, lib. ii. cap. xiii., Lipsiæ, 1832, p. 134.

Απαντα γὰρ πιστεύπμεν ἢ διὰ συλλογισμοῦ, ἢ ἐξ επαγωγῆς. Ἐπαγωγὴ μὲν οὖν ἐστι καὶ ὁ ἐξ ἐπαγωγῆς συλλογισμὸς τὸ δθι τοῦ ἑτέρου θάτερον ακτον τῷ μέσω συλλογισασθαι. — *Aristot. Analyt. Prior.*, lib. ii. cap. xxv. p. 138.

Φανερὸν δὲ και, ὅτι, ει τις αισθησος ἐκλελοιπεν, ἀνάγκη, καὶ ἐπιστήμην τινὰ ἐκλελοιπέναι, ἢν ἀδύνατον λαβεῖν ειπερ μανθάνομεν ἢ ἐπαγωγῆ, ἢ ἀποδείξει. Ἔστι δ' ἡ μὲν ἀπόδειξις εκ τῶν καθόλου ἡ δ' ἐπαγωγὴ ἐκ τῶν κατα μέρος ἀδύνατον δὲ τὰ δαθόλου θεωρῆσαι, εἰ μὴ δι' ἐπαγωῆς (ἐπεὶ καὶ τὰ ἐξ αφαωέσεως λεγόμενα εσται δι' ἐπαγωγῆς γνώριμα, ἐάν τις βούληται γνώοιμα ποιεῖν, οτι ὑπάρχει ἑκάσρω γένει ενια, καὶ εἰ μὴ χωριστά εσριν, ἢ τοιον δι εκαστον) επαχθῆναι δὲ μὴ ἔχοντας αἰσθησιν ἀδύνατον. Τῶν γὰρ καθέκαστον ἡ αισθησις ευ γὰρ ἐνέχεται λαβειν αὐτῶν τὴν ἐπιστήμην ουτε γὰρ ἐκ τῶν καθόλου ανευ ἐπαγωγῆς, ουτε διὰ τῆς ἐπαγωγῆς ανευ τῆς αἰσθήσεως. — *Aristotelis Analytica Posteriora*, lib. i. cap. xviii. Lipsiæ, 1832, p. 177

Καὶ ἡ μὲν καθόλου νοητή ἡ δὲ κατὰ μέρος εἰς αισθησιν τελευτᾷ. — *Analyt. Post.*, lib. i. cap. xxiv. p. 191.

All that Aristotle knew of induction is contained in these passages. What he says in his Metaphysics is more vaguely expressed, or perhaps the text is more corrupt. The early part of the first book may, however, be looked at.

THE NATIONAL REVIEW
1859, [R. H. Hutton]

Mill on Liberty

Liberty. By John Stuart Mill. J. W. Parker, 1859.
Religious Freedom: a Lay Sermon. By Francis William Newman. Holyoake and Co., 1859.

MR. JOHN STUART MILL'S essay on Liberty is a very melancholy book on a great subject. It is written in the sincere foreboding that the strong individualities of the old types of English character are in imminent danger of being swallowed up in those political and social influences which emanate from large masses of men. It might almost, indeed, have come from the prison-cell of some persecuted thinker bent on making one last protest against the growing tyranny of the public mind, though conscious that his appeal will be in vain, — instead of from the pen of a writer who has perhaps exercised more influence over the formation of the philosophical and social principles of cultivated Englishmen than any other man of his generation. While agreeing with Mr. Mill, as most thoughtful politicians must, in some at least of the most important practical conclusions at which he eventually arrives as to the fitting limits of legislative interference, and the proper bounds to the jurisdiction of that secondary tribunal which we call public opinion, we differ from him widely and fundamentally with regard to the leading assumptions from which he starts, and the main principle which he takes with him as his clue in the inquiry. Indeed, we believe that the whole character and tone of English politics would suffer deeply and permanently were the theoretic basis of Mr. Mill's political philosophy to gain general acceptance. But before we follow him into his political philosophy, we must explain why we think him totally wrong in the most important of his preliminary assumptions.

We differ widely from Mr. Mill as to the *truth* of the painful conviction which has evidently given rise to this essay. We do not for a moment doubt that English "public opinion" is a much more intelligible and homogeneous thing in our own day than it has ever been at any previous time; that it comprehends much fewer conflicting types of thought, much fewer distinctly divergent social tendencies, much less honest and sturdy controversy between diametrical opposites in intellectual theory. Sectarian lines are fading away, political bonds are sundering, even social attractions and repulsions are less marked than they used to be; and to this extent we willingly concede to Mr. Mill that considerable progress is rapidly making towards that universal assimilation of the social conditions of life which he so much dreads. "William von Humboldt," says Mr. Mill, "points out two things as necessary conditions of human development, — freedom, and variety of situations. The second of these two conditions is in this country every day diminishing; the circumstances which surround different classes and individuals, and shape their characters, are daily becoming more assimilated." No doubt this is true; and it is true also, as Mr. Mill says, that "the very idea of resisting the will of the public, when it is positively known that they have a will, disappears more and more from the minds of practical politicians." But to what do these facts point? Mr. Mill believes that they point to an increasing despotism of social and political masses over the moral and intellectual freedom of individuals. To us his conclusion appears singularly hasty, and utterly unsustained by the premises he lays down. If, indeed, Mr. Mill still holds, as many passages in his earlier works would seem to indicate, that there is no such thing as an inherent difference in the original constitution of human minds, — that the varieties in the characters of men are due entirely to the varieties of physical, moral, and social influence to which they are exposed, — then, do doubt, he must argue that the great assimilation of outward circumstances which civilisation necessarily brings, will naturally end in producing a fatal monotony in human character. But without entering into the intricacies of this discussion, for which we have no pretence, — though we suspect it has something to do with Mr. Mill's melancholy anticipations of the extension of a Chinese petrifaction to the western world, — we would suggest that any moral monotony which springs exclusively from the assimilation of social conditions is not only inevitable, but a necessary result of social and political *liberty*, instead of a menace to it.

And what *are* the varieties of character which disappear as the process of social assimilations goes on? Surely *not* individual varieties of character, — varieties, that is, proper to the natural development of an individual character; but simply class types, — the varieties due to well-marked sectional groups, — to widely-severed phases of custom, — to the exclusive occupations of separate *castes*, — in short, to some local or social organisation, the sharp boundary of which is gradually becoming softened or altogether dissolved by the blending and fusing influences of civilisation. That this process has been going on very rapidly during the last century, we believe. But so far from holding, with Mr. Mill, that it is a process fatal to the due development of individualities of character, we conceive that it has not contracted, but rather enlarged, the sphere of individual freedom. The country gentleman stands out no longer in that marked contrast to the tradesman or the man of letters which was observable in the days of Sir Robert Walpole; the dissenter is no longer a moral foil to the churchman; and the different shades of English religious opinion can not any more be mapped out as distinctly as the different counties in a map of England. But what individual freedom has any one lost by the fading away of those well-defined local and moral groups? That there has been a loss of social *intensity* of character in consequence, we admit. The exclusive association of people of the same habits of life and thought has no doubt a tendency to intensify the peculiarities thus associated, and to steep the character thoroughly with that one influence, to the exclusion of all others. But this intensification of local, or social, or religious one-sidedness is as far as possible from the development of that individuality of character for which Mr. Mill pleads so eagerly. Rather must the impressed force of such social moulds or stamps have tended to overpower all forms of individual originality which were not consistent with those special moulds or stamps. No doubt if there were any remarkable element of character in the individual which also belongs specially to the group or caste, we might expect that it would be fostered by such association into excessive energy. But any peculiarly individual element of character, on the other hand, would have been in danger of being overwhelmed. And it is therefore mere assumption to say that because there are now fewer striking varieties of type and class than there were in former generations, there is less scope for individual freedom. The very reverse must be the case, unless the assimilated public opinion of a whole nation be supposed to be more minute, more exigeant and irritating in its despotism, than the sectarian opinion of small local bodies or social castes.

The same explanation applies to that other statement of Mr. Mill's which we have also admitted, — the greater subserviency of statesmen in the present day to any ascertained or even suspected strong bias of political conviction. The true reason is not, in all probability, that statesmen are more cowardly than formerly, but that they cannot command the same unhesitating support from their own party; the individual freedom of politicians is greater, not less, than it was. Parties no longer move in phalanx. Statesman have to persuade the intellects of their followers, and to satisfy, therefore, a far greater variety of conditions than at any former period. But though this imposes a great restraint on the practical genius of statesmen, Mr. Mill fails to observe that it is a restraint imposed on them, not as individual thinkers or doers, but as *leaders* of the thought and action of others. It tells against, not in favour of, his theory of the gradual suppression of all individuality of character. What was the range of liberty permitted to the individual thought and action of a member of the Tory, or a member of the Whig, party in the last century? If he did not implicitly accept the policy imposed upon him by his leaders, he was "cast out" by one party, and suspected as a turncoat by the other. A more constrained political conscience could scarcely exist than that of the ordinary party-politician of the old type. The tyranny of sectional opinion was far greater than can now be easily imagined. In the present day no man, be he a statesman or a mere private politician, is punished for his individual eccentricities except by his individual isolation. Mr. Gladstone may follow out any vagaries that suggest themselves to his ingenious mind, and he loses nothing but influence by the amusement. Would Mr. Mill wish that statesmen should not only retain this individual liberty to judge for themselves, but the power of constraining a party to support them through all their windings? That would indeed be a strange application of the principle that free scope should be given to every man to follow the bent of his own individual character or genius. The political phenomenon Mr. Mill has pointed out is a clear indication of a diametrically opposite condition of things to that which he seems to infer.

But Mr. Mill may perhaps say that there is much more danger of tyranny from the unchecked power of a single homogeneous body of "public opinion" than there is from the local prejudices or conflicting political sects which formerly contended for the mastery. But this depends entirely on the mode in which this body of public opinion is generated, — whether it arise, as in England, from the genuine assimilation of opposite schools of thought, or, as in the United States, from the mere forcible triumph of a single class-creed, which, in consequence of democratic institutions, is unhappily able to drown by sheer violence the voice of all higher and more cultivated schools of thought. When people come to think more and more alike, simply because the same influences are extending from class to class, and the same set of reasons recommend themselves to the intellects of moderate men of all classes, — when this is the way in which a "public opinion" is formed, it is obvious that the restraint exercised by such public opinion, gathered up as it is from a *very wide social range*, is far less oppressive than the narrower and intenser type of opinion which pervades a single social class or political sect. In the United States, on the other hand, there has been nothing of this gradual assimilation of the different political convictions of different classes. Knowledge and civilising influences have not been the agents in giving predominance to that tyrannical type of thought which there goes by the name of "public opinion." The despotism of public opinion in America is not due to the gradual disappearance of local types of opinion and sectional habits of mind, and the natural fusion of political creeds which thus results, — but to the complete political victory which a false constitutional system has given to the largest and most ignorant class of the community over all those whose wishes and judgment were entitled to greater weight. A public opinion which is really only a special class-opinion, accidentally enabled to *silence* all higher elements of thought *instead of* assimilating them, is no fair specimen of that assimilation of view which is confessedly due mainly to the freer interchange of thought between class and class. And yet it is a pubic opinion formed, as he admits, in the latter fashion, which Mr. Mill thinks so much more menacing to individual liberty than those narrower and straiter forms of class-opinion and conviction which preceded it, and have been absorbed into it.

But while we thus join direct issue with Mr. Mill as to the effect which has been produced on individual liberty by the partial dissolution of those social castes and sectarian types of thought, and the gradual assimilation of the conflicting principles of political parties, — though we believe that never at any previous time were Englishmen at large so free to think and act as they deem right in all important matters, without even the necessity of rendering any account of their actions to the social circles in which they move, — we believe also that the intensity of character lost in this process is sometimes not counterbalanced by the gain in freedom. Mr. Mill has got into inextricable confusion between the strength or intensity of a well-marked type of character encouraged by every social influence to grow *out* prominently in certain directions, — and that individuality which is simply left at liberty to find and follow out its own perhaps not very defined bent. Massiveness and strong outline in character are certainly less promoted by the *laissez-faire* system Mr. Mill recommends than by the predominance of certain tyrannical and one-sided customs, and motives, and restraints, and schools of thought in the moral atmosphere by which men are surrounded. Mr. Mill is probably right when he complains that the character of the present age is to be 'without any marked character;' but for our parts, instead of ascribing it to that exigeant commonplace with which our author wages so internecine a war, we ascribe it in the main to the exactly opposite cause, — the dissolution of various stringent codes of social opinion and custom, which extended the variety of well-marked types of character *at the expense* of the individuality of those who were subject to their influence. We do not, therefore, practically differ from Mr. Mill, widely as we differ from his theory, when we find him saying as to the present state of the pubic mind —

> "Instead of great energies guided by vigorous reason, and strong feelings strongly controlled by a conscientious will, its result is weak feelings and weak energies, which therefore can be kept in outward conformity to rule without any strength either of will or of reason. Already energetic characters on any large scale are becoming merely traditional. There is now scarcely any outlet for energy in this

country except business. The energy expended in that may still be regarded as considerable. What little is left from that employment is expended on some hobby; which may be a useful, even a philanthropic hobby, but is always some one thing, and generally a thing of small dimensions. The greatness of England is now all collective: individually small, we only appear capable of any thing great by our habit of combining; and with this our moral and religious philanthropists are perfectly contented. But it was men of another stamp than this that made England what it has been; and men of another stamp will be needed to prevent its decline."

But, holding as we do that Mr. Mill ascribes this dead level of character to a cause nearly the reverse of the true cause, it is not surprising that we differ from him still more widely when he suggests his remedy. Mr. Mill sees no means of stimulating the individual mind to assert its own right to rebel against the tyrannous desire of average men "that all other people shall resemble" themselves. And so he sets himself to persuade average men that, whether with regard to their influence over legislation, or with regard to their share in forming the public opinion of the day, they must steadily resist the temptation of interfering at all to regulate the standard of individual morality, except so far as it touches social rights. This is the one object of his essay. It is not at present half so important, he says, to purify the public conscience, as to break down once and for ever its right to intrude its impressions on individuals. Having long brooded painfully over the evils which are involved in what he regards as the abject deference of individual thought to the "voice which is in the air," Mr. Mill proposes to impose on it a vow of complete silence with regard to all subjects affecting the individual only. He is so anxious to secure free action for human individualities, that he would interdict the "public mind" from expressing any opinion at all on some of the gravest topics that can be submitted to human discussion. He would, in short, emasculate public opinion, in order to remove one principal stumbling-block in the way of those who tremble to assert their own individual convictions in the face of that terrible tribunal.

Now we are far from denying that the power of public opinion is often a real and painful stumbling-block to men in the discharge of their duty. It is often hasty, and often ignorant, and often cruel. It sometimes crushes the weak, while it spares altogether the strong and the shameless. It continually "judges according to appearance and not righteous judgment." Its standard is conventional, and is yet generally applied with most rigour where it is, in fact, inapplicable altogether. All this is true, but is certainly no truer of that section of public opinion which regards individual duty than of that which regards social duty; and the remedy does not lie in the artificial proposal to warn Government and Society off the former field altogether. This, however, is exactly the position which Mr. Mill has written his book to defend. "Those who have been in advance of society in thought and feeling," he says, "have occupied themselves rather in inquiring what things society ought to like or dislike than in questioning whether its likings or dislikings should be a law to individuals." Accordingly his essay is an inquiry into the "nature and limits of the power which can be legitimately exercised by society over the individual;" and he does not confine it to investigating the legitimate degree of *State* interference, but, assuming that the principle on which society may claim to interfere with individual self-government by the infliction of social penalties is identical in kind, though not necessarily equally applicable in all cases, with that which warrants legislative interference, he makes it his object to establish that "the sole end for which mankind are warranted, individually or collectively, in interfering with the liberty of action of any of their number is self-protection," or "to prevent harm to others."

Before we follow Mr. Mill into his able exposition and defence of this principle, we wish to call attention to the new light thrown upon it by the position we have attempted to establish. We have affirmed that the loss of power and intensity which is observable in the typical characters of the present day arises not, as Mr. Mill affirms, from that galling slavery to Commonplace, under the name of Public Opinion, into which men, as it is said, have recently fallen; but from the partial disappearance of those narrow religious, social, and political organisations which formerly gave a more definite outline, and lent a more constant sustaining power, in the shape of strong class-sympathy, to the minds of those who were formed under their influence. But if this be so, — if the change be due rather to the dissolution of habitual social restraints, which, however irksome and oppressive to the young, soon wrap themselves like a second and stronger nature round the minds of the mature, than to any increase of paralysing influence in the mild public opinion of the present day, — then it would seem that the effect of even much stricter codes of social custom, and much narrower sectarian and political prejudices, than any now prevalent tended to sharpen rather than obliterate that edge, and flavour, and intensity which Mr. Mill so much admires and which he misnames "individuality." Suppose for a moment Mr. Mill could have emasculated the various petty "public opinions," confined to special castes and classes, which produced the well-marked characters of the last century, as he would now emasculate the wider and less definite public opinion of modern English society, what would have been the result? The very pith of every strong class-opinion was and is its ideal of *personal* excellence, that touchstone by which it proves the mettle of all its members, and by reference to which it accords its popular judgment of favour or censure. And not only is this true, but it is equally true that no qualities of character enter more deeply into such class-ideals of excellence than those termed by Mr. Mill purely "self-regarding qualities," — self-possession, courage, firmness, self-restraint, — which, according to our author, should be confined to the most solitary chambers of the imagination. Moreover, once admit that such virtues may and must enter into the very essence of popular standards of character, and you cannot prevent that severity of popular condemnation on the corresponding vices which Mr. Mill regards as a violation of the principle of individual freedom. Suppose, for instance, the country gentleman of the last century had been induced, in anticipation of Mr. Mill's philosophy, sternly to discourage all tyrannical social prejudices as to the so-called "self-regarding" excellences of the country gentleman; they would of course have discouraged any attempt to affix a social stigma on avarice, meanness, timidity in field sports, and so forth. But how could this have been possible without destroying entirely the strength, freshness, and clearness of outline, which has engraved that type of character so deeply in the English imagination? We are not now, of course, contending that such class-prejudices are not frequently unjust and injurious in their actual operation; but simply that that breadth and massiveness in the old English types of character which Mr. Mill deplores, was due to the stimulating power of a much *more* trenchant criticism on individual demeanour than now exists, and not to any habit of ignoring entirely the private principles of men's life so long as their duties to others were well observed. In fact, nothing is more remarkable as regards popular English standards of character than a certain undue esteem for purely personal gifts and excellences, and a deeper detestation of those deformities which imply a want of self-respect than even of those which imply a want of respect for others.

And we feel sure that Mr. Mill's proposal to encourage the growth of moral individuality by entirely warning off the conscience of a society or a class from any responsible criticism of this interior world, would have exactly the opposite effect to that which he desires. A strong type of character may be the result either of vivid sympathy or keen collision with the social morality it finds around it; but where the social conscience practically ignores altogether any sphere of universal morality, it will seldom be the case that individual characters will dwell with any intensity upon it. Social indifference will result, not in individual vitality, but in individual indifference. Personal morality, once conscious that society has suspended its judgment, will grow up as colourless as a flower excluded from the light. And if society do not suspect its judgment, it cannot but take leave to mark its approval and disapproval, to praise its heroes and to brand its outlaws. In spite of Mr. Mill's authority, we hold that if his object be, as he states, to encourage the growth of those more bold and massive types of character which he mourns over as extinct, it will be more wise, as well as more practicable, to select as his means to that end the purifying of social judgments from their one-sidedness than to attempt the complete suspension of them on certain tabooed subjects; to seek to infuse into them a truer justice and a deeper charity in estimating individual principles of conduct than to lecture society on the impropriety of passing any opinion on them at all. The "liberty of indifference" is the only kind of liberty which Mr. Mill's proposal would be likely to confer; and that is scarcely consistent with the massive and defined strength of purpose he wishes to restore.

But we have delayed long enough on the threshold of the subject. We cannot avoid touching slightly on Mr. Mill's moral theory, deeply interwoven as it is with his political principles; but we will do so as briefly as possible, and try so far as we can to discuss his social and political theory on its social and political side. Mr. Mill beings by disclaiming, as a utilitarian must, any appeal to abstract right. 'I regard utility,' he says, 'as the ultimate appeal on all ethical questions; but it must be utility in the largest sense, grounded on the permanent interests of man as a progressive being.' And the influence of this theory is marked throughout the book. For, starting with the assumption that there is no inward standard of right or wrong, no standard except that which is attained by studying the *results* of conduct, he is led to divide actions into two great classes, — those which affect exclusively or mainly the agents, which are therefore beyond the reach of any external criticism, since no one can know the full consequences except the agent; and actions which affect directly or at least necessarily the interests of others, which can be classified into right and wrong according as they would, if generally permitted, satisfy or interfere with the claims of others.

> "Self-regarding faults," he says, "are not properly immoralities; and to whatever pitch they may be carried, do not constitute wickedness: they may be proofs of any amount of folly or want of personal dignity or self-respect, but they are only a subject of moral reprobation when they involve a breach of duty to others, for whose sake the individual is bound to care for himself. What are called duties to ourselves are not socially obligatory unless circumstances make them at the same time duties to others. The term 'duty to oneself,' when it means anything more than prudence, means self-respect or self-development; and for none of these is any one accountable to his fellow-creatures, because for none of them is it for the good of mankind that he be held accountable to them."

And accordingly he classes cruelty, malice, envy, dissimulation, insincerity, love of domineering, as *immoral*; while cowardice, self-conceit, prodigality, and sensuality, so long as they infringe no one else's rights, he regards as beyond the bounds of morality proper. Their evil, he maintains depends on their evil consequences. Those consequences, we may think, indeed, that we discern, but they are really experienced only by the mind of the agent; while the evil consequences of the former class of dispositions, on the other hand, are directly measurable by the disturbing influence they exert on the well-being of others. Mr. Mill is consistent, therefore, as a utilitarian, in drawing the broadest distinction between the faults and crimes which aggrieve others, and those which directly hurt, or are supposed to hurt, none except those who commit them.

Mr. Mill is perfectly consistent, we say; but what conscience can acquiesce? Insincerity, he says, is an immorality; lying is a *vice* properly visited by an extreme social penalty; and a fraud is a *crime* properly requited by a severe legal penalty: for lying and fraud invade the rights of others; it is an obligation to others to tell the truth and to act the truth, for others are relying upon you. But sensuality, unless it trespasses on the rights of others, is a "folly," a "want of self-respect," a carelessness as to "self-development;" but, "to whatever pitch" it may be carried, it "does not constitute wickedness." We cannot wonder at this inference from the utilitarian ethics; but we do wonder that so marvellous a result should not stagger any great thinker as to the justice of his premises. The truth is, that Mr. Mill is deceived by the epithet of "self-regarding," which he assigns to the various evil dispositions and actions thus intended to be exempted from social criticism. "Prudence," "self-respect," and "self-development," against which alone he considers them to be transgressions, convey no sense of obligation. A man may sacrifice his own good, indulge little in self-respect, or even have erroneous notions as to the best direction of self-development, without any sense of guilt. None of these phrases in the least describe the origin of the self-reproach which accompanies any kind of evil self-indulgence, moral or sensual. The reason why the term "self-regarding" is so misleading, is not because there is any error in supposing that these things do primarily affect ourselves, but because it seems to indicate that there is a real distinction in kind, which there is not, between the inwards moral conditions of this kind of evil disposition or action and those of dispositions or actions which affect primarily others than ourselves. Were Mr. Mill's theory, and the special epithet of "self-regarding" which represents it, a copy of any characteristic inward feeling, — then any habit of self-indulgence, such as that of anger or envy for example, which directly tends to infringe the rights of others, would be separated by a broad moral chasm in our own minds from any other habit of self-indulgence, moral or sensual, which directly tends only to affect our own nature. But this, as Mr. Mill knows, is not the case. The consideration as to whom any guilty act will mainly strike is an *arrière pensée* of the mind, not the least involved in the primary sense of guilt. The classification may be important to the politician, but to the moralist it is utterly artificial. There is as much, and usually far more, sense of a violated claim in the first impurity of thought, which does not seem to go forth into the external world at all, than in the first passionate blow or the first malignant insinuation, which are clear self-indulgences at the expense of another. However important, therefore, may be the distinction between what Mr. Mill calls "self-regarding" faults and what he calls immoralities affecting others in result, it is simply an error to suppose that it is a *natural* distinction, which is recognised by the self-accusing and self-condemning power in man. In both classes of moral evils alike the sting of self-reproach is entirely inward; and is not removed by any demonstration that no *injury* to society has resulted, or is likely to result. Of neither class of evils, again, is it a true account of the matter to say that they lie absolutely within us; for, quite apart from any theological conviction, in both classes of offences alike there is the same sense of transgression of some deep invisible claim on us, which we have no power to release as we can release any mere right of property of our own. We advance these things only for the sake of showing that Mr. Mill's classification is in no sense a classification of wrong dispositions and actions according to the kind, or even degree, of guilt with which they universally impress men, in no sense a moral, but only a political classification. In this, of course, we are at direct issue with Mr. Mill; since, as we have seen, he applies the word "immoral" to the one class, and entirely excludes the other class from any share in that epithet.

But notwithstanding this broad distinction in our ethical theory, it is clear that Mr. Mill's case may be argued, as, indeed, he generally argues it, without any explicit logical reference to his utilitarian creed. For the object of the essay is not to discuss the amount of moral penalty to the individual which difference classes of faults ought to entail, but only that portion of it which social custom or political law is justified in *inflicting* for the purpose either of retribution or restraint. Now, even for those who hold that Mr. Mill's classification of "self-regarding" and non-self-regarding faults is morally an artificial one, it is quite a tenable position that the only legitimate ground for social or political penalty ought to be an injury to society or the state. This, accordingly, is Mr. Mill's position; he denies to society the right to intimidate by any intentional combination, even by the combined expression of moral opinion, those whose practice evinces a great divergence of moral principle from the accepted standard, so long as the practice at issue has no bearing on the rights of any other than the offending persons. We have a right, he says, to choose our own society according to our own tastes, and we may therefore avoid the society of a man who offends those tastes; but we have no right to inflict any social penalty upon him by inducing others to do the same, unless his offence be one which threatens the social rights of others.

> "It makes a vast difference both in our feelings and conduct," says Mr. Mill, "whether he displeases us in things in which we have a right to control him, or in things in which we know that we have not. If he displeases us, we may express our distaste, and we may stand aloof from a person as well as from a thing that displeases us; but we shall not therefore feel called on to make his life uncomfortable. We shall reflect that he already bears, or will bear, the whole penalty of his error; if he spoils his life by mismanagement, we shall not on that account desire to spoil it still farther; instead of wishing to punish him, we shall rather endeavour to alleviate his punishment by showing him how he may avoid or cure the evils his conduct tends to bring upon him. He may be to us an object of pity, perhaps of dislike, but not of anger or resentment: we shall not treat him like an enemy of society. The worst we shall think ourselves justified in doing is leaving him to himself, if we do not interfere benevolently by showing interest or concern for him. It is far otherwise if he has infringed the rules necessary for the protection of his fellow-creatures, individually or collectively. The evil consequences of his acts do not then fall on himself, but on others; and society, as the protector of all its members, must retaliate on him, — must inflict pain on him for the express purpose of punishment, and must take care that it be sufficiently severe."

Hence if a man should come to live in a society where his life offends the moral principles of all, but yet without injuring them by any invasion of their rights, each may individually avoid him, or remove from his neighbourhood; but any attempt to excite the disapprobation of others, — any attempt to awaken the conscience of the society to any organic sentence like that of the individual conscience on his mode of life, — is an act of social tyranny; and, moreover, prejudges questions in which the social conscience is far more likely to err than the conscience of individuals.

"For," says Mr. Mill, on "questions of social morality the opinion of the public, that is, of an overruling majority, though often wrong, is likely to be still oftener right; because on such questions they are only required to judge of their own interests, of the manner in which some mode of conduct, if allowed to be practised, would affect themselves. But the opinion of a similar majority, imposed as a law on the minority in cases of self-regarding duty, is quite as likely to be wrong as right; for in those cases public opinion means at the best some people's opinion of what is good or bad for other people; while very often is does not mean even that, the public, with the most perfect indifference, passing over the pleasure or convenience of those whose conduct they censure, and considering only their own preference."

This contains, we believe, the substance of Mr. Mill's argument. First, an injury to society is the only legitimate ground of social or political punishment; since any other fault or vice expiates itself, and we can only claim to inflict penalty from that principle of social resentment which is implied in the right to self-protection. Next, if society does transgress this rule at all, the chances are that it will be on the wrong side; since society is some judge of its own interests, but will judge simply by accidental liking or prejudice as to things which do not affect its own interests. Again, the individual is the best judge of his own self-development; and to fetter him by social restraints in what does not affect society is to menace the principle of free self-government. And finally, to the argument that every thing which hurts the inward life and purity of the individual necessarily reacts on society, Mr. Mill replies that he does not deny it, but that the principle of mere authority has had at least an adequate trial during the period of early education, when no one would argue for absolute liberty, even in "self-regarding" acts: but there must be some limit to interference; and if society is to interfere with the self-government of the mature, on the ground only of the infectious nature of all moral evil, there will be no secure sphere of individual freedom at all.

We must keep in mind, in discussing this argument, that Mr. Mill applies it as much to any combination of social opinion which tends to prevent or to render painful the assertion of individual freedom as to political legislation. His test of what such social combination is, seems to be this: any act of which it is the intention to discourage a social heresy of this kind, is a social persecution if the heresy menace the rights of no one but the heretics. Individual disapproval may show itself, as a mere offended taste would show itself; but if you try to put an end to it at all, if you do more than simply withdraw your own countenance, and express your own opinion when natural occasion offers, you are guilty of a social persecution. You may disapprove of gambling or fornication, — you may even perhaps punish those who live by offering inducements to these vices, for that is a social act, which may possibly, at least, trench on the rights of others; but you may not (even socially) punish those who commit them in the exercise of their mature discretion; for the evil falls on themselves, and not (except through the moral infection) on society. You may avoid them yourself; you are bound not to do any thing with the intention of discouraging such a life, except by expressing temperately your individual opinion and regulating your individual conduct. You may not try to excite public censure against these things, — to bring them under the ban of society; as you might a furious temper or an envious and dishonest tongue. In the latter case, the heavier the social penalty you bring down the better. Society must be protected against it. But the evil of "errors" which are visited exclusively on the head of those who commit them ought not to be increased, but if possible alleviated, by lookers-on: and they may not be errors, after all; there is no worse judge than a society on whose rights they do not trench, and which is actuated only by prejudiced "likings" or "dislikings" of its own.

We have done our best to state Mr. Mill's case, where we have not actually used his own words, with the precision and force of thought of which his book gives us so many examples. Certainly his theory does not lose any thing for want of power of exposition. Still it seems to us to fail miserably in furnishing even the ground-plan of a sound political philosophy. In the first place, few can read the book without feeling that, with all

its elaborate defence of liberty, there is no element so utterly
absent, from the first page to the last, as any indication of
sympathy with the free play of a national or social character in
its natural organic action. Mr. Mill's essay regards "liberty"
from first to last in its negative rather than its positive
significance. But in that sense in which the very word "liberty"
is apt to excite the deepest enthusiasm of which human nature
is capable, it means a great deal more than the mere absence of
restraints on the individual; it implies that fresh and unconstrained play of national character, that fullness of social life
and vivacity of public energy, which it is one of the worst
results of such constraint to subdue or extinguish. But any
sympathy with a full social life or fresh popular impulses is
exactly the element in which Mr. Mill's book is most deficient.
The only liberty he would deny the nation is the liberty to be a
nation. He distrusts social and political freedom. There is a
depressed and melancholy air about his essay in treating of
social and political organisms. He thinks strongly that
individuals should be let alone, but virtually on condition that
they shall not coalesce into a society and have a social or
political life that may react strongly on the principles of
individual action. Of course in saying this we do not use Mr.
Mill's language, nor probably would he accept it as a true
description of his doctrine. We only describe the ineffaceable
impression it has produced upon us. An aggregate of individually free minds, if they are to be held asunder from natural
social combinations by the stiff framework of such a doctrine
as Mr. Mill's, would not make in any true or deep sense a free
society or a free nation. For any thing this essay contains to the
contrary, a nation might be held to possess the truest freedom
though there were no indication in it of a common life, no sign
of a united society, no vestige of a national will. It is strange
that, while Mr. Mill's lays so much and such just stress on the
liberty of individual thought and expression, he should quite
ignore the equally sacred liberty of social and national thought
and expression, and even invent a canon for the express
purpose of discouraging any action of society at all on topics
where he would think it dangerous to the liberty of the
individual. In England we should regard the mere absence of
interference with individual opinions and actions as a poor sort
of liberty, unless there were also due provision for the free play
of social opinion, a suitable organ for the expression of those

characteristic thoughts which elicit a response from the whole nation, a fit instrument for the timely assertion of England's antipathies and sympathies, hopes and will. If it be in reality a far truer mode of thinking to conceive individuals as members of a society, rather than society as pieced together of individuals, it is certain that true liberty demands for the deepest forms of social thought and life as free and characteristic an expression as it demands for the deepest forms of individual thought and life.

But, says Mr. Mill, what business has society to interfere with actions which do not in any way infringe on the rights of others? "If the consequences of any act can be shown to be purely individual, not social, then that act must be considered as beyond the range of social criticism." We reply that, even if the consequences of what Mr. Mill calls "self-regarding errors" can be admitted to be individual only, yet that it is not by the consequences that even the agent himself judges his own action, and therefore not by the consequences that the society of which he is a member can judge it. Both the individual and society feel that the inward principle which is violated in many of these "self-regarding errors" is of infinitely more importance in estimating their relation both to the individual character and to the constitution of society, than the immediate consequences can ever be. The distinction between "self-regarding" consequences and consequences to society is not usually a distinction naturally suggested to the agent, but a distinction taken afterwards on his behalf by astute advocates. And if not a distinction which the individual conscience can always recognise as morally important, then also not a distinction which the social conscience — if a society may be permitted a conscience — can recognise either. Mr. Mill speaks as if those who violate the laws of social morality could properly be conceived as *outside* the social body, as mere invaders of society, and their guilt estimated by the amount of immediate social confusion it tends to produce upon others than themselves. Again, with regard to those whose social guilt or innocence is in dispute, Mr. Mill reasons in the same manner; he thinks of them as external to society, and then asks himself the question, Will the actions of these people in any way disturb the equilibrium of the rest of society? If not, we may retain our opinions as individuals as to the impropriety of what they do, but we are not justified as a society in objecting. Now this is a completely artificial and deceptive mode of thought. Individuals who in any special point reject the moral authority of the society in which they live, are none the less members of that society. Their act is not an invasion, but a rebellion. In other words, it has a double influence, which the aggressive acts of mere invaders never have, — the external and the internal, — the directly injurious results, which, even though they fall exclusively upon their own heads, still fall upon living members of a society who cannot suffer without injury to the whole; and again, the still more important influence of the practical protest put forth by living members of a society against the social principle they have violated. If that principle be one really essential either to social unity or social purity, it is clear that society cannot treat either the immediate ill consequences or the practical protest as if it came from an external source.

If there be any transgressions of social morality which are conceived, as well by the individual as the social conscience, as momentous, not nearly so much because of their immediate results as because they soon extinguish that sense of the inviolable sanctity of social life which is its best and most distinctly religious bond, then surely society, if it have an inward life and constitution and conscience at all, has even more right to express itself in open resentment and displeasure, than in the case of offences which happen to affect the external lot of others of its members. Mr. Mill will not deny that there are offences not trenching on the rights of any other member of society, which yet do more to relax the strength of that spiritual tie which holds society together, than many offences which are direct aggressions upon the rights of others. He can scarcely doubt that the moral dismemberment of Greek and Roman society, for instance, was due in a far higher degree to the impurity which had already spread so fearfully in the age of Plato and of Juvenal than even to the growth of insincerity, dishonesty, and rapacious desires. Yet because offences of the former class are, in the first instance, sins only against that hidden conscience, or rather that overshadowing power, which constitutes the true spiritual bond of society, while offences of the latter class are also visibly traced in unjust violence or defrauded claims, Mr. Mill would call an organic expression of social displeasure towards sins of the one class a tyranny, and towards sins of the other class a needful and justifiable resentment. It is, we suppose, because Mr. Mill denies the

existence of any moral standard of action, except consequences, in the individual, that he is also unwilling to admit the
existence of any inward social principles apart from consequences against which members of a society can offend. Were it
not so, he would see as clearly as we see that the danger of
severing the spiritual roots of social purity and unity is the true
danger to society, and needs even more sedulous and organised
protest in cases where there is no one person specially
interested in raising it, than even in those cases where some one
is directly wronged, and therefore certain to call in the aid of
others in his own behalf. Social liberty, or liberty for the free
play of social character, is quite as sacred as individual liberty;
and it cannot exist at all if the deepest principles which form
that character are to be kept in abeyance out of respect for the
liberty of those who infringe them. How far the individual
should be compelled, *otherwise* than by the free expression of
social opinion, to respect such moral laws, is quite another
question, which involves a large class of new considerations.
But to propose that social opinion should spontaneously put
itself under unnatural restrictions, with regard to principles
which go to the very root of social life, in deference to
individual liberty, is to ask that society should renounce its best
impulses, in order that individuals may indulge their worst.

We shall not, we trust, be understood to deny that such a
thing as social tyranny — quite apart from legislative enactment — is very common and very dangerous. No doubt society
often does interfere with the proper sphere of private individual
liberty. We only maintain that Mr. Mill's principle altogether
fails properly to distinguish the two spheres, and practically
denies any inward life and character to society altogether;
turning it into a mere *arbiter* between individuals, instead of
regarding it as an organised body, in the common life of which
all its members partake. Mr. Mill thinks society a competent
judge of its own *external interests*; but that its moral likings
and dislikings are mere tyrannical sentiments, which it will
impose at pleasure on any unfortunate minority within its
control. No doubt societies, like individuals, are disposed to
bigotry. No doubt majorities will at times strive to impose their
coarser tastes and poor commonplace thoughts on minorities,
instead of desiring to know and try the principle opposed to
theirs. But what is the true check upon social bigotry?
According to Mr. Mill, the only guarantee against it is to erect,

by common consent, every individual human mind into an impregnable and independent fortress, within the walls of which social authority shall have no jurisdiction; the functions of the latter being strictly limited to arbitrating questions at issue between all such independent lords, and prohibiting mutual encroachments. Now we do not deny that such a total withdrawal of individual duty and morality from the circle of social questions might secure against bigotry; but at what expense? At the sacrifice, we believe, of that mediating body of social faith and conviction which connects together the more marked individualities of different minds, interprets them, and renders them mutually intelligible and useful, — at the cost of that social unity of spirit which alone renders the diversity of individual gifts capable of profiting by each other. Mr. Mill's essay may be said to be one long *éloge* on individuality — its importance in itself, and its paramount importance to society. This we accept as strongly as Mr. Mill. But individuality may suffer in either of two ways: from the too great rigour or from the too great looseness of the social bond, — from the tyrannical domination of custom and commonplace over the individual; or from that paralysis of social life which permits individual modes of thought and conduct to diverge too widely for mutual influence and aid. What is it that really makes strong individualities of character and thought so important to society, but their real power of increasing the moral and intellectual experience of general society? And how could this be, if they were not kept constantly in living relation with general society by the sense of social authority over them? It is this moral authority exercised by social opinion, and this alone, which obliges the innovator to remember, and, if he can, to appreciate, the body of diffused social conviction, even while modifying, deviating from, and expanding it. People of strong one-sided individualities are always in danger of losing their full and fair influence on society; nay, of losing even the full advantage of their special characteristics, from want of adequate sympathy with the society which they wish to influence. For example, it is not easy to avoid the conviction that Miss Emily Brontë had all, and more than all, the *specialities* of genius which gave her sister Charlotte so great and deserved a celebrity, but fell short of her sister in real artistic power owing to the excess of these qualities, or rather to the deficient sympathy with the more homely tastes and interests which gave the latter a large common ground with the world she was to address.

And what is true of intellectual characteristics is far more uniformly true of moral characteristics. Those who ignore entirely the restrains of the code of social morality under which they live, are never likely to deepen, widen, or elevate it. Moral heretics may often render a great service to the world, but only where they feel acutely where it is that their creed diverges from that of the world, and on what grounds it thus diverges; only if they recognise the moral authority of the social creed to the full so far as it is sound, and dispute it on the one point on which they have tested its unsoundness. Mere groundless eccentricity, — which Mr. Mill, with less than his usual good sense, goes into a special digression to extol, — had more effect, we believe, in aggravating the social bigotry of Commonplace, and rendering men suspicious of all genuine individuality, than any other influence. Proper individuality is any thing but eccentricity; it is a development — one-sided perhaps, but still a development — of convictions and characteristics the germs of which are common to all men. If social conviction on all questions of individual conduct and morality could be struck dumb, so as to leave individuals to themselves, moral heresies would no doubt multiply more freely; but by losing their intimate relations with the wider experience of society and with the broader convictions of the social conscience, they would not only lose a certain restraining and tempering influence, but also the power which that greater breadth and temperateness gives of reacting upon society which regard to all points on which social opinion has passed a false or narrow and inadequate verdict.

If now Mr. Mill asks us what we regard as the true check upon that oppressive social bigotry which so often gives rise to weakness and moral cowardice on the one hand, and to unjust social excommunications on the other, we should reply, that there is the same check on the tyrannical treatment by society of what he calls "self-regarding" heresies as there is on similar social tyrannies towards what he admits to be justly punishable social immoralities. Society is apt to be quite as despotic, and the results of that despotism are apt to be quite as disastrous in inspiring moral cowardice and the arrogant spirit of excommunication, in the latter class of cases as in the former. Cases of real or fancied dishonesty, insolence, breach of faith, pride, are quite as often misjudged and over-punished as are those cases of "self-regarding error" with which, in Mr. Mill's estimation, society has nothing to do. That society is an imperfect judge of right and wrong, is true enough. Is it likely to improve under the exhortation to give up thinking of right and wrong altogether, and to calculate instead the tendency of human actions to produce external social disturbance? Is it likely to be more charitable and less unjust when told that it must no longer try human action by a practical human standard; that it must take pains to distinguish between actions with evil social consequences and actions with evil individual consequences only; and while disregarding the latter altogether, it should administer the unwritten law of social instinct upon the former with all the deterrent rigour it can command? When we look Mr. Mill's proposition directly in the face, it is impossible not to wonder that with so deep a despondency as to the inward spirit of English society he should combine so strangely sanguine an estimate of the power of theory. He thinks that if society would but confess that it has no social right to set up any concrete standard of moral duty, if it could but be persuaded to confine its criticisms to that abstract idea of his, "social man", and to plead absolute incompetence to deal with the "self-regarding" duties of human life, — that then individual minds would begin to play freely, and health to return to the whole social system. We believe, on the contrary, that if Mr. Mill's prescription could be carried out at all, which it cannot, the result would be exactly opposite. The individuality of individual life would be paralysed by this artificial indifference on the part of Society to its proceedings. The social morality of social life would lose all depth and seriousness by being thus unnaturally dissevered from the deeper judgments of the individual conscience. Social morality, striving to judge of actions simply by their effects on the rights of others, and ostentatiously excluding all the natural canons of moral criticism, would become arbitrary, conventional, formal. In proportion as it relaxed its hold on the individual conscience, it would become pharisaic in its anxiety about the rights of others. Professing to judge men only by this rigid test-formula, 'What is the net social result of your action?' instead of by any natural human conception of good or evil, social morality would wander farther and farther from the natural principles of justice, and soon substitute a *doctrinaire* social bigotry of

its own, in the place of that moral bigotry in judging of
individual conduct from which Mr. Mill hopes to redeem it.
Indeed, Mr. Mill's own writings contain sufficient indications
of this risk. There is one social offence of which he writes with
sustained and profound indignation, in a tone sometimes rising
to the eloquence of patriotic resentment, sometimes to the
judicial severity of the bench. That offence is early marriage on
the part of men unprovided with certain means of supporting a
family, — the social crime of contributing to over-population.
He speaks of this repeatedly in his various works as the offence
which society ought to resent with its bitterest social penalties;
nay, which the law itself should punish as soon as social
opinion is ripe for such a consummation. We do not wish to
take moral thoughtlessness of any sort, or the injustice arising
from thoughtlessness, under our protection; but it is important
to point out practically the sort of moral result in which Mr.
Mill's doctrine issues. Impurity of heart and life, and all those
forms of it which avenge themselves primarily and externally
on the heads of the individual offenders alone, he holds that
society, as such, has no business to interfere with, — no right
by social penalties of any sort to discourage or resent. But on
the imprudence, — or, let us admit at once, the injustice, — of
hasty and improvident marriage he would bring down, if he
could, the ban of something like social excommunication.[1] Yet
with which class of evil has the social conscience the most real
and intimate concern? Mr. Mill's essay is in many parts a
continuous wail over the tendency of the individual mind to
succumb to the conventional prejudices of a social creed; but
could any better illustration be required than we have here
given that his own theory, if accepted, would lead to a yoke of
conventional social morality far heavier and more oppressive to
the individual conscience than that which he conceives to be
already almost beyond endurance? Thus to supersede social
morality by intellectual formula will prove, we take it, a harder
task than to regenerate it by the natural method of moral
influence. Mr. Mill is very hard upon those who try to change
the "likings or dislikings" of society instead of to convince its
reason. But few caprices of social liking or disliking could be
conceived less reasonable than the intellectual caprice which he
wishes society to adopt as its rule in dealing out its

---

[1] Political Economy, vol. i. p. 445; Essay on Liberty, p. 194.

discouragements, its censures, and its bans; for he asks society to neglect, on principle, the cancer at its heart, while he would have it amputate without scruple the slightly injured limb.

Mr. Mill is well aware that the principal recommendation of his social theory to ordinary minds is not likely to consist in its inherent strength half so much as in its inviting logical affinity to one very important and very direct application, which English thought has already, on other grounds, heartily accepted; we mean the perfect liberty of individual opinion, and the evil of any sort of social excommunication of mere heresy. So well aware is he that the persuasiveness of his theory will lie mainly in its seeming adaptation to yield this already established conclusion, that the ground we have hitherto disputed with him, though it is the key of his position, is not that which he takes the most or the first pains to fortify. On the contrary, he trusts mainly to the indirect argument we have indicated. Here, he wishes his readers to feel, is a principle which is recognised by the highest and noblest minds, which is deeply ingrained in English politics, and is every day more generally acceptable in English society, — the principle that men's honest individual opinions and beliefs ought not to subject them to any persecution, explicit or indirect, political or social. Accordingly he spends the first half of his essay on reconsidering this principle, and developing it beyond its already familiar political aspects into its purely social bearings. He sees that there is much chronic social intolerance left which ought to be eradicated, and he perhaps justly thinks his theory of society well adapted to educe an extension of this principle, to prove the inadmissibility of those social excommunications which religious heresy still frequently draws down. If society has no further right than to protect itself against practical transgressors of social duties and claims, how clear that it has no right to stir up any sort of social resentment or arm prejudice against a man who has simply used his own individual liberty of thought to form his own individual convictions! And what theory of society but that of self-protection would be likely to leave the sphere of individual thought so inviolable? How closely connected are individual opinions on religious or moral matters with the individual conscience! and if we are once to admit that public opinion about right and wrong has any thing at all to do with the sphere of government, or even with the exercise of social authority, how can we prevent endorsing all sorts of claims to punish men for their opinions? Only if we admit that there is an absolute sphere of individual liberty which society is not warranted, on any pretence whatever, in infringing, can we feel sure that we have a theory of society in perfect harmony with this important principle.

Thus, as we believe, or in some similar strain, Mr. Mill has reasoned with himself. Unfortunately, however, for his social theory, he ought to separate the right to form individual convictions from the right to *propagate* them. The two rights, he freely concedes, are practically inseparable; yet the two certainly do not bear the same relation to his social theory. So long, indeed, as the convictions formed have no direct bearing on the admitted rights of others, — so long as they are religious, or belong only to the "self-regarding" class of moral duties, — so long his theory would justify their free propagation as well as their free formation. But once let them have a revolutionary tendency in their bearing on social life, — once let their adoption have evil consequence which would fall primarily on *others*, — and he feels at once that the "self-protecting" theory of society would justify both government and social opinion in interfering to punish or to excommunicate the propagandist. Mr. Mill does not attempt to get over this difficulty. He knows that government ought to interfere only with evil actions, not with dangerous opinions. He knows that social feeling itself ought to draw a broad distinction between evil actions and those opinions which merely encourage and impel to evil actions; but his theory will not admit this distinction. If "self-protection" be the duty of society, it ought surely to discourage in the germ those views which endanger its existence, and not to wait till the risk has borne fruits of serious evil.

Mr. Mill is obliged to draw a distinction between opinions so expressed "so to constitute a positive instigation to some mischievous act," and abstract opinions with the same tendency: "An opinion that corn-dealers are starvers of the poor, or that private property is robbery, ought to be unmolested when simply circulated through the press; but may justly incur punishment when delivered orally to an excited mob assembled before the house of a corn-dealer, or when handed about by the same mob in the form of a placard."

With this doctrine we entirely agree; but if it be taken

absolutely, what does it really amount to except a complete abandonment of Mr. Mill's own theory, and a virtual admission of our position that, after all, it is the judgment of the social conscience, and not any technical formula derived from a right to protect itself against external disorders, which justifies society in the infliction of political and social penalties, and the expression of social resentment? For if, as Mr. Mill contends, society is the best and only proper judge of what is inimical to its own interests, and is bound to watch over and protect them without regard to the principles of individual morality involved, how can he regard as any thing but positively praiseworthy its attempt to stifle at once, — if not by law, at least by the expression of stern displeasure on the part of the public, — all teaching that would directly tend to subversive actions? On the principle that prevention is better than cure, — on the principle on which society engages police to watch the dangerous classes, as a wiser measure than calling in the military to defeat them when once in force, — no one can deny that to brand the propagation of opinions dangerous to the constitution of society with social opprobrium would be a much safer measure than to punish those who act them out. If an opinion is advocated "that corn-dealers are starvers of the poor," and it is possible, by uniformly frowning upon and, if needful, excommunicating the advocates of such subversive opinions, to prevent the assemblage of that unruly mob before the corn-dealer's door altogether, how much more merciful this course would be than to let the doctrine reach that degree of influence and then punish its propounders! Mr. Mill makes reply, as we understand him, that he admits this consequence; that, strictly speaking, society has the right to guard itself against revolutionary opinions, even while only abstract; but that it wisely waives this right for the chance which always exists that by habitually listening to all abstract opinions, it may occasionally be induced to reconsider its own view, and give in its adhesion to what it at first erroneously deemed subversive doctrine. In short, society, he thinks, properly runs the risk of delaying for a while to protect itself against many really dangerous opinions which may gain ground and become practically threatening, in order that it may protect itself against the alternative and worse risk of overlooking the truth contained in some seemingly but not really dangerous opinions. This is, however, practically leaving it to the discretion of society whether in any given case it regards the practical risk or the chance of new light as the greater. The right of self-protection always exists; and if it is waived, it is only because society does not fear so much as it hopes. Mr. Mill, on his theory, could not charge French society, for instance, with any inconsistency, looking to the past, in prohibiting or punishing the propagation of such doctrines as Proudhon's, that "property is robbery." The chance of new light from such doctrines is infinitely small. Socialism has had its trial, and been condemned. The risk of social commotion from such doctrine is proved by experience to be great; if society elects to excommunicate such teachers, and crush the almost certain evil in the bud, society is quite justified on Mr. Mill's theory. It prefers to protect itself against the physical danger rather than against the possible ignorance which free discussion might remove. It regards the risk of the former as very great, and the risk of the latter as infinitely small. Accordingly political and social intolerance is certainly clearly admissible, — on the theory that the only duty of society is to protect itself, — in the case of all opinions which seem to threaten, in the opinion of the majority, much more social danger than their investigation could possibly bring new light. After all, then, Mr. Mill's doctrine does not exclude considerations as to the degree of social unanimity against an opinion, and the nature of the apprehensions excited by it, from the problem as to the right or wrong of exercising tolerance towards it. "Self-protection" is a duty which is found to require much judgment; and different lines of conduct are justified by it in different countries and under different social conditions.

Moreover, Mr. Mill's theory does not only leave large room for social and political intolerance, but in those cases where it does admit intolerance at all, it admits it in the highest degree. Suppose society convinced — say by bitter experience, such as that of revolutionary France — that it had far more danger to apprehend from the spread of exciting doctrine on any particular subject than enlightenment to look for from the discussion, it will be warranted in using the most effective social measures for its extinction. That is but poor "self-protection" that only half does its work. The earlier the blow is struck, the more entirely theoretic the stage in which the social heresy is extinguished, the farther it is from any actual criminal intention at the time, the better. So far from waiting till the mob is before the corn-dealer's door, according to the true principle of self-protection, society would raise a hue and cry against the social heretic when first he began to intimate that to destroy granaries of corn in order to raise the price of the remainder is a selfish and unprincipled act. Once let the teaching take the form of a popular cry, — once let selfish ends become interwoven with it, — and it might be too late. The theory of self-protection, then, will not only justify intolerance to social heresies in given cases, but in those cases will justify it at the point farthest removed from practical action; while the intellectual error, and that alone, is the danger to be feared.

Now let us compare these results of Mr. Mill's theory as to the limits of social authority with what we may call the natural theory, which gives the social conscience both liberty and right to express itself strongly on all moral points sufficiently simple, and sufficiently clear of individual elements, to be within its comprehension. We maintain that this, no doubt very commonplace and practical, but not the less, we believe, true, mode of looking at the duty and province of society, will be found to justify Mr. Mill's candid but not very self-consistent admission, — that merely abstract opinions tending to mischievous social acts ought to be absolutely unfettered and free, whereas "opinions so expressed as to constitute a positive instigation to those acts" should be punishable as social offences, — far better than his own theory. Once make it the very essence of the law of right acknowledged by society to take measures for mere self-protection, and we cannot refuse it the privilege of judging how that end will be best accomplished. Mr. Mill says it is the only guarantee for the soundness of a practical principle that its theory should be always entirely open to attack, and yet should have endured uninjured all such attacks as may have been directed against it. But make self-protection your only rule, and society can scarcely be denied the right to judge for itself in this matter, especially after winning two or three expensive and exhausting victories over such adversaries. The theory of self-protection will not admit account to be taken of individual purposes or motives, except as an element in the probable danger to society. A very good and innocent fanatic, dealing in abstract opinions only, may be very dangerous; and a very guilty and mischief-meaning scoundrel, with selfish ends close in view, may choose his ground so ill as to be very harmless. In this case, according to

Mr. Mill's theory, society would be bound to punish the former, even though his instruments were abstract opinions only, but likely to work powerfully; and to ignore the latter, even though his opinions were "so expressed as to constitute a positive instigation to mischief," but yet were inefficient opinions, likely to have no practical effect. But once let us see that society will not really protect itself best by making self-protection the one end and aim of its law of right, — once admit that if it act on the natural principles of individual justice, and strive to judge mischievous acts by the degree of individual ill-intent they involve rather than by the risk to itself, it will really be better protected than if it think only of self-protection, — and it will at once follow that opinions should never be judged purely by their mischievous tendencies, — should never be punishable, in short, socially or politically, except when in the closest possible relation to the acts they seem to justify. To take Mr. Mill's own illustration: so long as the doctrine that "corn-dealers are starvers of the poor" is a mere theory, it may have risen from a thousand sources of intellectual and involuntary error, — from confused political economy, confused theories of society, and so forth; but no sooner is the actual deed of violence which that doctrine would justify vividly present to the eye in a real individual case than we feel assured, in ninety-nine cases out of every hundred, that any man who had not the mind of a common robber would shrink back from the consequences of his own theory; while the hundredth man, though possibly an innocent fanatic, cannot expect to have the law made for his exceptional case. This is the only real distinction between an abstract opinion and an opinion giving birth to an action. It may be quite possible for an innocent opinion to justify a very criminal action; but scarcely so if the two are brought into such immediate relation of cause and effect that the mind of the merely speculative thinker fully realises all the elements present to the mind of the criminal doer. We maintain therefore, that the just ground for permitting the free propagation of such abstract opinions as, if they took the concrete shape of recommending specific actions, would be justly punished, is that in the one case they often involve no kind of guilt at all, but merely intellectual confusion and want of imaginative power; while in the latter case, if the social judgment be not itself utterly distorted, they can rarely be free from a deep stain of guilt. But on his own theory of the merely self-protective right of society, Mr. Mill would be obliged, we maintain, to make large and important exceptions to the very just principle he lays down with respect to the difference between mischievous opinions and "opinions so expressed as to form absolute instigations" to mischievous acts.

We hold, then, that Mr. Mill's own theory does not permit nearly so clear a distinction between opinions and actions as is absolutely necessary for any true guarantee of social tolerance. Measure Wrong by the mere amount of tendency to imperil the admitted rights of others, and you cannot draw any satisfactory distinction between the intellectual and the practical tendencies which imperil them. Measure it, on the other hand, by a practical standard, the purpose and circumstances of the wrong-doer, and there is the broadest distinction between a theory and an instigation, — an impersonal conclusion of the intellect, and a practical recommendation which realises the whole actual significance of the injurious theory. Of course, if what we have called the natural theory of social right be the true one, — though the indignation of society ought to fall only on such teachings as come into the very closest relations with evil acts, — there is no reason why it should not fall as much on teaching of this sort when it corrupts only the moral conduct, as when it tends to invade the social rights of others. Mr. Mill's doctrine would not only exclude the *legal* punishment of preachers of such socialist doctrines, for instance, as advocate the promiscuous intercourse of the sexes, — for there we should agree with him, not because we deny government the right to interfere, but because, in England at least, we doubt if society would not have far more power to interfere efficiently by social means only, — but it would prohibit any manifestation of social feeling against them as an intolerance. We hold, on the other hand, that there can be no greater offence against the true principles of liberty than to deny society the right, admitted to individuals, of expressing the convictions of the social conscience freely and strongly on all subjects of this kind on which the social conscience can adequately judge.

How, then, Mr. Mill will ask, do we provide against that religious and social intolerance which, as his own essay most eloquently shows, is still so deadly a poison in English society? It we contend that the social conscience should be as free to judge and speak as the individual conscience, how are we to protest with any force against that miserable bigotry which *always* professes to speak from the impulses of a pure moral zeal, and very generally really is closely connected with the moral nature? So long as a social prejudice or exclusive piece of bigotry can assert that it is grounded in moral feeling, we shall have no means of assailing it except on its most hardened side; — we shall not, like Mr. Mill, be able to attack it in the rear; on the ground, not that it is wrong, but that it is out of place, and interfering in a region where it has no proper title to interfere at all. If a sabbatarian-minded society, for example, wishes to impose its own sanctimonious rules on a protesting minority, Mr. Mill would set to work to oppose it, not by contesting the right to interfere on this particular subject, but by trying to establish a general canon of social right, which, if accepted, would on examination be found to deny the power to dictate on the question. We, on the other hand, could only fight the battle separately on each particular point as it occurred. We admit fully this inferiority, if it be a real inferiority, in the advantage of our position; but seeing that all the triumphs of social and political tolerance have been practically gained in this way, and not in Mr. Mill's, — have been gained, we mean, by convincing society or the State that men of the highest moral and social virtue have differed in their religious or biblical tenets, and that therefore the conscience of society could not be said to have determined these points at all, — we exceedingly doubt the inferiority of our position to Mr. Mill in respect to any practical advantage. Mr. Mill instances the fundamental questions of the belief in God and a future state, and intimates that the conscience of a vast majority would stoutly affirm it an immorality to reject these beliefs — in fact, a symptom of moral deformity. It may be so; but we strongly believe that, if it be so, the way to convince society that it is in error is, not to deny that its conscience has any right to judge of individual conduct, but to exhibit the many great complexities of intellectual constitution which have prevented, and do prevent, men of pure life and stainless integrity from accepting these faiths; and to point out, moreover, that one of the greatest obstacles in their way is the uncharitable excommuncation to which society in its pharisaism dooms them. This would be a victory over the social conscience gained by an appeal to the social conscience, and therefore, we believe, would be much more likely to be firm and permanant than one gained by merely persuading society — which it would be hard to do — that it has no concern with the individual principles of life and action, as such, at all. We always mistrust these indirect victories over either individual or social opinion. The social conscience, like the individual conscience, will not submit to be merely out-manœuvred; it takes the liberty, after all, of forming its judgments, with reference to the rights of a question, on those rights. The best answer to Mr. Mill on this point will be found in the admirable lecture of Professor Newman which we have placed with his own book at the head of this article. No one can have felt more keenly than Professor Newman how grave an evil the narrow prejudices of the social conscience may be; — how injurious, first and mainly to the intolerant Society, next, and also grave, to the sufferer from social bigotry. Yet no one could have expressed more truly and profoundly the ground which it is wisest to take in struggling to remove this narrowness of social opinion; no one could have explained more ably why it would be foolish as well as unjust to deny the social conscience its just jurisdiction over individual life, and how much more hope there is of undermining social bigotry by enlarging the view and rectifying the judgment of society than by attempting to dispute its right to interfere in individual morality at all.

One of the most striking passages in Mr. Mill's essay appears to us to tell very strongly against his own view. No more graphic picture of the predominant modern phases of social bigotry could well be given than Mr. Mill gives in the following words:

"But though we do not now inflict so much evil on those who think differently from us as it was formerly our custom to do, it may be that we do ourselves as much evil as ever by our treatment of them. Socrates was put to death; but the Socratic philosophy rose like the sun in heaven, and spread its illumination over the whole intellectual firmament. Christians were cast to the lions; but the Christian church grew up a stately and spreading tree, overtopping the older and less vigorous growths, and stifling them by its shade. Our merely social intolerance kills no one, roots out no opinions; but induces men to disguise them, or to abstain from any active effort for their diffusion. With us heretical opinions do not perceptibly gain, or even lose, ground in each decade or generation; they never blaze out far and wide, but continue to smoulder in the narrow circles of thinking and studious persons among whom they originate, without ever lighting up the general affairs of mankind with either a true or a deceptive light. And thus is kept up a state of things very satisfactory to some minds, because, without the unpleasant process of fining or imprisoning any body, it maintains all prevailing opinions outwardly undisturbed, while it does not absolutely interdict the exercise of reason by dissentients afflicted with the malady of thought. A convenient plan for having peace in the intellectual world, and keeping all things going on therein very much as they do already. But the price paid for this sort of intellectual pacification is the sacrifice of the entire moral courage of the human mind. A state of things in which a large portion of the most active and inquiring intellects find it advisable to keep the genuine principles and grounds of their convictions within their own breasts, and attempt, in what they address to the public, to fit as much as they can of their own conclusions to premises which they have internally renounced, cannot send forth the open, fearless characters, and logical, consistent intellects who once adorned the thinking world."

This is most true and most graphic. But how does it tell on the theory that social opinion ought not to interfere in any way with individual life and conduct? that if individual morals or creeds excite social resentment, that resentment is neither to be expressed nor fought against, but rather to be suppressed or burked in conformity with the canon that social opinion should not meddle with such matters at all! Why, Mr. Mill's theory of an ideal public mind seems to us to be exactly what should lead to the state of things described above. If Society is to be made to feel that it is to have no social judgment, no social conviction, no social likings and dislikings, on individual morals and creeds at all, — if the social mind is simply to *abstain* from all corporate acts of conviction which might carry the weak along with it, or intimidate the cowardly into base compliance, — how could we have any thing but "heresies smouldering in the narrow circle of studious persons among whom they originate"? What is it that makes opinions "blaze out far and wide," and "light up the affairs of mankind with either a true or a deceptive light," except a profound conviction on the part of the social conscience that it *is* concerned in those convictions, and *has* a real relation to them, either in the way of cordial belief or of as cordial rejection? If Mr. Mill had looked for a theory of society which, if adopted, might have the effect of prolonging so undesirable a condition of things, he could not have invented any so excellently adapted to that purpose as his own. It is the belief that society, as society, has a common life, liable to be vitally influenced by the acceptance or rejection of religious and moral faiths; it is this true belief that favours those hearty battles between conflicting sections which are so much better and healthier a sign of the times than "smouldering" orthodoxies and equally smouldering hetero-doxies. If, as Mr. Mill believes, society has no such common life, it is impossible that the enunciation of truths or errors could stir up in it these elevated moods of social emotion. If common opinions are to be debarred all active expression, all signs of either approval or censure, for fear they may subdue the cowardly or silence the timid, it is impossible that the conflict between truth and error can be any thing but a weak and dropping fire carried on by individual marksmen. Mr. Mill uniformly advocates an unsocial conception of liberty which exactly corresponds to the condition of things he so eloquently condemns.

We have not been able to enter, as we had intended, on the discussion which Mr. Mill's book raises, though only as a secondary question, — the true limits of political as dis-tinguished from social authority. There are, of course, many considerations which would limit the interference of positive law with "self-regarding" actions, which do not apply in any way to the authoritative influence exerted by social opinion, custom, and faith. Of these, one of the most important is the absence of any *natural* prosecutor in the case of offences which do not infringe the rights of others, and the natural indisposi-tion of English law to lend any sanction to mere informers. Another great limitation on the interference of government with other classes, as well as with this class, of offences, is the general and healthy conviction that our criminal law should exact something *less*, not only than the average moral *standard*, but even than the average moral *practice* of the community, while social opinion may, and generally does, represent something either quite up to the average or even above it. It is by no means desirable that law should be nearly up to the level of a nation's conscience; were it so, indeed, criminals would be rather the rule than the exception. And besides this, beyond a certain point conscience ceases to concern itself with actions and broad purposes, and goes into those complex shades of motive where law neither can nor ought to follow it, and yet where the influence of the social conscience can sometimes penetrate with effect. All these and many other considerations limit the proper sphere of legal authority very closely; and yet not even as regards this much more limited sphere is Mr. Mill's theory at all likely to be absolutely admitted. The worst and most unnatural crimes which are punished in England, which certainly need the brand of legal as well as social infamy, would go untouched if his doctrine, that purely self-regarding actions are beyond the authority of society, were to be admitted.

But we must conclude. We have purposely kept in view as the point under discussion, the limit of *social* rather than of legal authority, because it was the characteristic feature of Mr. Mill's book to raise this larger question. Indeed, the points on which we differ from him most profoundly affect the essential principles of political philosophy; which they could not do if they merely determined the proper limits of legal interference, instead of the limits of "the power which can be legitimately exercised by society over the individual." We have sought to show that, notwithstanding his running eulogium, Mr. Mill has missed something of true respect for individual liberty, exactly because he has systematically and profoundly under-rated the significance and value of social liberty. In his effort to guard an absolute sphere of liberty for the individual, he would put most unwarrantable constraints on that social freedom which is quite as necessary to all mighty and rapid currents of human faith. Mr. Mill maintains, in fact, that every individual mind should be surrounded by an element that is a perfect non-conductor of social authority; a private sphere, from which social life should be jealously excluded. We maintain that this would be as fatal to the due development of individualities as to the due growth of social and national life. We hold that society has, and ought to have, a common life, which sends its pulses through every individual soul. If St. Paul's teaching, that different men are all "*members*" of one body, appears to represent insufficiently the independence of moral and individual character, yet the opposite conception of society as a mere aggregate of independent units implies a much more delusive and much commoner mistake. There *is* a common life and common conscience in society; and every individuality soon becomes a mere loose atom of eccentricity which does not feel, acknowledge, and show clear indications of its influences. The man who is most willing to open his mind to the stirrings of social faith and social conscience, is the one whose individual thought and powers will react most strongly upon society. Mr. Mill, in trying to exclude the influences of the one, has been unconsciously exerting himself to famish and paralyse the other.

THE WESTMINSTER REVIEW
Vol. LXXII, No. CXLII, 1859
[Robert Bell]

Spiritual Freedom

1. *On Liberty*, by John Stuart Mill. London: John W. Parker and Son. 1859
2. *Signs of the Times: Letters to Ernst Moritz Arndt, on the Dangers to Religious Liberty in the present state of the World.* By Christian Charles Josias Bunsen, D.D., D.C.L., D.Ph. Translated by Susanna Winkworth. London: Smith, Elder, & Co. 1856.

It is significant, perhaps an ominous fact, that within three or four years two men of such wisdom and authority as Chevalier Bunsen and Mr. Mill should have felt themselves constrained to address their countrymen in tones of solemn warning, if not sad foreboding, on the subject of our liberties, and emphatically on that liberty which we Englishmen are accustomed to regard, with pardonable pride and thankfulness, as the most dearly bought and highly prized of our privileges — the freedom of thought and conscience. The illustrious foreigner surveys the recent movements and tendencies of thought and action that have been, and are, exerting themselves, with the most influential and characteristic effects, on the field of European civilization, and finds —

> "A state of things certainly very similar to that in which the Roman Cæsars ascended the throne of the world's empire, but wanting in the fact of universal empire. . . . The prevailing mood of men's minds throughout Europe is everywhere, and not only on the Continent, decidedly that of uneasiness. . . . The north is being invaded by those despairing views of the world prevailing in Southern Europe, which have found voice in the immortal lyrics and meditations of the noble Leopardi. . . . The unimpeachable results of investigation are rejected as infidel, and that which has essentially proceeded from a deep moral and religious

earnestness stigmatized as godless. . . . The pretensions to a divine right of the clerical office over conscience, and as far as may be over the whole mental culture of the human race, are everywhere the same. . . . Every one feels that the most opposite extremes, indeed, apparently, at least, the most fundamental principles of truth — are standing face to face in an attitude of absolute defiance; that decisive conflicts are preparing; that a new order of things is shaping itself. But opinions are everywhere divided as to what is destined to remain at the close, or whether, perchance, that close may prove to be the end, if not of the world, yet of the existing civilization and social arrangements of Europe. The fears of one party are the hopes of the other; selfishness and passion not only step boldly into the foreground, but bear unblushingly on their brow the sign of the highest and holiest. The incredible, in one form or other, appears to all parties and peoples credible, nay, the impossible, probable; few or none of the existing powers or faiths are held to be secure."

He sees on all sides gloom and menace. He does not despond, but his hope seems grounded, less on any definite evidences of progress or coming light and peace, than on a deep Christian faith in the moral order of the universe, human advancement, and the general triumph of good over evil.

Still more cheerless and discouraging is the prospect on which the eye of our countryman looks forth. In "the Signs of the Times," Bunsen beholds the fortunes of civilization and freedom menaced by turbulent and destructive forces. The author of the "Essay on Liberty" sees causes of apprehension of our civilization expiring through sheer want of inherent vitality, by the suppression of an informing, quickening intellect and morality. Energy, however misguided, is preferable to inertia; it has life. And activities which, in their first irruption, might level existing institutions, might yet lay the foundations of another and better social structure. Nothing, on the contrary, can be more absolutely unpromising than a state of fixity and rest, in which change is ignored as either desirable or possible. When development is arrested by prescriptive custom, when accomplishment supersedes education, and all fresh vital effort is repressed into a dead mechanical uniformity, then the established routine itself is insecure; even the level that is reached and considered as standard must ever tend to sink, as it ceases to be sustained by those powers through the agency of which it was attained.

"There is only too great a tendency in the best beliefs and practices to degenerate into the mechanical; and unless there were a succession of persons whose ever recurring originality prevents the grounds of those beliefs and practices from becoming merely traditional, such dead matter would not resist the smallest shock from anything really alive, and there would be no reason why civilization should not die out, as in the Byzantine empire."

Public opinion appears to him with iron tyranny to be crushing out all individuality and original character. Yet "the initiation of all wise and noble things comes, and must come, from individuals."

"Already energetic characters on any large scale are becoming merely traditional. . . . The greatness of England is now all collective; individually small, we only appear capable of anything great by our habit of combining; and with this our moral and religious philanthropists are perfectly contented. . . . We have a warning example in China — a nation of much talent, and, in some respects, even wisdom, owing to the rare good fortune of having been provided at an early period with a particularly good set of customs, the work, in some measure, of men to whom even the most enlightened European must accord, under certain limitations, the title of sages and philosophers. They are remarkable, too, in the excellence of their apparatus for impressing, as far as possible, the best wisdom they possess upon every mind in the community, and securing that those who have appropriated most of it shall occupy the posts of honour and power. Surely the people who did thus have discovered the secret of human progressiveness, and must have kept themselves steadily at the head of the movement of the world. On the contrary, they have become stationary — have remained so for thousands of years; and if they are ever to be farther improved, it must be by foreigners. They have succeeded beyond all hope in what English philanthropists are so industriously working at — in making a people all alike, all governing their thoughts and conduct by the same maxims and rules; and these are the fruits. The modern *régime* of public opinion is, in an unorganized form, what the Chinese educational and political systems are in an organized; and unless individuality shall be able successfully to assert itself against this yoke, Europe, notwithstanding its noble antecedents and its professed Christianity, will tend to become another China.'

Prognostications so gloomy, words of warning and appeal so grave and earnest, and issuing from quarters so influential, demand a review of privileges we are perhaps too ready to assume as established, in order that we may truly apprehend our real position in respect to free thought and action.

What is liberty? What do we mean, — what object do we present to ourselves when we laud and claim liberty? How few men would agree in giving a rational and consistent answer to that question. We all have a vague idea of liberty, but with almost all it is only a vague idea. Yet it is of the last importance that our conceptions on this subject should be definite and fundamental. Mr. Mill concisely traces the origin of the notion. It is first seen conspicuous in early history in the contest between subjects and their governments. By liberty was then meant protection against the tyranny of the political rulers. The rulers were conceived as distinct from, and antagonistic to, the ruled.

"The aim, therefore, of patriots was, to set limits to the power which the ruler should be suffered to exercise over the community; and this limitation was what they meant by liberty. It was attempted in two ways: — First, by obtaining a recognition of certain immunities called political liberties, or rights, which it was to be regarded as a breach of duty in the ruler to infringe, and which, if he did infringe, specific resistance, or general rebellion, was held to be justifiable. A second, and generally a later expedient, was the establishment of constitutional checks, by which the consent of the community, or of a body of some sort, supposed to represent its interests, was made a necessary condition to some of the more important acts of the governing power."

From being viewed as consisting in restriction of an external and opposed governing power, liberty next appears in the idea of self-government. When the community came to be regarded as including the ruler, and the interests of the two identified,

immunity seemed thereby secured from an oppressive government. And so it would, were the identity complete. But the
identity is one of civil and social relations only. What belongs
to a society is not the aggregate of all that belongs to its
individuals. Certain properties and interests are sacred to the
individual with which society has no concern, while the
common council and executive have rights and powers no
individual can arrogate. As in the logical concept, increased
comprehension is accompanied by diminished extension, and
vice versa, so here, the higher the function, the narrower the
field of its exercise. Liberty now, therefore, comes to mean the
defence from encroachment on the part of the people in a
governing capacity beyond its legitimate sphere.

"It was now perceived that such phrases as 'self-government'
and 'the power of the people over themselves,' do not express
the true state of the case. The 'people' who exercise the
power are not always the same people with those over whom
it is exercised; and the 'self-government' spoken of is not the
government of each by himself, but of each by all the rest.
The will of the people, moreover, practically means, the will
of the most numerous or the most active *part* of the people;
the majority, or those who succeed in making themselves
accepted as the majority; the people, consequently, *may*
desire to oppress a part of their number; and precautions are
as much needed against this as against any other abuse of
power. . . . Like other tyrannies, the tyranny of the majority
was at first, and is still vulgarly, held in dread, chiefly as
operating through the acts of the public authorities. But
reflecting persons perceived that when society is itself the
tyrant — society collectively, over the separate individuals
who compose it — its means of tyrannizing are not restricted
to the acts which it may do by the hands of its political
functionaries. Society can and does execute its own
mandates; and if it issues wrong mandates instead of right,
or any mandates at all in things with which it ought not to
meddle, it practises a social tyranny more formidable than
many kinds of political oppression, since though not usually
upheld by such extreme penalties, it leaves fewer means of
escape, penetrating much more deeply into the details of life,
and enslaving the soul itself. Protection, therefore, against
the tyranny of the magistrate is not enough; there needs

protection also against the tyranny of the prevailing opinion and feeling; against the tendency of society to impose, by other means than civil penalties, its own ideas and practices as rules of conduct on those who dissent from them; to fetter the development, and, if possible, prevent the formation, of any individuality not in harmony with its ways, and compel all characters to fashion themselves upon the model of its own. There is a limit to the legitimate interference of collective opinion with individual independence; and to find that limit and maintain it against encroachment, is as indispensable to a good condition of human affairs as protection against political despotism."

The precise ascertainment of this limit — "the fitting adjustment between individual independence and social control" — is the problem to which Mr. Mill addresses himself, and of which his solution is, — "that the sole end for which mankind are warranted individually or collectively in interfering with the liberty of action of any of their number is self-protection."

In this conclusion, he adopts and carries out in application to unorganized social influence the principle of a merely negative function, so eloquently advocated by W. von Humboldt, in relation to State action.

Before we are prepared either to coincide with or dissent from this doctrine we think there is required a more radical explication of what liberty essentially is. In limiting our consideration to one side of human life, we must be careful lest we should obtain results that are partial and inadequate. To eliminate what may be merely temporary, special, or accidental, we must endeavour to ascertain the fundamental idea of all liberty, — that essential quality in proportion to the presence and recognition of which, however in actual legislation modified by the difficulties of the particular case, any freedom is genuine and perfect.

According to Mr. Mill, the ideal of liberty, as we have seen, was first consciously realized in a political relation, as a fence and barrier thrown up against the exercise of ultra-official power by Government. It is easy to see how readily and naturally it would come to be regarded simply as antagonistic to Government, — and to laws, the organ through which Government finds expression. In other relations, the same crude and indiscriminate generalization would not fail to be

carried out, and Law and Liberty be regarded as in their
natures opposed and contradictory, — as standing to each
other in an inverse ratio, so that the measure of freedom we
enjoy is less or greater, just as we are in a greater or less degree
subject to law. But this is only the confusion of loose thinking.
It is not government in itself that liberty is opposed to, but only
government *ultra vires*, — only to an oppressive extension of
its power beyond its proper sphere. The antagonism is not to
Law as law, but to those laws only which the State is
transgressing its true office in enacting. Constitutional law is
not only in harmony, but, to its extent, is identical with
freedom. But constitutional law, in theory however far astray
from this it may go in practice, is but an authoritative
declaration and adjustment of the rights of its subjects. Law,
therefore, so far as it is just and fulfils its end, has its
foundation in its subjects, and, ideally considered, creates
nothing, is nothing, but an artificial embodiment and
expression of what has its real existence in them. It is only the
counterpart and recognition of those rights, in the due exercise
of which we are free. The vulgar misconception of the natures
of Law and Liberty, and of their mutual relations, as
incompatible and contradictory, is subversive of both. Keenly
alive to individual claims, and impatient of impediment, we
revel, at the expense of law, in what we deceive ourselves by
calling liberty, merely because it is not restraint. Or, deeply
impressed with the sense of a beauteous order, we deprecate
freedom as a thing unruly, and likely to disturb that harmony
and beauty, and so check the spontaneity, which thereon
confers its highest quality as vital and unmechanical. Lawlessness
is not liberty, but anarchy and chaos. Liberty is to be permitted
not to do as we please, but to do as we ought. Law, based in
truth and nature, in nowise interferes with legitimate Liberty, but
is its bulwark, and, indeed, the very condition of its existence. As
little does Liberty contradict Law; it depends upon laws, and is
their natural and necessary offspring, — is but the result and
expression of the harmony of laws. So far from there being any
antagonism or incompatibility between them, the one is rendered
possible only by the other. "Law alone,' says Goethe, "can give us
freedom."[1] Every infringement of law is a violation of liberty;
every extravagance of liberty is a law broken.

[1]   Nur das Gesetz kann uns die Freiheit geben.

To take up this question fully, would far exceed the necessary limits of the paper. But some of its more general aspects may be indicated, as a guide towards a broad and comprehensive definition of Freedom. The essential connexion of Law with Liberty, viewed in their most general aspects, will become apparent by a consideration of what law really is. A clear statement of what is meant by law is the more requisite, as this is a term used in such various and ambiguous senses. We talk of divine law, of human law, of natural law, of physical and of moral law; and often without any clear or precise meaning attached to any of these phrases. So far as law can be truly predicated in these several relations, there must be a sense in which it lies at the root of them all, a view of it in which they are all comprehended. Here, then, the term is employed in its deepest and universal signification, as expressive of that constitutive and regulative principle in the Universe, in virtue whereof lies its organization and cosmical subsistence. It is therefore divine, inasmuch as its primary source and author is Deity[2] — inasmuch, indeed, as it is nothing else than the method of God's own working in His creatures. Natural also it is, in respect of its being the reflex of the principle or essential *virtus* operating in each creature, the expression of that wherein the being, as such, is — the nature with which its Creator has endowed it. Whatever is truly human, is included in it, as being a part of creation, one sphere of nature. But human law, when by that is meant the administrative enactments of men, finds a place under this broad general idea of the expression, only in so far as those enactments are the faithful reflexion and outcome of natural God-given law. Νόμος is not δόγμα πόλεως, but τοῦ ὄντος ἐξεύρεσις.[3]

We trace everywhere around and within us system and order; and these imply law. An order must have a principle or arrangement; a system must have a method of development, and a central connexion. In its highest generic aspect, therefore, law is that principle of consistence and relation

2 It is not intended here to express an opinion that God's will is the ground or origin of law, or that He is not Himself necessarily subject to law, nor indeed, to raise this question at all, but simply to affirm that the law is divine, as being that with which, in conformity with His own divine nature, the Father and Maker of all has informed His creatures.

3 Plato — Minos.

which gives to the great system of things — to creation — its completeness and harmony of method, its individuality and inter-dependence of parts, its unity in variety. Viewed more specially, it is that which confers on its own department, considered in itself as a whole, that same harmony, uniqueness, and character, which belong to the entire system. Contemplated in its most particular and circumscribed operations, it is that which regulates the particular *virtus* of the individual, in other words, the character of that *virtus*, the essence wherein the individuality subsists. Regarding it, therefore, in the sum of its aspects, we observe a regular series, as in ordinary genera and species, varying, as to its extremes, inversely in depth and breadth; presenting under the one, the greatest comprehension of parts, and consequently the most complex individuality in its subject, and under the other, the most particularly determined activity, and the simplest unit. Starting from any stage within the whole range of being, we find the same law operating in all the individuals on that stage, asserting and working out in each his own life. On a higher level in the scale, these individuals may cease to be units, and combine, as parts, with others, to form higher individuals, according to a more general law. And so on. Thus the lower laws are taken up, and harmoniously subordinated to higher ones; which again similarly find converging points in still higher; till the apex of all is reached, which is nothing else than the loftiest and most general expression of the universal constitution. Looking from the summit downwards, we see the great all-comprehensive idea, of which the actual order of things is the phenomenal development — we see the principle, the αρχη, branching off into restricted and departmental laws, and affording them their mutual harmony and unity; and these again spreading out into still more special limitations; and thus downwards, until, through science or imagination, the lowest units, the true elements, are reached.

The existence of such laws — or law, for it is but one variously modified[4] — is seen alike in the satisfaction it affords

---

[4] "In fact, the diversity of laws conceals an analogy so perfect, that, taken separately, they are nothing more than the various formulas of one single law. God created the original law; and the world, with all its bright expansion, has thus been filled with harmony. In this law everything was included." — M. Jules Simon's "Natural Religion," translated by J. W. Cole.

to the demands of our intellectual nature, and in the results of experience and investigation. So soon as the very conception of this fair world is awakened within us, we postulate, not always very consciously, but still decidedly and inevitably, its regulation by law. We cannot think of its forces as moving capriciously or arbitrarily, or without design and fixed method. What the method is we may be very far from knowing; but the existence of some regulated plan is given us as immediately in the conception, as is the axiom that a whole is equal to all its parts, in the knowledge of what a whole and a part are.

What is thus *á priori* postulated, is not only in science *á posteriori* verified, but what the law is, is ascertained. This regulated uniformity is the foundation of science. The bare knowledge of an isolated fact is not science, nor any number of such knowledges. Relation, uniformity, necessity, and universality are required; otherwise science would be an impossibility. Science, in fact, is the knowledge of Nature in her laws. Their existence and operation are therefore assumed by science as its necessary condition, and proved by its actual development. To enlarge on this would be superfluous and tedious; it is on all hands admitted and acted on.

To say that these laws are universal does not of course imply that each particular law is boundless in its operation: their plurality and difference disprove that. But each is limited only by its fellows. Each is universal with respect to its own province, and there is no sphere of creation without its law. Every living being, every natural unit or individual, has a law of being, a principle of organization, in conformity with which it is developed and maintained as an individual, and which is no sooner overborne and rendered inoperative than it ceases to exist as such. "Life is the principle of individuation," says Coleridge — as said Schelling before him. Every power in nature is regulated by such a law, otherwise it would be characterless and indefinite. Every faculty of mind is so, otherwise it could have no specific action, and could never rise above the naked level of indeterminate possible energy. So is every physical object which is a whole, which is not fragmentary, and in that respect dead and passing away to form other combinations; in which case, the inherent regulative principle is to be traced in the laws proper to the several elements, or in those of the new combinations. Every truth of science affords an illustration. Look to atomics: the law of definitive proportionals directs every combination. One part of hydrogen chemically combined with eight of oxygen invariably forms water, and no other proportions of these or of any other elements can be constrained to do so. By law the crystal smooths its facets, and points its angles. The orbs of heaven are rounded by law, and move in curves and with velocities by law prescribed. Movements that long appeared anomalies are now resolved into the more recondite exponents of law. In the vegetable world branches are sprung at definite angles; leaves are clipped and veined at the same angle no less definitely: the leaf repeats the tree, and owns the same regulative principle. No art or science can constrain the acorn to produce aught but the oak — the oak aught but the acorn. And in higher forms of life, if the laws are more complex, they are not less certain. Each animal produces in likeness of itself. An egg, however hatched, becomes always a bird the same in kind as the hen that laid it. It may rot, and may become subject in its various elements to their respective laws; but if its life is quickened at all, it is the same life. Each kind of animal has its own normal form and contour, its own normal action and function. - The universe and all its several parts are instinct with vitality, and no life can be without a law.

No portion of the universe, we say, is without its law, without its order; there is no want of form, no void. That the form, however, may be broken, that there may be *de*formity, we know. But the very fact, that such is acknowledged to be deformity, confesses the reality of a norm that is therein being outraged, and in that very outrage displaying its sanctions. And what are those sanctions? The law, we have seen, is nothing else than the formula of individuality. It is the rule and condition of life and being to its subject. The disturbance of normal action must therefore result in the life and individuality being lost or impaired. Dissolution of the creature must be the consequence and penalty of utter defiance of the law. The being is no longer the individual it was: vital unity is extinguished. Thus, if the law of water be interfered with, water exists no longer — only oxygen and hydrogen. If the law of animal life be interrupted, the animal as such ceases, the organism is resolved into its constituents, "the dust returns to the dust, and the spirit to God who gave it." Conscience is injured by every infraction of the moral law, and by habitual and permanent disobedience, would surely become extinct. If the law of the spiritual nature obtains no respect, is not the judgment death?

It may seem as though we were insisting unnecessarily on a question so commonly considered an established point, as the government by law of all nature, animate and inanimate. If we have dwelt upon it, we have done so with the view, not merely of asserting the existence of such laws, but of guarding against an erroneous conception as to their nature and seat, as fatal as it is common. We refer to that false metaphysical conception that prevails of Law as something external, an entity different from the being itself, as "thetical and positive,"[5] instead of natural and inherent. It is not with loose and popular thinkers alone that this view finds favour. It numbers its adherents in the highest rank of science. In his discussion with Geoffroy St Hilaire on the unity of composition in the animal kingdom, Cuvier asks, "Wherefore should Nature always act uniformly? What necessity could have constrained her only to employ the same organic forms, and always to have employed them? By whom could this arbitrary rule have been imposed?" Elsewhere he declares that St. Hilaire's "pretended identities" would, if true, reduce nature to a kind of slavery.[6] According to this conception a rule or ordinance is instituted, and certain creatures placed under its edicts; or a race of creatures have a law *made* for them, and promulgated; and to secure the observance of its precepts — which in this view of the matter carry with them, considered in themselves, no inherent obligation or authority — a certain penalty or punishment is *attached* to their non-observance, which, by appealing to the capacity in its subjects for the painful and abhorrent, aims at goading them

---

[5] Cudworth.

[6] See Mr. G. H. Lewes's "Comte's Philosophy of the Sciences," p. 53, where he exposes this error as to the nature of law. He objects to the expression "laws of nature" altogether, as involving a mechanical theory of the universe, and tending to mislead us in speculation. But grant there is order, then law follows as its abstract expression. To say there is a law according to which a plan is worked out, no more implies that the law is prescient of its end, than in analytical geometry the use of "the equation of a curve" implies either a foreknowing or a controlling power in the equation.

into doing what they feel no natural, constitutional obligation to do. All natural law, on the contrary, is within the creature, and is authoritative just because it is the principle of the creature's nature. Beings are not affected from without by forces acting according to certain laws; but they are endowed, each with its own proper inherent law, its constitutive principle, in virtue of which it is what it is. Natural action, whether material intellectual or moral, does not take place according to any compulsory power *superimposed*, and having its seat elsewhere than in the vital activity itself. The universe does not have laws impressed upon it; it is not the object of law; not the *materia circa quam*, but the *materia in qua*. It is the subject of laws by which it is informed and unfolded, and which are revealed and expressed in its varied life and action. It is, therefore, in the beings themselves that we are to look for and discover these laws. They are to be ascertained nowhere else than in the constitution of their subjects. Their actual spheres of operation are their own statute-book. By study of each life is to be learned its own law. Obvious as this may seem, it would appear from the evidence of history to be one of the latest lessons to be learned, and one of the most difficult rules to be practised; but important and valuable as it is difficult; for the disregard of it is one of the most fruitful sources of broken law, and of liberty unattained. The history of science is the history of our training and slow advance towards its recognition and observance. Men have ever shown themselves prone either to forget the existence of law altogether, or to seek for and hypothetize it from without. The consequence of this to man is ignorance, false science without foundation in reality, a failing to subdue and control external nature as he ought, or to regulate or be himself. For God-given laws are perfect, and can be disregarded only with peril and loss. Whosoever does not recognise and bow to them, they will crush; and failing patiently and humbly to watch for and accept them, we never are what we ought to be, nor do we stand in out rightful relation to God's other works. And so to discover and learn them, our first and never-to-be-forgotten lesson is, that every constitution alone authoritatively proclaims the law of its own life — that not only the human nations, but every creature of God, "is a law unto itself, and will show the work of the law written in its heart."

Here an objection may occur which must be met. The

principle attempted to be established, it may be said, would constitute the existent and actual into the rightful and legal, and would necessitate the alternative, that either bondage or law is but a name and a fiction, — that broken law is impossible and a contradiction, since the actual state expresses the law and legalizes itself. But it is the constitution, not the present condition, that declares law. The actual often declares most plainly, that it is not a state of consistence and vitality, but of decay and disintegration, — not of progress and discharged function, but of incompleteness and arrestment or relapse. We do not mean to argue that phenomenal permanence is a certain condition of fulfilled law; the reverse. Here all is progress, and this can be attained only through the casting off of the old, and the putting on of the new; an advance towards the higher that lies before, by a retirement from the lower that is to be left behind. New life is only possible through death; and the law which determines the being as a whole, subordinates those of the several parts which pass through the various stages of development necessary to the perfection of the creature. The law, in the nature of its action, may be terminal and conclusive, and like a converging spiral, running in to a point. But this, which is the perfect implementing of the law, is not to be mistaken for the abrupt arrestment of its action, any more than the shattered column for the capitalled pillar. There is no difficulty in distinguishing the searing of the seed-pod after its contents are matured and ready for delivery, from its untimely withering before its work is done; or the dying of the seed in the act of springing up into new vegetation, from premature, unproductive deadness.

Now if law, in any particular instance, fail of active operation, — if the idea it would express attains inadequate or no exposition, it must be from one of two causes.

It may be from inherent weakness; the vital principle may be too languid for the organism, and its phenomenal determinations consequently weak and undecided. In animal or vegetable life we say the creature is sickly, morbid, dying a natural death, that is, death springing from causes within itself. The law is not fulfilled, because the quickening principle in itself, and apart from any counteracting influence, is too weak to run out into the full occupation of its sphere. The lamp is not forcibly extinguished, but fails for want of oil. The law is the *sine qua non* of the being, and from mere negativeness and inability of self-assertion the individual ceases and disappears.

On the other hand, constitutions the most lively and healthy may be attacked by forces foreign and external, so that the vital energy is either wholly repressed, or so bound and constrained as to attain only a dwarfish and deformed development. The law is in a greater or less degree not given effect to, and the creature is correspondingly abnormal. As the deviation, in the former case, from the fulfilment of the law, arising from internal weakness, implies disease when the observance is imperfect, and death when there is no observance; so here, in the departure resulting from counteracting force, when the law finds no expression, we have murder or violent death; when only a partial expression, slavery.

Liberty may, therefore, be defined the necessary external conditions of Law — as Health may, those which are internal and necessary. A creature is free when so conditioned *ab extra* as fully to permit the working out of the law of its own being. The fulfilling of it is ever the witness of liberty and health; its infraction results from the absence of one or other, or both of these. But non-observance is of two kinds; we may either exceed, or fall short, of the legitimate limits. On the one hand, vital energy may be deficient, or a greater foreign potency may repress and hinder its action; or, on the other, it may be uncontrolled, licentious, aggressive. But oppression and bondage are correlative; and although expressive of contraries, relative to the subject, may, in the general question, be considered together. For tyranny in one quarter implies an exactly corresponding slavery in another; so that the transgression of any excursive power beyond its proper sphere, may always be studied in the invasion to which another's domain is subjected. There is no natural void, all is replete with life: and in their normal adjustments the sphere of each faculty adjoins and bounds those of others.

In reviewing Mr. Mill's doctrine in the light of the results we have obtained, the question arises whether, and if so, in what character and measure, society in itself, as distinguished from its components, is real, natural, and positive. We have spoken of lower laws finding a common head and unity in a superior and more general law; but corresponding to this law there must be an entity of which it is the abstract formula, and which through it acquires unity and "individuation." Society in this

view is not a mere collection of individuals, as a heap of sand is
the aggregation of its particles, but is a body, has an organized
existence and a life. That life does not jar or interfere with the
several lives of its members, but rather, as they essentially
involve in their nature certain social elements, completes and
enriches them. What the constitution and life, therefore, of
society exactly is, would fall next to be inquired into. But this
would open up the whole field of social science; and instead of
attempting even in the slightest manner to enter upon a
province so large and difficult, we purpose, in the space that
yet remains to us, limiting our consideration to a special sphere
of individual liberty, in examining which we shall endeavour to
illustrate and exemplify the principles we have enunciated.

Before passing, however, we may remark that in recognising
in society a real and natural existence, finding its expression in
a positive law, we inevitably differ from the view of a merely
negative function which Mr. Mill assigns to it. With respect to
Government, in so far as it is regarded as an artificial and
economic arrangement, and therefore having only a factitious
existence, its character and duties would fall within the
negative class. Viewed, on the other hand, as the representative
head and embodiment of national life, while it may be artificial
and temporary in form, it is in its substance real and
permanent, having its root in nature.

Among our liberties, those of thought and conscience stand
first alike in importance and order of connexion. As intelligent
beings, thought is the ground which underlies all our actions,
or the condition under which they are consciously realized.
Slavery here, therefore, taints whatever springs hence. Conscience, regarded as the regulative organ or faculty of our
moral nature, cannot be held in bondage without disorder
ensuing throughout that nature. If violence be offered to this
regulating power, hollowness and untruth pervade the whole
character. As more internal to the man, too, both it and
thought seem more intimately our own than anything else,
more nearly ourselves; so that both on account of their close
personal relationship and wide influences, it is round these
spheres of our activities that the question of freedom revolves.
It is for these liberties that men have ever first and most
determinedly fought; it is these, the enjoyment of which, to
whatever other servitude a people may be reduced, still cheers
and sustains them with the conscious dignity and self-respect of

men; and, deprived of which they harden into a mechanical and perfunctory existence, if haply they sink not to a lower and more savage nature, however great the other privileges they may possess.

It is to this branch of his general subject that Mr. Mill first and chiefly directs attention. It occupies a third part of his whole treatise; and at his hands it received a masterly, and, so far as he has occasion, to entertain the problem, a thorough and comprehensive treatment. The question he proposes to himself leads him to consider only the relation of society to the individual, and, as this bears on the free exercise of thought and conscience, the rights of the individual have never received a more enlightened and dispassionate advocacy. But there is another field on which, beyond all others, these rights are most frequently violated, and where their vindication is the more called for because the injury is less patent. If a great wrong is done when society by law or force of custom represses our free activities of thought and conscience, or rather (for this it cannot very directly do) interdicts their natural issue in speech and overt action, the evil is at least readily felt and recognised; but it is quite otherwise when a man tyrannizes over himself. Yet is he not more free, but rather less, in the latter case than in the former. It is of secondary importance who the oppressor may be; the question is as to the state of slavery endured — only, the character of the one may throw light on the other; and as society, to quote our author's forcible words, "may practise a social tyranny more formidable than many kinds of political oppression, since, though not usually upheld by such extreme penalties, it leaves fewer means of escape, penetrating much more deeply into the details of life, and enslaving the soul itself;" so self-tyranny is above all to be dreaded, as carrying with it all these formidable qualities in a superlative degree.

As we have seen, Mr. Mill shortly indicates the growth of the idea of liberty to that stage in which it is opposed to "the tyranny of the majority." But why stop here? May it not be traced further? Considering society as the higher unit, the several members are the elements. But it is no new idea to transfer the analogy of the body politic to the body natural, where the individual is the State or community, and his several faculties its members. And here is it not equally true that "the majority, or those who succeed in making themselves accepted as the majority, may oppress, and that precautions are as much

needed against this as any other abuse of power?" The
passions, avarice, hatred, lust, ambition — not by virtue of any
natural authority or right to dictate — the reverse — often
tyrannize over both reason and conscience. How often does
fear unman us? the appetites enslave us? How often is the
whole order and constitution of the inner man reversed, every
mental liberty outraged, and the nobler functions arrested,
perverted by the excess of lower faculties? Just as politically
considered, it has been found that society, though rid of its
monarchical misrulers, has still to stand in dread of itself as its
governor; so viewed individually, we have not only to be
defended from society, but to guard against ourselves. Three
stages of development in the conception of liberty are
recognised, corresponding to that by which it is contradicted
and defined: — by the despotism of superior rulers, then by the
oppression of a political majority in representative governments, and next by the unlegalized, but not less tyrannical,
intolerance of custom. Why not another in which it finds its
negative in an unwarrantable predominance of some of the
powers and faculties of the individual over others, analogous to
the undue authority claimed and wielded by a real or so-called
majority in the political state? Of these four positions Mr. Mill
has reached only the third, and the fourth, though often
handled partially from the point of view of the practical
moralist, has yet to receive articulate statement and scientific
consideration as a phase of liberty.

By our author, liberty of thought and liberty of discussion
are considered together, as practically inseparable; and in
general usage we find that when free thought is spoken of, it is
free speech that is meant. It is, no doubt, true that in actual life
they stand so related to each other than the former does not
flourish apart from the latter. But the practice of identifying
them has had this disadvantage, that when we have vindicated
and secured the one we think we have made good the other
also, and leave our work half done. The privilege and exercise
of free speech by no means implies the enjoyment of free
thought, or even the recognition of its true character, or the
conditions under which alone it is possible. On the topic of
religious freedom our minds naturally recur to the mighty
struggle it occasioned three hundred years ago throughout
western Europe, and a better representative instance could not
be found than in it and the movements to which it has given

rise, of how the very essential of individual liberty of thought and belief is lost sight of behind its more palpable and obtrusive social counterpart of free profession and advocacy.

Protestantism claims to have thrown off the yoke of the Pope, and to have vindicated the right of private judgment. It asserted individual life, and aimed at union through the combination of units, not at Catholicity to be attained in the suppression of individuality. This was the vital principle, and as an idea, ever so dimly apprehended, was an immense advance. But how has this idea been realized? Has it not, to a considerable extent, been forgotten, and even when kept in view, has it not greatly failed to receive a thorough-going application to human life? The form has been changed, but the spirit is often the same. The former tyranny is revolted from, but are the laws of our constitution more revered? The despotism may be more enlightened, and may aim at another order and arrangement of things, and may, accordingly, enact other and less severe laws; but the order may not be that of free natural development, nor the laws native and proper. Protestantism revolted from Papal authority, only, it would seem, to adopt that of a book, and while freeing us from others (even where it has succeeded in this), has forgotten to carry out its principles and deliver us from ourselves.

Care must be taken not to confound things that differ. Protestantism in idea, Protestantism fairly represented, sustaining its implied character, and carrying out its original aim and effort, may be very different from what it has now very much come to be. It may be that the majority of Protestants very unworthily uphold the name, and exhibit an ungenuine and perverted Protestantism; they may have exposed it to charges to which it is not essentially liable. But if Protestantism is to be regarded, not as an idea and possibility, not merely as a system of doctrine and the results that ought legitimately to flow from it, but as a historical movement of human life, how is it to be dealt with, if not in its prevalent living embodiment? It is not Protestantism as it ought to be, or as it might be, but as it is to be seen generally manifested that is here spoken of. Many, and the best, Protestants will, no doubt, repudiate the belief of such an absolute, oracular character in the Bible, alike for themselves and their church. But whatever the sentiments of certain individuals and the *professed* teaching of the church, it cannot, looking to our religious history during the last two centuries and a-half, be denied that the prevalent view of both laity and clergy among us has been that the Scriptures are the most unconditional, irrelative embodiment of truth. The vagueness of the line of demarcation that fences the canon is by most apparently unthought of. The question of purity of test has been supposed to be of insignificant practical bearing. In spite of exposed contradictions, of misstatements of fact, notwithstanding what is irreconcilable, incredible, its perfect infallibility has been maintained, and the whole, without exception, unflinchingly imposed on the human intellect and conscience, which, on any symptom of opposition or impatience, have been too often summarily silenced by a "get thee behind me, Satan!" The depravity of the human heart is in nothing more seen, it is alleged, than in its unwillingness to receive the Scriptures, and the readiest reply that can be made to any objection to them is a reminder of Adam's fall and our descent. It might, no doubt, very plausibly, on parity of reasoning, be asked, if our faculties, are so crippled and uncertain in their action that they cannot be heard in opposition to the Bible, how they can safely be trusted in the ascertainment of its perfect truth. But consistency, as well as freedom, is occasionally at a discount.

That this is no misrepresentation, no unfair or exaggerated statement, might be shown by pages upon pages of our popular religious and theological literature. In selecting the one citation we shall adduce, from a pamphlet by one of the prize Burnet essayists, who enjoys a certain reputation of being "advanced and liberal," we cannot be considered as straining our point. His lecture,[7] which professedly, and so far, from the author's position, representatively, sets forth the principles and spirit in which many of our religious teachers are being trained, doubly bears us out — now by explicit corroboration, and again by affording in itself an example.

"Is the truth to be held unquestioned and unquestionable in *any* outward formula, — at the simple dictation of *any* outward power? or is it ever only — for our time as for all time — the product of *two* factors — of Scripture and Reason, of Revelation and Free Inquiry? It is the implied

7 "Theological Tendencies of the Age," Inaugural Lecture, by the Rev. J. Tulloch, D.D., Principal and Primarius Professor of Theology, St. Mary College, St. Andrew's. 1855.

principle of all genuine Protestantism that it is the latter. It is, however, we are forced to confess, the practice of much of our Protestantism to hold it for the former. And what is remarkable, and might be instructive to the Christian student is, that this practice is especially characteristic of certain sections of our Protestantism that consider themselves the furthest removed from all taint of Popery, as they are certainly animated by the most loud-voiced zeal against it. . . . However it (the party these sections form) may profess to acknowledge the right of private judgment, there is nothing less known, and nothing less tolerated by the adherents of this school than any free and fruitful exercise of this right. *Authority*, in fact, has here, in certain cases, established itself in a far more inflexible, as in a far less dignified and impressive form than in Catholicism."

Meant as in contrast, he thus describes the position he himself fills and advocates.

"But while we assert the validity of the subjective critical element in theology, there must yet ever be recognised in Scripture on *objective* element, entitled not merely to inform, but altogether to guide and *rule* the other. If the original revelation of reason is not to be rejected, but to have its right freely acknowledged, the later objective revelation in Scripture must withal remain the standard and arbiter of the truth. To the law, and to the testimony, must ever be the final appeal. Here alone is the invariable *norma fidei*. . . . The Bible must be acknowledged as not only co-ordinate with reason, but as forming, in all points of religious truth, the ultimate *determining* authority. For us, whatever may be alleged to have been the case with the early Christians, there can be no genuine Christian doctrine or sentiment apart from the Bible. It, and it alone, under God, is the *source* of divine wisdom and divine life."

He then strangely enough adds, —

"It (the Bible) is a symbol of sacred meaning, which never changing itself, may yet ever be read anew, under richer lights, and yield a deeper significance to the reader. Infallible itself, it lays no restraint on the freest inquiry. It, indeed, alters no more than the great symbol of nature; but just as we are ever finding, under the light of common science, a more glorious meaning in the latter, so, under the light of an advancing and wiser criticism, may we reach a more harmonious and perfect meaning in the former."

How such a view of the Bible can be maintained by men professing to fight for freedom under the banner — susceptible of illiberal and exclusive interpretation enough, no doubt — of the rights of private judgment, it is difficult to understand. Only, it may be regarded as a temporary phase of the struggle — as one of those failures that intercept, but prepare for, ultimate success — one of those eddyings into which rapids sweep, when, having spent their force dashing over the steeps, they meet the mass of deeper waters, before they settle into renewed and steadier current towards the sea — one of those side movements which make up the zigzag path by which we onward toil and tack. The weak but struggling sometimes call in the assistance of another and foreign power, to aid in repelling the invading foe, and are for a time at the mercy of their helpers. The tyranny of the Church in certain realms of thought was resisted only by the strength and support obtained, through the revival of letters, from thinkers of the heathen world, to whom, for this service, men in return swore fealty; and in acknowledging the greatness of the power, that effected their deliverance from a yoke they had themselves failed to throw off, owned their inferiority, and yielded to that of the governor, till his more enlightened sway gradually raised them to assert their independence. So, in another sphere, men may have felt themselves so under debt to the power they obtained through the Bible, to defy the Pope, whom, without its aid, they had been unable to withstand, that they have abjectly clung to it as their only safety, their rightful lord and master.

The absolute infallibility and authority of the Bible, indeed, is no less contrary to liberty than is the infallibility of the Pope. They are equally cases of subjection to foreign law. Abstractly considered, wherein lies the difference? The sources are different, the edicts are different. The one is fixed and stereotyped, the other variable and capable of accommodation, and the world in its revolution may and will carry it along with it. The ordinances of the Bible may be much nearer an accordance with the innate law of the creature than papal bulls — may, let it be said, be in perfect accordance. Then their dignity, truth and influence depend upon that accordance. But this is not the authority and infallibility claimed. It is a controlling, regulating authority, a standard and criterion that is contended for; while the true standard and authority must ever be to each creature its own law and constitution. To attempt to constitute any Scripture into such a law for man, is to enslave him in every sphere of his nature to which that Scripture is addressed.

Such a doctrine interrupts the laws of thought, and presents a check to free inquiry. What Protestant doubts the painful effects of papal infallibility in this respect? And the principle is the same here; — it silences inquiry by determining the result. It will not do to say that the one is really infallible while the other is not; that the claim of the Pope is unfounded and false, but that the claim in behalf of the Bible is no more than is true; and that, consequently, by an acknowledgment of the former we debar ourselves from the truth, whereas by owning the latter we prevent our aberration from it. Were this otherwise tenable, it would not be to the point. Belief in infallibility is objected to, as an obstacle to freedom of inquiry. But the reply is, that by admitting this doctrine we secure our attainment of the truth, not by the exercise but by the exclusion of free inquiry. This promises the possession, only by denying the pursuit. "Did the Almighty," says Lessing, "holding in his right hand truth, and in his left search after truth, deign to proffer me the one I might prefer; in all humility, but without hesitation, I should request search after truth." But, that we have perfect truth offered us in any set of documents, is an assumption of the whole matter, and aims at settling the question by starting from the conclusion. Nothing could more betray the very spirit and principle of Popery, nothing could more trample under foot any real and distinctly Protestant right of private judgment.

The right of private judgment, indeed, like many more watchwords, whatever significance it may have had originally, has come to be little more than a mere watchword. For, if the Bible be regarded as the certain standard and arbiter of truth, without appeal, what does this much-vaunted title and privilege amount to? It involves a twofold action. It may stand related to the Scriptures simply as preliminary and positive, or as expository and applicative. In the former relation, it has to examine the claims to infallibility, to decide that there is a sure and perfect canon, and to draw its line of demarcation; in other words, it has to sign its own death-warrant. Like the insect that lives but to produce its young, it is roused to activity, only to elect its successor, and in that one act to yield all title ever to act again. In this office its sole duty is to choose its executioner. Its interpretative function, on the other hand, is permanent. Having once for all examined and accepted the Bible, as an infallible guide and rule, to supersede and control itself, it has then to treat it in the way of criticism and analysis, to interpret and apply the rule, and bring forth its guidance into contact with every varying human life. But is inquiry, limited to these functions, peculiar to Protestantism, or does it serve any of the great ends claimed? Does it protect us on any one side from the invasion of our liberties? Or is it not rather the engaged servant of our oppressor, labouring first to establish and impose the external rule, and then to explain and enforce it? Popery in its most unmitigated intensity could desire nothing more.

Criticism, in so far as it is merely explicative of the meaning of a symbol, and not a judging of its truthfulness, is inquiry, not regarding, but on behalf of, that symbol — a service rendered to it, not a test of its serviceableness. To this the most abject traditionalist could offer no objection, the most servile apostle of authority could desire nothing else. That the symbol should be examined and sifted of any foreign and fallible elements, with which in course of time it may have been mixed up, that its meaning should be set forth, its difficulties explained, any apparent inconsistencies in it reconciled, is all in favour of the cause. Criticism thus far is but labouring in behalf of that to which it is applied; like farmers separating any chaff there may be from the grain, irrespective of the nature or quality of what it winnows. So soon as it proceeds to test the grain itself, to criticize and discuss the symbol thus purged and sorted, then where is infallibility?

For what, in any case, are the grounds on which infallibility may be attempted to be established? As a matter of fact, the immense majority, in claiming that character either for Pontiff or Scripture, only conform to old custom or prevalent fashion; they believe it, because their fathers believed it before them. But this is not universal, nor could it have been so originally. To man the first grounds of credibility are his own immediate consciousnesses, his inborn undeniable beliefs, and to these must all ultimately be referred. The most absolute tradition-alism, carried to its fullest consequences, must find its let somewhere, and, whether of church or γραφη, has its appeals to human faculty for credibility. How thorough-going soever, it must either have a higher traditional authority, and that a still higher, and so on, or must set forth its evidences, and submit its claims to be judged of by the human mind. Accordingly, we have our formally drawn up "evidences" — evidences external and internal, drawn from miracle, prophecy, and promise, from the nature of the contents of the books themselves, and from the supposed necessity of the case. And the Papists have their arguments and machinery of persuasion; and so far as the necessity of the case is concerned, Bellarmin and his coadjutors can hardly be thought less successful than his opponents.

This necessary recourse to appeal to human faculty, requiring it, the fallible, to judge and bear witness to the infallible, is a yielding of the whole question. It is attempting to raise an indestructible superstructure upon a tottering foundation. It is submitting to our judgment that which, by the necessity that is claimed for it, is presupposed to be quite beyond our judgment. It is calling on man to decide regarding that to which, if it possess the character asserted, he needs himself to refer for decision. Man it is said is fallen, and prone to err. He requires a guide free from a similar liability, and to supply this want, he is offered, in the one case a *Papa*, and in the other a Book, for the infallibility of which he is himself the sole guarantee.

What is infallible, there is no need to ascertain; doubt or question is already excluded, and *hors de combat*. If it is already known to be infallible, there is no room for inquiry. If not, no investigation and decision of ours can establish it to be such. To do so, would imply our prepossession of what we desiderate. If we are to examine the Bible in detail, and to judge of the unmixed truthfulness of its contents, we must have the standard by which to try divine verities, and so have within ourselves what we are seeking from without, and which, therefore, we do not need. To endeavour to establish its infallibility on any averments or claims of the writings themselves, or by any deductions from their statements, would be to admit the testimony of a document, while itself *in statu probandi*, as already authoritative and conclusive — a clear case of *petitio principii*. Evidence from sources external to the book will serve no better. Collect and heap these evidences to the utmost, they can never amount to such a weight, but that their balance may be found in the book itself. A single contradiction is stronger against it, than all external testimony conceivable in its favour. Whatever is unthinkable, no evidence can prove. So far then from these, or any writings being a canon and authority to us, it is we who examine and admit their title and authority. Nor can what is thus conferred ever rise superior to its source. So that if any human faculty (unless it be a faculty which, by man's constitution, ought to be controlled by the understanding), ever clash or jar with their declarations, they can have no right to overrule.

The bondage of this infallibility has in some quarters been recognised, and inquiry has asserted its freedom. The firm and secure advance of science has in many directions exposed the truth of nature too palpably to be doubted by reasonable and educated men. By many, accordingly, the dogma of an all-comprehensive infallibility has been conceded; they have narrowed their ground, and limited the claims of infallibility to a certain class of subjects. Thus, Archbishop Whately says:—

"In matters unconnected with religion, such as points of history, or natural philosophy, a writer who professes to be communicating a divine revelation, imparted to him through the means of miracles, may be as liable to error as other men, without any disparagement to his pretensions."

Similarly writes Bishop Hinds:—

"It is not truth of all kinds that the Bible was inspired to teach, but only such truth as tends to religious edification; and the Bible is consequently infallible, as far as regards this and this alone."

Bishop Hampden goes beyond this; he yields even morals:—

"So independent is the science of ethics, of the support and ennobling which it receives from religion, that it would be nothing strange or objectionable in a revelation, were we to find embodied in its language much of the false ethical philosophy which systems may have established. This, I conceive, would appear to those who bear in mind the real distinctness of religion and moral science, nothing more objectionable than the admission into the sacred volume of descriptions involving false theories of natural philosophy."

Such a position may be found as untenable, as it is unsatisfactory. These concessions are not enough. Our liberty is as precious in theology, as in physical science and ethics; and progress is as much the law of our life in the one as in the other. Humanity cannot be congealed. " 'The heavens journey still, and sojourn not,' and arts, wars, discoveries, and opinions go onward at their own pace. The new age has new desires, new enemies, new trades, new charities, and reads the Scriptures with new eyes." The reflex and scientific recognition of the religious life wherein theology consists, must so far depend upon our general culture and modes of thought. With these it must in the march "Excelsior" keep time, otherwise it will fall out of the rank, and be left behind. A realm of active thought will be vacant, its law hushed — or peopled only with the embalments of a former life, which we morbidly cherish, like the nations that refuse to bury their dead out of their sight. A theology to be other than a dead drag — between which and our general life there can be any harmony and reciprocity, must be progressive. But this it never can be so long as we bow to a fixed, infallible, and complete expression of theological doctrine.

Such a progressive character implies no uncertainty, no arbitrariness, no negation of real truth. That there is danger of a wilful, unscientific theology, if the Bible were not held as an infallible standard and rule, is not to be denied. That the lifeless and fixed theology, which alone such a doctrine of infallibility can secure, is not much better, is, perhaps, as little to be denied; and that such a danger would threaten, is only in accordance with the common condition of all liberty. If we look to what is not law, but its violation, at what is not essential, but incidental and accessory, not to the universal, but the singular, neither certitude nor advance can be attained. So long as it is accounted a glory and a privilege, a token of salvation and of God's special favour, to be exceptional and select, while actuated by the spirit of thankfulness that we are not as other men, and till we believe that none of God's creatures are common or unclean, the results that will be evolved in religion and theology, will be as grotesque and disorderly as, under similar conditions, those in any other sphere of life. If we cherish and value peculiarities of endowment and "experience," if we indulge wilfulness and licentiousness rather than own law and liberty, unless we rest on our common humanity — in perfection realized in its Head and Fountain — universality and truth, manhood, and the knowledge of the Kingdom of God, are not to be expected. But, because we may do wrong, is no reason why we should be debarred from doing right. Because a man more accustomed to external than self-restraint, is not unlikely, especially on being first left to himself, not too scrupulously to observe peace and order, — this can hardly be considered sufficient ground for depriving him of his liberty by anticipation, the more so, that the longer he is deprived, the greater will be the difficulty he will have in learning rightly to use his freedom when he gets it. The theological developments of our own time afford warning of the peril; but without under estimating that peril, liberty is to be asserted, in the faith that it is our inalienable right, and God's will, and that it will prove its own vindication. The advance, the capability of extension and correction of other sciences in nowise makes them less determinate, less sure, less scientific. Has chemistry or astronomy become more capricious and fanciful, more dependent upon the fluctuations and inconstancies of individual, national, or secular character, since Bacon's time? Or have they not only since then attained their character of certainty, irrefragable truth, lawfulness, in a word, science? Why should it be otherwise with theology? It can be unscientific and untrue only when we neglect to study the laws, the operations of which it professes to set forth, and seek to find the principle of its determinations elsewhere, whether in our own whims, fancies, and emotions or in the recorded thoughts and feelings of others. The soul is surely not less lawfully constituted, less orderly, less divinely moved, than the material atoms that surround it; nor are the dignity and trust-worthiness of science and law the less, the nobler the subject. Science, in itself, is not vacillating and arbitrary; it is based on eternal law; but to us it is and must be progressive; for while the law ever *is*, our relation to it ever changes.

"For I doubt not through the ages one increasing purpose runs,
And the thoughts of men are widened by the process of the suns."

Science — knowledge of laws — can advance only when we condescend to learn law — where alone it is authoritatively taught — in the constitution of its subjects. To seek it anywhere else must result in failure; to attempt to impose anything else is despotism. As a science, Theology is the product of the mind in form, and of the object of that science in matter. Now the Bible is not the subject of spiritual law, and cannot therefore be the proper object of Theology. That object is God's dealings with man. It is no true parallel to argue that, as physical science is to be promoted only be careful investigation of external nature, so, patient and exclusive study of the Bible is the proper means to perfect Theology. The Bible is not the field of operation of spiritual law, and is not therefore its direct effluence and product; it is not pretended to be such — only a reflex expression of it; and when that expression is held to be already perfect, progress is impossible.

But the evil of the thraldom appears in its full magnitude only when we consider its influence on spiritual life. It is bad enough in paralyzing our Theology, but unspeakably worse in its effects on that, of which Theology is but the scientifically elaborated expression. And it is remarkable that in this relation, where the denial of freedom works most perniciously, the necessity for an external infallible rule is mainly insisted on. While the Scriptures themselves everywhere point us to the true and sovereign fountain of divine life, how often do we persist in making them the measure and the mould into which it must unfold itself, and sometimes even in upholding them as its source — forgetting that "where the spirit of the Lord is, there is liberty." How often are they used not as a lesson-book, but as a teacher; not as a mere teacher, but as an oracle! How often are they taken, not as the "man of our counsel," but as our Lawgiver! And all this is done as the only means of accomplishing that which, if accomplished at all, is so, notwithstanding and irrespective, if not despite of, these appliances so misused; just as animal life sometimes resists and discharges the poisonous medicine which friendly hands administer. The subtle life of the spirit may, by the very galling of its chains, be roused with irresistible might to vindicate itself, and burst its fetters, as many a struggling soul in these our days is doing, nobly often, but often too, alas! not without self-injury and wound; or, penetrating less within the reflective intellectual arena, it may, as was perhaps more commonly the case with a former generation, elude the grasp that would enslave it, by keeping beyond its range, and avoiding those positions where alone its influence could be felt. But any way, and under any circumstances, the natural and proper issue of an enforced external rule, without regard to inner law and principle, however correct an exponent of the principle that rule may be, cannot be spiritual growth; and this has the more urgently to be insisted on, since for such teaching the main plea is its influence.

Whether ostensibly or not, the real argument for this doctrine is its utility, and in this it is eminently Romish. Its chief attraction is the supposed character of its practical tendency. The good it does, the difficulty of doing without it, — this, and not its truth, is the ground-reason of its being so strenuously maintained. Men have been led to it, not by fearless, trustful, unbiassed inquiry, desiring only truth, but by the want they felt of such a revelation and guide; and just in proportion as they lose sight of the true light that has come into the world, and of a present revealing of their Father to themselves, will they more and more substitute for the ever-living WORD of God this expression of a past revelation to others. We have felt it to be desirable, and have argued ourselves into its belief. There must be some certain rule and guidance. Many things seem to point to this as such. This *must* be it. Therefore this *is* it. It hardly admits of a doubt, that if the need, the usefulness, of an external infallible canon were no longer felt, there would be much less anxiety shown for the assertion and recognition of its existence. How indifferent should we become to it, though still as true as before, if it ceased to minister to aught, save our pure chaste love of truth. This fond belief begotten in secret by expediency has been nourished by fear, and prudential considerations are the staff of its old age. Oh! that we had the courage to look things in the face. We have valued it for what it could do for us, rather than for what it is. And have we missed our reward?

That an external authority may be of a certain service and benefit is not to be denied. Where all is open, flagrant outrage of order, it may restrain outward action and secure a certain superficial regulation; — a service not to be lightly esteemed, both for the protection it affords to the weak, and for the reflex influence the outward decorum may exert upon the character. Considered in its outward and social results, the establishment of order, by whatever means, is desirable. Whether it at all improve the aggressor, it at least provides protection and safety for the oppressed. But, in relation to the offender, the operation of enforced order may be in one or other of two directions, according to the class of character to which it is applied: it may be hardening or reformatory. It may provoke resistance and an assertion, with intensified energy, of individual determination; or it may meet with compliance, and may mould to its pattern. In the one action it only accelerates the catastrophe of utter dethronement of law and extinction of liberty in the individual; and even in the case of its best and most softening effects, the order of Nature is inverted; and the only good it can do is to awaken the inner life to take up its rightful position, in other words, to render the external authority useless, by securing the outward observance without its assistance. Its position and character, therefore, in reference to the repressed power, is but temporary and provisional, if not altogether without advantage, while, in the general system, it occupies the place only of a substitute and makeshift.

In religious matters, however, there can be no such variety of action. As religion is personal, and not between man and man, the element of constant good, which, in the social problem, may be traced in enforced law — to wit, the protection of the aggrieved — is here out of the question; and, in its bearing on the individual on whom the rule is imposed, an outward conformity can have no inward beneficial reaction; because outward life, which, in the social consideration, is the issue and consummation of the law's action, forms no part of religion; and while an outwardly moral conduct has its value, from whatever motive it may proceed, the rites and ceremonies of religion, if performed only in compliance with external authority, and unless they are but an utterance of the hidden spiritual life, are worthless, if not worse, by being and begetting a species of hypocrisy. Any reflex influence it may exert is detrimental.

Here consequently, either way, whether it call forth opposition or is submitted to, its tendency is injurious — and in the case of submission especially so; for, what is the necessary mode of its imposition?

In establishing a social order, brute force may be employed: conformity, with the alternative of physical suffering, is proposed; and if a man cannot be compelled to obey, he may be walled in from disobeying; but within the sphere of the spirit, force is of no direct avail. By torturing the flesh, by threats, or by bribes and seductions, we may subdue him to the profession of certain religious doctrines, but by no such means can we make him really believe them. Persecution wielded by

the material hand of Might, may be a most outrageous
violation of civil rights and individual liberty, but can effect no
direct entrance within spiritual precincts, and is therefore,
although proceeding on the ground of a profession of faith,
really outside religion altogether, and falls to be considered
rather as an invasion of civil than of religious liberty. While
certain forms of word or deed, held as of religious import, are
taken as the occasion to call it forth, yet it has nothing of
religion in its own nature and operation. In a certain sense it is
a curtailment of spiritual freedom; for, from the harmonious
and sympathetic constitution of human nature, as a whole,
expression is, in a manner, the natural complement of the
spirit's action. Without utterance nothing is complete and
coordinate with general life, but seems to belong to the
generations yet unborn into the world of form. The genial
atmosphere favourable to full expansion is awanting, when
expression is denied. Still the real and immediate limitation of
spiritual freedom takes place, only when the unfolding of the
Spirit's own law is interfered with, and for this, something
more subtle and penetrating is necessary than vulgar force or
coarse materialism. The world of thought and feeling can be
fought only by like powers. External authority can obtain
internal application only through the instrumentality of the
mind itself. A traitor within the camp is required here to
impose the yoke, and in such imposition consists true direct
mental bondage.

Spiritual bondage consists in the soul's action being controlled by a rule, if not originating in the mind itself, yet
applied through the intervention of one of the mind's own
faculties, which, though internal to the man, is external to the
spiritual organ. Thus sense may completely overlie and stifle
spiritual life, so that the unseen is treated as the unreal, the
doubtful, the unsubstantial. Symbolism is elevated from its
secondary and ministering place, to be essential and primary.
Sinai has no glory, unless crowned with the terrible manifestations of physical power. Miracles are cogent, not the still
small voice. The prevalent form in our own time is perhaps the
substitution of logic and calculation for faith, the inability to
believe, the glory and boast of not believing, save what is
proved; and the introduction of futile syllogisms into fields that
underlie the deepest premiss, and mock the widest notion; and
the blundering attempt to bring within the measuring line of

the understanding, the illimitable, the infinite, all that belongs to the soul; — which, the further conceptionally traced, becomes only the more untraceable, and issues ever into profounder and more awful faith- and soul-nourishing mysteries.

The revolt from such a tyranny may not secure true freedom and unimpeded action of the native law, but it will, at least, effect immunity from that particular yoke, and give assurance of a vitality and vigour which may be hoped eventually "to work out its own salvation." The danger is that common to all violent reactions — that the extreme servitude may be recoiled from only for an excess of license. Rejecting the cramping form illegitimately imposed, the spirit may spurn all order and restraint: bursting its prison-doors, it may rush forth in fear and disgust at any limitation of the expanse, and wander homeless. How many, cooped up within creeds too narrow for their expanding souls, have escaped, not to fitter habitations, but to dwell desolate among the tombs. Yet, even in such cases, there is much ground of hope; they have life and strength; and the impulses of their own nature, which urged them forth from their bondage into exile, may bring them back, after weary wanderings in the wilderness, to their fatherland. The prodigal may return, and in the home of his birth become a truer son than his brother, who never left it. Hence at once the prevalence of what is called the infidelity of our times, and the hopeful and healthful character by which much of it is distinguished. Vigorous and earnest minds disdain the circuit prescribed to them, and with centrifugal impetuosity rush forth at a tangent, from which, haply, they may in time deflect into curves of wider sweep suited to their natures; and although we should not be able to trace them falling into regular orbits, is not even this independence a token of something better than mere passivity and negativeness? It at least shows life and power, which may yet be regulated and legalized; and of such a consummation it gives the greater promise, that this outburst is referable to the elasticity of the inner law to resist compression. It is the full tide of life breaking forth, and cutting out a channel for itself — which is surely better than that its waters should stagnate, pent up and still. There is no greater mistake than to class much of the present rejection of popular forms of religion with the superficial, heartless, thoughtless, free-thinking of a former century. It is often a mark of fundamental soundness

and robust spiritual constitution. Unspeakably sad and dis-
tressful were it ultimate and final; yet, when not manifestly
passing into anything more mature and perfect, may it not
often be a pause or arrestment (by a sudden and, to our eyes,
untimely withdrawal of the process from our ken) in the
advance towards perfect life, rather than any real permanent
aberration from it?

Passive acquiescence, on the other hand, when the inherent
strength sinks under the despotic sway, has little to redeem or
alleviate its evil. For whatever the enactments of the foreign
rule, free natural growth is impossible. True liberty consists in
such a relation, as provides the external condition necessary for
the legitimate operation of internal law. Dictation, therefore,
to our spiritual nature from any source extrinsic to itself —
whether in the result different widely or not from the working
of its own law — is, in principle, and abstractly considered,
quite contrary to freedom. The greater the divergence, of
course, the greater the evil. But how coincident soever in the
resulting objective action, the very principle of liberty is
outraged, when the basis and origin of that which regulates the
action is external. The vital principle is transferred from the
soul to something without it, in other words, all real life in the
soul is suppressed, and it reduced to the condition of a puppet
and an automaton, and this, equally, whether the automatical
movements be in close imitation of the natural action or the
reverse. The very idea, therefore, of spiritual freedom is
ignored, and equally ignored, whether we constitute the Pope,
or the Bible, or anything else, the authority for our spiritual
development. Nothing but the laws of the soul's own divine
constitution can legitimately authorize its action; any
impression or controlling influence from without, save such as
it is of its own nature to receive, and which, by that adaptation
to its nature alone, is ratified, can prove only an interference
with the operation of its normal energies, and a cause of
deformity. It is not the mere abstract idea of liberty which is set
at nought. That is something: truth is precious in and for itself.
But the practical working is altogether injurious, and so far
from calling forth and training the spirit's life, crushes and
distorts it. Let the authority be in the interest of the most
perfect form of spiritual development, its influence is baneful.
The attainment of such a development is desirable, but not by
such means. By such means, in fact, it cannot be attained *as a*

development; the form would be a thing imposed, not unfolded. It would, therefore, be a form put on it, but not its form, and, therefore, a form through which no quickening life could circulate. The principle of non-intervention is as sound here as in politics; it is essential to all liberty that no one power shall dictate to another. Any attempt to force the constitution of any state upon another has ever proved fruitless, if not disastrous. However sound its principles, however skilfully contrived its machinery, it will, at the best, hamper and lie as a clog upon the free energies of any other people, than that out of whose national life it has sprung. Most assuredly, there are eternal principles of government, and what is essential can nowhere, and under no circumstances, from what is good be awanting; because humanity is one. But not only, along with what is radical and essential, must each particular case have its own varying complement of the adventitious and circumstantial, but the degree in which, at any time, and under any circumstances, the necessary and universal can healthily find development in different cases, cannot with impunity be interfered with; so here, as elsewhere, it is wisdom and duty to

> "Trust the spirit
> As sovran Nature does, to make the form;
> For otherwise, we can only imprison spirit,
> And not embody. Inward evermore
> To outward."

Still while the real moulding constructive power lies within, it is of the nature of life to derive nourishment, and even means of subsistence, from without; while the nature and amount of food, as well as the forms into which it must be elaborated, to become instinct with life, depend on the inner vital principle itself, it again is dependent on what is out of itself for the means of support and growth. It is nothing self-included, independent, and exclusively subjective, that is argued for. The divine life must be within, supreme, welling up from the inscrutable and infinite depths, where our being has its root; but the means and conditions of its manifestation, work, and culture lie beyond and about itself. Whatever can contribute to the attainment of these ends, therefore, must not be neglected or undervalued. Every vehicle of enlightenment, of strength, of growth, is to be welcomed, and used with thankfulness; and it is in this capacity that the Bible finds its true place and service.

This, and not that of an infallible canon, is its rightful relation to us; and in such a relation it is a pearl beyond price.

Such a position and agency, alike the constitution and requirements of man, and its own nature, assign to it. It claims on oracular character, no more, than the freedom of our souls could admit such a claim. It nowhere assumes to be an infallible canon, but line upon line would teach us otherwise. It has neither the subject-matter, nor the tone, and form of an inflexible standard and absolute guide. Much of the greater portion of it could not by any exercise of ingenuity be represented, or misrepresented, as a fixed, stereotyped pattern, after which to conform human life. A large portion is devoted to the history of a marvellously privileged, but withal a very wicked nation. It contains the narrative of the lives, the doings and sayings, the thoughts and utterances of men of like passions as ourselves; and of one Life "in all things made like unto his brethren," yet "without sin;" but even this, only as seen through the vision of men themselves sinful. It abounds in passages both of national history and individual biography, which we dare not imitate, and which can teach us only as implied warnings. It lays before us alike the good and the bad, and appeals to our own consciences to discriminate, and to approve or disapprove. In straightforward terms it relates to us the domestic history of Isaac and his family, but leaves us to form our own thoughts, and draw guidance for ourselves, from the picture of the weak, deceived old man, of the artful wife, and unjustly partial mother, of her apt son, the subtle supplanter, and of the bold, manly, reckless hunter. It shows us Jacob, the exile and adventurer, outdoing by his patient affection, and not too scrupulous worldly shrewdness, the insincerity and avarice of Laban. It shows us Jacob, the successful man, of calculating spirit and mean heart, conscious of his past injustice, seeking by gifts to appease the wrath, the full-hearted, forgiving Esua, does not cherish. It tells us of David, the man according to God's own heart, the murderer, the adulterer. It records his struggles against sinfulness, his failings, his penitence, his exultation, his "*suspiria de profundis*," but gives us no reason to suppose that all he spoke, and wrote, or sung, was true and pure, any more than all he did and thought. It reveals a centre Life, the wonder and the joy of ages — One who spake, indeed, with authority, yet appealed ever to the latent life and suppressed law — of which he himself was the hidden Head and Fountain — that yet lingered within the breasts of those about him, making them still human. We see in it the little band He had chosen, dimly, imperfectly, falsely conceiving the truth, painfully struggling towards its apprehension. Farther on, we find them differing, quarrelling among themselves; but it offers no umpire for their disputes. It never warns us that although they in their own lives erred, although they sometimes taught their contemporaries wrong, it was impossible they should leave to posterity anything but unblemished truth. On the contrary, in it they argue and address themselves to our own power of discussing the truth, instead of enunciating verities to be accepted implicitly as such, as to which natural faculty has no relation. As a canon it has no clear line of demarcation. Many writings, which on its own testimony are of equal authority, and, indeed, on some points are quoted as its authority, are lost. As a perfect, infallible canon it is therefore incomplete; and, as in some parts it is deficient and secondary, so, it has often been thought to include more than it ought. By far the greater portion of it has no direct didactic statements. Much is certainly highly figurative, much is open to question, as to whether figurative or literal, much is hard to be understood, if not unintelligible. Not only are the matter it contains, the forms in which it present that matter, and the tone in which it addresses us, unsuitable to an infallible canon, but it contains statements impossible and inconsistent with well ascertained facts, and is even self-contradictory. To impose such a set of writings on us as an infallible absolute *norma* of our faith, is as tyrannical towards the human mind, as subversive of the real uses and value of the Scriptures.

But these features, which as much disqualify it from being an infallible rule, as such a rule is unnecessary and undesirable, in nowise render it less adapted to the uses for which it is required and intended. Quite the contrary. The life-law, overborne and silenced, cannot be stimulated and roused to self-assertion by a mere rule, however perfect, but only by the pleadings of the same law, working more freely in a corresponding sphere; and this is what the Bible, as being the words of "holy men of old who spake, moved by the Holy Ghost," displays to us. Every good and just man, in a greater or less degree, shows us the same thing, and, so far his life is an evangel. The Bible is the collected records of such lives, or rather it exhibits such lives in contact and conflict with all that is evil and at enmity with their law, now overcome, now triumphant, and working out that law in various degrees, from — it may not be said who is lowest — to that Life, which was the fulfilling of the law, the victory over Death and the Adversary. It has no speciality in kind. But, that it shares its character in common with all the gifts of our great Teacher, cannot detract from its dignity or degrade its office or efficiency. Its glory is, that in doing this common work it rises conspicuous above all else, in that it does it in measure beyond comparison. It is special, and stands *per se* in its teaching, not because there is any reason to believe its dogma alone authoritative and infallible, but because, as a matter of experience, it accomplishes the end altogether incomparably. And this it does, just because it is the accumulated expression of the noblest fulfillings of humanity's law, which our race, in its progress of millenniums, has achieved. Not by its enforcement as a rule of faith and practice, at once necessary and perfect, not by its being professed as an indispensable and unfailing instrument of salvation, not by its being fastened by any cord ever so finely intellectual, and worn as an amulet, can it do any good. It can prove a means of eliciting law into actual life, only by its own appeals to the law. The seeing the law more perfectly fulfilled in another can teach us, only in so far as it is recognised to be such.

Wholly at variance with this is it, that ourselves or another should argue us into its implicit belief, and the necessity of its unqualified acceptance. That it thus by the understanding should be presented and applied to the soul, is to supersede and paralyse spiritual life. What is desired is to nourish and stimulate that life, and the Bible is offered as the food God has given for this purpose. Such an end it can subserve, only through the spontaneous acceptance and appropriation of it — not as it is crammed into us, but as it is digested and assimilated. But in this, reference must be had to the condition of the recipient. St. Paul himself warns us to discriminate between those who, as babes, require milk, and those to whom, as grown men, strong meat is suitable. Food — even wholesome food — may, under certain conditions and to certain constitutions, prove in effect little else than poison. So far as it is unassimilated and incapable of assimilation, its introduction must be injurious. Not only must we avoid the presentation of what is noxious and false, but we must be careful against urging home upon ourselves or others, by weight of any authority, even what is true, if it fails to be apprehended as such. What we cannot recognise as truth, whatever it may be, is to us, until we can so recognise it, practically untruth; and to press it — however exalted and pure others may see and feel it to be — by force of argument, that is, by the authority of the understanding, on a power to which the understanding has no title to dictate, is not to foster, but to do utter violence to our love of truth — to do our best to trample it out, and to replace it by a love of opinion. If anything in the Scriptures, therefore, contradict our higher intuitions, it must be impossible to produce conviction that such a statement comes from God, unless the whole order of our being be perverted and overturned, in the subjection of these intuitions — these whisperings of God to the soul — to the mere notional understanding. Let evidence, for example, be ever so accumulated, it can yet afford no proof that the prophecy of Deborah, in what appears to many its obvious meaning, is of divine inspiration, so long as God gives the power to believe in Himself, as just and righteous. Whenever conviction ensues, faith is so far lost in God, as "the Judge of all the earth who will do right," or power is so far lost, to recognise and appreciate moral distinctions. To require of ourselves, if ever such a collision should occur, to ignore our most undeniable beliefs, to silence the deepest utterances of "the man within the breast," to set at defiance the most imperious dictates of conscience, and disregard the most urgent claims of duty, in compliance with any writing, the authority of which is established only on the lower basis of cumulative evidence, is abject slavery — is a *religio*, not to Truth and Right, but to the usurped supremacy of our own understandings — at the best, to a symbol which, however good in itself, when worshipped becomes an idol.

This, as it is the degradation of what is noblest in man, is the deepest of all slavery, and the encouragement and furtherance of it, the most terrible of all persecution. It may be the least palpable, but only because so insidious, the more to be dreaded. Against physical compulsion, even when submitting, a man may inwardly protest. The soul may be turned towards Jehovah, while the body is bent in the House of Rimmon. But when the mind is enslaved the protesting power is itself in fetters. Who can reckon the nights of anxious tossing and the days of sorrow and self-torture, or tell of the settled gloom and despair, the misery and the madness, of the crime, the mortal anguish, and the lost lives this slavery has caused? It is, indeed, a thraldom to which a man, while true to himself, can never be reduced, and so far, therefore, his freedom is in his own hands. But others may repress healthy efforts, and tighten the cords. His weakness or want of balance may be taken advantage of, and it may be, with the most benign intention, turned against himself. It is a slavery and persecution which no civil enactment, no law but the law within, can prevent, because it presents no tangible result to be seized and dealt with as an offence. There cannot be free intercommunication between man and man, and the mutual exercise of intellectual and moral influence, without suasion to evil being as possible as suasion to good — destruction as instruction. We cannot enact that all teaching shall be of a given character, and tending in a given direction. Thus to legislate would presuppose our knowledge and agreement as to what alone is good, and what alone could operate for its furtherance. Nor could any political machinery reach and test personal influence. This life is too fine and delicate to be safely guarded by Act of Parliament. The greater need, therefore, for jealousy and watchfulness against any encroachment with which it may be threatened. The influence to enslave must just be met by a counter effort, with the same powers, to deliver. All that the free can do is to exhibit in themselves the free and joyous working of constitutional law, appealing with quickening sympathy to the repressed law in others. The constitution of man owns a spirit of progress, and reason and conscience must advance to the perfect assertion of their inalienable rights and liberty. Philosophy, in her progress towards emancipation, in her first successful rising, fell subject to the authority of antiquity, in throwing off the yoke of the Church. Religion, perhaps not unnaturally, oscillated from the same bondage in the first instance, only into another servitude, from which it must in turn recoil. It has certainly not been prompt to make very vigorous movement in the direction of that recoil. Any attempt has been either partial in its nature and aim, or confined to a few scattered rebel minds. Yet mutterings of the coming struggle have been heard, and the crisis seems approaching for the determination of "this momentous question, which," as Dr. Arnold says, "involves in it a shock to existing notions, the greatest, probably, that has ever been given since the discovery of the falsehood of the Pope's infallibility. Yet it must come, and will end, in spite of the fears and clamours of the weak and bigoted, in the higher exalting and more sure establishing of Christian truth."

THE RAMBLER
Vol. LIX, No. CCCLIII, May, 1859
[Thomas Arnold]

Mill on Liberty[1]

Any book of Mr. Mill's which professes to lay down fixed
principles, applicable to important questions of social and
individual ethics, deserves to be as carefully studied by those
who possess known landmarks and unalterable methods for
the guidance of life and the discipline of the soul, as by those to
whom all questions of the kind are still open. The Catholic
faith places a man in the best position for forming a sound
ethical code, and extending it to new cases and exigencies as
they arise: but it does not itself explicitly include such a code.
The leading rules and distinctions of ethics form no part of
divine revelation: no one ever laid them down so clearly as
Aristotle: and from him, in the middle ages, saints received
them, to blend them into one harmonious whole with the
truths of revelation. Even now all the work is not done to our
hand, for the ethical philosophy of Catholics is not unpro-
gressive; and therefore a work like the Essay on Liberty,
though chiefly interesting to Protestants, concerns us also. A
denial of this would go far to justify the imputations of mental
torpor which are so freely made against us. Although ethical
principles do not change, the *applications* of those principles
may vary with changing circumstances and relations. The
moral relation between a child and a father changes as the child
grows to be fifteen. Slavery may be, under one set of
circumstances, justifiable; or, under another set, abominable.
So with liberty of thought and of action. It may be that, under
the social conditions of former ages, a degree and kind of
repression of error might advisably, because successfully, be
employed; which under modern conditions would, if
attempted, cause more evil than it would cure.

Perhaps there is no single moral question upon which a
greater medley of opinions is afloat among Catholics than that

---

[1] *On Liberty.* By John Stuart Mill. J. W. Parker and Son, 1859

of individual liberty. This by itself shows the disputable nature of the whole subject; for upon articles of faith it is notorious that there is no such discordance. Yet the *data* possessed by a Catholic places him in a peculiarly favourable position for solving difficulties. But to recommend his views to others, he must neither spare the labour of thought nor shrink from the arena of discussion.

The occasion of Mr. Mill's Essay is to be found· in the relation of the rationalist party in England to the prevailing state of opinion. As far as external indications go, rationalism in England is less influential, less progressive, than it was twenty years ago. In these last years, such wild outbursts of spiritual rebellion as the *Nemesis of Faith* no longer rise to startle the religious world from its propriety. Fifteen years back, the popular book on cosmogony and geology was the *Vestiges of the Natural History of the Creation*; now it is the *Testimony of the Rocks*. Among the Reviews of that school, some, like the *Prospective*, have vanished altogether; others, like the *Westminster*, contrive to exist, but with a stationary circulation, and less than the old pugnacity. The *Examiner* has dropped its racy diatribes upon Anglican Bishops, finding probably that they would not suit the soberer tastes of its present pubic. In 1834 the Church Establishment appeared to be tottering under the blows of a legion of enemies; in 1859 it seems to be as secure against a crash as the Bank; and yet in spite of these appearances, it is certain that rationalism is not less, but probably more widely spread. The thinking, reasoning persons in a nation must always form a small minority; and when the mediocre majority are attached to orthodox opinions, or what they deem such, while the social fabric is steady and the social bond strong, the dissenting or rationalist opinions can only find favour among the thinking minority. Now in England it is probable that a considerably larger proportion of this small class belongs to the rationalist camp at the present day than twenty years ago. On the Continent, at least in France, the course of things I believe has been the reverse. Meantime the majority, little suspecting the true movement of the currents of thought, are so well pleased with themselves, and their national character and religion, that, with the usual insolence of ascendency, they are gradually becoming more intolerant of marked divergence on either side from the popular standards. For the system of the Catholic is no less offensive in their eyes than that of the rationalist. Strange to say, English Protestantism is tending to a sort of unity, which may be described as a common national sentiment, strong enough to cause the special differences between sects to be felt as very small matters. In vain do a few hundred clergymen, and a few rural coteries, point to the language of the Liturgy, insist on the value of the old fringe which · Martin still bears upon his coat, and utter solemn warnings against the sin of schism. In Mr. Carlyle's language, "the Puseyite logic runs off John Bull like water;" and he answers, in no gentle tone, "In spite of all your formularies, Protestant I am, and Protestant I remain."

Against this disposition of the majority to encroach upon the freedom of thought and action of dissenting minorities, Mr. Mill, on the side of the rationalists, has skilfully chosen his ground. In some ways, the yoke of the dominant system is more oppressive to rationalists than to Catholics. We are, indeed, liable to be treated with unjust suspicion, to have our children proselytised, and to experience in the court of law and in the board-room the intolerance of the half-educated masses; but, at any rate, we are not now persecuted into conformity. But rationalists, having no external organisation, are left under the full pressure of the popular system in many things where it is most irksome. They may think that marriage should be a revocable contract; yet public opinion renders a marriage before a registrar ordinarily inadmissible. They may consider baptism an idle ceremony; yet few of them will brave social opinion so far as to deprive their children of it. Thus opinion exacts a conformity to the usages of the popular religion, which rationalists cannot but feel to be humiliating. In order to mitigate this rigour of opinion, Mr. Mill correctly judged that a direct attack upon the received system would not advance his object. But he took up the cry which the received system loudly utters, and prefixing the name of Liberty to his essay, he claimed for the thing its full application in the domain of law and of opinion.

In his introductory chapter, Mr. Mill traces the gradual development of the idea of human liberty. The first epoch of the struggle between liberty and authority is marked by the establishment of definite rights and immunities, wrung by the subjects from the governing few with the view of protecting themselves against abuses of power. Such was the law erecting the tribuneship of the commons at Rome; such the Magna Charta of our ancestors. A further step in the same direction consisted in the establishment of constitutional checks, mainly through the contrivance of a system of representation, and by committing to the representatives a control over the public expenditure. When power was so limited by checks that it ceased to be formidable, it was perceived that antagonism between the governors and the governed was, after all, no necessity of nature; that when the idea of representation is completely carried out, the distinction would be obliterated by the people coming to be their own governors. Since, then, the powers of the government had come to emanate solely from the governed, the necessity for multiplying checks on its exercise seemed to be superseded; for why should the people require to be protected against itself? But experiments have made it evident that new dangers to liberty have emerged. "The 'people' who exercise the power, are not always the same people with those over whom it is exercised; and the 'self-government' spoken of is not the government of each by himself but of each by all the rest. The will of the people, moreover, practically means the will of the most numerous, or the most active, *part* of the people." Hence arose a new species of tyranny, the 'tyranny of the majority' — as manifested either in the acts of the public authorities, or in the *social* intolerance habitual to a majority. "Protection, therefore, against the tyranny of the magistrate is not enough; there needs protection also against the tyranny of the prevailing opinion and feeling, against the tendency of society to impose, by other means than civil penalties, its own ideas and practices as rules of conduct on those who dissent from them; to fetter the development, and, if possible, prevent the formation, of any individuality not in harmony with its ways; and to compel all characters to fashion themselves upon the model of its own." The object of the Essay, therefore, is, "to assert one very simple principle, — that the sole end for which mankind are warranted, individually or collectively, in interfering with the liberty of action of any of their number, is self-protection." Our ideas of our neighbour's good may justify our remonstrating with, or counselling him; "but not our compelling him, or visiting him with any evil, in case he do otherwise."

In the second chapter Mr. Mill states four grounds on which he infers that it is necessary to the welfare of society to allow the liberty of thought and discussion in the fullest extent. First, the opinions prevailing in society may be false; but unless a free examination and pubic discussion of their grounds be permitted, they cannot be disproved. Secondly, the received opinion may be partly true, partly false; while the dissenting opinion, though also partly false, may contain the truth which is wanted to complete the popular half-truth. Thirdly, though the received opinion is wholly true, yet, unless it be vigorously attacked from time to time, so as to elicit equal vigour in its defence, it may become a mere prejudice, a matter of habit, not of understanding. And lastly, the meaning of the received doctrine itself may be lost or enfeebled: it may become a mere lip profession, ineffectual for good, only obstructing the growth of other truths which might be held with real conviction.

Mr. Mill, in the third chapter, inquires whether the same considerations do not require that men should be free to *act* on their opinions, provided it be at their own risk. Here the chief difficulty is, that the end to be attained — individual spontaneity of conduct — is so little valued; that few even comprehend William Humboldt's dictum, "the end of man, or that which is prescribed by the eternal immutable dictates of reason, and not suggested by vague and transient desires, is the highest and most harmonious development of his powers to a complete and consistent whole." Not that each man is to aim at independence of self-development, so as to undervalue the teachings of experience; on the contrary, education is unceasingly to communicate them to us. But afterwards the individual should be free to use and interpret experience in his own way, instead of having some customary rendering imposed upon him. Conformity to custom, merely *as* custom, even though it may happen to be good, involves no practice of the faculties, no moral choice. "It really is of importance, not only what men do, but also what manner of men they are that do it." To choose his plan of life, and follow it, demands the employment of all a man's faculties, judgment, observation, activity, discrimination, decision, and firmness. This makes him more of a man, and his life ampler, more eventful, and more richly stored, than the life of the slaves of custom. His desires and impulses, "the raw material of human nature," are strengthened; and their possessor is made capable, perhaps of more evil, but certainly of more good.

In early stages of society individuality was in excess, and the difficulty was to keep the passions of individuals within the bounds of the general interests of society. But in our own day "society has got fairly the better of individuality." The danger lies now in the uniform mediocrity which threatens to become the almost universal type of character; even in amusements men "like in crowds;" "until, by dint of not following their own nature, they have no nature to follow, their human capacities are withered and starved."

Is such a state, he asks, desirable for a human being? It is so according to the Calvinistic theory, which makes obedience the one duty of man, and self-will his one offence. Yet surely, he argues, it is more religious to believe that a good Creator gave all human faculties that they might be cultivated and unfolded, not rooted out and consumed. In what follows, the author confounds Calvinism with Christianity; but a nobler passage succeeds:

> "It is not by wearing down into uniformity all that is individual in themselves, but by cultivating it and calling it forth within the limits imposed by the rights and interests of others, that human beings become a noble and beautiful object of contemplation; and as the works partake the character of those who do them, by the same process human life also becomes rich, diversified, and animating; furnishing more abundant aliment to high thoughts and elevating feelings, and strengthening the tie which binds every individual to the race, by making the race infinitely better worth belonging to. In proportion to the development of his individuality, each person becomes more valuable to himself; and is therefore capable of being more valuable to others. There is a greater fullness of life about his own existence; and when there is more life in the units, there is more in the mass which is composed of them" (p. 113)

If genius is necessary to mankind, the soil in which it grows must be preserved. "Genius can only breathe freely in an atmosphere of freedom." The present ascendency of society, and the power of the masses, was perhaps inevitable; but still, "the government of mediocrity is mediocre government." "The initiation of all wise or noble things comes, and must come, from individuals; . . . the honour and glory of the average man is, that he is capable of following that initiative." The

increasing tendency of European society is to frown down
individual diversities of character and practice, and to gravitate
towards the state of things which prevails in China and all
oriental countries, which, though once progressive, have for
many ages, been properly speaking, without a history, because
they have become stationary and inanimate under the numbing
despotism of custom. This tendency must, it is argued, be
resisted before it is too late, by asserting the claims of
individuality.

Having now stated the doctrine of individual freedom, Mr.
Mill considers what restraints on that freedom are permissible,
and where the line is to be drawn between the authority of
society and the liberty of its individual members. His principle
is simple: "To individuality should belong that part of life in
which it is chiefly the individual that is interested; to society,
that part which chiefly interests society." The individual
(supposing him of legal age and of sound mind) should be free
to act in any manner that pleases him, so long as the interests of
others are not directly injured. But how to apply this principle?
Is a person who is grossly deficient in the "self-regarding" as
distinct from the social virtues, — in industry, sobriety,
frugality, and the like, — yet who directly injures no one else
by his conduct, — to be in no way amenable to society? Such a
person is amenable to society in respect of the *spontaneous* and
natural consequences which flow from his conduct, viz. the
displeasure, contempt, and avoidance of his neighbours; but
not in respect of positive penalties. If, indeed, he is so deficient
in his duty to himself as to become disabled from discharging
some definite duty to others, he may become the fitting subject
of moral reprobation and punishment. But for the merely
contingent or *constructive* injury which his conduct may cause
to society, it is better that society should bear the inconvenience
than that the principle of liberty should be infringed; especially
as it will generally happen that society itself is partly to blame,
in having neglected to provide for the education of the offender
to a right understanding of his duties and opportunities as a
human being. Ill-judged attempts at the coercion of conduct
generally end, as in the case of the Puritan government before
the Restoration, in a strong rebound in the contrary direction.
With reference to certain cases, in which the free action of the
individual or the minority might appear disputable, as in the
abhorrence felt by a Mohammedan society for the practice of

eating pork, the disgust with which a Catholic population regard a married clergy and a heretical worship, the horror with which Sabbatarians are inspired by Sunday amusements, or teetotalers by dram-drinking, — the author argues that the only principle which will apply to all these cases, and defend the weaker body against coercion into conformity to the tastes of the stronger, is this, "that with the personal tastes and self-regarding concerns of individuals the public has no business to interfere."

To the doctrine of human freedom, thus explained, I am disposed to give a decided general adherence. That doctrine is, that the liberty of thought and of its expression should be entire; and that the liberty of tastes and modes of living should be only limited by the single condition, that the rights and interests of others by respected. By liberty, I mean absence of accountability of any *temporal* authority; and, with Mr. Mill, I understand by the subjects of this liberty persons of full age and of sound mind. And my thesis is this, that although, in bygone states of society, the employment of coercion in order to bring recusants to conformity may have been occasionally defensible, as producing, on the whole, more good than evil, the circumstances of modern society are such as to render the use of such coercion inexpedient and reprehensible, because certain to produce more evil than good.

It is objected that such a doctrine is suitable enough to the circumstances of a Catholic minority in England, but that no English Catholic would advocate its application to the case of the Catholic majority in Austria, or France, or Spain, or adapt to the latitude of Vienna the rule which he approved for the latitude of London. I answer, that I make no mental reservations. Having faith in my thesis, I am prepared beforehand for the extension of the principle laid down to every variety of circumstances.

Mr. Mill himself, in defining the range of his doctrine,

"leaves out of consideration those backward states of society in which the race itself may be considered as in its 'nonage' (p. 23). Liberty," he says, "as a principle, has no application to any state of things anterior to the time when mankind have become capable of being improved by free and equal discussion. When the wisdom of the governors is far in advance of the wisdom of the governed, and the means do not exist, by the communication and comparison of ideas, of equalising the two, it is desirable and right that the subjects should be coerced, if necessary, to their own good."

In the employment of coercion; whether directly or by penalties attached to non-compliance, to bring men to the true faith, I believe that the test of lawfulness is success. To exact the hollow profession of the truth, while the heart internally rebels, so far from being a success, is a more disastrous failure than acquiescence in open recusancy. Coercion *succeeds* only when it produces higher moral results to the persons coerced than were attained under toleration; only when they, or at least the majority of them, are brought to admit the expediency of the coercion, and are visibly benefited in their moral nature by having embraced the true and discarded the false opinion. To such success I conceive three concurrent conditions are requisite:

First, that the persons coerced should not be persons of full-developed intellect, but in that immature mental state, akin to the case of children, which justifies, in Mr. Mill's own opinion, the use of despotic means to effect their improvement.

Secondly, that there should exist a body of teachers on the side of that true faith to which men are to be coerced, sufficiently wise, zealous, and virtuous, and also sufficiently numerous, to ensure that the true doctrine shall be exhibited in its proper light to the persons coerced; that they shall be led to see its intrinsic superiority to the falsehood which they had formerly embraced, and, partly through that insight, partly through the moral elevation caused by contact with the wise and good, attain to a higher and more developed state of being than they had formerly known.

Thirdly, that there should not exist, in the neighbourhood of the scene of coercion, a civilised community or communities of persons, who, having themselves repudiated the true doctrine, will sympathise with those who are being coerced to accept it — will encourage them to make resistance, active or passive, to the coercive measures employed, and will nourish in them a feeling of ill-usage, and of suffering unjustly in a good cause, if the resistance is unsuccessful.

Only when these three conditions meet can coercion be really successful, and therefore legitimate. It is not difficult to show that, at various times in the history of the Church, all three conditions have concurred. For three hundred years Christianity suffered from coercion, but could not inflict it. The laws and administration of Theodosius were the first attempt on a large scale to employ on the side of the true faith the weapons which had so often been turned against it. Heresy was made a crime punishable by the civil tribunals; the pagan worship was prohibited, and its temples transferred to the use of the Church. On the whole, this coercion was successful: its partial failure was owing to the imperfect fulfilment of one or other of the first two conditions. There were many individual cases in which the objects of coercion, being persons of fully-developed faculties, were irritated, not rendered submissive, by the treatment they received: and there was in many parts of the empire a dearth of good and wise Christian teachers to make the faith a living reality to the pagan multitude who were forced to profess it. Hence we read of individual Donatists and Priscillianists filled with a bitter and burning sense of wrong at the operation of the imperial laws: and also of numbers of the poorer classes relapsing secretly into paganism in remote districts, doubtless to their own grievous moral degradation, — because the truth had come to them in name only, and not in power.

St. Augustine's letter to Count Boniface (Epist. 185) on the complaints of the Donatists, to whom the severe laws of Theodosius had been applied to compel them into submission to the Church, is an exceedingly remarkable production. Defending the employment of coercion towards the Donatists, the saint makes use of language which has been on the lips of persecutors ever since; citing, for instance, the text, "compel them to come in," and the prophecy that 'the kingdoms of the world are become the kingdoms of the Lord and of His Christ;" and referring to the conversion of St. Paul as a case of compulsion exercised by the Lord Himself. Yet, if we read this letter attentively, and note the heavenly and loving earnestness, which it breathes, as of one bent to win souls to God and truth, we shall see in it not the narrow intellect and flinty heart of the persecutor, but the earnest love of a father, rejoicing that even by chastisement his erring children are brought back to the paths of duty. To restore to the wanderer the priceless treasure of the truth is his one thought; and if the severity of law will effect this, where persuasion would have failed, he welcomes that severity. Moreover, he distinctly testifies that the coercion used *has* been successful; that crowds of schismatics, humbled and penitent, have been received back into the Church, to their immense moral gain: "Multis profuit (quod experimento probavimus et probamur) prius dolore vel timore cogi, ut postea possent doceri." On the whole, therefore, this experiment with the Donatists seems to have succeeded. Yet there were individuals among them whom it was useless to treat like children, and who maintained the right of the human mind to liberty; they said (I quote from the same letter), "Liberum est credere vel non credere; eni vim Christus intulit? quem coegit?" and I cannot feel the answer of St. Augustine to be satisfactory.

Again, in the case of our Saxon forefathers, and other Teutonic tribes, whom the authority of their princes compelled to relinquish heathenism and embrace the true faith, as all the three conditions were indubitably present, so the act of coercion was eminently successful, and therefore legitimate. So far as it failed, it was in consequence of the inadequate fulfilment of the second coincident; teachers could not be found in sufficient numbers to instruct in the Christian doctrine the obedient crowds who came to receive baptism.

The coercion of the Albigenses is too mixed and difficult a question for me now to discuss. That of the Lollards, though perhaps in the main successful, is yet a doubtful case; partly because, through the prevalence of ecclesiastical corruptions, the second condition was imperfectly fulfilled, partly owing to the extravagant nature of the coercion itself. The statute *De hæretico comburendo*, made for the use and behoof of the Lollards, indicates an increased degree of severity in coercion, at the very time when advancing civilisation was making even the minor degrees of questionable utility. The cases, under the early Christian emperors, of the capital punishment of heretics are exceedingly rare. One memorable instance is that of Priscillian, executed under the sentence of a civil court in 384. On this occasion the great St. Martin (I quote from Fleury) "implored the Emperor Maximus to spare the blood of the guilty ones; saying that it was quite enough that, having been declared heretics by the judgment of the Bishops, they should be excluded from the churches: finally, that there was no precedent for bringing an ecclesiastical cause before a secular judge." The notion that it can be either right or advisable to kill one man, in order to convince others that he and they are in the wrong, seems to me one of the most singular hallucinations which ever had a firm hold on the imagination of mankind.

An examination of the various conditions presented by the chief cases of religious coercion which have occurred since the time of Constantine would fill a volume. I will refer to one more instance, that of the coercion of the French Protestants under Louis XIV., culminating in the revocation of the Edict of Nantes. If ever, in modern times, coercion to the true faith stood a chance of success, it was now. And, in truth, it was very *nearly* successful. The mass of the Huguenot population held their opinions traditionally, and certainly did not stand on so high a grade of intellectual cultivation as the French Catholics. Many even of their ministers, so long as the coercion to which they were subjected did not proceed to extravagant lengths, and no extraneous sympathy came to their support, were led to enter into themselves, to meditate calmly, and either embrace, or approach very nearly to Catholic communion. Thus the first condition was tolerably well fulfilled. The second was fully carried out in some parts of France. What Protestant could feel any humiliation in yielding to the massive intellect, the glorious eloquence, the apostolic charity, of the great Bossuet? Accordingly, through all the coercive measures of the government, until they reached an extravagant height, the diocese of Meaux under Bossuet, like that of Hippo under St. Augustine, was the scene of innumerable *real* conversions, placing the converts in a higher state, morally and intellectually, than they were before.[2] In other parts of France, which then could boast of an unusually large number of holy and enlightened Bishops, things took, though less strikingly, the same course. But there were districts where instruction was wanting, or grossly defective; and here coercion produced lamentable results. However, its average operation had tended to produce good rather than evil, until the time when, overstraining the bent bow, it endeavoured, by one grand *coup*, to extirpate the remaining recusancy of France. The third, negative, condition, which had hitherto been fulfilled, immediately broke down. All the neighbouring Protestant communities took the alarm, and expressed by every means in their power their sympathy with the sufferers, and their indignation at the treatment they were receiving. England

---

[2]   For particulars I refer to the admirable Life of Bossuet by the Cardinal de Bausset.

received them with open arms, subscribed for them, wrote for them, fought for them. Thenceforward the coercion employed could obtain at most a political success.

Ever since the revocation of the Edict of Nantes, the party of literature, and the non-Catholic communities of Europe, have been incessantly on the watch to detect any attempt at coercion to the true faith which may be made in any part of Western Europe, and to encourage the objects of this "persecution" to every species of resistance, material and moral. Evidently therefore, the third condition of success does not and cannot exist in Europe; whence I conclude that, in our times, coercion to the true faith is impossible.

Again, every year that passes renders the first condition less easy of fulfilment; because advancing civilisation develops the general intellect, and alters that childlike condition of the human mind to which alone compulsion can be applied with moral benefit. In Asia and Africa it is still possible that occasions may arise when coercion may be employed with profit; in Europe, that period seems past for ever.

The whole case may be illustrated by the laws of parental discipline. It is obvious, that although in the early years of boyhood punishment is often the best means of effecting moral improvement, it becomes ever less and less expedient as the boy is passing into the youth; until a time arrives when the attempt to inflict it, so far from tending to good, is attended with the worst moral consequences to both parties. The early stage of the boy's education answers to my first condition. But there may be cases in which a father may find punishment inexpedient, even before the arrival of the time when it would become so in the course of nature. Suppose that a son, whom his father had just chastised, instead of being left to himself to reflect in loneliness upon his fault and upon the means of regaining his father's favour, were to be immediately surrounded by a number of his playmates, assuring him that he had done nothing wrong, condoling with him for what he had suffered, inveighing against the unjust severity of the father, and suggesting to him measures of resistance for the future. The case is not imaginary; a similar occurrence is related in Johnson's *Travels in New Brunswick*, of a family that removed from Canada into the United States. The consequence will be, that unless the boy is endowed with more than ordinary firmness and humility, he will adopt the view of the case suggested to him: — he will mutiny internally, if not openly rebel, against any future attempt on the part of his father to coerce him by punishment: and any such attempt, if made, will have a hardening and lowering effect on his moral nature. This is an exact illustration of the present state of European society. Any attempt to spread what is deemed the truth by coercive means, raises up at once a swarm of sympathisers, who denounce the employment of these means as persecution, and encourage and assist the sufferers. I do not pretend to decide whether this state of things is desirable or undesirable, but only to state the fact. If it tells against coercion used *by* Catholics in one place, it checks coercion used *against* them in another. If it helps Protestants in Tuscany and Austria, it helps Catholics in Sweden, Denmark, and Poland. But from these facts the inference is inevitable, that coercion cannot succeed in Europe at the present day, and is therefore illegitimate.

I do not shrink from any consequence of this doctrine, however apparently startling. It may be said, "Would you, then, abolish the censorship of books by the civil power in Catholic countries, and allow not only foreign heterodox works to be imported, but those of home growth to be published? Would a Christian government which so acted, consult as it ought for the faith and morals of the people committed to its care?" I answer — not, with Mr. Mill, that restraints on reading and publishing such works may possibly keep out the truth; not, with Protestant divines, that every individual has a moral right to construct his religious creed for himself, and therefore ought to have an unshackled freedom, whether of choice for himself, or of suggestion for others: — but simply this, that experience shows that, at the present stage of European civilisation, these restraints do more harm than good. In spite of prohibition, works of this class are sure to make their way into any country where there is a demand for them; and the difficulty and secrecy which surround their perusal, lend additional zest to the doctrines which they contain. Under such circumstances, a writer inclined to heterodoxy will spread a film of orthodoxy over every page; but the practice which the Germans call "Zwischen den Zeilen lesen" then arises, and sympathising readers see in his guarded statements all the audacious things which the author would have said if he dared, and often a great many more. Nor is the practical difficulty of finding proper censors a slight one, as

Milton pointed out long ago in his *Areopagitica*. A dull man will imagine that to be dangerous which is only novel; and will prevent new thoughts from coming into the world, because to his own torpid intellect they seem unsettling. Hence a twofold mischief: the suppression of a — perhaps important — truth, and the discouragement of an ardent soul from the pursuits for which God and nature designed it. An unfair man will have one rule for this writer, another for that. But even if it could be ensured that all censors should be saints and men of genius, the evils inseparable from restraint would remain.

Once for all, coercion is an educational instrument which Western Europe has outgrown; and the citizens of her commonwealth of states are all bound to assume, — and must be permitted to assume, — the burdens and the dangers of freedom.

All this reasoning applies, it must be observed, only to coercion by *temporal* authority. Coercion by ecclesiastical censures, proceeding in the last resort to excommunication, is inseparable from the idea of the Christian Church; all that my principle requires is, that such coercion should not be enforced by penalties inflicted by the temporal authority. I may have to refer to this matter again, when I come to speak of Mr. Mill's view of the neutral character, in a moral sense, of human opinions.

From an examination of the general doctrine of the Essay, it was my intention to proceed to the discussion of two or three of the more prominent questionable statements which it contains. But as the space at my disposal will not permit of my bringing these considerations to a close in the present Number, I propose to postpone the remainder of my remarks to the next *Rambler*.

Mill on Liberty

Agreeable to the plan proposed in page 75 of this volume, certain particular propositions contained in Mr. Mill's Essay have now to be examined.

The line of argument followed in the first part of this article tends, though by a different road, to the same general conclusion with that of the Essay, namely, that the *liberty* of thought and discussion should be entire. For it need hardly be said that if the lawfulness, at the present day, of coercion *to* the true faith be denied, the lawfulness of any coercion from it is denied *á fortiori*. That, indeed, could not at any time have been legitimate, according to the premises laid down, since the third condition of success could by no possibility be fulfilled in the case of the coercion of Catholics by Protestants. No Lutheran or Anglican, however convinced he might be of the truth of his own opinions, could deny the existence of a large external body, ready to extend its sympathy to any Catholics whom he might attempt to coerce, and to encourage them in at least moral resistance. Protestant coercion cannot, therefore, by the nature of things, attain to more than *political* success. But to maintain that discussion ought to be perfectly *free*, is quite a different proposition from maintaining, as Mr. Mill does, that it is essentially necessary to the profitable holding of any truth. Mr. Mill speaks as if human improvement were entirely dependent on the culture of the ratiocinative faculties. In his view, an opinion is profitless to the holder if believed merely because others believe it; unless we know the adversary's case, we do not properly and efficaciously know our own. This would be true, if it were granted that whatever opinions a person may hold are either false or but partially true; for then discussion would either bring out the falsehood, so inducing us to renounce it, — a decided gain, — or it would make us appreciate and mentally appropriate the complemental truth, which would be also a gain. But assume that the opinion is entirely true, and also that it relates to matters in which the deepest and most vital interests of the soul of man are concerned. The utmost that the exercise of the ratiocinative faculties can now effect, will be to induce the conviction that the balance of probability lies on the side of the opinion. For, from the nature of the case, since the opinion relates to matters removed from the criticism of the senses, or of any faculty judging according to sense, physical or scientific certainty of the truth of the opinion is unattainable. Take as an obvious instance the opinion of the immortality of the soul. But now, if the ratiocinative faculties be not appealed to, is the opinion therefore necessarily a sterile encumbrance on the mind, and a clog on its free working? Evidently not. There are other faculties, — the contemplative, the illustrative, the imaginative faculties, to say nothing of the sentiments and emotions, — which may be freely and largely exercised, while all the while the absolute truth of the opinion is assumed; and it cannot be denied that the exercise of these, no less than of the ratiocinative faculty, is calculated to deepen and enlarge the mind. Any one who understands what is meant by religious meditation will see at a glance the truth of what is here asserted, that a man's belief, though its grounds be not questioned, may be to him a vital and invaluable possession. He who, without questioning, has *realised* his opinion, holds it at last, not because it is the custom, not because others hold it, but because he has made it his own, and feels it by the testimony of his own consciousness to be true. Meditation upon it has brought out relations, before unperceived, with other truths; has presented it under various images, and illustrated it by various analogies; has seen it hold water under a wide range of circumstances, and tested its purifying and elevating influence upon many various natures.

The question of the abstract reasonableness of assuming the truth of any proposition prior to proof cannot be here entered upon; that would involve a long discussion having little bearing on the immediate subject of this article. It is here assumed that it *is* reasonable to take certain propositions on faith antecedently to proof; and if that be granted, it has been shown, that the propositions *being* true, they are capable of being of incalculable value to the mind, although no discussion of their grounds be engaged in.

The illustration used by Mr. Mill, when treating of this supposed *necessity* of discussion, does not appear, when examined, to be strictly relevant. "The greatest orator, save one, of antiquity," he said (p. 66), "has left it on record that he always studied his adversary's case with as great, if not with still greater intensity than even his own." A mere advocate, in whom there existed no internal connection between the side of the case he supported and his own inner life, might reasonably do so; or again, if such connection did exist, the mastering of his adversary's case might be necessary, not for *his own* benefit, which is what Mr. Mill's argument requires, but to enable him to make a successful counter-impression on his hearers. An apter illustration may perhaps be found in the case of the possessor of a property whose title is impugned by a rival claimant. If perfectly satisfied of the soundness of his own title, he will give himself no trouble about the nature of his adversary's claim; nor will his *enjoyment* of the property be at all impaired by such neglect, but rather the contrary. This seems exactly a parallel case to that of the holder of some great religious truth, upon whom there rests no obligation to controversy; he enjoys and is nourished by that truth not one whit the less because there are many disputants abroad who suppose themselves to have demonstrated its untenableness. Mr. Mill must be well aware of all this; and when he speaks of the necessity of perpetually discussing all received opinions, it is evident that his secret meaning is, that those opinions are in a great measure *false*, and that unembarrassed and fearless discussion would disclose their falsehood. For if they were wholly or mainly *true*, he could not but allow that constant medication upon them, rather than constant discussion of their grounds, should be recommended as the best means of again penetrating life and character with their spirit.

Again, to maintain that in the present state of society it is desirable that every man should be free to form and express what opinions he pleases, is a totally different thing from maintaining that opinions have no moral colour, — that whatever a man *has a right* to think and express (relatively to society) he *is right* in thinking and expressing relatively to God and conscience. Mr. Mill seems to imply this doctrine of the moral neutrality of opinions in several passages of the Essay; nor, indeed, is he inconsistent in so doing, since he is an avowed upholder of the doctrine of philosophical necessity. In the second volume of his *System of Logic* (p. 480) he says:

> "The doctrine called philosophical necessity is simply this: given the motives present to an individual's mind, and given likewise the character and disposition of the individual, the manner in which he will act may be unerringly inferred; that if we knew the person thoroughly, and knew all the inducements which are acting on him, we could foretell his conduct with as much certainty as we can predict any physical event."

To this doctrine Mr. Mill expresses his adherence. But if it be assented to, it is evident that there is no place for culpability to come in, either in character, action, or opinion. For "character and disposition" are partly born with us, partly formed by the mutual action and reaction between ourselves and the external world; "motives" are mainly supplied to us by our passions and desires. At the beginning of action, therefore, the contact of motive (which is of physical origin, and therefore not culpable) with the character (for which, as it was born with us, we are not then morally responsible) produces, according to this doctrine, inevitable results in conduct. This inevitable conduct inevitably tends to mould the character into a certain form; and so the process goes on; and as this doctrine of necessity denies the self-determining power of the will, there is no place, from the beginning to the end of a life's actions, in which to insinuate any thing like culpability or moral turpitude. Opinions will of course, follow the same rule. But those who believe in free-will in the sense in which the Church teaches it, in the sense in which Coleridge explains it in the *Aids to Reflection*, as a spiritual super-sensuous force in man, as a self-determining power, the existence of which justifies the solemn ceremonial of human justice, and authenticates the doctrine of a final judgment, — can never admit that man is not responsible for the regulation of his passions, and for the course which the formation of his character may take. And since our opinions are notoriously influenced in a high degree by our passions and our character, it follows that we are morally responsible for our opinions also. Let it not therefore be supposed that he who maintains the non-amenability of the individual to *society* for his opinions — provided their expression does not directly tend to injure others — is in any way restricted from maintaining most emphatically his amenability for them to a higher tribunal.

The last and most vital question, upon which I should desire to express a wide divergence from the views of Mr. Mill, regards the estimate which he has formed of the Christian, or, as he would prefer to term it, theological morality. Mr. Mill considers (p. 92) that "the Christian system is no exception to the rule, that in an imperfect state of the human mind the interests of truth require a diversity of opinions." It too, he things, is a half-truth, and requires to be supplemented by a morality derived from quite other sources than the New Testament. "Pagan self-assertion," he says elsewhere, quoting from Sterling, "is one of the elements of human worth as well as Christian self-denial." "Its ideal" (that of the Christian morality) "is negative rather than positive, passive rather than active, innocence rather than nobleness, abstinence from evil rather than energetic pursuit of good."

There are few Christians of any denomination who would

not dispute the accuracy of this description. If Mr. Mill had said, "*holiness* rather than nobleness," he would have stated the Christian ideal correctly; but holiness is not a negative conception, and therefore the word would not suit his purpose. It is enough to refer to the parable of the talents, and to that of the barren fig-tree, for proof that the Founder of Christianity enforced the necessity of *active* goodness at least as strongly as any moral teacher whom the world has ever seen. But if by the expression "half-truth" it be meant that Christianity does not embrace within its scope a moral code adapted to all the various conditions and circumstances of human life, the proposition may be granted without the slightest prejudice to our maintaining that the Christian morality is divinely revealed. Be it remembered that morality is *natural* to man; its leading principles are impressed by the Creator, independently of a direct revelation, upon the conscience; and the natural reason is able to deduce from these original principles rules of conduct fitted to guide the individual in the emergencies which the conditions of life present. God does not *reveal* to His creatures that which the constitution with which He has endowed them enables them to discover for themselves; and hence it is no disparagement to the revealed morality of the Gospel to say that it is not a complete ethical code. Christianity reveals to us the true relation between man and God, and man's destiny beyond the grave; the Christian morality accordingly is simply that part of morals which teaches man so to pass through this life as to attain his true destiny in the next. In every moral principle which the Gospel proclaims there is a constant reference to a life to come, — to a scene where all partial or apparent wrong will be set right, and compared to which the concerns of the present life are mere vanity and futility. The distinguishing device of the Christian among other men is, *Credo vitam æternam.* He cannot prize this life and its so-called realities at a very high rate, who, taught by religion, steadily fixes his eyes on the one fact, that in a few short years his puny being will be swallowed up in the immensities and splendours of God. The Christian ethics, therefore, are designed for a being placed at the Christian stand-point. Their main principles are:

1. The deliberate preference of the heavenly to the earthly life, of the future to the present.

2. The principle of love or charity, prescribing a heavenly temper, the exact opposite of the selfishness which Mr. Mill charges upon Christian morality.
3. The regulation of the passions, by the aid of the light afforded by the first principle, and of the example of Christ.
4. Entire purity of thought and act, of mind and body.
5. Humility, consisting partly in a child-like reception of the revelation of God, partly in the imitation of the lowly and suffering life of Jesus.

This is the morality of the Christian as such: he can dispense with any other while thoroughly in his life realising this. One thing is *necessary*; and multitudes of persons of either sex, in every age, have deliberately given up the world as an object of pursuit, in order that they might pursue the life eternal; and have gone through life guided by this morality alone, without ever finding the want of any other, or repenting of the choice which they had made. The practical inconsistency which prevails among Christians, and which furnishes the ground for Mr. Mill's strictures, arises from this, — that many, who are thoroughly addicted to the pursuit of temporal good, *pretend* nevertheless to walk in conformity to this Christian morality, and to need no other ethical rules than those which the Gospel furnishes. It is as if Dives, in the midst of his money-getting, were to affect the detachment and mortification of Lazarus. It is indisputably true, as Mr. Mill says, that the Koran contains excellent moral precepts which are not found in the New Testament; he might have added that Aristotle has yet more excellent maxims than the Koran. But what is the reason? These maxims are all fitted to aid man in arriving at his *natural* ideal, namely, "the harmonious development of all his powers to a complete and consistent whole." As reason is capable of discovering this ideal, so it is capable of ascertaining the ethical principles which subserve to its attainment. The morality of the temporal life, in all its parts, — that of the public assembly, that of the bar, that of the counter, or that of the farm, — is capable of being ascertained by human reason unaided by revelation, and for a large part of it has been so ascertained. So far, then, as an individual is bound, or inclined, to bear a part in the world's work, — so far as he cannot, or will not, give himself up wholly to God, — so far it is his duty to guide himself by the best and wisest ethical rules which he can find, from whatever source derived, applicable to that particular department of the temporal life in which his station is. The higher Christian morality which he possesses will often enable, nay compel, him to *revise* ethical judgments which have been arrived at independently of religion; but it will not serve him, in these worldly matters, as an exclusive code.

But when Mr. Mill speaks (pp. 88, 89) of the Christian morality as being, "not the work of Christ or the Apostles," but gradually built up by the Catholic Church of the first five centuries," — when, again, he speaks of its having "received additions in the middle ages," which the Protestant sects merely cut off, substituting fresh additions of their own, — one cannot but wonder at so strange a distortion of the facts. That the leading principles of the Christian morality, as above defined, were taught by our Lord and His apostles, is so palpably true, is so easily established by a multitude of texts, that it were waste of words to go about to prove it; that the same principles were taught by the Catholic Church of the first five centuries is also notorious; it is equally certain that these are the main principles of Catholic morality at the present day. Mr. Mill ought to inform us what were the additional principles invented in the middle ages. Some such might be found, perhaps, by culling extracts from mediæval writers, after the fashion of Mosheim's citations from St. Eligius (see Newman on *Popular Protestantism*), but certainly in no other way. The separated bodies have, indeed, either impaired these original principles, or joined to them, as Mr. Mill says, "additions adapted to the character and tendencies" of each. By setting up the State as the supreme power in the Church, the Anglican body has impaired the testimony of its members to the first principle; many of them have had already, and will have again, to choose between the edict of Cæsar and the command of God; while their position as a separate body disposes them, in the case of collision, to prefer the former to the latter. The Methodists have added to the morality of Christ a kind of morbid self-inspection, which is perpetually asking itself the questions, "Am I right with God or not? is my inward state satisfactory? shall I be saved, or shall I be lost?" The Antinomian sects have, to say nothing of what they have added, abandoned the second and third principles, — purity and the regulation of the passions. Lastly, all have, in different ways and degrees, abandoned the principle of humility, and added various kinds and forms of pride. Dryden, it will be remembered, challenged Stillingfleet to name a single Protestant work on humility; and when his adversary produced one, it proved to be in the main a translation from a Catholic treatise.

The last chapter consists of "applications" of the general doctrine of the Essay, one of which only can here be noticed. Although not strictly belonging to the subject of the Essay, which is social liberty, not political enfranchisement, Mr. Mill has handled in this chapter the question as to the limits of the interference of government in the business of society. There is often a misuse of words here which leads to confusion of thought. English popular writers, when they hold up England as a pattern of political liberty to foreign nations, generally mean that we have a right to vote for a member of parliament, which they have not; a right to tax ourselves for local purposes, which they have not; together with many other privileges of the same kind. On the other hand, there are those who, revolted by the self-satisfied air with which these privileges are paraded, and detecting an ambiguity in the terms used, are apt to speak slightingly of these supposed advantages. These persons say, "Why attach the name of liberty to functions which we are by no means impatient to exercise? If government officials will undertake the laying of our water-pipes, and the cleaning and lighting of our streets, we shall thank them for relieving us of a task which the wider knowledge and experience they can command enables them probably to execute better than ourselves. Certainly we shall not regard their interference as an invasion of our *liberty*. Nor, again do we think it essential to our liberty that we should have a voice *valeat quantum* in the election of the members of the Legislature, in preference to any other mode of appointment. Continental experience proves that towns can be made beautiful and healthy as well, perhaps better, by a centralised than a localised administration. Nor does our vaunted parliamentary machine always work smoothly or profitably; it economises neither time nor money. What we understand by liberty is exactly what Mr. Mill understands by it, namely, the power of managing our own life as we please; of reading what books we like; of unhampered locomotion; of cultivating and developing our own and our children's minds by the methods we think best, provided we do not trench upon the rights of others. If we think an institution wrong, — slavery, for instance, — we desire the liberty of publishing our thoughts without being tarred and feathered; if we prefer one style of religious worship to another, we would prefer to be free to practise it without constraint either from a government or from a mob. The charter of our civic rights may include all the fine openings for fussy self-importance that you describe, and perhaps many more; yet without the species of liberty we have insisted upon, we shall not be free in any sense that seems to us worth caring for."

A tendency to such reasoning as this is often perceivable on the part of the Catholic minority in England, and not unnaturally so. Local self-government and the representative system do not work favourably for English Catholics. Although they form more than one-twentieth of the population, they can command only one six hundred and fifty-fourth part of the parliamentary representation, and even that happens through a fortunate accident. The same is the case, as a general rule, with all municipal offices. Every where in England Catholics are in a minority; and minorities, being unrepresented under the present *régime*, cannot get their man elected, nor cause their voice to be more than imperfectly heard. The positive prejudice also which disqualifies Catholics, as such, in the general English mind for posts of honour and trust is still, though with diminished intensity, powerfully operative. It might seem, therefore, at first sight, to be our policy rather to aid in accumulating power in the hands of the government than in the maintenance and extension of the system of local management. Government officials, it may be said, are more or less accessible to reason; they are mostly raised by education above the sway of mere blind prejudice; if we can make out a clear case of hardship to them, they will redress it. But the blind unreasoning bigotry of the bulk of the English middle class is unimpressible and unassailable; to attempt to extract fair concessions from them, when the Pope is in the case, is, as Sir John Fortescue would say, to go "scheryng of hogges," with the old result of "moche cry and little wole."

All this is true; yet still Mr. Mill is probably right when he says, that the more narrowly government interference in local concerns can be circumscribed, the better. First, for the sake of the great principle, that "though individuals may not do the particular thing so well, on the average, as the officers of government, it is nevertheless desirable that it should be done by them rather than by the government, as a means to their own mental education, — a mode of strengthening their active faculties, exercising their judgment, and giving them a familiar knowledge of the subjects with which they are thus left to deal" (Essay, p. 196). Secondly, because Catholics have no cause to despair of being able ultimately to work round free institutions more to their advantage than they seem to be at present. Let them show themselves the equals of their Protestant fellow-citizens in public spirit, in intelligence sharpened by education, and in acquired knowledge, — in short, in the whole circle of the civic virtues and qualifications, and they may reckon on not being always excluded from posts of trust. This book itself, the weighty maxims of which are destined to leaven very extensively, if we mistake not, the general sentiments of society, will contribute to dissipate the intolerance which defeats their just claims. Thirdly, the precariousness of favours obtained by a minority from a government has to be considered. When we stand with our countrymen man to man, we know where we stand. We may be disliked and suspected at first; but if we can once get a footing, and satisfy them that we personally are a decent sort of people, and that our claims are just, we shall have gained a success which can never afterwards, unless through our own fault, be wrested from us. For all experience shows that rights thus gained are progressive, and that their expansion can only be arrested by external constraint; on the other hand, the concessions which a government has made to a minority in a time of quietness may be revoked in a time of excitement. Are examples needed? Look at the seeming prosperity of English Catholicity under the government of Charles I. before the year 1640, and again under James II. In each case the relief afforded by the government was given in defiance and in advance of the general sentiment of the nation, and was soon swept away beneath a torrent of penal inflictions; but to take advantage of more equal laws, and to disarm by sensible and spirited conduct the inveterate prejudices of individuals and of local coteries, is, *pro tanto*, to alter the general sentiment itself.

BRITISH QUARTERLY REVIEW
1860

On Liberty. By John Stuart Mill. Crown 8vo. pp. 207. London: J. W. Parker and Son.

'The subject of this Essay,' says Mr. Mill, 'is not the so-called liberty of the Will, so unfortunately opposed to the misnamed doctrine of Philosophical Necessity; but Civil or Social Liberty; the nature and limits of the power which can be legitimately exercised by society over the individual. A question seldom stated, and hardly ever discussed, in general terms, but which profoundly influences the practical controversies of the age by its latent presence, and is likely soon to make itself recognised, as the vital question of the future.' It may surprise some of our readers to learn that the subject of liberty, 'civil or social,' has been 'seldom stated and hardly ever discussed in general terms.' Nor is it true if, by 'general terms,' were meant merely the utmost limit within which society has a right to restrict, and interfere with, the freedom of the individual by the expression of its will in the shape of law and legal penalties; for this question has been often discussed, even if no universal concurrence has yet been obtained as to the precise limits within which such restriction or interference is warrantable. In our own country, however, we have *practically* come, at least, to the universal recognition of the right both of free thought and free discussion.

But if by 'general terms' he meant, as Mr. Mill is careful to show he means, that the discussion is to include all *possible* methods of restricting individual freedom, — not only those of a legal character and which are enforced by legal penalties, but those also of a moral nature, and the limits within which society has a right to appeal to any of these last, — then it is quite true that the question has been 'seldom stated' and 'hardly ever discussed;' one reason of which, we imagine, is that it is hardly possible to attain any practical results, except so far as we *can* fairly make such things questions of law and legal penalties; and this cannot be done, in the great majority of cases, except by endangering far more liberty than it could secure. In illustration of these remarks we shall, by-and-bye, take a few examples.

That there are several difficult and unsettled questions as to the limits of a rightful, or, if rightful, expedient action of government in restriction of individual liberty, or that of any fraction of society, there can be no doubt. And from the ability with which Mr. Mill treated portions of the subject in his chapter on the 'Limits of Government Interference,' in the second volume of his *Political Economy*, we should have been very glad to receive a careful discussion of it, in its entire length and breadth, at his hands. But such questions are only touched upon in this Essay, and rather indicated than fully argued. That there is also such a thing as social 'tyranny,' sometimes exercised by the community at large, for the repression of certain opinions or restriction of certain acts on the part of individuals, is most true. But on the most important of these last cases, and on the possibility of any legal action being taken with regard to them, or the limits of such action, if possible, we find little in this volume. The 'tyranny' exercised by 'Trades Unions', the 'tyranny' of opinion, again, in America, (especially in relation to slavery,) are passed by, while the principle of the 'Maine Liquor Law' is slightly touched. We have already hinted that where law cannot interpose (either because it has no right, or, if it has a right cannot expediently use it), we have doubts whether very much can be done by mere discussion; we doubt it for reasons which we shall shortly assign. Still, some questions above indicated, would undoubtedly have given room for profitable discussion as to how far they *might* be, or why they ought *not* to be, the object of legislative action. The remarks of Mr. Mill on 'Government Education' form an exception to the general insufficiency which which these subjects are discussed; but even this is dismissed in a few pages. Indeed his whole chapter of 'practical applications' consists of less than forty very moderate-sized pages.

Meantime, he has expended nearly half his little treatise in vindicating the 'Liberty of Thought and Discussion,' which we had vainly imagined was pretty well understood and enjoyed among us.

Mr. Mill seems to think otherwise; and as this is the subject to which he has, after all, principally devoted his book (other points being, as we have intimated, very briefly treated), we shall, in this article, confine our criticisms for the most part to the chapter on 'Free Thought and Discussion.'

Mr. Mill seems to think that there is still a great deal to be done before we can be said fully to enjoy this inestimable right. We cannot agree with him. As far as legal penalties go, we are as free as any people can well be. For any remaining inconveniences which may attend the patron or champion of unpalatable or obnoxious opinions (not from the *hands*, for they are tied, but) from the looks or even tongues of his fellow-men, or from any other methods of showing aversion that cannot be recognised or repressed by law without greater social 'tyranny' than the law can ever cure, we do not flatter ourselves that Mr. Mill, or any one else, can devise a remedy; further, we doubt whether it would be good for the progress of truth (partly on Mr. Mill's own showing), if exemption from all such opposition could be secured for its champions. This we shall endeavour to make out by-and-bye; meantime, as regards civil liberty, we do not see that Englishmen can learn much from Mr. Mill's long chapter on 'Freedom of Thought and Discussion,' however useful it might have been if published (supposing it *could* have been published) in Italy, or Spain, or Portugal. Mr. Mill, indeed, hints that even legal exemption from pains and penalties for the expression of opinion, is not quite secured to us; and in illustration alludes to that great 'Pooley' case, of which Mr. Buckle attempted to make so much use in a recent number of *Fraser's Magazine*, but which proved a fatal *ignis fatuus* to that enterprising gentleman, and finally plunged him into as deep a bog as ever controvertist was smothered in. Mr. Buckle's essay was valuable, however, as a piece of triumphant self-confutation; for it not only showed, in contradiction to Mr. Mill, that Englishmen may use all proper freedom 'of discussion,' but a great deal more; and that the greatest declaimers for liberty are but too apt to resort to the worst vices of that 'social tyranny' against which they protest — abuse and vituperation. All this Mr. Buckle proves by his gross insults to Sir J. Coleridge and his son, and thereby gives us a curious idea of that peculiar felicity which may be expected under the millennium of 'free discussion' for which he pleads. It was indeed an unfortunate exhibition of Mr. Mills' principles; for a more truculent specimen of that overbearing, imperious, and prejudging temper, in which 'social tyranny' originates, it has not often been our lot to encounter. However, we flatter ourselves that if Mr. Mill had known all the circumstances of the great 'Pooley' affair, as afterwards detailed by Mr. Coleridge, he would not have made that luckless allusion which led to so sad an escapade on his disciple's part, who assuredly had a 'zeal' for liberty, 'but not according to knowledge.' In spite of any such rare instances as that of Pooley, we are still disposed to say that, practically, no great increase of our liberty of 'discussion' is possible. As Mr. Coleridge justly argues, people are not to be permitted to scribble blasphemy and obscenity on our gates and walls, for the expression of 'free thought' or the vindication of a 'liberty' that is certainly neither 'civil nor religious;' any more than a Christian is to be permitted to dangle a lump of pork before the nose of a Jew along the street by way of expressing his superiority to the Jew's religious prejudices. Such things cannot be allowed by way of vindicating individual liberty; and so, in spite of an occasional great 'Pooley' case, it is quite true (and, we think, every day sufficiently confirms it) that there is, practically, in this country the most unfettered freedom of discussion. We heartily wish indeed that every remnant of obsolete law which savours of forcible repression, may be abolished, if only for consistency's sake; but we cannot say that, practically, any serious let or hindrance is given to the most free (if only tolerably decent) discussion of any opinions, however paradoxical or obnoxious. Of this we think we have *more* than fair proof — say in Mr. Buckle's diatribe against Sir J. Coleridge (for that is not decent), and in Mr. Holyoake's lucubrations, for a similar reason; and a *fair* proof in Mr. Mills's own book, and in innumerable others, teeming with paradoxical speculations on all sorts of subjects. Mr. Mill, for example, has certainly given free expression to his opinions respecting the Christian ethics. Yet, we suppose, no one thinks it would be desirable to lay any interdict on the freest expression of such opinions. It is a little inconsistent, indeed, that, while in the very act of proving the liberty of discussion, men should grumble at society as though it had denied it. So far, however, are we from apprehending any harm from Mr. Mill's expression of opinions, that we shall quote them *in extenso* — not for the purpose of confuting them (thought we may, perhaps, make an observation on one or two points), but just to show we have no objection to convince our readers by a practical proof that we have not spoken without reason when we said that Mr. Mill cannot consistently complain of want of freedom in avowing his opinions. He is certainly as much at issue, in the following passage, as it is well possible for him to be, with the general feeling of the mass of his countrymen. As to his statements, we have no fear of their making any wrong impression on any who are really well acquainted with the New Testament morality. We trust that Mr. Mill will be duly sensible of the liberality which not only does not seek to 'gag' him, but actually gives his opinions a chance of a wider circulation.

> 'What is called Christian, but should rather be termed theological, morality, was not the work of Christ or the Apostles, but is of much later origin having been gradually built up by the Catholic Church of the first five centuries; and though not implicitly adopted by moderns and Protestants, has been much less modified by them than might have been expected. For the most part, indeed, they have contented themselves with cutting off the additions which had been made to it in the Middle Ages, each sect supplying the place by fresh additions, adapted to its own character and tendencies. That mankind owes a great debt to this morality, and to its early teachers, I should be the last person to deny; but I do not scruple to say of it that it is, in many important points, incomplete and one-sided; and that unless ideas and feelings not sanctioned by it had contributed to the formulation of European life and character, human affairs would have been in a worse condition than they now are. Christian morality (so called) has all the characters of a reaction; it is in great part, a protest against paganism. Its ideal is negative rather than positive; passive rather than active; innocence rather than nobleness; abstinence from evil rather than energetic pursuit of good; in its precepts (as has been well said) 'thou shalt not' predominates unduly over 'thou shalt.' In its horror of sensuality, it made an idol of asceticism, which has been gradually compromised away into one of legality. It holds out the hope of heaven, the threat of hell, as the appointed and appropriate motives to a virtuous life; in this falling far below the best of the ancients, and doing what lies in it to give to human morality an essentially selfish character, by disconnecting each man's

feelings of duty from the interests of his fellow-creatures, except so far as a self-interested inducement is offered to him for consulting them. It is essentially a doctrine of passive obedience; it inculcates submission to all authorities found established; who, indeed, are not to be actively obeyed when they command what religion forbids, but who are not to be resisted, far less rebelled against, for any amount of wrong to ourselves; and while, in the morality of the best pagan nations, duty to the State holds even a disproportionate place, infringing on the just liberty of the individual in purely Christian ethics, that grand department of duty is scarcely noticed or acknowledged. It is in the Koran, not the New Testament, that we read the maxim, 'A ruler who appoints any man to an office, when there is in his dominion another man better qualified for it, sins against God and against the State.' What little recognition the idea of obligation to the public obtains in modern morality, is derived from Greek and Roman sources, not from Christian; as even in the morality of private life, whatever exists of magnanimity, high-mindedness, personal dignity, even the sense of honour, is derived from the purely human, not the religious, part of our education, and never could have grown out of a standard of ethics in which the only worth professedly recognised is that of obedience.

'I am as far as any one from pretending that these defects are necessarily inherent in the Christian ethics, in every manner in which it can be conceived, or that the many requisites of a complete moral doctrine, which it does not contain, do not admit of being reconciled with it. Far less would I insinuate this of the doctrines and precepts of Christ himself. I believe that the sayings of Christ are all that I can see any evidence of their having been intended to be; that they are irreconcileable with nothing which a comprehensive morality requires; that everything which is excellent in ethics may be brought within them, with no greater violence to their language than has been done to it by all who have attempted to deduce from them any practical system of conduct whatever. But it is quite consistent with this to believe that they contain, and were meant to contain, only a part of the truth; that many essential elements of the highest morality are among the things which are not provided for, nor intended to be provided for, in the recorded deliverances of the Founder of Christianity, and which have been entirely thrown aside in the system of ethics erected on the basis of these deliverances by the Christian Church.' (pp. 88–91.)

Whether it can be said, so exclusively, that the 'appointed and appropriate' motives presented by Christian moralists are 'the hope of heaven and the fear of hell,' those will judge who have read the New Testament; but it if *were* so, it certainly seems curious to find a resolute 'utilitarian' moralist like Mr. Mill finding fault with such a system; for if all men would but act on it, and so attain 'eternal good,' in compliance with the rather extensive love of the *'utile'* thus proposed as a motive, it would certainly be attended with the 'greatest happiness of the greatest number;' and thus the object of utilitarian ethics would be very effectually attained. However, we suppose that those who remember what sort of place the Christian 'heaven' is represented as being — what sort of *happiness*, that of perfect virtue and purity, it mainly proposes to its inhabitants — what the *qualifications* of those who alone can enter it — or the motives of gratitude, love, hope, and the lofty aspirations to be 'holy even as God is holy,' to which the New Testament appeals, — will think either that Mr. Mill's memory is very short, or his tongue very long, when he thus ventures to characterize the all but exclusive motives to Christian virtue. Similarly, whether 'abstinence from evil rather than energetic pursuit of good' is the main feature of New Testament morality, may also be left to the decision of every reader of the Gospels or the Epistles. Almost any of the summaries of duty given by Paul will confute it; and by the time the reader has 'done' (as well as 'forborne') all that the Apostle enjoins him, we much doubt whether 'many' (or any) 'essential elements' of a true ethical character will be found wanting in him. As to that wonderful addition to the moral code, for which Mr. Mill says to triumphantly that we are indebted to the Koran, and not to the Bible, the Koran is quite welcome to whatever honour is involved in stating it; but, in truth, it is no addition to a moral code at all, but just one of the applications of a general maxim to practical details, and which (more or less important) might be multiplied without end; for example, that he 'who employs a dishonest or incompetent shoemaker or breeches-maker, when he might employ an honest and efficient one, *pro tanto* sins against society.' The principle of a thousand such cautions must, in any code of ethics, take its place in a general maxim. Such maxims are as easily found in the Bible as anywhere; but if a code of morals has not all 'its essential elements' without such details, the statutes at large would not be so voluminous as a code of human duty. Meantime, we fear that this inestimable and pithy sentence of the Koran has done little or nothing for the nation to whom it was given; for of no nation can it be said that their government has more flagrantly violated it. If the Turks have the maxim, they certainly have needed it. Unluckily, they do not act upon it more than those who do not expressly include it as a formal proposition among ethical *first principles*.

However, to leave the question whether England has the privilege of free thought and discussion so far as exemption from all legal penalties is concerned, let us further consider — and this is the principal object we have in view — whether the sort of social immunity our author would advocate for the champions of unpalatable truths or errors is not an imaginary one; whether, in truth, his principle is not *nugatory*, and whether if it were practicable, it would be beneficial.

That it is possible, as Mr. Mill remarks, for society to exercise a very stringent repressive power in relation to both opinions and practices that are obnoxious to it, without appealing to law at all, is very true; that this power may, by putting the individual under the ban of society, make him feel very uncomfortable, much 'as a toad under a harrow,' as the saying is, that it may, perhaps, if he be a coward or faint-hearted, compel him to a very unwelcome silence and inaction, and lead him 'to hide his light under a bushel,' is equally true. That this power in society may, in a given case, be exerted very unwisely, and inflict great hardships, may, in fact, be a 'tyranny of the majority,' is also undoubted. But we do not, we confess, see any direct remedy, supposing each man does only what his undoubted legal rights permit him to do, and the law remains impartially indifferent on both sides, that is, merely compelling all to keep the peace. We see no remedy, we say, except that of enlightening the public on the very questions on which the said power of moral repression is supposed to be inequitably exercised; that is, the persons who hold the obnoxious tenets, or plead for the obnoxious practices, must face all the obloquy, whatever it is, of proclaiming the one, and doing the other — the protests and frowns of society notwithstanding. Society, of course, cannot be compelled to listen with patience to what it had rather not listen to; nor can people be compelled to associate or hold parley, or, if you will, only fair and candid discussion, with men whom it abhors; or to think no worse of them if they chance to hold opinions which, though not punishable by law, the said society deems in the highest degree profligate, impious, or seditious, necessarily leading to vice and immorality.

Mr. Mill, it is evident, would be as averse as any man, to any such vindication of individual liberty as would, in fact, be the slavery of society at large; and, of course, neither Mr. Mill nor anybody else would be so absurd as to plead for anything of the kind. It is, we admit, very proper that every man should be at perfect liberty to speak his opinions and sentiments, whatever they may be; and, in spite of Mr. Mill and Mr. Buckle, we cannot see that this is a liberty which is not pretty well understood and practised among us. But it is at least equally proper that another man should run away from him if he thinks it best to do so, or close his ears, or refuse to have anything to do with him, or warn other people against him, and in a thousand other ways, if he thinks proper, show his displeasure and his aversion.

Now here we confess to a difficulty; and Mr. Mill's principle, by which he would limit the power of society over the individual, seems to us far too vague to be of any real value. Mr. Mill says that no restriction, in the way of moral coercion, on individual liberty, is justifiable except as prompted by 'self-protection.'[1] But, then, who shall define the limits of what is morally justified by 'self-protection?' The vague generality conveys nothing. Let us try it upon a single and simple case;

---

[1]   The following sentences from Mr. Mill's Essay will show his meaning: 'The object of this Essay is to assert *one very simple principle*, as entitled to govern absolutely the dealings of society with the individual in the way of compulsion and control, whether the means used be physical force in the form of legal penalties, or the moral coercion of public opinion. That principle is, that the sole end for which mankind are warranted, individually and collectively, in interfering with the liberty of action of any of their number, is self-protection. That the only purpose for which power can be rightfully exercised over any member of a civilized community, against his will, is to prevent harm to others. His own good, either physical or moral, is not a sufficient warrant. He cannot rightfully be compelled to do or forbear, because it will be better for him to do so, because it will make him happier, because, in the opinions of others, to do so would be wise, or even right.' — p. 21, 22.

and see whether it can do anything for us. Let us take the case of an atheist, with full power (as we would certainly grant him), of publishing his opinions, and making any proselytes he can. Now every conscientious theist will regard his sentiments as of the most deadly and pernicious character, and recoil from them not only with disgust and fear, but horror and indignation. In the exercise, then, of *his* undoubted liberty, and what he believes due to self-protection, has he a right to decline the acquaintance of the said atheist? or, though previously a friend, to *cut* his acquaintance on his becoming such? to refuse him access to his own house, to refuse to meet him at the houses of others? to point him out as a man to be shunned and avoided by his children — his servants — his dependents, — all, in short, over whom he has influence? to refuse to argue with him, if he pleases; or, if he argues, to give vivid and natural expression to his abhorrence of atheistical sentiments? Why, yes; Mr. Mill himself appears to concede all this; for he says:—

'We have a right also, in various ways, to act upon our unfavourable opinion of any one, not to the oppression of his individuality, but in the exercise of ours. We are not bound, for example, to seek his society; we have a right to avoid it (though not to parade the avoidance), for we have a right to choose the society most acceptable to us. We have a right, and it may be our duty to caution others against him, if we think his example or conversation likely to have pernicious effect on those with whom he associates.' (p. 139.)

But then, if every theist does the above-mentioned kind of things — and we think no one can challenge his moral right to do them with not unreasonable notions of 'self-protection' — then, since the atheist is as one to ten thousand in any community, nay, in a much less ratio, he will as effectually be under the 'ban' of society, as though sentence of excommunication had been pronounced against him. The full power of 'discussion' is still left to him, only he must 'discuss' in solitude, or if men listen at all, in defiance of the universal frown and aversion of society; and thus he will be placed under that so-called 'tyranny' from which, as it seems to us, Mr. Mill would vainly seek to deliver every apostle of an unwelcome or abhorred dogma. Yet is any one to blame? Is not the conduct of society what naturally flows from its honest view of the nature and consequences of the proscribed doctrine, and in strict consistency with the undoubted legal rights of every individual member thereof? Mr. Mill's principle, therefore, appears to us to be too vague to be of service. The notions of 'self-protection' will undoubtedly depend on the degree of intensity with which the opinions proscribed are deemed odious and pernicious; and the stringency of the moral coercion which society, quite involuntarily and necessarily, will employ, will be in proportion.

None will contend, we fancy, that any such modes of limiting the freedom or repressing the exuberance of individual action, as have been above enumerated, can be the legitimate subject of law. Now, if so, whether the action of society be a hardship or not, we see no other way of dealing with it than the one already stated, namely, that the very parties whose opinions and practices, for the present, are obnoxious, shall heroically persist in avowing the one and doing the other, till they convince society (if it *can* be convinced) that the one are true and the other beneficial — or at least harmless: that is, they must, through the usual modes of persevering agitation, succeed in turning the *minority* into a *majority*, by convincing the reigning majority, that it is mistaken. During the process of doing this we see not how the moral 'penalty,' such as it is, can be evaded. The true mode of laying the spirit of opposition, is by convincing it that the particular tenets or practices that rouse its displeasure, are not worthy of its censure or aversion. But, in order to do this, those who undertake the task of undeceiving the public, and of chaperoning a suspicious opinion into the world, must necessarily encounter all the storm of obloquy which will attend the utterance of what the public is intensely averse to, and the doing what it will unsparingly condemn; and so the position of the patron of supposed error, or heterodoxy, or immorality, will, in the very nature of things, he a very uncomfortable one; and if it be called 'persecution,' it is such 'persecution' as all the Essays on Liberty in the world cannot obviate, being the result of the constitution of human nature itself.

Mr. Mill, if we apprehend him rightly, seems to think that the alleged tyranny of society against obnoxious opinions or practices, can be put down in some other way; by general reasoning, for example, on its being wrong to do anything in the way of restricting the liberty of the individual which is not dictated by 'self protection;' by inculcating the duty of listening with candour to anything that everybody has to say for his opinions; by telling us to be always ready obligingly to reopen our own convictions to a renewed sifting on every summons of a new objection, or a renewed statement of an old one; by reminding us of our fallibility, or by exhorting us not to use any of the curt, perhaps discourteous, methods of closing argument when we *think* we have examined enough, and have made up our minds; which last at present is undeniably a great saving of time and patience, but which may be thought, by a pertinacious champion of an imagined novelty, one of the most annoying, as it is certainly one of the most common, ways of restricting his sphere of propagandism. But we apprehend that Mr. Mill's view of the efficacy of any such general exhortations, where men conscientiously believe that truth, important truth, is concerned, is an illusion. The real difficulty is to convert them to the opinion that the opinion which they think immoral, pernicious, fraught with deadly consequences to their children or their country, is one of which they may as calmly discuss the *pros* and *cons*, and let those over whom they have any influence, do the same, as of an opinion about the prospects of the coming harvest, or the practicability of a proposed machine. But this cannot be so long as a man really believes that such and such opinions are of deadly quality. Could we respect him, if, merely on the general ground of his hypothetical fallibility, he were willing to listen to everything that could be urged for them as readily as he would to arguments for the undulatory theory of light, or the possibility of a planet outside Neptune? Mr. Mill may say, that an intellectual being singly intent on truth, ought so to listen; but man is *not* a mere intellectual being — but a being of conscience, emotions, passions, as well as intellect; and so strongly, that even in purely *scientific* questions, or at all events having only scientific issues — as, for example, the value of any new discovery, or the claims of him who is thought to have made it, we have proof every day that it is not possible to make a man a mere 'reasoning mill,' — to use Voltaire's expression of Samuel Clarke.

We repeat, that the only effectual method of sheltering an obnoxious speculator from the aversion and contempt of the community at large (from all substantial injury, all 'penalties', we suppose the law to secure him) will be found to be that of convincing society of the falsity of its conclusions; and this will not and cannot be done, except as those who think them false shall face all the odium that may be implied in endeavouring to confront and to confute them. That they should have the liberty of asserting as loudly, as clearly, and as frequently as they please, these unpalatable truths (or falsehoods) is conceded.

As long as the public *conscientiously* holds such and such opinions fraught with such and such consequences, you cannot show that they are *not* fraught with them, except by persevering, in the face of obloquy, in advocating them; the *effects* of conviction cannot be wrought before-hand by bespeaking those effects anterior to it. And now comes a seeming puzzle, which, however, experience easily enables us to answer. If it be said 'How is a man to convince or convert those who won't listen?' a sufficient answer would be to ask, 'And how shall they listen except some one shall speak? How shall they believe without a preacher?' And if he *does* speak, then of course will come the necessary conflict of feeling to which we have adverted so often. But to the question, 'How shall a man convince or convert others if the public in general will not listen?' the proper answer is, 'Just as in other cases where the world has been heretofore disabused of errors, and those as inveterate as any that are likely to be dissipated by our modern *illuminati*; that is, by persevering in the assertion of obnoxious opinions.' It is the old course, often taken in the face of much greater opposition than any that now threatens the *soi-disant* Reformer; of legal penalties, torture, and death itself, superadded to the most stringent moral repression which contempt and neglect, or the most intense aversion could produce. If a man cannot face even these last, it is pretty clear that he is not predestined to be an Apostle of the Truth.

At all events, it cannot be helped. These obstacles must be faced. For none will say, we presume, that it is 'tyranny' to refuse to listen to listen to the 'voice of the charmer, charm he never so wisely;' that it is tyranny, if a man is allowed to publish a book, unless men will also read it; that it is tyranny if he be allowed to express what opinions he pleases, so long as people will get out of the sound of his voice; or, if they remain, frown or look displeased, or laugh or hiss, or shrug their shoulders, or persuade their neighbours not to listen. No; if we

vindicate the right of a man to say what he pleases, we must
also vindicate the right of his neighbour not to listen to him if
he pleases, or, listening, to turn away with the natural
expressions — natural as long as he remains in the same state of
mind — of dislike or indignation. Good breeding, or pity, or
even contempt, may sometimes modify or disguise the
expression of these feelings; but they will exist and whether
expressed or not, we apprehend that the practical difficulties of
the would-be Reformer will be much the same, and that no
general discussion can mend the matter. To attempt to amend
it by enforced suppression of feeling is what we should all
deprecate, as killing much more liberty than it would save. But
we humbly think that, even the suppression by universal and
conventional consent would also kill more freedom than it
would save; for it would demand the repression of natural
feeling on the part of the many in behalf of the few, and must
far more imperil that brusque 'individuality' for which Mr. Mill
pleads so strongly, than the present state of things.

'Hands off,' is fair play, and there we must stop. Meantime,
of course, every advocate of a crotchet will be disposed to
complain if he may not pour his merciless discourse into your
ears, or hold you by the button as long as he pleases; or if,
having once inflicted on you the same or similar arguments, he
sees you bolting as soon as you hear the inevitable harangue
begin, or taking little pains, or none at all, to conceal your
aversion and disgust.

If a doctrine be really true, and important, perseverance
through evil report and good report will have its reward at last;
by little and little animosity and prejudice will be disarmed,
advocates gradually enlisted, and favourable conjunctures
secured for disseminating the once obnoxious tenet more
rapidly. These propitious results, as experience shows, will
come at last; but in the very nature of things they must be
waited for, and, in some degree, generally suffered for; it is the
inevitable penalty which, for the reasons already given, must be
paid, unless men (which would surely be the last calamity that
could befal them) were ready to listen to what they deemed the
most pernicious doctrines and the most beneficial truths with
the same unenviable equilibrium of feeling. He who would
convince them that these feelings ought to be reversed must
count the cost; if he decline the payment, there is no smooth
path, 'no royal road' of ease by which he can attain the same

end. A man cannot be 'nursed and dandled' into a Reformer. This was the old way, and we suspect must ever be the way of spreading either unwelcome truth or unwelcome error in the world. Nor, in truth, can we wish it to be otherwise; though if we wished it ever so much, it could not be otherwise. It is impossible to suppose any one holding with any firmness views, on the maintenance of which he conscientiously believes that the best interests of his country, the virtue, the morality of his children, of his family, in short, of everybody, are involved, consenting to hear them impugned with the same *sangfroid* as he would listen to doubts as to whether or not Jupiter be inhabited, — though even *that*, it seems, from recent experience, requires some patience on the part of controvertists who take the other side! Take, for example, the case of the theist as opposed to the atheist. It is quite certain that any devout theist believes in the existence and intimate presence of a Personality unspeakably more worthy, in his estimation, of veneration and affection, than the dearest earthly friend. He might be quite willing, for what he deemed the truth's sake, to enter into discussion as to whether such a Being exists, though even *that* is painful to him; and it is best done, where it generally is done, in books, and without personal collision. But it can hardly be expected, because it is hardly possible, that he should permit any unnecessary communion with an atheist; it is reasonable that he should keep himself as much as possible out of the atheist's company, and take care that all over whom he has any control should be kept out of it too. Mr. Mill may say, perhaps, that this is very illiberal; we reply that it follows, naturally and necessarily, from the man's views of the moral importance of the doctrine he holds and the pernicious consequences of the contrary doctrine. It is in vain to say, 'Yes; but these views of the moral importance of such doctrine have led to legal persecution — to burning men's bodies for the good of their souls;' for it is conceded that the atheist is at liberty to publish doctrines as loudly and as widely as he pleases; we vindicate his full liberty; but we can go no further without impairing the liberty of *others*. We cannot prevent the natural expressions of aversion which doctrine so obnoxious to the generality of mankind must produce. Be it recollected that a sincere theist would sooner hear his dearest friend calumniated, his father's or his mother's honour assailed, than the existence of that Infinitely Good Being in whom he believes, called in

question; above all, lightly and scornfully. If we vindicate him
for showing the liveliest feelings of indignation or aversion in
the former cases — we mean, of course, within the limits of law
— can we blame him in the latter? To suppose a theist quite
unmoved in the matter would be to suppose that he was really
in a state of scepticism or indifferentism; a state which, as it
seems to us, the sort of moral toleration which Mr. Mill's
theory requires, necessarily presupposes, or would infallibly
lead to.

Take, again, the case of a sincere Christian. He believes, if
really such, that to Christ, as a personal Friend, he is more
indebted than to all other friends put together; that neither
'father nor mother, nor sister nor brother,' can or ought to
come into competition with Him as to claims upon trust and
devoted affection. We are not speaking about the justness of
these convictions, (though of course we believe it,) for it makes
nothing to the argument; for an illustration drawn from a
sincere Mussulman's regard for Mahomet — provided he
would allow (as *we* would) everybody else to be, and to avow
himself of what religion he pleased — would equally answer
our purpose. But, to keep to the case of the Christian; how is it
possible for such a man to listen to the arguments which
declare that this greatest of all Benefactors is an impostor, or a
fanatic, — or the history which records Christ's life and
sustains the disciples' faith a forgery or fiction; arguments
tending to destroy that which he believes to be the most
precious heritage of humanity, without the strongest revulsion
of feeling; without endeavouring to draw a *cordon sanitaire*
around his children, his family, and his dependents, and
insulating them from what he deems a moral pestilence? He
may be perfectly willing that those who hold the above views of
Christianity should be free to express and publish their
sentiments, and get anybody to read that will. But he must
equally use *his* liberty of closing his own ears, and as many
more pairs of ears as he can against them. To suppose
otherwise, is again to suppose that the man really does not
believe what he professes to believe; that he is in a state of
indifferentism with regard to the truths which he can so lightly
hear contested.

And so it must be with every other opinion which men
conscientiously believe involves the vital interests of society and
humanity. So far as the liberty of publishing obnoxious

opinions is concerned, there is no question; no legal penalties whatever should be attached to this act. But similar liberty, on the other side, implies that men so publishing must be prepared to face all that opposition on the part of society which Mr. Mill (if we understand some of his representations) would regard as a sort of moral persecution; while yet in other passages, as we have seen, he seems to allow to society the right innocently to do all which really involves it; — so fruitless, because so unpractical, seems to us this discussion.

Mr. Mill argues that the majority should be more willing to give a ready hearing to opinions accounted 'heretical,' inasmuch as those who hold them, being the minority, are generally a much weaker party. This is a very good reason why they should be permitted to express them to as many as they can induce to listen to them; but no reason at all why, if their doctrines by thought pernicious by the bulk of the community, the moral repression should not be stringently exerted. Numbers have nothing to do with this question; if it has, then a single individual, though holding the most ludicrous and pernicious moral paradox, ought to be heard with most patience and indulgence. This is not an appeal to reason, but an *argumentum ad misericordiam*. The degree in which the moral repression, so often spoken of, is exerted, will depend on quite other things; its energy will be simply in proportion to the degree in which doctrines are sincerely deemed — wrongly or not — deleterious to truth and man's well-being; and it must be so unless, as we have said, the community has already become really callous to the importance and significance of the views it professedly holds, and has already resolved on betraying the citadel while nominally manning its walls.

Nor, again, must it be forgotten that the terms on which the parties usually meet are not equal. It is generally but too easy for him who takes the *negative* side to be perfectly tolerant of the opinions of his neighbour, and to be most philosophically calm, that is, indifferent, whether his reasonings are accepted or rejected. 'Vacuus viator cantat;' he who believes that all religions are equally false, or none certainly true, is, no doubt, well qualified by his scepticism to hear with edifying impartiality the arguments for any, and in turn to dispute smilingly against all. The thing does not, in his esteem, involve any consequence which should ruffle his feelings, or disturb the serenity of his Pyrrhonism. The same reasons make him comparatively indifferent about proselytism; and though he is, like all human creatures, not quite indifferent on that point, he is usually quite unwilling to run any great hazards of loss of reputation, or 'the cold shoulder' from his friends, by indiscreet avowals. Hence it is that infidelity not infrequently exists, as Mr. Mill affirms, among those who are not suspected of it by the world, but perfectly known to be infidels among their intimate friends. A negative creed has always tended to form this Nicodemus sect of disciples — men who come to visit the oracle by night, and are reluctant to visit it by day. This species of moral cowardice is very naturally connected with a creed that cannot easily stir enthusiasm, far less make men willing to be martyrs for it. But if, (perfect liberty of speech and expression being granted them,) men cannot prevail upon themselves to endure even the moral stigma of preaching unwelcome doctrine, we see not such merit in this negative creed as to make us carpet the rough road by which all triumphant truth has hitherto trudged its way in the world.

But now, let a man believe any religion to be true and divinely revealed, and his whole position is essentially changed.

In like manner, the theist and the atheist cannot meet on equal terms. The atheist has no profound emotions stirred by his stolid Fate, or his capricious Chance. It is not a person, but an abstraction, that is in question. But, in the sincere theist's estimation, the atheist's dogmas are necessarily more hard to bear than any amount of personal abuse. It is impossible for the atheist 'earnestly to contend' for such a faith as terminates in an abstract 'law,' from which all idea of a Personal Lawgiver has been somehow eliminated, and he can afford, if need be, to be silent about it; and therefore would generally prefer a diatribe against the hardships of any man's being thought the worse of for holding such sentiments to a courageous avowal and defence of them — courage which almost all religions, however false, can inspire, but which a negative creed seldom teaches. Hence the pleas for a more easy style of proselytism.

But the test is inevitable; and those who hold sceptical or negative views, if they wish them to prevail, must learn to face the ordeal — it is very moderate in our days — of being at least active missionaries and confessors, and, if need be, moral 'martyrs;' that is, so far as the title can be earned by merely allowing their neighbours to exercise the undoubted right of disregarding or despising their claims.[2]

Again; we can hardly suppose the world at large really acting on some of the principles here laid down, if we suppose them to hold any previous convictions at all; either a general state of doubt must be presupposed to make men thus act, or an incipient treachery to their convictions, which must tend to such a sceptical state. If we understand Mr. Mill, no man has a full right to rest satisfied with his opinions unless he has examined, and is prepared to refute, every objection that can be brought against them. We suspect that even if they recognised any such principle, men would much sooner practise silence on all sides, that is, become indifferent to the truth, rather than live such a life of logical torments. But let us hear Mr. Mill: 'However unwillingly a person who has a strong opinion may admit the possibility that his opinion may be false, he ought to be moved by the consideration that, however true it may be, if it is not fully, frequently, and fearlessly discussed, it will be held as a dead dogma, not a living truth.' (p. 64.)

Again:—

'A man who knows only his own side of the case, knows little of that, *His reasons may be good, and no one may have been able to refute them*. But, if he is equally unable to refute the reasons on the opposite side, if he does not so much as know what they are, he has no ground for preferring either opinion. The rational position for him would be suspension of judgment. . . . Nor is it enough that he should hear the arguments of adversaries from his own teachers, presented as they teach them, and accompanied by what they offer as refutations. That is not the way to do justice to the arguments, or bring them into real contact with his own mind. He must be able to hear them from persons who actually believe them. . . . He must know them in their most plausible and persuasive form.' (p. 67.)

---

2   We observe that some writers of our day think that Mr. Mill's doctrines ought to be carried much further before a true freedom can be enjoyed. 'Bibliolatry,' we observe, they denounce as a tyranny great as that of the Papal authority which the Reformers abjured. They forget that this 'Bibliolatry,' let them suppose it ever so much an error, happens to be *voluntary*, and the Papal yoke was *compulsory*, which makes all the difference. But many infidels write as though they thought it tyranny over *them* that *we* persist in believing the Bible to be authoritative.

Query. May not a man be justly a believer in the Copernican theory without knowing a tenth of what *may* be said for the Ptolomaic? Or reject the Mahometan religion, without knowing a twentieth of what is said for it? If not, we fear that, whether men be atheists or theists, Christians or infidels — in short, hold any opinion or the contrary (out of the mathematics) — there is not a single well-grounded opinion in the world, and never will be.

However, we must be content to deal with the possible; and if men were ever so willing to entertain all objections, lest haply there should be some they had never met with, and could not refute, and so their opinions be vitiated, the necessities of life will not permit this logical Quixotry. Let us suppose a man, for example, fully convinced of the truth of Christianity, after reading one or two (or one, if you please) of the best works for it and against it, is he to renew the examination every time a new theory is started, or an old one better stated? That is, is he to peruse every treatise which promises anything of novelty in the objections, before he is fully warranted to repose upon his conclusions, and act upon them with undoubting confidence? Is he to regard his 'rational position,' that of 'suspension of judgment?' Observe, we do not say that, if he has difficulties, he should not endeavour to settle them; let him do so if he can; but if he has none, or if what he has cannot, he believes, affect the balance of evidence on which he has already once deliberately decided, is he yet to reopen the question to everybody who summons his attention to a new light? If so, he would never have the chance of a stable conviction. The controversy has been carried on for the last eighteen hundred years, and it cannot be said (though the arguments of infidelity have been repeated *ad nauseam*) that some new objections are not found out, and from time to time propounded to the world. May not a man act on the assumption that he has moral certainty until he has actually done far less than examine and refute all the objections that have been discovered even up to this time? If not, we suppose it must fare much the same with every form of infidelity also; for there is no lack of new objections for the infidel to examine! And indeed it must be the same with every form, whether of truth or error, for not one man in a million has leisure or ability to obtain this sort of knowledge of the grounds of his opinions, — certainly not in any of the professions, law or physic, for example, — on which, nevertheless, it is imperative that a man should act. The very attempt of men of all opinions thus to verify them would soon lead, in weariness, to the habit of scepticism to which we have so often alluded, and indispose to action in the same proportion; *or* to a condition of universal and intolerable wrangling and contention, which would make the world a positive nuisance, and which would equally impede action by consuming in debate the time which should be given to action.

What, then, we ask, is a man who has fairly examined evidence, and is fully convinced of the justice of his opinions, to do? Must he always be repeating the process when he finds that something has been said which he either had not seen, though said before, or is said now for the first time? Human life is not sufficient for this otiose investigation. If this sort of examination is obligatory, 'never ending, still beginning,' the condition of the inquirer under this 'law of liberty' seems, after all, about as happy as that accorded to us by some of the High Churchmen, who concede the right of 'private judgment' in words, but, at the same time, deny the thing. It is a right to *inquire*, they say, but only to come at last to a foregone conclusion. Are you satisfied that *that* is true which they think not so? 'Inquire again, dear neophyte,' they say. You inquire again, and come back in the same mind. Still the remedy is the same. Meantime, it is pretty plain that the unhappy inquirer will never, in the estimate of his High Church oracle, have inquired enough, till he has inquired himself into the belief of the said oracle. We shrewdly suspect it would be much the same with any one who conceived that it was his duty to listen candidly to every form of novel objection to his views which any opponent could manage to invent. He would rarely be found to have inquired enough, till he had conspicuously signalized his logic and candour by adopting the views of his opponent.

And even if a perfectly prompt and equally courteous hospitality to all sort of opinions could be exercised without implying culpable indifference to them all, many may, even on Mr. Mill's own showing, doubt whether it would be good for Truth to have this fair-weather passage through the world. Mr. Mill contends that, as a general fact, all dogmas are the most vigorous when militant — while they are being fought for; and that as soon as the truth is established, and at last universally acquiesced in, that moment it is apt to be forgotten.

'It is illustrated in the experience of almost all ethical doctrines and religious creeds. They are all full of meaning and vitality to those who originate them, and to the direct disciples of the originators. Their meaning continues to be felt in undiminished strength, and is perhaps brought out into even fuller consciousness, so long as the struggle lasts to give the doctrine or creed an ascendancy over other creeds. . . . From this time may usually be dated the decline of the living power of the doctrine. We often hear the teachers of all creeds lamenting the difficulty of keeping up in the minds of believers a lively apprehension of the truth which they nominally recognise, so that it may penetrate the feelings and acquire a real mastery over the conduct. No such difficulty is complained of while the creed is fighting for its existence; even the weaker combatants then know and feel what they are fighting for, and the difference between it and other doctrines.' (pp. 72, 73.)

From these sentiments, taken in their literality, one would imagine that it was best that truth should never be established at all; that, like the fox, it was worth nothng but to be chased; made, not to be eaten, but to be hunted. For, according to this doctrine, at least those who contend for a truth are in earnest about it, while, once hunted down, friends and foes give it the slip altogether. But against such inferences from his doctrine Mr. Mill guards himslef (pp. 79, 80), though we cannot honestly say that the harmony of his statements is altogether made out.

But, whether the extreme inference is more in consistency with Mr. Mill's general principles, or his disclaimer of it, we cannot now stay to inquire. Meantime, experience at least teaches thus much; that the actual establishment of any unwelcome dogma is not to be effected without much struggle and contention, and that, while compelled to fight for a footing, and to face at least the moderate obstacle which is implied in the expressed aversion of those who do not sympathize with it, it is apt to gather strength,because really earnest emotion is involved in the matter. It would not, therefore, be well that any patron of a novelty should have that luxurious and easy course, which the complete ascendancy of the principles of this Essay would secure for him. He would certainly stand a poor chance if the principles of that same

Essay be true; since it seems that it is only while in some degree
'militant' that any novel truth — or falsity — can gather omens
of success.

Mr. Mill pleads thus strongly on behalf of those whose
'reticence,' as regards certain opinions, is the effect of their
timidity — a fear of a too stringent public opinion. He tells
us —

> 'Our merely social intolerence kills no one, roots out no
> opinions, but induces men to disguise them, or to abstain
> from any active effort for their diffusion. With us heretical
> opinions do not perceptibly gain, or even lose, ground in
> each decade or generation; they never blaze out far and wide,
> but continue to smoulder, in the narrow circles of thinking
> and studious persons, among whom they originate, without
> ever lighting up the general affairs of mankind with either a
> true or a deceptive light. And thus is kept up a state of things
> very satisfactory to some minds, because, without the
> unpleasant process of fining or imprisoning anybody, it
> maintains all prevailing opinions outwardly undisturbed,
> while it does not absolutely interdict the exercise of reason
> by dissentients afflicted with the malady of thought. A
> convenient plan for having peace in the intellectual world,
> and keeping all things going on therein very much as they do
> already. But the price paid for this sort of intellectual
> pacification is the sacrifice of the entire moral courage of the
> human mind.' (pp. 59, 60.)

The last sentence is certainly a singlular paradox. It is a new
thought that 'moral courage' is *sacrificed* by the circumstances
which test its presence or show that it does *not* exist, and that it
will exist and be manifested so soon as there is no occasion for
it! The state of things which demands a little moral pluck —
and it is *very* little that is asked in the present day — may be
bad or good; but assuredly it is not answerable for *extinguish-
ing* the courage which will only be brave when there is nothing
to be faced. It may reveal the cowardice of the 'heretics' who
dare not speak, but certainly does not quench their zeal; for
that, *ex hypothesi*, must be non-existent.

For our own parts, we confess we have no faith in any
apostle who, when relieved from all fear of legal pains and
penalties for the expression of opinion, is so great a 'coward'
that he dares not face prejudice or scorn, for what he deems

important truth. In general, where there is any earnestness in behalf of any truth people are ready enough to confront these things. Mr. Mill, indeed, tells us that we do not know what we lose by the 'reticence' of those who hold what society would deem 'heretical' opinions; and we quite admit that we do not know, nor are likely to know, unless they speak; but, for our own parts, we are quite ready to put up with that loss, whatever it is, if the price to be paid for their speaking be a general habit of hearing any opinions, seem they ever so pernicious, with the same ceremonious indifference. There are limits to suavity in these matters which Mr. Mill's negative creed, we imagine, does not give him a due conception of.

It is curious to see how Mr. Mill really concedes the impossibility of dealing with the hardship, if it be one, to which his argument seems mainly directly — that repressive action of society against certain opinions which arise out of its general repugnance to them. Of intemperate language and vituperation, though often the most definite and specific form in which aversion to such and such opinions is manifested, he truly says that it is generally impossible to deal with it, and to 'bring it home' to a man. We apprehend that just the same will be found of every other mode in which, where liberty of thought and expression is fully allowed, men will show their displeasure at novel heterodoxy, or what they deem such. He says (p. 96):—

> 'Undoubtedly, the manner of asserting an opinion, then, though it may be a true one, may be very objectionable, and may justly incur severe censure. But the principal offences of the kind are such as it is mostly impossible, unless by accidental self-betrayal, to bring home to conviction. The gravest of them is, to argue sophistically, to suppress facts or arguments, to misstate the elements of the case, or misrepresent the opposite opinion. But all this, even to the most aggravated degree, is so continually done in perfect good faith by persons who are not considered, and in many respects may not deserve to be considered, ignorant or incompetent, that it is rarely possible, on adequate grounds, conscientiously to stamp the misrepresentation as morally culpable; and still less could we presume to interfere with this kind of controversial misconduct.' (pp. 96, 97.)

There is one speculation of Mr. Mill on which we must say a

few words. However plausible in general, its application to our own day seems more than questionable; contradicted, in fact, in the most emphatic manner by all the phenomena around us. He says that high civilization tends in a certain degree to make men all alike — to repress unduly the manifestations of individuality and spontaneity, and to operate prejudicially by inducing men to stifle their genuine sentiments and convictions, and to think and act just as the majority about them are thinking and acting; in other words, to yield to what some would perhaps call the 'tyranny of society.' We should indeed demur to call it by such a name; we should rather visit it on the *individual*, and say the tendency originated in mere indolent love of quiet or in moral cowardice. But as to the *fact*, that there is generally some such tendency in high civilization, we should not care to deny it. And we may remark, that if anything could *increase* it, it would be a too solicitous courtesy in listening to the expression of all sorts of sentiments — even those most abhorrent from our deepest convictions of truth. It *is* one of the characteristics of the high conventional regard for the feelings of others engendered by much social refinement, that men only too often *suppress* what they deem unpalatable truths. Let there be no opinions so unpalatable that everybody will not be perfectly at his ease in listening to and expressing them, and it could only be by the prevalence of a general indifferentism. If there could be an unreserved expression without giving offence to others of any and of all kinds of opinions (though it is just as likely that people would hold their tongues from the same indifferentism), it could only be because society had already arrived at the *ne plus ultra* of the alleged ill effects of a high civilization; could listen with equal and imperturbable calmness in the spirit of the required mental freedom, only because it was indifferent to all opinions, and because strong '*individualism*' had ceased to exist. The result of *this* kind of freedom would be mainly favourable to every species of scepticism. Whether the sceptic succeeded in imposing silence on all such subjects, or induced society in general to listen to the unrestrained expression of opinion without any wincing or vehement reclamation, the business of the propagandist of scepticism would be equally well done.

But, whatever may be the general effect of a high civilization, with its multitudinous conventional restraints, in repressing an exuberant 'individuality' (and we are fully disposed to think that the *general* effect is as Mr. Mill states it), there does seem something droll in the notion that these repressive tendencies are at all a feature of the present day. On the contrary, we should say that never, since the world began, so far as history informs us, has there been an epoch distinguished by a greater *flush* of all sorts of opinions, even the most reckless and absurd. We can hardly see the 'green ground' in Truth's meadow for the dandelions, thistles, and poppies that have sprung up in it. Never has there been a period in which men have either given expression to a greater number of speculative monstrosities, or avowed them with greater freedom or more enviable superiority to modesty and shame. Why, there is hardly an extravagance, in either political or theological speculation, from the extremes of Communism to Despotism, from the extremes of Atheism and Pantheism to Mormonism — no folly of pseudo-philosophy, from Table-turning and Spirit-rapping to Biology and Clairvoyance, that has not graced our era. The present age, in Germany and in England, exhibits a perfect Babel of opinions. As *we* read the present day, every eccentricity of speculation seems obtruded on the world without a thought of patient investigation, or any attempt to ascertain whether it is worth while to plague the world with it at all; every man has a 'psalm,' every man a 'doctrine,' of his own, and incontinently sings the one and says the other in the ears of the unfortunate public. It is, in truth, a very Pentecost of the spirit of speculative error, with the correspondent 'gift of tongues.' We do think that for the present, 'individualism,' at least in the direction of *speculation*, inflicts far more on society than society inflicts on it.

BENTLEY'S QUARTERLY REVIEW
Vol. 2, 1860
[R. W. Church]

Mill on Liberty[1]

Every one who feels interest in truth, and who tries to 'enlighten his practice by philosophical meditation,' must feel thankful when a bold and powerful thinker like Mr. J. S. Mill takes in hand one of those latent but embarrassing difficulties, which few think of putting into words, but which underlie whole tracts of discussion, and are for ever coming up in the commonest questions of practical life. We run against them, or they against us, at any moment: but because they are so common, and we feel sure that they must occur to every one round us — and yet no one seems to think them worth special notice — we fancy them too trivial to be made the distinct subject of our thoughts, and allow the feeling of the difficulty to haunt us obscurely, and often to inflict an indefinite but serious sense of dull worry. One of these usually unanalyzed difficulties is the question, which most people must have practically encountered some time or another, of the influence to be exercised by any means short of or beyond direct argument, on other people. In the present Essay, Mr. Mill undertakes to discuss this question, or, as he states it in its broadest terms, 'the nature and limits of the power which can be legitimately exercised by society on the individual.'

The value of such an attempt is not to be measured simply by the conclusions arrived at. A man must be very sanguine who should expect to see a question, which he must have found for ever recurring in human history and pervading his own experience, closed and settled, even by a thinker like Mr. Mill. Only very young speculators, who, in their earliest attempts at thought, turn in their simplicity to logic, or to Locke on the 'Conduct of the Understanding,' for an infallible specific which

---

[1] *On Liberty.* By John Stuart Mill. London: J. W. Parker and Son. 1859

shall insure their thinking and reasoning right, believe that such final solutions are anywhere to be looked for. At any rate, only those who are very easily satisfied, or are very servile admirers, will admit that it has been arrived at in Mr. Mill's Essay. The gain is in the treatment of such a subject at all by one so competent to handle it. The distinctness, the daring, the vigour of the discussion, the novelty which it throws round what is old and trite, the reality into which it quickens what is inert and torpid, even the peril and menace which it not obscurely discloses to convictions which may be matters of life and death to us, act as a tonic to the mind, and awaken, exercise, and brace it, even if they do not, as they well may, elevate the heart and widen the range of its ordinary contemplations. The reading of a book like this ought to be an event in a man's mental history. It is a challenge to him to analyze much that is vague and confused in his thoughts and current notions; and it is at the same time a help and guide in the process, by presenting the problem itself as conceived by a mind of greater than average reach and clearness. The discussion is important, too, in other ways, whether or not we are convinced by its argument, or even whether we can get any satisfactory and consistent answer to the question at all; for it shows us the term to which difficulty and inquiry have reached on the subject, on what scale the debate has to be carried on, and under what conditions; and, possibly, within what limits an approximately sufficient truth may be hoped for at present. It is both interesting and important as a measure of the grasp and strength of one of the foremost thinkers of his time. And perhaps its use is not the least, if it teaches us something more vividly of the real power or inability of the human mind to penetrate and master the complicated elements of our social state, and of its success in bringing them into a harmony, which we can feel to be both philosophically complete and also answering to the fact.

The subject of social liberty may be said to belong by special appropriateness to Mr. Mill, and to have a natural claim on him for a thorough sifting. Mr. Mill, as every one knows, regards democracy as the inevitable and beneficial result to which society is everywhere tending. In this he is not singular; but he differs from the majority of those who think with him, in the great clearness with which he discerns the probability, and in the extreme uneasiness with which he regards it, that as the dangers of political oppression of the many by the few disappear, the dangers of social oppression of the few by the many will increase. The foresight of this result does not, indeed, in any degree shake his full faith in the democratic principle; but it presents a serious abatement of the benefit which he hopes from it, and he loses no opportunity to show his ever-present sense of the danger, and of the necessity of providing means to counteract it. No one can have looked through the collection recently published of his review articles, extending over a considerable period, without observing how early he became alive to the substantial magnitude of the peril to individual freedom which seems to wait of necessity on the triumph of the power of the majority, and how continually this menace recurs to his mind, as the dark shadow attending on it, and as the heavy price to be paid for it. It is true, he notices with a sarcasm Sir Robert Peel's use of De Tocqueville's phrase, 'the tyranny of the majority.' But into no man's mind has the import of the phrase sunk more deeply than into his own, and no one's words sound more impressive to us, in bidding us watch its nascent influence and be prepared against its more formidable growths. But hitherto his allusions to the subject, though full of meaning, have been incidental; and so serious a matter required to be treated by itself. The question as relating to the great concomitant drawback to a progress, otherwise as promising as it is certain, deserved special examination from one to whom, both as a philosopher and as a practical man, the acceleration of that progress had been the object of life. What Mr. Mill has written on the political tendencies and prospects of these times would not be complete without a full discussion of the most menacing tendency of future democracy; one which, if predominant, would kill all improvement even more surely and relentlessly than the old-fashioned tyrannies. The Essay on Liberty may be regarded as a democrat's protest against the claim of the masses, sure to be advanced, in proportion as they grow stronger, to impose their opinion and will without appeal, and to beat down and trample out all self-assertion and independence in minorities and individuals. One who hopes everything from popular ascendancy also fears it, and tries beforehand to establish in the opinion of society some well-recognized line round private life and private freedom, before the foreseen power of democracy arrives, to invade and confound all limits by blind usurpations to which there can be no resistance, and by a wayward but inexorable interference from which there will be no escape.

But Mr. Mill's aim is not wholly prospective. He thinks that the control of society over individual opinion and action is at present far too stringent; that it is illegitimate and exorbitant in its pretensions and mischievous in its effects. And as he is markedly distinguished from the common run of representatives of liberal doctrines in another point besides the one just alluded to, that is, in thinking very meanly of the men, the society, and the opinions of this generation, and in holding cheap the measure of improvement to which it has reached, he finds the yoke all the more intolerable. His Essay is directed not only to provide against anticipated dangers, but to abate what he feels to be an existing evil. Having but little respect for the opinions which hold sway over present society, and which it sanctions and arms with its influence, he is anxious at once to cut from under them the ground on which their power over the separate units of society rests. The path of thought and truth and individual development is, he holds, miserably encumbered with ignoble entanglements, with maiming and crippling snares, with arbitrary and cruel restrictions, arising out of the interferences of society and the deference or the fear which it inspires. It is the purpose of his Essay to reduce within much narrower limits these customary and hitherto recognized rights of interference, as he finds them exercised now; and to lay down a rule for the jurisdiction of society over the individual, grounded on a clear and definite principle; lightening the weight with which society presses on its members, and destroying the prerogative by which its accidentally prevailing opinions impose themselves with irritating or degrading peremptoriness on those who wish to have, or ought to have, opinions of their own.

His claim for individual liberty is of the very broadest, and involves serious consequences. Adopting William Von Humboldt's maxim, that the great purpose of government and society is the completest development of the individual, according to his own proper nature and tendencies, he demands for the individual every liberty compatible with the same liberty in others, and with the preservation of that society which alone makes any real liberty possible. After remarking that in laying down the limits between individual liberty and social control 'almost everything yet remains to be done,' and

that 'in general, those who have been most in advance of
society in thought and feeling' have left 'the present state of
things unassailed in principle, however, they may have come
into contact with it in some of its details' — occupying
themselves rather 'in inquiring what things society ought to like
or dislike, than in questioning whether its likings or dislikings
should be a rule to individuals' — he thus states his principle:—

> 'The object of this Essay is to assert one very simple
> principle, as entitled to govern absolutely the dealings of
> society with the individual in the way of compulsion and
> control, whether the means used be physical force in the
> form of legal penalties, or the moral coercion of public
> opinion. That principle is, that the sole end for which
> mankind are warranted, individually or collectively, in
> interfering with the liberty of action of any of their number,
> is self-protection. That the only purpose for which power
> can be rightfully exercised over any member of a civilized
> community, against his will, is to prevent harm to others.
> His own good, either physical or moral, is not a sufficient
> warrant. He cannot rightfully be compelled to do or forbear,
> because it will be better for him to do so, because it will
> make him happier, because, in the opinion of others, to do
> so would be wise or even right. These are good reasons for
> remonstrating with him, or reasoning with him, or persuad-
> ing him, or entreating him, but not for compelling him, or
> visiting him with evil in case he do otherwise. To justify that,
> the conduct from which it is desired to deter him, must be
> calculated to produce evil to some one else. The only part of
> the conduct of any one, for which he is amenable to society,
> is that which concerns others. In the part which merely
> concerns himself, his independence is, of right, absolute.
> Over himself, over his own body and mind, the individual is
> sovereign.' — Pp. 21, 22.

Such a statement is vague and ambiguous enough, and may
mean very different things according to the extent given to its
limiting terms: and this vagueness, inevitable, perhaps, from
the nature of the terms employed, attaches, as it seems to us, to
all Mr. Mill's attempts to lay down the formula of the liberty
for which he contends. But if the abstract statement might be
accepted by many of very different ways of thinking, his own
conception and application of this principle are plain enough.

In his view, society as it now exists, and by the maxims on which it acts, crushes and dwarfs the individual. There was a time when the individual was too strong for society, and by his lawlessness, self-will, or merely by the excessive accumulation of power in his hands, set at nought its fair influence, and hindered its healthy growth. But that time, in England at least, is long past. Society for many centuries has been slowly and surely gaining on the individual, till it has come at last to be, not merely his protector but his taskmaster, pedagogue, and even Pope, It has established a hold on his thoughts, opinions, and belief, justifiable only on a claim to infallibility. It has formed a number of moulds for his character and plan of life, and of some one or other of these it compels him to make his choice, as the shape into which he is to force and squeeze his whole nature. The individual, according to the received understanding as to its rights and its claims to submission, has no chance with society. Neither has he any escape from it. It is everywhere: it surrounds him: it penetrates into his own retirement, cows his reason, unnerves his own self-reliance, discredits and shakes his faith in his own clearest convictions, intimidates his purest purposes. Conscious of its invisible presence, he dares not think, he dares not like, as he would. Society 'executes its own mandates;' and its penalties as they are more elastic and comprehensive than those of law, so are they more exquisitely adapted to their end, for they reach the soul and subjugate the will. Mr. Mill does not stint the strength of his words in characterizing the effect of this despotism of society. If we did not remember that he writes in view of a very high ideal, we should find it hard to resist the continual impression that his language, though it might be very well in a satire, a sermon, or a novel, is singularly unmeasured for a grave discussion of one of the most complicated questions of human life. It is the sort of view which recommends itself to a mind with a twist in it, or with a humour of its own, a view which we bear with as being its humour, not as if it were even meant to be taken as true. We might almost fancy, at times, that we were reading a description of some debased or declining condition of society, such as is popularly supposed to have been in the later ages of Rome or of the Greek empire. Men accept dogmas, but do not believe. They conform, but they disguise their doubts. They are afraid of contesting, but not ashamed of not caring. They submit to an unexamined morality, not from conviction but from tameness. They echo the cry of improvement, without knowing what improvement is. They have left off their fathers' vices, but have lost their fathers' strength. Their standard is high, but their conscience is torpid. They do good, but they do not do it well. There is a level average disposition to what is right, but no character. They hold themselves bound to the paths which they find laid out, but excused from the labour, almost forbidden the glory, of striking out nobler ones. Custom is never too heavy a burden on them, but reasons, and the questioning of custom are. What energy there is, is absorbed in business, with a little residuum for philanthropic 'hobbies.' The world is full of 'a multitude of promising intellects combined with timid characters,' who dare not pursue any difficult subject, lest it should land them in what seem immoral or irreligious consequences. England is no longer 'a place for mental freedom;' and the 'open fearless characters and logical consistent intellects have disappeared, who once adorned the thinking world.' We are at peace, but 'the price paid for this intellectual pacification is the sacrifice of the entire moral courage of the human mind.' Afraid of energy and individual impulses in their genuine strength, we 'reject the stuff of which heroes are made;' we 'lose all that is rich, diversified, and animating in human life' — all that 'strengthens the tie which binds any individual to the race, by making the race itself infinitely better worth belonging to.' 'The men and women who at present inhabit the more civilized parts of the world,' he writes, 'are but starved specimens of what nature can and will produce.' His hopes are but limited as to what the existing generation can do for that which is to succeed it, to make them wise and good, 'because it is itself so lamentably deficient in goodness and wisdom.' A dark shadow rests on the present and future of English society. 'The greatness of England is now all collective: individually small, we only appear capable of anything great by our habit of combining; and with this our moral and religious philanthropists are perfectly contented. But it was men of another stamp than this that made England what it is; and men of another stamp will be needed to prevent its decline.'

These are incidental, but not less significant expressions of a conviction which evidently is one of the deepest and most pervading in the mind of the writer. We will add at full length a passage, written expressly to enforce the same idea.

'In our times, from the highest class of society down to the lowest, every one lives as under the eye of a hostile and dreaded censorship. Not only in what concerns others, but in what concerns only themselves, the individual, or the family, do not ask themselves — What do I prefer? or, What would suit my character and disposition? or, What would allow the best and highest in me to have fair play, and enable it to grow and thrive? They ask themselves — What is suitable to my position? What is usually done by persons of my station or pecuniary circumstances? or, (worse still), What is usually done by persons of a station and circumstances superior to mine? I do not mean that they choose what is customary, in preference to what suits their own inclination. It does not occur to them to have any inclination, except for what is customary. Thus the mind itself is bowed to the yoke: even in what people do for pleasure, conformity is the first thing thought of; they like in crowds; they exercise choice only among things commonly done: peculiarity of taste, eccentricity of conduct, are shunned equally with crimes; until by dint of not following their own nature, they have no nature to follow; their human capacities are withered and starved: they become incapable of any strong wishes or native pleasures, and are generally without either opinions or feelings of home growth, or properly their own. Now is this, or is it not, the desirable condition of human nature?' — P. 110.

Such statements, so remarkably opposed to all that ordinarily meets us of judgments on our time, and coming from a writer who shows every disposition to weigh his words, are matters for serious thought. We are no doubt sufficiently well satisfied with ourselves to hear with advantage some plain and stern speaking. Similar statements, in other schools of thought, have before now been severely judged, as evidence of a reactionary spirit, and disloyalty to the present. Against Mr. Mill there can be no such suspicion. But even from such a writer, a picture so highly charged excites suspicion. It may certainly turn out to be the result of a more perspicacious and more comprehensive review of the facts of society than ordinary men can at first appreciate. But there seems in it oversight, and overstatement. Great classes of facts, passed over in it, rise up to our minds, which require to be taken notice of and allowed their weight in any account which claims to correspond to the real truth. The contrast, indeed, between the men of this day and those of days past and to come, is a very hazardous one for any man to make who is of the generation which he assumes to judge. He must be very confident in his power of placing himself at a mental distance from it; very confident in his superiority to secret disappointments and disgusts, very confident in his power to disabuse his judgment of the influence exerted by the crowd of petty familiar details which lower the living, and by the illusions which magnify the dead; of his power to make just allowance for the actual, and just abatements from the ideal and the possible, — to be able to pronounce a judgment of real weight on the comparative place which his age holds along with others. Whether we are better or worse, whether we have more or less character, than other times, we really cannot tell: it seems to us a fruitless and insoluble question. But we can ascertain something positive of what is going on round us; and on this ground it seems to us that we recognize in Mr. Mill's picture but a partially true representation of what is. Custom is very powerful, but not omnipotent. The current which runs through society is neither so uniform nor so irresistible as he makes it. On the contrary, the face of society appears seamed and traversed in all directions by a vast number of currents, different in their course, strength, and tendencies, pressing on one another or violently conflicting; accelerating, diverting, retarding, with endlessly varying results from day to day; and, as in the sea and the atmosphere, each strong current infallibly provoking its balancing counter-current. Such a state of things is consistent with much respect for custom, but it is inconceivable without also a large amount of activity of mind and resistance to custom. We cannot help feeling that if in these later days we have seen many lamentable exhibitions of stupidity, selfishness, and lowness of mind and feeling, we have also witnessed scenes, and on no narrow scale, which for the wisdom, manliness, and self-devotion displayed in them, ought to have exempted the time from the unqualified charge of 'rejecting the stuff of which heroes are made.' At least they have done this: they have produced in the public mind, and in the literature which reflects, and by reflecting confirms, its impressions, a singularly hearty — many people think a one-sided — recognition of the worth of the bold, enterprising, self-reliant qualities of character. And in the domain of mind, a representation is surely not an adequate one which leaves behind the impression of a prevailing servility and submission to intimidation. To take one point, and that an important test — has criticism, the criticism which is most sought for and listened to, made no advance, in largeness, in fairness, in temperateness, in the manifestly sincere effort to discharge a judicial office in a judicial spirit? Is not the criticism which now finds favour, and is regarded as answering to its true ideal, one which shows the sense of responsibility, which conscientiously endeavours to appreciate the strength of an adverse case, which is not afraid of a fair statement on both sides, which admits instead of slurring over difficulties, which aims at expressing its own real thoughts modestly but with independent firmness? Are the past periods of history, or the marked characters which appear in them, examined and judged simply by our received beliefs about them, and by our own standard and ideas? or has the tendency set in with indubitable force, to re-open, where any call appeared; the most settled historical traditions, to search for and weigh with the utmost care all new evidence, to admit a reversal of the strongest prepossessions, to do the fullest justice and render the heartiest sympathy to men and times not only most different, but in spirit and rules of action most opposite to our own? A generation which has produced, and which has listened attentively to Mr. Carlyle, Mr. Froude, and Mr. Buckle, cannot be charged with shrinking blindly from independence of thought. Again, we have had some keen controversies. For some of them, Mr. Mill cannot be expected to feel much respect or interest; they probably appear to him as sad wastes of life and time, lamentable aberrations of mental power, which might have been more healthily and hopefully employed. But at least they are evidence against that stagnant condition of thought which he thinks so fatal and so characteristic of this time. There has been shown in them, that which he cannot find, a disposition to ask for reasons for what had been taken for granted, a refusal to be led by powerful popular prejudices, a readiness to accept and defend, on examination and supposed evidence, positions at once highly unpopular, and regarded as absolutely indefensible. At least there was some boldness and independence of mind in the course which, in Popery-hating England, has led so many educated Englishmen of our day, freely and on conviction, towards Rome or Romish ideas, to the utter sacrifice, in many cases, of that which Englishmen of any intellect value most, position and influence among their countrymen. Nor surely have ideas of another kind been refused a hearing, or remained without effect. Certainly no inconsiderable amount of the intellect of the country — we state it simply as a fact — is seeking for satisfaction and speaking its mind in a very free way; and, as far as we can see, if people listen with hesitation, and it may be with alarm, to bold and eventful speculation, do they as a body shut their ears to it, if it comes in a shape which challenges respect? Widely apart as the two men are, Mr. Francis Newman has left his mark on people's thoughts, as well as his brother of the Oratory. And we should have thought that any one who had watched the gradual moulding and transformations of public opinion, as far as they can be approximately judged of, would have recognized the imperceptible infiltration into it, the silent but sensible influence, and perhaps, at last, the unquestioned currency, of portions of those systems which are most antagonistic to the prevailing doctrines of society. No one acquainted with human nature, or the vital processes of human thought, will expect that people at large will surrender at once to a clever argument which they cannot answer, or to a commanding and compact system which is beyond their mental grasp, and defies their resources to overthrow. But in a state of things where there is thought stirring, even while they are holding out, they are moved. Mr. Mill must have lived long enough to have seen his contemporaries, not indeed turned into Benthamites, but distinctly and forcibly impressed by much of what Bentham said. The degree of readiness at the present time to canvass on their merits and to accept new doctrines, must be a matter of opinion. The characteristic cry of modern thought, in art as in literature, for the unconventional, the real, the true, the strong, may be a deception. We may be mistaken in thinking that there has been no lack of as bold experiment in writing, if not in life, as in any age. But we find it difficult to reconcile the aspect which society presents to our eyes with the sweeping statement of its slavery to custom, and indifference or indisposition to what is spontaneous and original, on which Mr. Mill's Essay is founded.

But however this may be, Mr. Mill's estimate of society as it is forms the pressing reason with him for calling attention to principles, which, true as he thinks them, at all times, are

especially necessary now. They are needed, he maintains, for
practical and immediate relief. Society actually presents
hindrances to the individual development which is the end of
life, and so, to that perfection of the race, which can only be
with that of the individual; and these hindrances must be met
by a strong and clear assertion of the principle of liberty. And
what is that principle? It is that in everything relating to
themselves as individuals, and to their own interests, men
ought, without any interference from society or other men,
from authority or from custom, to think and speak as they like,
to act as they like, and to combine among themselves as they
like. The only limit to this absolute liberty is, in other
individuals the same liberty; in society the right of self-
preservation. With respect to the liberty of thought, as it can in
itself, in Mr. Mill's view, infringe on no other rights, it does not
require limitation; and with it, is to be joined the liberty of
expressing thought, which, though not standing exactly on the
same ground, must practically go with it. The general grounds
on which he rests his principle, that no opinion ought to be
forbidden, and that any, or almost any, opposition to existing
opinion ought to be allowed, are — that since men, not being
infallible, cannot be certain, the forbidden opinion may be
true, or the protected opinion may be false and ought to be
overthrown; — that even if the protected opinion is true, as
men cannot know the truth of a true opinion without knowing
what can be said against it, opposition is needed to ascertain its
truth, and, as they are apt to go to sleep on a received opinion,
to give it life; — and, lastly, that since what is most probable is,
that the opposing opinions share the truth between them, and
each is partly true and partly false, the mixture cannot be sifted
otherwise than by liberty of discussion. To these he adds
special grounds, from what he considers the actual uncertainty
and imperfection of what are accounted the most unquestionable of protected opinions. He argues for unrestricted liberty of
action, on the ground that unless men are allowed to desire,
choose, and act for themselves, there is no possibility of
individual development and character; that experiment, in life
and conduct, is necessary as a test between good and bad; and
that even if customs are good ones, resistance to custom, *as
such*, is necessary, to prevent society from becoming stationary. But liberty of action is liable, in a way that liberty of
thought is not, to come into conflict with the wills, the interest,

the welfare of others. It must have limits; and these limits are, that in all cases directly affecting society or others, society may step in, by law or by opinion, to restrain liberty, or punish it if abused; but that in what relates, first, to acts of individuals regarding self, and next, to habits and dispositions, as such, society may not step in at all by law, and only partially by opinion, to control them. If men chose to ruin themselves by folly and excess, all that naturally results from our not liking them or despising them, they must be content to bear; but for these, which Mr. Mill will not call immoralities, direct and intentional social punishment is illegitimate. Against vices which directly threaten the interest of others, such as envy or avarice, we may deliberately direct our disapprobation and abhorrence, though we cannot make laws against them. To the objection that, in the long run, these private vices, though primarily only hurtful to the individual, do mischief to others and to society, by example and otherwise, he replies, that even so, it is a greater good, in the long run, to maintain liberty; that society has no business to be hard on what it could and ought to prevent by education; and that there is the enormous probability, that if it interferes, it will interfere wrongly. On the liberty of combination, which flows from the preceding positions, he only touches, in speaking of some of the practical applications of his doctrine.

The argument itself, both for liberty of thought and liberty of action, is nothing new. Its main points are common to all writers of the liberal school; what is remarkable in it is the vigour with which the chief reasons of this philosophy are condensed and brought to an edge, the formidable consistency and uncompromising completeness with which they are unfolded and connected with their consequences, and still more, perhaps, the moral colouring and earnestness which pervade the whole statement. Whether, even in Mr. Mill's hands, the liberal philosophy exhausts the facts and meets all the difficulties in human affairs, is doubtful. The perplexing jar of liberty and authority, of the uncertainty of knowledge and the necessity of action, still remains, even after Mr. Mill's trenchant method of settling it, a harsh and importunate discord, in human speculation as much as in human practice and society.

No one can undervalue the strength and clearness with which Mr. Mill has stated the argument for liberty of thought in its largest sense. If it leads to the unpleasant consequence, that society may do and is doing too much for what we hold to be truth in religion and morality, its ground, at least, in the fallibility of man is but too undeniable to any one who reflects either on himself or others. Opinions, says Mr. Mill, must neither be proscribed nor protected, because we none of us can be certain for others, however we may practically be for ourselves, that we are right: opinions must be left to find their level, persons must be left to make them out for themselves, because there is no public and universal test of certainty to which men can appeal against their opponents; and each man can but fall back, as the last resort, on his own reason. The elaborate and exhaustive reasoning with which Mr. Mill pursues this line of thought is good, as regards those who have the power, and on whom therefore falls the responsibility, of forming opinions. As between them, one man's reason must be held as good as another's, and the only possible way in which one opinion can fairly prevail over another is by balance of argument, which balance may be reversed to-morrow. All who appeal to reason must accept the known conditions of reason, must abide the consequences of their appeal, must admit the possibility of their being wrong, the possibility in theory, however it may seem not worth taking account of practically, of their strongest and most important convictions turning out unfounded. There are difficulties attending on this aspect of the case, even as regards those who do and can reason, which we should have liked to see noticed by Mr. Mill; not the least of them being, how that cautious consciousness of the conflict of probabilities which is forced on us by reason, is to be reconciled with the unhesitating will and earnestness which is the prime element of all high and successful action. But however the case may be to those who can think, what about those, who not only do not, but in honest truth cannot think?

If there are schools of opinion, which in treating practically of the conduct of life, would make authority its almost absolute guide, the tendency in the opposite ones is to treat the same subjects as if training, capacity, and leisure to examine and judge were the average condition of mankind. It has always struck us that this is eminently the characteristic of Locke's able treatise 'On the Conduct of the Understanding.' He writes as if he was writing of a world of thinkers, or at least where all might be thinkers but for their own fault; he hardly allows it to escape him that he is aware how very different the actual world is, and must be, at least for a long time to come; and how absolutely inapplicable his rules are — admirable as they are where they apply — to what is possible or conceivable, in the use of the understanding, in the majority of mankind. And the same feeling revives on reading the arguments of one who is not unworthy to be Locke's successor. His supposition, like Locke's, in one part at least of his argument for intellectual liberty is, that the comparatively intellectual and reasoning people, for the conflict of whose opinions he lays down conditions, may be taken as practically identical with the mass of society. But is the supposition sufficiently near to the truth for a general theory to rest upon, which recognizes no distinction between the parts of society where reasoning may go on, without limit as to its subjects, upon grounds approximately respectable and with the prospect of fruit, and parts where it cannot? It seems to us as inconceivable that all men should think out their opinions, as that the world should ever improve if none did; as absurd to require even in theory, that all should know enough, and have time and intelligence enough to stand on their own ground, as to bind those who can to foregone conclusions. And if so, what is to become of those whose independent reason and judgment will not serve them to find their place in the world? The wise and thoughtful may claim liberty for themselves, but what liberty are the mass to have among themselves, and what is liberty to do for them? We said that Mr. Mill presupposes, in one part of his argument, that the thinkers represent mankind, as they are to be regarded in a question of this kind; but his practical estimate of the majority is of a very different kind, and it lies at the foundation of his appeal for immunity from all accountableness to their judgment on behalf of those who do use their reason. 'That miscellaneous collection of a few wise and many foolish individuals called the public,' how are they to get on in the strife of opinions which they cannot master, and among reasons about which they are totally incapable of judging? In one of the most striking passages in his book, Mr. Mill tells us that human affairs would be almost desperate, but for the fact that errors are corrigible.[2] Well, but they would be almost

---

[2] When we consider either the history of opinion, or the ordinary conduct of human life, to what is it to be ascribed that the one and the other are no

desperate, if the mass of people, the ninety-nine out of the hundred, had nothing else that they could legitimately trust to, but the opinions they could think out for themselves, and the truths which they could see with their own eyes; unless common men might hope that they are not quite deceived in their ideas of truth and good, in their sense, however fallible, and however they come by it, of right and wrong, and had some sure instinct for teachers and rules of life, which at the time, at least, were found to respond to these ideas. Things

worse than they are? Not certainly to the inherent force of the human understanding; for, on any matter not self-evident, there are ninety-nine persons totally incapable of judging of it, for one who is capable; and the capacity of the hundredth person is only comparative; for the majority of the eminent men of every past generation held many opinions now known to be erroneous, and did or approved numerous things which no one will now justify. Why is it, then, that there is on the whole a preponderance among mankind of rational opinions and rational conduct? If there really is this preponderance — which there must be, unless human affairs are, and have always been, in an almost desperate state — it is owing to a quality of the human mind, the source of everything respectable in man either as an intellectual or as a moral being, namely, that his errors are corrigible. He is capable of rectifying his mistakes, by discussion and experience; not by experience alone. There must be discussion, to show how experience is to be interpreted. Wrong opinions and practices gradually yield to fact and argument; but facts and arguments, to produce any effect upon the mind, must be brought before it. Very few facts are able to tell their own story, without comments to bring out their meaning. The whole strength and value, then, of human judgment, depending on the one property, that it can be set right when it is wrong, reliance can be placed on it only when the means of setting it right are kept constantly at hand. In the case of any person whose judgment is really deserving of confidence, how has it become so? Because he has kept his mind open to criticism of his opinions and conduct. Because it has been his practice to listen to all that could be said against him; to profit by as much of it as was just, and expound to himself, and upon occasion to others, the fallacy of what was fallacious. Because he has felt, that the only way in which a human being can make some approach to knowing the whole of a subject, is by hearing what can be said about it by persons of every variety of opinion, and studying all modes in which it can be looked at by every character of mind. No wise man ever acquired his wisdom in any mode but this; nor is it in the nature of human intellect to become wise in any other manner. The steady habit of correcting and completing his own opinion by collating it with those of others, so far from causing doubt and hesitation in carrying it into practice, is the only stable foundation for a just reliance on it; for, being cognizant of all that can, at least obviously, be said against him, and having taken up his position against all gainsayers — knowing that he has sought for objections and difficulties, instead of avoiding them, and has shut out no light which can be thrown upon the subject from any quarter — he has a right to think his judgement better than that of any person, or any multitude, who have not gone through a similar process.

would no doubt be desperate without the correction of errors, without remedy and medicine. But to live only on the correction of errors, to live only on medicine, is desperate too. And if the argumentative worth of their reasonings is all that men, as a body, have to trust to, they are in a bad case indeed: for of the imperfection of these if of anything, reason is a competent judge, and its witness is decisive against them.

If liberty be claimed for those who can use it by having the power to think for themselves, we should have thought that at this moment they have it in most ample measure, as far as is compatible with their living at all in a society of most various and complicated relations; and that they have it in a daily-increasing degree. If the same conditions of liberty, extending to the very foundations of belief and morality, are required to pervade the whole body of society, and to be realized among the masses of common men, it seems to us that this is as impossible as it is undesirable. By that liberty is understood, in Mr. Mill's book, not merely absence of the restraints of law, but much more, the absence of the restraints, more subtle but as efficacious, of social opinion. Society in the mass, the society of active life and intercourse, the society of those who have little time for thought, must take many things, and many things of the utmost importance, for granted, and take them for granted as the exclusive truth. Men in general cannot be expected to be, at the same time, examining things and admitting the possibility of their being false and wrong, and acting upon them. How many, indeed, of those whose training is of a higher kind, can face the fact of a principle being open to question, and yet act earnestly upon it as if it were true? To preserve this true balance between thought and choice, is the fruit of the highest education of the whole man, in the highest sense of the word. And common men want beliefs, principles, rules of action, and supports of life, as well as those who can think them out for themselves; and where are common men to get them, except from the common stock, which has its warrant from the society in which they live? Unless they are to pass their lives drifting to and fro on a sea of doubt among the conflicts of opinion and argument, helpless navigators and hopeless of ever acquiring the art, they must stick on to something: they may, no doubt, choose to stick on to a stronger mind; but if they may do this, they may at least as legitimately stick on to the current beliefs and ideas sanctioned by public and general agreement around them. And, on the other hand, these current beliefs and ideas which society sanctions, it does not sanction at random. It takes for or against certain views, because, at the time, the evidence seems on the whole to preponderate that way, to those who have power to win the confidence of society, to those who seem to it the wise and good; because it thinks, according to its light, that the ideas are, not merely useful, but sound and the best, and believes itself faithful to the truth disclosed to it in accepting and maintaining them. But what society accepts in this way, it must accept with an exclusiveness, a peremptory universality, which is out of place in the schools of inquiry and independent thought. It is impossible that it can be otherwise. Whatever be the opinion come to, the weight of society adopting it — which, it is to be observed, is different in moral authority from the mere weight of numbers — invests it with the finality of a law, deferred to implicitly as a rule of action by those who seek support from it, hostile to those who oppose it. Society must come to some agreement, must have some general belief for the mass of its members, about chastity: whichever way it decides — and decide it must — it must inevitably press on a disagreeing minority. If it is in favour of chastity, it must take a practical tone which restrains liberty in those who do not adhere to its ruling views, and which they will call intolerant: if it is indifferent about it, those who go along with society will resent and proscribe, and punish with the penalties which flow from the disapproval and contempt of society, opinions of a severer and less indulgent tendency. In either case — rightly or wrongly as we may think — from the very nature of a social standard, than which the mass of ordinary men in the ordinary course of life can have no other, there must be that assumption of being right, and that moral pressure to maintain and enforce what is so assumed, and to repel the invasion or corruption of it, which would be absurd and out of place, as soon as men feel themselves qualified, and bring themselves to consent, to raise the question from the beginning, and debate it as a matter of simple argument. Abridgment of liberty is the natural and necessary consequence of the prevalence round us of strong practical opinions; and unless there are strong practical opinions, opinions which merit the name of deep and earnest convictions, it is hard to see how society can go on.

Of course, society may be wrong, or may take wrong modes

of imposing its opinions and enforcing its social principles. It may be corrupt or misled; and it may be oppressive. Its beliefs and usages are shaped and consolidated not only by the wise and good, but by the foolish, and yet even more, by the half-wise and the half-good. Everybody knows how often society has wanted reform and renovation before, and may well believe that it may need it in his own time: and, doubtless, when men, singly or in crowds, have made up their minds decisively and feel strongly, they are apt to persecute. But there is a natural counterpoise for this stringency of social authority, a natural remedy for its stagnation or degeneracy, a natural antagonist to its overzeal. It is the liberty, intellectual and moral, not of all, whether they can use it or not, but of those who *can* use it: not a chimerical and impossible liberty, proposed in theory to those who, if they would, cannot by the nature of things live in society and really use it, but a liberty, proportionate to and coextensive with each man's power to examine, to judge, to form his own opinions. That which is the salt of society, that which is the source of all improvement in it, and the antidote to the stiffness and hardness which grow out of belief and usage left too long to themselves, is the play and collision of minds, thinking their own thoughts and standing on ground of their own choosing or making. Society has been kept alive, and saved when on the brink of perishing, by an independence and originality, which were the opposites to its own habits of thinking in masses, and of taking for granted the authoritative and traditional. For such thinkers liberty may be claimed — claimed in as full measure as Mr. Mill makes the claim. As little as we can see what the preaching of such liberty as the paramount idea of society at large, could do, except make its present confusions worse confounded, so strongly do we feel the force of Mr. Mill's arguments for liberty among those who have earned their right to it. We cannot see any great harm in society keeping down with a pretty strong hand much that pretends to be original and independent. It may, doubtless, make great mistakes; but it has also a strong good sense, more often right than not, which detects this very cheap and very common form of imposture and conceit; and nobody ought to complain if society is hard, and hard in proportion to the consequences of the question, on one who starts a novelty which he cannot make a good fight for, or who opens a question which he is manifestly incompetent to handle. But when men show that they know what they are talking about, their right to such freedom as is consistent with the freedom of others seems unquestionable. Let those use it, at all risks, who can show a title to do so. If men and society were perfect, if all men were equally able to think for themselves, this freedom would be coextensive with society; of course it will spread and penetrate into society, in proportion as men learn to know and think for themselves. But it is from the way in which those who can, and those who cannot, think, are mixed and jumbled together in the world as we know it, that the difficulty consists in stating and adjusting this question of liberty fairly — fairly to the individual and to society, fairly to the established and invaded, and to the invading and tentative opinions; justly to the indefinitely varying degrees of aptitude and qualification for independent thought, uninvidiously to that vast mass of serious, conscientious, and active conviction, which calm judgment must pronounce in the main unreasoning, though by no means necessarily destitute of the support of reason.

We should have thought, however, that in this country, thinkers *are* their own masters, at least to a much greater extent than Mr. Mill seems to admit. The thinkers are their own masters on their own ground. They may think and say what they please, as thinkers; and not only so, but, in spite of prejudice and clamour, they are sure of a hearing from those whose judgment is most worth appealing to, and is ultimately of the most weight with society. There is nothing that we know of to prevent in England any man of seriousness, straight-forwardness, and average courage, from proposing for consideration any theory on any subject in the range of human thought and we may be pretty certain that if he says what is worth attending to, there will be people, people whose attention is worth having, who will attend to it. There is no direct external impediment to a man fairly putting out his whole strength, in defence or in attack of any opinion, viewed simply as a matter of opinion and argument. Unless what is asked for is absolute indifference on the part of society, or a covert favouring of a cause because it is new and weak in numbers, we do not see what else there is to be given. No doubt many views have to contend with dislike and discouragement in public opinion. They are looked on by society, or by large parts of it, with every hostile feeling from suspicion to abhorrence: and their obnoxiousness may certainly be said to be an obstacle to their success. But it must be remembered, and it is not always remembered, that liberty cannot be one-sided, even for a minority. Liberty does not mean absence of opposition; and the opposition, even of a majority, must not be confounded with curtailment of liberty. Those who fight must expect to be fought with; and so that they are not unfairly dealt with, have no right to expect their opponents to forego advantages, or make the ground easier for them: and men may fairly be expected to take, not merely the consequences of their arguments, but the consequences of the bearing of their opinions on the existing state of things. For if one man may speak his mind against religion, another man may speak his, not only *for* religion, but also about the results of speaking against religion; and if society is on the side of religion, we do not see that the assailant has any business to complain, if, leaving him to speak as he will, it looks with dislike or suspicion on him. Unless opinions are of no practical consequence, a thinker ought to make his account for moral opposition as well as intellectual, the opposition, which is the real and genuine one, the opposition of the *whole* man, the disapprobation of the heart as well as the dissent of the reason. He may overcome it, if he can; it has been often overcome; but he has no right to represent it as weighting unjustly the cause which he supports, or as any more an infringement on his own liberty than purely intellectual opposition. It may be said that the opposition ought to be confined to pure reasoning. But pure reasoning is a very slippery term, when applied to subjects which are in question in a discussion on liberty. No one, except a mathematician, or the driest of metaphysicians, confines himself to pure reasoning: he is, perforce, a rhetorician as well as a logician; he appeals to feeling and moral judgments; he would move the heart; he would persuade as well as convince; he does not hesitate to invoke the feeling of mankind against what he opposes — their scorn or indignation or fear; he tries to set in motion the weight of serial opinion against what he represents as base or cruel; and he cannot complain of being met on the same ground, and with the same effect. The evidences of truth are sought for in what engages our sympathies, corresponds to a supposed ideal of character, approves itself to what are regarded our highest but practical principles. We cannot fight against this condition of things, unless we would fight against the nature of man. And results, however by themselves an unfair argument for or against a doctrine, cannot, if we would, be entirely put aside in judging of it. If, then, a man sets before me a view which lowers and degrades me, or seems to destroy my hope in life, he has no right to expect that I should suppress my judgment of the effect of his speculations, or be unmoved by it: nor, if he feels intimidated and embarrassed himself, by my judgment, or that of other people, being strongly against him, has he a right, while he is still allowed to speak as he pleases, to cry out about liberty. And further, it seems to us that there is a good deal to be said for the reluctance of society at large to listen to argument, which may powerfully affect the more thoughtful of its members; and that people who feel themselves strong in argument, and think that they have a clear case, are unreasonable in their demands for the effect of their argument on society. Society, that is, the great body of mankind, who can but think imperfectly, hesitatingly, interruptedly, must and ought to assent to new argument slowly. Not only, should the argument be one of eventful consequences, will society have much to re-arrange and settle, if it does assent — not only, since it must go by general understandings, and cannot go by every man's view, as it comes accidentally urged with some unusual strength, ought it be cautious in altering the clear understandings by which it goes at the time, — but it may well be doubted whether any revolutionary argument was ever put forth, on the complicated subjects of moral interest, of such strength, completeness, and cogency as that it ought at once to have commanded general assent. The practical experience of mankind has not found that the seeming an invincible demonstration at the moment was a test of the ultimate truth. And, on the other hand, nothing is more common than a strong sense of the unsatisfactoriness of an argument which yet is very clever, and to us unanswerable, and of which we cannot see the fallacy, if there is one. It is the long run which must practically decide the strength of a theory or a doctrine. If it has much to say for itself, and yet is long in prevailing, and meets with obstinately recurring opposition, the probability is that there is something still unexplained, unsettled, unaccounted for in it, which keeps it back. The sum is not right, even if it is nearly so; and it is returned to be done over again. But in the long run, argument, if it is sound and true, will carry the day, and will find at last its right shape, one which meets the difficulties which have impeded it. But not necessarily at first. And when new arguments challenge assent, the common sense of mankind, though perhaps with but a vague consciousness of the grounds on which it rests, remembers the history of opinion, and is, not unwisely, suspicious of quick assent. The battle of opinion in the world is not like that in the schools: here, if an argument is not answered, it claims the victory in the debate; there, people wait for the long run; they know that it does not follow, because an argument is not at hand, that it does not exist: they know that the disputant may be wrong, though he has all the advantage of present ability, and though the aspect and balance of argument may be now entirely in his favour: they know that unless men are to be ever learners and never coming to the knowledge of the truth, unless they are to be the sport of every wind of doctrine, they must not change to every temporary variation in the intellectual power of different advocates: they know that it is absurd to give up their assent to the first thing which they cannot answer, though it is very reasonable, and incumbent on them, to bear in mind, that this is something which they have not an answer for. Opinions, in the hands of those who know the difficulty of truth, have no right to complain of this long and severe testing; of any opposition, social as well as argumentative, by which they are met, short of being absolutely gagged and stifled. 'If all mankind minus one,' says Mr. Mill, 'were of one opinion, and only one person were of the contrary opinion, mankind would be no more justified in silencing that one person, than he, if he had the power, would be justified in silencing all mankind.' True enough. Let the one man speak against the whole world; but let the world think well before it parts with its convictions from any immediate show of argument in his words. The world and truth will both be gainers by the delay; if they do not come together so soon, they will not do so less surely and less safely at last.

We repeat, then, that if what is asked is liberty of thought and speech for those who wish to think for themselves, we cannot see in what respect they are seriously hindered in it. The question of the limits of opinion in bodies, which avowedly profess to be united on a common standard of principle or belief, is a separate one, which cannot be argued simply on the grounds of liberty in society generally. And the law of the land which forbids a man to annoy his neighbours by wantonly and

pertinaciously outraging what they hold dear, or which takes
for granted, in administering an oath, that all men believe in a
divine ruler,[3] is but a small weight on the liberty of holding and

[3] Mr. Mill's remarks on this subject are hardly marked by his usual calmness
   and exactness. He mentions three cases, where persons were rejected as
   jurymen or witnesses because they refused to take an oath, having no
   theological belief; and he proceeds to comment on them:— 'This refusal of
   redress took place in virtue of the legal doctrine, that no person can be
   allowed to give evidence in a court of justice who does not profess belief in a
   God (any god is sufficient), and in a future state, which is equivalent to
   declaring such persons to be outlaws, excluded from the protection of the
   tribunals; who may not only be robbed or assaulted with impunity, if no
   one but themselves, or persons of similar opinions be present, but any one
   else may be robbed or assaulted with impunity, if the proof of the fact
   depends on their evidence. The assumption on which this is grounded, is,
   that the oath is worthless, of a person who does not believe in a future state;
   a proposition which betokens much ignorance of history in those who
   assent to it (since it is historically true that a large proportion of infidels in
   all ages have been persons of distinguished integrity and honour); and
   would be maintained by no one who had the smallest conception how many
   of the persons in greatest repute with the world, both for virtues and for
   attainments, are well known, at least to their intimates, to be unbelievers.
   The rule, besides, is suicidal, and cuts away its own foundation. Under
   pretence that atheists must be liars, it admits the testimony of all atheists
   who are willing to lie, and rejects only those who brave the obloquy of
   publicly confessing a detested creed, rather than affirm a falsehood. A rule
   thus self-convicted of absurdity as far as regards its professed purpose, can
   be kept in force only as a badge of hatred, a relic of persecution; a
   persecution, too, having the peculiarity, that the qualification for under-
   going it, is the being clearly proved not to deserve it. The rule, and the
   theory it implies, are hardly less insulting to believers than to infidels. For, if
   he who does not believe in a future state necessarily lies, it follows that they
   who do believe are only prevented from lying, if prevented they are, by the
   fear of hell. We will not do the authors and abettors of this rule the injury of
   supposing that the conception which they have formed of Christian virtue,
   is drawn from their own consciousness.'
      We are sorry to hear, and hestate to believe, even from Mr. Mill, that so
   many whom we respect are secretly, nor merely unbelievers in Christianity,
   but (for this is what his argument requires) atheists. We did not know it
   before; and we cannot help thinking it a sadder piece of news than to be put
   in as an incidental retort in an argument of this kind. But he seems to us
   invidiously to overstate the case, when he represents the effect of the legal
   doctrine to be that 'atheists must be liars,' and that 'he who does not believe
   in a future state necessarily lies'. The law no more implies this, than it
   implied that Quakers were liars, before it allowed them to substitute an
   affirmation for an oath, or than it now implies that the scrupulous
   Christians, who refuse oaths and are set aside in courts of justice, are liars.
   It is not implied that these persons, or that atheists necessarily lie; but that
   we have nothing by which we can be satisfied whether they will tell the truth
   or no; which is an entirely different thing. The whole question of oaths,
   their rightness and their usefulness, is a fair one for debate. Christianity is
   not very favourable to them; and their success in securing truth has not been

expressing convictions. But if what is asked for is, that all opinions should be treated by society as they would be among pure abstract thinkers; that all should be relieved from all social disabilities; that no opinions, however apparently false and immoral, should be at any disadvantage from the stigma of society; that society and all its members should deal with all alike, as if all alike might be true and all alike might be false; that no opinions, as such, should be, so to speak, *tabooed*, marked with special reprobation, thwarted, discouraged, stunted in their development, by that mixture, often a very confused one, of reasoning and sentiment, called pubic opinion, — such a state of things, if seems to us, never could be, and if it could, it would be fatal to the well-being of society. It never could be, without men ceasing to feel and think together; — without ceasing to have common principles, settled ideas and rules of life, joint objects, interests, and sympathies, convictions to stand the vicissitudes of things, a public spirit, a national character. And if they could lose these, a temper of indifference and uncertainty, a general sense of the dangers of choice, of the precariousness of truth, of the doubtfulness of duty, a temper incompatible with all sympathy and all high purposes, would be a high price to pay for having got rid of that degree of narrow-mindedness, and of positiveness without producible premises, which, hitherto at least, we have had to put up with, when men have done anything great and worthy, either by themselves or in company. Mr. Mill has elsewhere set forth the importance of that complex social phenomenon called national character. He has shown, in striking and admirable terms,[4] that whenever habitual submission to law is reconciled with a vigorous and manly independence — and in no other case can there be true greatness in society — there must be a definite and powerful education, a feeling of allegiance and loyalty to some

perfect. With numbers of men everybody feels them to be unnecessary. But mankind have felt that for the *average* of men, some unusual sanction was wanted; and if so, it must be universal, and the religious one has been the most obvious and natural one. We cannot accept a man as a witness, and take his word, simply because we know him to be a good man. We cannot see why it is persecution, if we decline to accept an atheist, and be satisfied with his word, merely because he is an atheist.

4   Article on Coleridge in his collected 'Dissertations and Discussions,' vol. i. pp. 416–421.

unquestionable principle, and a strong and active bond of cohesion — that cohesion, which comes with the mutual sympathy of men, who feel themselves one in purpose and in their view of life and its ends. He is quite alive to the necessity, in the state, of something settled, accepted, permanent, and not to be questioned — 'something which men agree in holding sacred' — open to improvement, of course, but having some fixed point, without which nothing can be improved, but only destroyed, to make way for something else. He quite admits the idea that society is in some sense the guardian of certain principles and a certain spirit, which belongs to its very essence and constitution. Can, then, the opinions and sentiments belonging to such a state of things fail to frown down those which are at variance with and destructive of it? Will public feeling in a democracy look tamely on, content with bare unimpassioned argument, at the insidious encroachment of an adverse opinion? Can it be expected, that social force will not put forth its power against doctrines, which imperil what is permanent, and invade 'what all agree in holding sacred?' Will not society — we do not say necessary stifle and silence the discussion of them — but, from the instinct of self-preservation, inevitably present to their free course those formidable barriers of disapproval or condemnation, which are quite compatible with leaving individuals unmolested to think and speak as they please? Rightly or wrongly it may be; we only say that it is natural to society to have certain characteristic principles, and, as long as it cares about them, to protect them by a social ban on their opposites. And our objection to Mr. Mill's way of putting the argument for liberty of opinion is, that he puts forward the individual only, and takes no account of society; that he draws no line between questions which are open to the schools, and those which society must close, or go to pieces; that, on his theory, there can be no closed questions whatever; and that on that theory it is hard to see how society has any right to resent and reprobate — at least without each time giving, or, at any rate, seeing all its reasons — a defence of lying, of selfishness, of cowardice, or of bigotry.[5]

---

[5] 'Strange it is, that men should admit the validity of the arguments for free discussion, but object to their being "pushed to an extreme;" not seeing that unless the reasons are good for an extreme case, they are not good for any case. Strange that they should imagine that they are not assuming

In truth, the difficulty of such speculations is to fit a theory, which presupposes genuine argument and real inquiry, to a world where the mass of people cannot really either inquire or argue, yet must act, and where questions are so difficult. This is illustrated by that part of the Essay which sets forth how much an opinion gains by being controverted, even if it is true. Nothing can be more admirable than the way in which Mr. Mill unfolds the truth contained in the old French proverb, which tells us, that

'Tout contraire en son contraire
Prend vertu pour soi refaire.'[6]

He points out, that, where there is an opposite opinion possible, as there is on every subject except mathematics, we cannot know the truth of our own, unless we are as familiar with the arguments which may be brought against it, as we are with those which support it. Unless we know the objections and their real force, we cannot know how far they are met by the answers to them; and we cannot know their real force except from those who are in earnest in urging them; unless, that is, there is real and not collusive discussion, and we make ourselves acquainted with it. Further, he points out how discussion is necessary, not merely for knowing the grounds of our opinions, but for keeping opinions alive. He calls attention to the fact, 'in the experience of all ethical doctrines and religious creeds,' that as soon as controversy ceases, and the belief has won its place, the lively apprehension of it, the energy with which it inspires its adherents, declines also. 'The words which convey it, cease to suggest ideas, or suggest only a small portion of those they were originally designed to communicate. Instead of a vivid conception and a living belief,

infallibility, when they acknowledge that there should be free discussion on all subjects which can possibly be *doubtful*, but think that some particular doctrine or principle should be forbidden to be questioned because it is so *certain*, that is, because *they are certain* that it is certain. To call any proposition certain, while there is any one who would deny its certainty if permitted, but who is not permitted, is to assume that we ourselves, and those who agree with us, are the judges of certainty, and judge without hearing the other side.' — P. 41. 'If the arguments of this chapter are of any validity, there ought to exist the fullest liberty of professing and discussing, as a matter of ethical conviction, any doctrine, however immoral it may be considered.' — P. 32.

6   Quoted in *Friends in Council*. Second Series.

there remain only a few phrases retained by rote: or if any part, the shell and husk only of the meaning is retained, the finer essence being lost.' When the necessity for argument is over, and intellectual vigilance is dispensed with, 'the mind is no longer compelled to exercise its vital powers on the questions which its belief presents to it;' then comes the 'dull and torpid assent,' 'dispensing with the necessity of realizing the belief in consciousness or testing it by personal experience, till it almost ceases to connect itself at all with the inner life of the human being.'

> 'Then are seen the cases, so frequent in this age of the world as almost to form the majority, in which the creed remains, as it were, outside the mind, encrusting and petrifying it against all other influences addressed to the higher parts of our nature; manifesting its power by not suffering any fresh and living conviction to get in, but itself doing nothing for the mind or heart, except standing sentinel over them, to keep them vacant.' — P. 74.

He contrasts the Christian precepts of the New Testament, with the unreal and reserved way in which they are accepted by Christians now; he observes how the common sayings about life remain truisms, till made realities by experience. The 'fatal tendency of mankind to leave off thinking of a thing, when it is no longer doubtful, is the cause of half their errors;' and he quotes with approbation the expression which speaks of the 'deep slumber of a decided opinion;' though, if we substitute for 'decided opinion,' 'strong conviction,' the phrase will lose something of its truth. Admitting to a certain extent the gradual approach of mankind to agreement, the cessation 'on one question after another of serious controversy,' he still maintains the necessity of debate and discussion, to keep alive our real knowledge of the grounds of our agreement. The Socratic dialectics and the middle age scholastic disputations were powerful educational helps of this sort, which we have lost without anything to replace them: a remark which is true enough, though the force of it is qualified by the liability which every man is under now, who lives in public or takes interest in public concerns, of having opposite opinions, very ably supported, forced upon his notice. Where the advantage of actual opposition is no longer to be had, 'I should like,' he says, 'to see the teachers of mankind endeavouring to provide a substitute for it; some contrivance for making the difficulties of the question as present to the learner's consciousness, as if they were pressed on him by a dissentient champion, eager for his conversion.' No one can deny the force of what Mr. Mill urges, though he overlooks the very important fact that the meaning of religious and moral doctrines is kept up, not only by the activity of the intellect, but by realizing them in the life and acting on them: and that many a man has a vital belief in God, and is admirable in his social duties, whose mind has never been disturbed by doubt, and who could give but a poor account of the grounds of the morality which he illustrates. But, allowing for this, take Mr. Mill's argument, in his own forcible words, for listening to what can be said against our own views:—

'But, some one may say, "Let them by *taught* the grounds of their opinions. It does not follow that opinions must be merely parroted because they are never heard controverted. Persons who learn geometry do not merely commit the theorems to memory, but understand and learn likewise the demonstrations; and it would be absurd to say that they remain ignorant of the grounds of geometrical truths, because they never hear any one deny, and attempt to disprove them." Undoubtedly: and such teaching suffices on a subject like mathematics, where there is nothing at all to be said on the wrong side of the question. The peculiarity of the evidence of mathematical truths is, that all the argument is on one side. There are no objections, and no answers to objections. But on every subject on which difference of opinion is possible, the truth depends on a balance to be struck between two sets of conflicting reasons. Even in natural philosophy, there is always some other explanation possible of the same facts, some geometric theory instead of heliocentric, some phlogiston instead of oxygen; and it has to be shown why that other theory cannot be the true one; and until this is shown, and until we know how it is shown, we do not understand the grounds of our opinion. But when we turn to subjects infinitely more complicated, to morals, religion, politics, social relations, and the business of life, three-fourths of the arguments for every disputed opinion consist in dispelling the appearances which favour some opinion different from it. The greatest orator, save one, of antiquity, has left it on record that he always studied his adversary's case with as great, if not with still greater, intensity than even his own. What Cicero practised as the means of forensic success, requires to be imitated by all who study any subject in order to arrive at the truth. He who knows only his own side of the case, knows little of that. His reasons may be good, and no one may have been able to refute them. But if he is equally unable to refute the reasons on the opposite side; if he does not so much as know what they are, he has no ground for preferring either opinion. The rational position for him would be suspension of judgment; and unless he contents himself with that, he is either led by authority, or adopts, like the generality of the world, the side to which he feels most inclination. Nor is it enough that he should hear the arguments of adversaries from his own teachers, presented as they state them, and accompanied by what they offer as refutations. That is not the way to do justice to the arguments, or bring them into real contact with his own mind. He must be able to hear them from persons who actually believe them; who defend them in earnest, and do their very utmost for them. He must know them in their most plausible and persuasive form; he must feel the whole force of the difficulty which the true view of the subject has to encounter and dispose of; else he will never really possess himself of the portion of truth which meets and removes that difficulty. Ninety-nine in a hundred of what are called educated men are in this condition; even of those who can argue fluently for their opinions. Their conclusion may be true, but it might be false for anything they know; they have never thrown themselves into the mental position of those who think differently from them, and considered what such persons may have to say; and consequently they do not, in any proper sense of the word, know the doctrine which they themselves profess. They do not know those parts of it which explain and justify the remainder; the consideration which shows that a fact which seemingly conflicts with another is reconcilable with it, or that, of two apparently strong reasons, one and not the other ought to be preferred. All that part of the truth which turns the scale, and decides the judgment of a completely informed mind, they are strangers to; nor is it ever really known, but to those who have attended equally and impartially to both sides, and endeavoured to see the reasons of both in the strongest light. So essential is this discipline to a real understanding of moral and human subjects, that if opponents of all important truths do not exist, it is indispensable to imagine them, and supply them with the strongest arguments which the most skilful devil's advocate can conjure up.'

But there is another side to the picture. Nothing can be more admirable than this, as applied to those whose proper business it is to think. And can anything be more unreal, when applied to the mass of people, of whom society is composed? Take a man engaged in the affairs of life, an average professional man, or man of business. He has plenty of good strong common sense to take him through life. He has the power and the will to be a useful member of society, a source of help, of elevating and improving influences, to those around him. He has a fair right to take his side in the practical discussions which go on in the social or political world in which he finds himself. But place him in the midst of those hard questions which lie at the root of our knowledge, our morality, our religion. They have as yet proved very trying to the deepest and strongest thinkers of our race. Place him among them, and call upon him to take hold of them and follow them out. Suppose, and this is what Mr. Mill's view does suppose, that his 'Times,' or his weekly journal assiduously brings before him, not as an occasional matter, but with the frequency proportioned to their importance, and as part of the staple subject of daily debate, all that may be thought or said on our condition and destiny, on immortality, on duty, on a Divine Being; all the subtle difficulties and refined explanations that keen and bold minds have busied themselves with, all the doubts and uncertainties, all the conflicting probabilities, and siftings of evidence, about what he is every day obliged to decide upon and to do. Can anything be conceived more ludicrously and pitiably helpless than he would be, fought for and dragged hither and thither by contending arguments, of which he was unable to master the grounds and consequences, perplexed and distracted by rival proofs which he was told it was his duty to weigh, but which his mind vainly endeavoured to take in, oppressed and confused with difficulties in which he too clearly felt himself out of his depth, but which he must for very shame, as a rational being, suppose himself able to find some way through.

Or is it conclusive against the honesty and fair strength of a man's mind, that he is confessedly unable to handle, and unwilling to meddle with, everything that may be made the subject of question? Surely there is common sense in making the difficulty of a subject a limit to its promiscuous and ordinary discussion. This is not discouraging discussion, where people are equal to it. Let there be discussion as much as people please; but let there also be a sense of the uselessness of incapable discussion — of the fitness of some, and the unfitness of more to undertake discussion. Let thinkers write, as they used to write, for those who will read them: this is a healthier plan than enlarging on the abstract necessity of wholesale debate and inquiry. They were not eminently happy times, when the rage for free discussion of difficult questions invaded those who were manifestly unfit for it; when things which ought to be kept for the most grave and anxious, as well as powerful, thought came to the surface; when grooms and cooks, courtiers and gossips, filled the shops and saloons of Constantinople with the sound of theological terms and distinctions; or when the mysteries of free-will and grace were the daily subject of metaphysical wrangle at the tables of hard-headed Puritans, as acute and practised dialecticians for the argument, as they were deficient in largeness and reality for the ideas they argued about. They were not happy times; not is it a happy thing, at any time, to see a great and wide question, full of life and of many sides, taken in hand by a poor and narrow intellect, profoundly unconscious of the depth and extent of it, and drying it up, distorting and hardening it. There is discussion enough among us, for the amount of apparent power to do justice to it. In spite of Mr. Mill's fears, there seem to us to be no symptoms of its being on the wane. Those certainly who look on it with jealousy do not think so. The temptations of our day to heresy may well be set against the temptations to orthodoxy. If there is, as we think there is, an increasing considerateness and sense of responsibility in opening great questions, there is no want of disposition to open them, and to do it very boldly. And if society has the inert weight, it is the single thinkers who have the moving power.

In attempting, then, to simplify and generalize the doctrine of liberty, and to lay down a principle which should decide without difficulty the 'endless jar' between society and individual liberty, and cut away with a clean sweep the usurpations of the former, Mr. Mill seems to us to have given too little weight to considerations which make the application of his principles far from simple. The points which chiefly strike us as overlooked by him are two. First, the way in which the mass of the people *must* depend more or less on society for their opinions. In urging and claiming liberty you must suppose power; and though he himself certainly does not suppose it, as a matter of fact, in the minds of people at large, his argument does. *That* supposes a state of things where people of the same average capacity and training are going through life, each for himself, without needing guidance or help besides his own; and where society does not want for itself settled principles, acknowledged standards, and a pervading spirit. The reality is far otherwise. He allows that his theory of liberty, as it is not applicable to children, so it is only but very partially applicable to many previous states of society, which have been only too happy if they had 'an Ackbar or a Charlemagne' to give them that guidance which they could not give to themselves. Things are greatly different now, of course; but the change, however estimated, is only one of degree. There are many, doubtless, who can judge for themselves; many more who do not, but who might and ought to do so; and the relaxing of authority is, in fact, gradually going on, in proportion as men become more and more qualified to judge for themselves. But the time is certainly not come yet, nor does it seem within view, when the many can cease to lean upon each other, or upon society, for their knowledge and principles, as the few can. And till that time comes, it seems useless to talk of abrogating or ignoring an authority which practically justifies and enforces itself. The second point is, that of the interests of society and of others seem to us far too closely interwoven and entangled with those of individuals to allow of that clean division which Mr. Mill's theory requires. The limits of individual liberty are, he says, from society, self-preservation; from other individuals, what concerns themselves. Suppose the rule is admitted in words, though we do not think that this is the only or the best way of expressing the truth, what endless questions open, about what 'self-preservation' in society means and involves, and as to how the concerns of one individual are affected by what another is and does. Surely these limits are not so clear at first sight as to be capable of being made the basis of a ready and sweeping test between liberty and encroachment. It makes a difference to

society and to others what opinions a man holds, just as truly
as it makes a difference to him what amount of liberty society
allows him. Society is deeply interested in what men believe,
and in what rules they go by; and if society may legitimately
aim at creating and fostering a national character, a common
spirit; if society may, as Mr. Mill says it ought to, cultivate a
certain cast of character,[7] that is favour one and discourage its
opposite; if society may *educate*; — the principle seems to us
conceded, that it may take measures to make people, within
large limits, it may be, yet in some real sense, good, both for
themselves, and, because its own interests are involved in what
they are, for its own preservation and well-being. In each case
of conflict between the individual and society, the question as
to the effect and tendencies of the liberty claimed will raise a
debate, and, as far as we see, must in each case be decided on
its merits, and with reference, it may be, to many cross and
complicated interests. Doubtless society may draw to itself
what does not belong to it; but the individual may quite easily
judge in his own cause partially, and refuse to see how deeply
what he alleges to concern only himself concerns others also.
What *does* concern the individual only? is the very question to
be answered in a discussion on liberty.

All that he says about the importance of individuality, and
the necessity of guarding jealously its limits, so as to leave room
for it to put forth its energies and grow, is forcible and
important. We may differ from him as to the extent to which
individuality is, as he alleges, stifled and crushed among us. He
underrates, as it seems to us, the degree to which individuality
of any value has a fair chance to assert itself; and he does not
attend sufficiently to the fact, that the forced and stimulated
individuality of mediocrities would simply be a pest and
nuisance, without any countervailing advantage. But estimates
and measures of these matters of fact in our contemporaries are
doubtless precarious things; custom, and laziness of mind, and
dull sluggish compliance, and the fear of man, and servility to
our circle or our party, and the insolence of vulgar and coarse
opinion, are great powers among us still; and even if Mr. Mill's
statements are one-sided and scornful, we may listen with
advantage to his warnings against the insidious weight of what
is established and customary, his sympathy with the fear, 'lest

[7] P. 108.

one good custom should corrupt the world,' and his indignant protests against the tyranny of opinion, blindly intrusive, meddlesome, and intolerant, overbearing the individual preferences of the weak, unforgiving to the manliness and courage of the independent. We may hesitate about the dignity as well as the truth of such unqualified assertions as that 'individual spontaneity is hardly recognized by the common modes of thinking, as having any intrinsic worth, or deserving any regard on its own account;' 'that spontaneity forms no part of the ideal of the majority of moral and social reformers, but is rather looked upon with jealousy, as a troublesome and perhaps rebellious obstruction to the general acceptance of what these reformers in their own judgment think would be best for mankind;' that there is a general unwillingness to admit 'that to possess impulses of our own and of any strength is anything but a peril and a snare;' that 'it does not occur to people now to have any inclinations, except for what is customary;' that the popular 'standard, express or tacit, is to desire nothing strongly,' and the popular 'ideal of character is to be without any marked character;' that even the intelligent part of the public have to be made to see — what, we should have thought, was almost one of the truisms of the day — 'that it is good that there should be differences, even though not for the better, even though, as it may appear to them, some should be for the worse.' Surely these generalizations, to be true, require large abatement. But this does not make the statement of the general principle less impressive in such passages as the following:—

'It is not by wearing down into uniformity all that is individual in themselves, but by cultivating it and calling it forth, within the limits imposed by the rights and interests of others, that human beings become noble and beautiful objects of contemplation: and as the works partake of the character of those who do them, by the same process also human life becomes rich, diversified, and animating, furnishing more abundant elements to high thoughts and elevating feelings, and strengthening the tie which binds every individual to the race, by making the race infinitely more worth belonging to. . . . To be held to rigid rules of justice for the sake of others, develops the feelings and capacities which have the good of others for their object. But to be restrained in things not affecting their good, by their mere displeasure, develops nothing valuable, except such force of character as may unfold itself in resisting the restraint. If acquiesced in, it dulls and blunts the whole nature. To give fair play to the nature of each, it is essential that different persons should be allowed to lead different lives. In proportion as this latitude has been exercised in any age, has that age been noteworthy to posterity. . . . There is always need of persons not only to discern new truths, and point out when what were once truths are true no longer, but also to commence new practices, and set the example of more enlightened conduct, and better taste and sense in human life. This cannot be gainsaid by any person who does not believe that the world has already attained perfection in all its ways and practices. It is true that this benefit is not capable of being rendered by everybody alike: there are but few persons, in comparison with the whole of mankind, whose experiments, if adopted by others, would be likely to be any improvement on established practice. But these few are the salt of the earth; without them, human life would become a stagnant pool. Not only is it they who introduce good things which did not before exist; it is they who keep the life in those which already existed. If there were nothing new to be done, would therefore human intellect cease to be necessary? Would it be a reason, why those who do old things should forget why they are done, and do them like cattle, not like human beings? There is only too great a tendency in the best belief and practice to degenerate into the mechanical; and unless there were a succession of persons whose ever-recurring originality prevents the grounds of these beliefs and practices from becoming merely traditional, such dead matter would not resist the smallest shock from anything really alive, and there would be no reason why civilization should not die out, as in the Byzantine empire. Persons of genius, it is true, are, and are always likely to be, a small minority; but in order to have them, it is necessary to preserve the soil in which they grow. Genius can only breathe in an *atmosphere* of freedom.' — Pp. 113–116.

But when Mr. Mill applies to particular instances his discriminating test — what concerns the individual, to liberty, what concerns society, to authority, to be enforced either by law or

opinion — when he points out cases of what 'may be called
moral police, encroaching on the most unquestionable liberty
of the individual,' the absence or the smallness of interest which
society has in the matter in question seems to us far too lightly
assumed, and certainly not to be so clear as to leave no room
for argument. The illustrations from the Mahometan feeling
about pork, and the exclusiveness of religious opinion in Spain
would have been better away. It seems hardly in place in a
discussion like this, to take the short and easy method of seeing
no difference between the 'moral police' of barbarous and half-
civilized people, and that of those of more advanced and
thoughtful ones; of people who have, to some extent at any
rate, admitted that questioning and testing of their principles
which Mr. Mill is recommending, and of those who have not
admitted it at all. *We* can see that Mahometan proscription of
pork and Spanish intolerance are unreasonable, on their own
merits, even if Turks and Spaniards cannot: and it seems
affected modesty to think our opinion on the matter no better
than theirs. And to say that we should have no common
ground but that of liberty, in discussing the question with
them, is no more than may be said of most discussions with
people more ignorant than ourselves. Dr. Livingstone found it
impossible to gain an argumentative victory over the South
African rain-doctor on the question of 'medicines' making
rain.[8] Fairer and better instances are 'Sabbatarian legislation,'
the Maine Liquor Law, and the public feeling with respect to
Mormonism. With respect to Sunday legislation and the Maine
Liquor Law, we agree with Mr. Mill; entirely as to the latter,
and to a great extent as to the former; and though we cannot
say the same about his view of Mormonism, his remarks on it
deserve attention. But on all these points, whether we agree
with his conclusions, or not, it appears to us that the debate
arises just on the very allegation which Mr. Mill takes as his
starting-point — the purely 'self-regarding' character of what is
interfered with. The interests of society are inextricably
interlaced with what in these cases concerns the individual; his
course acts upon and materially influences the general char-

---

[8] See the Conversation on Rain-making. Livingstone's Travels, p. 23. A
capital instance of the dialectical advantage of knowing less than an
opponent, which most people must have observed in arguing with the acute
and uneducated.

acter and spirit of society — whether well or ill, or, if either
well or ill, whether to such an extent as to warrant the action of
society upon him, is just the difficult question, upon which
opposite probabilities appear, and on which we require to find
their balance. They must each be decided on their own merits,
when all the interests involved have been fairly taken into
account. But in this part of the subject we seem to miss the
vigorous handling with which in the earlier part of the book
objections are taken up and discussed. Thus, as regards the
Maine Liquor Law, the secretary of the Alliance 'claims, as a
citizen, to legislate whenever his social rights are invaded by the
social act of another.' And he proceeds to define these rights;
'the traffic in strong drinks invades his primary right of
security, by constantly creating and stimulating social disorder;
his right of *equality*, by deriving a profit by the creation of a
misery which he is taxed to support; his right to *free moral and
intellectual development*, by surrounding his path with
dangers, and weakening and demoralizing society, from which
he has a right to claim mutual aid and intercourse'. The
question is, *does* it? If it does, the Alliance would have made
out something of a case, overweighing, according to its
seriousness, the *prima facie* claim and benefit of individual
liberty. This is the point in dispute. But it does not seem to be
settled by what is only, even for Mr. Mill, a rhetorical
exaggeration.

'A theory of "social right," the like of which probably never
before found its way into distinct language — *being nothing
short of this — that it is the absolute social right of every
individual that every other individual should act in every
respect exactly as he ought*; that whosoever fails therefore *in
the smallest particular*, violates every social right, and
entitles me to demand from the legislature the removal of the
grievance. So monstrous a principle is far more dangerous
than any single interference with liberty: there is no violation
of liberty which it would not justify: it acknowledges no
right to any freedom whatever, except perhaps that of
holding opinions in secret without ever disclosing them; for
the moment an opinion which I consider noxious passes any
one's lips, it invades all the "social rights" ascribed to me by
the "Alliance." The doctrine ascribes to all mankind a vested
interest in each other's moral, intellectual, and even physical

perfection, to be defined by each claimant according to his own standard.'

Really we cannot see how all these formidable consequences are involved in the secretary's theory. He asks for protection against *some* misconduct, which (rightly or wrongly) he alleges to be intolerably prejudicial to him. Cannot he do that, without the implication claiming the same protection against *all* misconduct? without claiming, as his 'absolute social right', that every other individual should act in every respect exactly as he ought, and 'that whosoever fails thereof in the smallest particular' should be regarded as 'violating every social right?'

We cannot entirely pass over a grave subject, which must be met with in an inquiry of this kind. With broad statements like those of Mr. Mill's Essay, on the exclusive claims of liberty, there always presents itself, as their inseparable correlative and anxious attendant, their bearing on the possibility of a religion. There would be nothing specially difficult in the question, if the world were made up of philosophers, or if only the religion of those who can examine and think were concerned. But religion is for the poor and weak. Religion must be a joint thing and a thing of faith. Men must believe together, and believe without doubt; be united in a common hope, and be united in full dependence on it, for those sympathies and harmonies to be developed among them by which they are supported them- selves, and support one another, in the darkness and dis- appointments of life, on a trust which goes beyond it. No one can look at the documents of Christianity and doubt that this religion was meant to produce the same ordinarily unquestion- ing faith as that, for example, of our family affections: and without that entire faith it cannot be the religion which we read of in the New Testament. If there is not faith, it may be philosophy, but not religion; and if there is faith, then, at some period or other, doubt of its truth must be cast behind. How such a state of mind is possible, either in the individual, who, on the ground of the fallibility of man and the infinite revolutions of opinion, keeps himself on continual guard against the too certain persuasion of what he holds, or in society, in which it is the normal and perpetual condition, that every conviction and belief is for ever held to be on its trial, and where public opinion, neutral about conclusions, discourages nothing but slackness of debate and the disposition to feel too positive, is a question — we are very far from saying, unanswerable, but which deserves an answer. Mr. Mill does not help us to one, or even as to whether one is to be hoped for. But throughout the discussion, we feel that it is, however latently, on uneven ground. *La partie n'est pas égale.* Mr. Mill's feeling about Christianity, respectful as it is, and just as he means it to be, is not that of those who feel that anything for life and death, to them and to the world, is involved in its truth. Christians believe that Christianity is as certain as anything given to men can be, for the very reason which Mr. Mill gives for any practical certainty; — that it *has been* open to question and denial, and that as yet no one has adequately produced on men at large the impression of its falsehood. They feel that hitherto nothing else has shown a *primá facie* case to compete with it. Of course, if the faith of civilized nations, or of those who are the teachers of their kind or generation, is shaken in it; if people feel that as a whole, or in any of its particular doctrines, it can be effectually and seriously challenged, it, or parts of it, will fall by degrees into the class of open questions. But so far it has stood a long test, one of a practical nature, and not of the most gentle kind. It is impossible to abolish the interest felt for issues like those of religion, or their power over the mind; or to make it as little hazardous to peace to discuss God and Christ, as to discuss monarchy and republicanism. Those, then, who value Christianity cannot look with indifference on the hazard of its going out in civilized society. Their own personal grounds for believing in its truth are no guarantee against this. If truth, as Mr. Mill justly remarks, may be endangered by persecution, it may also be endangered, not, indeed, by fair and honest inquiry, but by reckless, unscrupulous, and incompetent inquiry — by a spirit of mockery, indifference, or affected freedom. The saying that truth has nothing to fear from unlimited liberty is just as much a 'pleasant falsehood' as the dictum that it has nothing to fear from persecution. It *has not*, in the long run, any more than in the long run, from persecution. But it may be overborne at a particular time by accident placing intellect, as at another time, power, in the hands of its opponents: and they who rely absolutely on its intrinsic power forget that being able to argue and refute is, at any given time, a matter seemingly of chance, and that an argument which is a weak one in the hands of its present holders may prove a very different one in the hands of others. And that this danger is incident to any strong stimulus of a promiscuous and absolute liberty of thought throughout society, seems as evident, and as much attested by experience, as the danger of persecution from religious earnestness and enthusiasm. Mr. Mill makes no secret of his anxiety about the latter. Christians may be pardoned, if, feeling strongly the value of their religion, they are not without uneasiness as to the former.

There is one incidental comment of Mr. Mill's on Christianity which appears strange in a writer of his largeness of mind. We entirely assent to the truth, and not merely the truth, but the needfulness of his remark that 'if Christians would teach infidels to be just to Christianity, they should themselves be just towards infidelity.' But this very remark makes the grudging and stinted justice the more surprising, of his assertion that 'the ideal of Christian morality (so called) is negative rather than positive; passive rather than active; Innocence rather than Nobleness; Abstinence from Evil rather than energetic Pursuit of Good; in its precepts (as has been well said) "thou shalt not" predominates unduly over "thou shalt." ' The assertion is the more remarkable as it is not necessary for his argument. He is answering a supposed objection to his statement that the truths that we have are commonly half-truths, requiring the supplement of other and seemingly opposite truths — an objection drawn from the allegation, that Christian morality at least is not a half-truth. It would be perfectly true to answer, that in a sense it is: that there is no evidence, that the New Testament was meant to enable us to do without the morality of nature and experience; and that in the absence of that evidence, it is no disparagement to the authority of the New Testament to say, that we are not likely to go right, if we try to do without that morality. This is no more than has been said over and over again by Christian writers. It has been acted on in the chief schools of Christian education from the beginning to the present day, where the types of natural greatness and the masters of natural wisdom have been studied with fearless and hearty frankness: and any attempt to narrow this plan, to exclude them from their influence on character and moral ideals to confine the sources of moral truth even to the most sacred of its authorities, has been condemned by the general sense of Christendom. Such an attempt, more than anything else, was the ruin of the Puritans; and it has been energetically repelled in our own day in the Roman Catholic Church of France. It is surely a common-place among most Christian teachers of any authority, that Christianity, as such, was intended to each us what nature and the world could not teach us; but that there is much that we were meant to be and to do, which it does not, and was not intended to teach us, because we were meant to learn it elsewhere. Of course, even *its* teaching would be imperfect, if it has not that supplied to it which it presupposes. As regards our Lord's own words, Mr. Mill makes in effect this answer. But he goes on to draw a distinction — a just one, if fairly stated — between Christian morality as taught by Him, and that which has grown up into a system in the Christian Church. Of this latter the same remark holds good as of the former: it is a system which primarily has in view objects not of this world, which, doubtless, often really, and more often apparently, clashes with what is wise and great for this world, but which, in the hands of its best expounders, has always sounded in harmony with, and implied the co-existence of, whatever was excellent in this world. It also needs something besides itself to complete, it may be, to balance it. This was enough for Mr. Mill's argument. But he goes beyond it, and as it seems to us, out of his way, to urge his unfavourable estimate of Christian morality. And we must repeat we read it with ever-increasing surprise. Mr. Mill, strangely enough, seems to take Calvinism as the type of Christianity; and when he wants an example of Christian greatness, to compare with and set below the heathen greatness of Pericles, he chooses John Knox: yet even the characteristic features of the Christianity of John Knox, with its rugged and inflexible zeal that stirred up the world, do not tally with a supposed ideal which is 'negative rather than positive — passive rather than active — innocence rather than nobleness — abstinence from evil rather than energetic pursuit of good.' But Mr. Mill need not be told that there is a larger, more ancient, more human conception of Christian morality than that of so-called Calvinism. Let us take this where we will, in its early or its later expressions. Whether sketched, assuredly with no narrow outline, by its greatest apostle — 'Finally, my brethren, whatsoever things are true, whatsoever things are honest, whatsoever things are just, whatsoever things are lovely, if there be any virtue, and if there be any praise, think on these things' — or exhibited even in the middle ages, in scholastic systems which incorporated with their theories, and co-ordinated with the 'Graces' of the New Testament, the Virtues of Aristotle, and in poetry like that of the 'Divina Commedia,' which catches life from everything that is living and that is great in man — or, lastly, more calmly analyzed and enforced by preachers and moralists like Bossuet and Butler, — it must have suffered a strange eclipse to the mental eye, which sees, as the predominating mark in it, a negative fear of evil, and cannot see in it, except in a subordinate degree, the appreciation and love and 'energetic pursuit' of good. Such misapprehensions are among the most impressive mementos of the limited grasp of the human mind. That a man like Mr. Mill should have made such a statement; that he should express himself, 'that what little recognition the idea of obligation to the public obtains in modern morality is derived from Greek and Roman sources, not from Christian;' and that 'in the morality of private life, whatever exists of magnanimity, high-mindedness, personal dignity, even the sense of honour, is derived from the purely human, not the religious part of our education, and never could have grown out *a standard of ethics in which the only worth, properly recognized, is that of obedience;*' — is only to be explained by remembering how great phenomena are often unrealized, even by the most powerful minds, when foreign to their usual ways of thought and life. It is an illustration, to be taken note of, and borne in mind when we are disposed to be uncharitable, of the real difficulties of fairness.,

We close Mr. Mill's book, not without great admiration for much clearly and nobly said, but yet with disappointment. Nowhere has the obligation been more strongly urged on those who are responsible for truth in society, of giving a fair hearing to opposite opinions; nowhere the advantage more forcibly set forth, to opinion and belief, of collision with real opposition. He has added one more to the varied testimonies which meet us on all sides, to the indispensable importance, in an age in which public opinion is so strong of individual character being proportionally free and strong, self-determined and self ruling. He recals, and forces us to reflect upon, in comparison with what we see and are, — the old type of manly grandeur, independent, fearless, and great in purposes, attempts, and deeds. And the protest is not unseasonable, which he enters against what is likely to be in increasing measure the evil of modern society, the intrusiveness and impertinence, as well as the oppressiveness, of social interference and narrowmindedness. And it is a rebuke to our lazy ways of thinking; a challenge to those, who have minds fit for it, to use them in serious conflict with the difficulties of thought and life. But we cannot find in it the clear line drawn, which it was written to draw, between liberty and the claims of society. It seems to us that, after all, our philosophical view of liberty is but slightly improved; that we must still work out its problems by experience, and find their limits by mere rule of thumb, and by taking out the scales, as each case arises for settlement, first from one side and then from the other, till the balance hangs even, as we do when measuring sugar against pound weights.

The value of a philosophical doctrine depends on the completeness with which it meets various and opposite difficulties of the case. It is not enough, that it states clearly and impressively the facts of one side, or that it wraps up and contains in itself a vast amount of important truth. If it does not lay this out in order and unravel it distinctly, so that the limits of each expression of truth are truly and clearly given — so that we are not obliged to take the truth in a lump with a whole tangle of possible ambiguities and misunderstandings hanging around it, it so far fails in its claim and utility as a philosophical doctrine. Aphorisms, as Mr. Mill has said elsewhere, contain truth in this manner — unanalyzed, unlaid-out, undiscriminated, unqualified, unbalanced. But a philosophical theory professes to do just what aphorisms do not. It professes to take account of difficulties, to meet exceptions, to give full prominence and due meaning to counter-appearances, to reconcile seemingly inconsistent facts, so that we feel that they *are* reconciled, and their fair and real weight given to each. If it does not do this, it is so far unsatisfactory; and however alluring and captivating at first glance, it must ultimately fail of its purpose, because it will more and more be felt to be not really available for the handling of practical questions.

And we cannot but feel that, with much that is true and admirable, this is the case with Mr. Mill's Essay. It is vitiated by the principle on which, according to it, the jurisdiction of society is to be regulated. That principle seems to us to leave but one great side of human nature, which is as clearly to be taken into account as the one on which Mr. Mill's theory lays stress, — the way, namely, in which by natural and inevitable laws, we *do* take account of the good of others, and feel ourselves bound to look after it and promote it, even in cases where they are indifferent or hostile to it. By the only conditions of human life and society with which we are as yet acquainted, we are invested with influence over others, over one another, of which we cannot divest ourselves, which we cannot help feeling, and cannot help using, ill or well. Mr. Mill is the last man to take mere abstract views of society. He must take things as he finds them, as they really exist — not as they would be under other imaginable circumstances, or as it might be supposed that they ought to be, under the supposition of man being a reasonable and responsible being. If he had stated the limits between the two principles, which often come into conflict, — the right of the individual to look after his own good, and the right and duty of others and of society to do so too, — he would have done good service; but to leave one out in theory is not to abolish it in nature, and to make a theory with one only, omitting the other as having no existence, is not to give us a sufficient philosophy. A theory of freedom, without also a theory of mutual action and influence, is but a theory of part of the social relations of men. He has told us a great deal about man, conceived as moving among others alone as an individual: he has not told us about man as a link in the network of society, necessarily acting as others, and acted on by them. People who are content with a vigorous, one-sided statement about liberty, may think that Mr. Mill has done enough. People who think that there is another side to the matter, besides individual liberty, will wish that it had been fairly dealt with by so powerful a mind, and will be of opinion that there is something still to be said and cleared up on the subject. We want those whose love of liberty is beyond suspicion to tell us the limits and benefits of custom and control; as we want those who do not undervalue authority to speak honestly and heartily of the claims and necessity of liberty.

THE DUBLIN REVIEW
Vol. 13 NS, 1869
[Edward Lucas]

Mill on Liberty

On Liberty, By John Stuart Mill. Third edition. London: Longmans, Green, & Co.

By the commonest consent of mankind, liberty is the very noblest of all the subjects which can occupy the human mind. In one shape or other, consciously or unconsciously, almost, if not quite, every sane man is engaged either in the defence of what he has already, or in the search for a yet greater liberty than falls at present to his share. The pursuit of wealth from the day labour of the poor to the great pecuniary operations of the rich; the clamour of parties; wars civil and foreign; the acquirement of knowledge divine no less than human; the self-discipline of saints and saintly men; in short, all efforts in every direction, have for their object either to escape the bondage of poverty and weakness, imperfection and sin; or to retain the present means, or enlarge the scope of action, spiritual, mental, or bodily; individual, corporate, or national.

Yet what is this thing which, in all ages, poets have sung, orators have lauded, philosophers have claimed as a right; for which patriots have worked and suffered; soldiers fought and died; and on which saints and theologians have insisted? Poets have exhausted their store of metaphors, one vying with another in boldness; orators have exaggerated every figure in rhetoric, philosophers have propounded the wildest theories, patriots and soldiers have worn out their lives in patient labour, or have fought at hopeless odds in its behalf; the air resounds with its praises. But what is it? The most despotic nations, referring back to ancient days, rest the traditions of their greatness upon struggles for this priceless blessing, without which it is held that life would not be worth the having. That we must have liberty at any cost is taken as too self-evident to need debate. The proposition is one to which direct appeal is seldom made; so obvious is it considered, that it is argued from by implication only. But yet once again we ask, in what does it consist? Some regard it as a political, some as a social good; if in one case the former be established, little is thought of the latter; or, again, unless the latter be secured, of what value the former? Some think it is for one class alone; some, for civilized nations only; some demand it for themselves and not for others; some would affix to it no bounds whatever, and some, who regard the thraldom of sin as the only slavery worth combating, rejoice in the glorious liberty of the bondage of Christ — deeming such bondage the best security for the widest freedom. Ideas regarding it are vague and contradictory. Men speak of it and write about it, but they do not define it. Nor is Mr. Mill an exception to this remark. In an essay of 200 pages, in which he professes to examine "Civil and Social Liberty, the nature and limits of the power which can be legitimately exercised by society on the individual," the reader looks in vain for a definition. This is the more astonishing because, in one of the early chapters of his book on Logic, Mr. Mill himself lays down what is tolerably self-evident that the first rule of logic is to see that terms be accurately defined. But, perhaps, like certain speakers in some well-known dialogues, Mr. Mill considers the word too plain to require defining. We propose here to review the Essay in question, for the purpose of seeing whether or no this be the case.

Like most other subjects in which men are interested, liberty has its two aspects. It may be looked at either in the abstract or in the concrete. A discussion on liberty may be taken either on its principles or on the practice of it. But it is clear there is no use in discussing its practical application without being first agreed on the principles by which we are to be guided. But in order to arrive at anything like a satisfactory notion of principles, we must first define the word itself. Now, as before remarked, this is precisely what Mr. Mill has failed to do. He leaves his reader at the disadvantage of having to pick out and joint together the detached pieces of his puzzle; to learn the map of liberty as we used to learn geography, with this difference, that under that system we knew when the whole map was complete, whereas Mr. Mill furnishes us with no means of such assurance. The only way open to us, therefore, is, to examine such principles as he asserts, either together or one by one, and so endeavour to make out his entire plan.

Now, after many pages he tells us the object of his Essay. "It[1] is," he says, "to assert one very simple principle as entitled to govern ABSOLUTELY the dealing of society with the individual, in the way of compulsion and control, whether the means used be physical force in the form of legal penalties, or the moral coercion of public opinion. That principle is, that the sole end for which mankind are warranted, individually or collectively, in interfering with the liberty of action of any of their number is self-protection. That the only purpose for which power can be rightly exercised over any member of a civilized community against his will is to prevent harm to others. His own good is not a sufficient warrant to justify compulsion: his conduct must be calculated to produce evil to some one else. . . . over himself, over his own body and mind, the individual is sovereign."

Again, he claims for every man[2] "absolute freedom of opinion and sentiment on all subjects, practical and speculative, scientific, moral, and theological; and of expression, as practically inseparable from opinion."

Moreover, he says[3] that the peculiar evil of silencing the expression of an opinion is that it is robbing the human race. For if the opinion be right, they are deprived of the opportunity of exchanging error for truth. If wrong, of what is almost as great a benefit, viz., the clearer perception of truth from its collision with error.

But in the next page he declares that we can never be sure that an opinion is false — and this he repeats in these words,[4] "An approach to truth is the amount of certainty attainable by a fallible being"; and this he again repeats[5] in almost the same words. Then[6] he says that he regards utility as the ultimate appeal on all ethical questions; but it must be utility grounded on the permanent interests of man as a progressive being. And in another place[7] he tells the world that the truth of an opinion

[1] P. 21.

[2] P. 26.

[3] P. 33.

[4] P. 41.

[5] P. 95.

[6] P. 24.

[7] P. 43.

is part of its utility. And again, he says,[8] "I altogether condemn the expressions 'the immorality and impiety of an opinion.'"

At page 22 he informs us that the principle laid down in the previous page is meant to apply only to human beings in the maturity of their faculties. And that[9] "despotism is a legitimate mode of government in dealing with barbarians, provided the end be their improvement, and the means justified by actually effecting that end."

Again, we are told[10] that "complete liberty of contradicting and disproving our opinion is the very condition which justifies us in assuming its truth for the purposes of action."

Moreover he elaborates the theory, that to silence any discussion is an assumption of infallibility. That is, it is not the being certain of the truth of an opinion, but the undertaking to decide a question for others, in which the assumption of infallibility consists. This agrees with the before quoted notion, that we can never be sure of the falsity of any opinion; and he argues that the assumption of infallibility is most fatal, precisely in those cases where the opinion is called immoral and impious, and he applies these remarks especially to the denial of the Being of God.

He declares further[11] that on any matter not self-evident there are ninety-nine persons totally incapable of judging of it for one who is capable; and that the capacity of the hundredth is only comparative.

From all this it will appear that Mr. Mill does not commence with a principle, and on it erect his superstructure.

His plan is rather to do that for which he condemns others, whose arguments, he says, on all great subjects are meant for their hearers, and are not those which have convinced themselves; who narrow their thoughts and interests to things which can be spoken without venturing within the region of principles. We venture to think that had Mr. Mill's character depended on this essay alone, he would never have acquired the reputation of a "logical consistent intellect." For it will be perceived, on carefully examining the foregoing passages, that

8   P. 45.

9   P. 23.

10   P. 38.

11   P. 38.

all he does is to take several of the current popular notions, which pass with the multitude for principles, and to push them to extremes, which are no doubt logical enough up to a certain point, but which fail absolutely when surveyed from a new point of view. The method is one with which every one who has argued much with Protestants must be perfectly familiar.

Thus, when he tells us that the sole end for which men can interfere with the liberty of their fellows is to prevent harm to others, we seem to have got hold of a principle; and when he further claims for every man the right, on this ground, not only to the most absolute freedom of opinion, but of expression, we seem to be making some progress. But the ground is cut from under our feet by his dictum, that utility is the ultimate appeal on all ethical questions. For we are driven back to consider what utility is, and how we are to judge of it. But here we are stopped again, for in the next sentence he affirms that it must be utility founded on the permanent interests of man as a progressive being. Now we have always supposed that an ultimate appeal must be to a first principle. But no; here we have an ultimate appeal based upon something as unsubstantial as itself, viz., upon "permanent interests," which are neither explained nor even alluded to any further, except to say that they are founded upon the progressive character of human nature. So that the "very simple principle," which is "absolutely to govern society" in its dealings with the individual, rests upon vague considerations of "utility," which rest again upon "permanent interests," which are vaguer still; and these upon a knowledge of human nature, which is still more vague; for, he says, we can never be sure that an opinion is false; an approach to truth being the amount of certainty attainable by a fallible being. These remarks, let it be remembered, are made to refer to a future state. Now, if the immortality of the soul be a matter of doubt, how can one be said to know anything definite of human nature in its entirety? His simple principle, therefore, has for its only foundation the old, exploded Pyrrhonism, the absurdity of which is no new discovery. For it is obvious that we cannot establish the principle that there is no certain knowledge, without declaring it certain that no certainty exists, which is a palpable contradiction. But if Mr. Mill is so clear that no certain knowledge exists, by what right does he come forward, and in a cloud of words proceed to delude his readers, admirers, and worshippers with talk about principles and rights and truth and utility? Why did he not being his Essay with the declaration that his whole system is a mere guess? that he *knows* nothing of what he is writing about; and that, as there must needs be many errors to one truth, the chances are a thousand to one that he is going to write absurdities?

One cannot understand how it is that Mr. Mill should be so sure that no certain knowledge is to be found, and yet that he should argue in a directly opposite sense. It cannot be denied that he has in no common degree a logical mind. He sees plainly enough where many of the weak points in his argument lie, and he stops up the holes through which an objection might enter with the greatest ingenuity, or rather with the cleverness which continual discussion and a perfect familiarity with popular theories and popular objections are calculated to impart. Nevertheless, after an argument of seven pages, commencing with the sentence already quoted, and ending with these words, "the beliefs for which we have most warrant have no safeguard to rest on but a standing invitation to the whole world to prove them unfounded," supplemented with the further declaration that "an approach to truth" is "the amount of certainty attainable by a fallible being"; and after telling us that he "regards utility as the ultimate appeal in all ethical questions," it does seem singular to find,[12] "the truth of an opinion is part of its utility." So that the ultimate appeal depends again upon truth, which cannot possibly be ascertained for certain. Moreover[13] we find, that holding the truth without knowing the arguments by which it is maintained, is not knowing the truth. But how can one know without being sure that one knows? Real knowledge is real certainty, and if certainty be denied, to talk of knowing the truth is a contradiction in terms. An ignorant man fancies he knows; but one who does know cannot be in doubt as to his knowledge, still less can he hold that all knowledge is doubtful. Acquaintance with the arguments by which an uncertain theory is maintained does not add one jot to the certainty of the theory itself, by the very condition of the case supposed. But Mr. Mill's actual words are, "We can never be sure that an opinion

[12] P. 43.

[13] P. 65.

is false." We do not see that a quibble can be raised on this, for if we cannot know what is false, neither can we know what is true; and if we know a thing to be true, we know its opposite to be false, and this is the possibility which Mr. Mill denies. This will sufficiently guard us against any charge of misrepresentation.

Here it might seem advisable to stop. It might fairly be said that any edifice built on such shifting sands will soon fall; and no doubt this is true. Another age will review with wonder this return to the hopeless Eleatic scepticism. It will search for some moral cause as alone sufficient to lead a man like Mr. Mill into that very world of universal doubt from which the old philosophers struggled with such melancholy impotence to get free. Some future biographer may perhaps draw a parallel between Mr. Mill rejected from the British Senate, and the founder of the New Academy banished from Rome on the demand of Cato. But in the mean time his books are read; and with all the more avidity, because he says many plausible things, and much that is true, and all in an attractive style; but chiefly because he brings into definite shape, and defends with more constructive power than others, the notions on which Protestantism is founded, and which have not hitherto been placed before the multitude upon a quasi-philosophical basis. Many of his remarks are, no doubt, what it is the fashion to call *suggestive*, and for these he is entitled to our thanks: they contain a foundation of truth, though, to be sure, like certain dishes, in a celebrated banquet —

Longè dissimilem noto celantia succum,

they indicate a want of skill in the preparation. His attack upon authority, though more uncompromising, and though conducted with less reserve than usual, is but the legitimate result of common Protestantism, and he is quite justified in remarking how strange it is that men should admit the validity of arguments, yet object to their being pushed to an extreme; as if reasons could be good for any case which are not good for an extreme case. While, therefore, Mr. Mill holds a kind of intellectual supremacy over the minds of so many, and while, on the one hand, attacks upon authority are increasing in number and audacity, and while, on the other hand, the class of men is daily augmented, who, weary of their labyrinthine search after truth, are craving to be led back to authority by a process of intellectual conviction, it seems not unreasonable to give some sort of reply to his attack.

It is satisfactory to know that Mr. Mill deprecates[14] "the fashion of the present time to disparage negative logic" — that which points out weaknesses in theory and errors in practice, without establishing positive truths, — "for as a means to attaining any positive knowledge or conviction worthy the name, it cannot," he says, "be valued too highly." We will not stop to do more than to mention the difficulty of acquiring positive knowledge, since no certain truth is, according to himself, attainable. But we will recur at once to passages already quoted, and will allow the reader to judge how far they are consistent one with another. The negative logic will be found very useful here. For a system inconsistent with itself cannot but be false. If, therefore, we can show such inconsistency, Mr. Mill's system falls to the ground; if not, the advantage will be with him.

As we have seen, he claims for every sane adult absolute freedom of opinion, and of expression as inseparable from opinion. He declares that to silence the expression of an opinion is to rob the human race; and also he condemns altogether the phrase "immorality or impiety of an opinion": and further, asserts that the assumption of infallibility, that is, the silencing of discussion, is most fatal in those cases where the opinion silenced is called immoral or impious.

It is evident, therefore, that should a schoolmaster open a school in which atheism is publicly taught, the State would have no right to put him to silence. To do so would be most fatal: his opinions being neither immoral nor impious, and being moreover possibly true, mankind would certainly be robbed, and might be deprived of the inestimable good of exchanging the false belief in God for the true belief in no God, should the latter be really true; for at present the world has not become prepared to receive so very recondite a doctrine. But, it may be said, though the State may not interfere with the schoolmaster, it may prohibit scholars from frequenting the school. This, however, would be to interfere directly with parents, and indirectly with the master too, and would be assuming the fatal gift of infallibility: whereas, we can never be

14 P. 81.

sure that either the belief or the disbelief in God is true, for we are not sure of the falsity of any opinion.

But suppose the State to be profoundly convinced that its whole authority is derived from God, and that if the belief in God be destroyed, the proximate result will be anarchy, what course must it take? Provisionally it *may*, even according to Mr. Mill, and it *must*, by every reasonable consideration, act upon its belief, upon its strong conviction; that is, it may silence the schoolmaster or public lecturer, for the case is the same, upon condition of giving him complete liberty of contradiction and disproving the opinion of the State, which is the most palpable contradiction. But Mr. Mill is a logician. He recognizes the fact that " it is far from a frequent accomplishment even among thinkers to know both sides." He expressly mentions mathematical and physical speculations, and he maintains that on no subject except these does any opinion deserve the name of knowledge, unless after either an active controversy with opponents, or an equivalent mental process. Having this conviction, he must therefore have passed through such a process himself. He cannot have neglected to do so. He is enamoured of the Socratic dialectics. By them he will test every philosophical assertion, and he is no doubt equally willing to be so tested himself.

Let us, then, see how he would stand a dissection — we will not say after the Socratic method, but after such fashion as to a man of average clearness of perception is possible. Let us repeat two passages already quoted, and let us examine them strictly. Mr. Mill is not the man to shrink from any proof, however strict. He courts trial. He is a hard hitter, and he does not expect any opponent to accept his challenge, which is offered to all comers, with the reverse of his lance: the combat is understood on both sides to be á l'outrance: ridicule and sarcasm are weapons which he does not disdain to use, and to which he does not object; and they are perfectly lawful. All that can be required is that the fighting be according to the rules of courtesy.

He says, — 1st.[15] "The only purpose for which power can be rightfully exercised over any member of a civilized community against his will, is to prevent harm to others."

---

[15] P. 22.

2nd.[16] "Despotism is a legitimate mode of government in dealing with barbarians, provided the end be their improvement, and the means justified by actual effecting that end. Liberty, as a principle, has no application till men have become capable of being improved by free and equal discussion."

Now every one who has ever read any of Plato's dialogues, either in the original or in a translation, knows that the first question which Socrates is always represented as putting has for its object on every occasion to get at a definition of common words used by the other interlocutors. The same may not be an inconvenient plan to adopt here, and as we have not Mr. Mill to interrogate, we must be content to assume, if possible, such meanings as he would not question. And first, as to the word "rightfully"; by this no doubt is meant justly, or according to justice; and justice, we may presume to be equally the right of all men; that could scarcely be denied: the words right and justice then are of universal application: they apply to all men, at all times, and under all circumstances, in one country as well as another: were they absent, the human race itself could not exist, for society would be impossible, because they are at the root and basis of all our mutual relations. This is an *abstract* idea of justice or right: in the *concrete*, in the practical application of justice, it will be admitted that as circumstances vary, so must the conduct change, which it is right or just to pursue under the circumstances. Thus, it is right to restore to a man his sword, but not if he be in a rage and likely to hurt himself or others with it; and so on in an infinite number of circumstances simple and intricate. So far then as to the word rightfully; and the meaning of legitimate, as used in the second passage quoted, appears to be synonymous with "rightfully." "Despotism," in the same passage, evidently means a government which actually interferes with the individual in a great degree, not merely in order to prevent harm to others, but for his own good.

It is obvious, therefore, that different forms of government are allowable or legitimate under differing circumstances. Now, as a perfectly free government is, according to Mr. Mill, the only rightful one in a civilized community, and as a despotism is legitimate in dealing with barbarians; and as there

[16] P. 23.

are many shades of national characteristics between gross barbarism and high civilization, Mr. Mill will no doubt admit that corresponding degrees of despotism or freedom must be as legitimate in their respective places, as either complete freedom or complete despotism. But opinions on civilization differ; scarcely will two men agree on a definition of the word: the Greeks considered all other men barbarians; the Chinese take the same view at the present time; and Europeans hold Chinese civilization very cheap. Whether any nation has arrived at the enviable condition of being capable of improvement by free and equal discussion, is simply a matter of opinion. It cannot be otherwise, for the facts are disputable in every conceivable case. Now Mr. Mill says, the only nations with which we need concern ourselves in this discussion have long since reached that condition. But the whole controversy turns on this very point. Have any nations, and what nations, arrived as a matter of fact at the condition contemplated? and if they have, who knows the fact, and how is it known? But Mr. Mill is laying down a principle. He cannot confine himself to this nation or that; a principle is of universal application, and the present principle concerns justice, which is the right of all mankind equally. But if it be alleged that he is speaking of the application of the principle only, we reply, the very use of the word "rightfully" implies something universal, and to confine it within the limits of what any individual may be pleased to call civilization, is to make justice a mere matter of opinion. And this is in truth what Mr. Mill does: the word, as he applies it, means this only, that *in his opinion* a nation or nations have reached a point at which a certain amount of freedom is a real right. He has not advanced the argument a single step. He must mend his definition, or give up his principle: he argues like a very Thrasymachus; he muddles together the expedient and the just in the old old style. He makes himself, or some other individual, the judge of when and whether a right which he declares to be absolute can be insisted on at a given time, or at all. We mean this: if interference be only just under certain conditions, it is because subjects have a right to reject interference under any other conditions; but who is the judge whether those circumstances exist or no? Whether the decision on that point depends upon rulers or people, Mr. Mill leaves undetermined, so that on this theory, justice (for these people) becomes, we repeat, a mere matter of opinion, which is absurd.

But more, "despotism is only legitimate provided the end be the improvement of barbarians, and the means justified by actually effecting that result." That is to say, a ruler is justified in his despotism to-day provided such despotism actually improves his subjects twenty or fifty years hence. But his experiment, made in perfect good faith it may be, is not justified if it be not successful. So that *he* can appeal *during* the experiment to Mr. Mill's dictum in support of his despotism, and his subjects can appeal equally to Mr. Mill's dictum against it *afterwards* in case his plan fails. In other words, what is just to-day is to-morrow proved by the event not to have been just, at the very moment when it was just. It seems positively astounding that a man of Mr. Mill's logical habit of mind should put his hand to such sentences as these. But perhaps the explanation is to be found in another remark quoted above,[17] where he says that ninety-nine men out of a hundred are incapable of judging of any matter not self-evident. He has, it would seen, a contemptible opinion of the human understanding as it exists at present. He takes it for granted, perhaps, that the ninety-nine cannot discover his sophisms, and that the hundredth will not expose them. His propositions are, to say the least not axiomatic. They do not strike the mind as truths at first sight; they require much patient investigation; and, after all, they are not convincing: the unquestionable ingenuity with which they are worked out would be a greater proof of genius were they original. But after all, they are, we repeat nothing but popular fallacies more skilfully stated than usual. And it is this which gives them their chief importance. There is no profound philosophy in them. At least, having no claim whatever to be the hundredth man; being only *unus multorum*, one who runs; we confess, we have no difficulty whatever in admitting our inability to understand this fabric without basis, this lever without fulcrum, this progress from no starting-place and towards no goal, this knowledge begotten of doubt, this logic without premises and without conclusion, or rather, let us say, this ocean of hypothetical propositions which yields before us and closes behind us, as though the whole intellectual life and activity of man were one infinite and eternal If.

So far as to Mr. Mill's principles. One or two other questions, however, suggest themselves for solution before we

[17]   P. 38.

conclude. Does Mr. Mill really mean to say that the bulk of mankind, of whom, according to himself, so very large a proportion is utterly incapable of comprehending any question not self-evident, is to refuse to accept premisses on authority? Leaving aside altogether the practical contradiction of requiring the unintelligent ninety-nine, the very persons who cannot take in a proposition even when it is furnished them, to invent propositions for themselves, one would like to know from whence Mr. Mill got his own knowledge of the meaning of simple facts when playing around his mother's knee? Did he take no premiss on authority? Does he deny that the learner is under obligation to obey? Will he assert that in any conceivable condition of society any very considerable proportion of mankind can become teachers? It would lead one very much too far to prove the profound metaphysical truth conveyed in those few words, *nisi credatis non intelligetis*, unless you believe neither shall you understand. Suffice it to remark, that this saying is as philosophically sound, as it would be practically absurd to call upon the multitude even of educated men, in the midst of the struggle for life, to be for ever questioning first principles of metaphysics, or philosophy, or even of morals. For it is to first principles we ascend when we discuss the question of authority. Mr. Mill himself, in denying the claims of authority, does so only after a very profound investigation. Or, if he refuse to admit this, of what value are his conclusions? We are told that, before writing his book on politics, Aristotle studied the constitutions of many states; and we must presume that Mr. Mill has not only done likewise, but that he would require a similar course of study in those who are to discard authority; but to ninety-nine men out of every hundred such a study would be the most wearisome labour, not to say an utter impossibility. So that they must be slaves to Mr. Mill's intellectual disc pline, in order that they may enjoy a liberty whose sweets they neither desire nor even understand.

Let us proceed now to make two or three remarks on the chapter on Individuality. In this chapter are many excellent ideas. But, unfortunately, even the pure metal often has not the true ring; it is like a cracked coin, which requires a searching test to prove its genuineness. Thus, when we are told that "*even opinions lose their immunity*" when expressed under circumstances calculated to lead to some mischievous act, we at once admit the truth of the remark, however oddly the word *even* may sound. But when this principle comes to be applied, infallibility is at once assumed. For if it be true that private property is robbery, that[18] "interest on capital is a permanent source of injustice and inequality," or that "machinery in the hands of capitalists is a powerful instrument of despotism and extortion," and that therefore "machines and all the instruments of labour ought to be in the hands of productive labourers," what justice can there be in suppressing the expression of those principles, however public, and what mischief in seizing property and destroying machinery belonging to the employers of labour? The object of this chapter, however, is to insist upon the necessity for the universal development of the faculties of the individual, and to protest against the tyranny of society and of custom over the individual. It is too true, as Mr. Mill says, that at present society weighs heavily upon individuality, and that from the highest class down to the lowest every one lives too much under the eye of a dreaded censorship. And Mr. Mill will, no doubt, agree that the only remedy for such a state of things is to cause true principles to predominate in the mind of society at large. As to the way in which this desirable result can be brought about, whether it be by the free expression of false principles, the encouragement of charlatanry, the diffusion of newspaper philosophy and the metaphysics of novels, or by a method of a diametrically opposite kind, he and we will not agree. Nor is this the place to enter into the discussion. In this paper we are only engaged in showing Mr. Mill's inconsistencies. The establishment of our own theory is too long a task to be entered upon here; and we shall conclude with pointing out that his "applications" are quite at variance with, what seems to be, his fundamental proposition, if any such proposition can be said to exist. We shall give but two specimens, and let the reader judge for himself.

At page 169 the maxim is laid down, "that for such actions as are prejudicial to the interests of others, the individual is accountable, and we may be subjected to legal punishment." Now here again we are placed in the difficulty of not having a definition of the word used. What, for instance, does Mr. Mill mean by "actions"? Is the publication of opinions an "action"?

---

[18]   Report of International Working Men's Congress in Brussels, *Times*, September 14, 1868.

If it be not, what is it? If it be, and if the general sense of mankind in favour of religion be founded in the truth, then it follows that to publish atheistical opinions should render the publisher subject to legal punishment. But no punishment for the expression of opinion is allowable, since the opinion may be true. Most likely Mr. Mill would indignantly disclaim the imputation of atheism if applied to himself; but we take it, that the question of the existence or non-existence of God is one on which the mind cannot remain in suspense. To doubt the existence of God is precisely the same, both intellectually and practically, as to deny the fact. Doubt excludes worship and the idea of religious obligation, quite as effectually as denial. You can neither worship nor feel responsible to a Being who may possibly not exist. Certainty is of the very essence of the recognition of responsibility or duty. A government must therefore be either atheistical or the reverse. Now no government has ever yet tried the experiment of professing atheism. Some have gone a long way in this direction, but none of which we ever heard has made the open profession; and till one is discovered which does not regard religion as the foundation of social order, the right to punish the publication of atheistical opinions cannot be denied in practice, even according to Mr. Mill's own maxim.

Again, Mr. Mill is an advocate for divorce in certain cases. Now he cannot deny that to pass a law legalizing divorce, or any other practice, is a direct encouragement to such practice. If therefore divorce be contrary to the law of God, to pass a statute legalizing it is to grant and encourage a liberty which is contrary to true liberty; and this cannot be, even on Mr. Mill's own showing, for he says, "the principle of freedom cannot require that a man should be free not to be free"; and by the same rule, a liberty which is contrary to true liberty is freedom in name alone, and not in truth; in other words, it is slavery to error. But, says Mr. Mill, the law of God on this point, as on others, is uncertain; and therefore the State has no right to restrict the liberty of the subject in the matter. That is to say, the State is bound, in behalf of liberty, to permit, and therefore to encourage, a practice which may be contrary to liberty!

We have done with Mr. Mill on Liberty. It is plain the English public at large views his Essay very differently from ourselves, for it has run through several editions. We suppose the explanation to be, that the great name of the author lends a sanction and an authority to notions which are the foundation of Protestantism, and the logical results of which have been obscured by the mist with which educational prejudice clouds the intellects of so many Englishmen.

THE FORTNIGHTLY REVIEW
Vol. 20, 1873
[John Morley]

Mr. Mill's Doctrine of Liberty

Mr. Mill's memorable plea for social liberty was little more than an enlargment, though a very important enlargement, of the principles of the still more famous Speech for Liberty of Unlicensed Printing with which Milton ennobled English literature two centuries before. Milton contended for free publication of opinion mainly on these grounds: First, that the opposite system implied the 'grace of infallibility and incorruptibleness' in the licensers. Second, that the prohibition of bold books led to mental indolence and stagnant formalism both in teachers and congregations, producing the 'laziness of a licensing church.' Third, that it 'hinders and retards the importation of our richest merchandise, truth', for the commission of the licenser enjoins him to let nothing pass which is not vulgarly received already, and 'if it come to prohibiting, there is not aught more likely to be prohibited than truth itself, whose first appearance to our eyes, bleared and dimmed with prejudice and custom, is more unsightly and unplausible than many errors, even as the person is of many a great man slight and contemptible to see to.' Fourth, that freedom is in itself an ingredient of true virtue, and 'they are not skilful considerers of human things who imagine to remove sin by removing the matter of sin; that virtue therefore, which is but a youngling in the contemplation of evil, and knows not the utmost that vice promises to her followers, and rejects it, is but a blank virtue, not a pure; her virtue is but an excremental virtue, which was the reason why our sage and serious poet Spenser, whom I dare be known to think a better teacher than Scotus or Aquinas, describing true temperance under the form of Guion, brings him in with his palmer through the cave of Mammon and the tower of earthly bliss, that he might see and know and yet abstain.'

271

The four grounds on which Mr. Mill contends for the necessity of freedom in the expression of opinion to the mental well-being of mankind are virtually contained in these. His four grounds are, (1) that the silenced opinion may be true; (2) it may contain a portion of truth, essential to supplement the prevailing opinion; (3) vigorous contesting of opinions that are even wholly true is the only way of preventing them from sinking to the level of uncomprehended prejudices; (4) without such contesting, the doctrine will lose its vital effect on character and conduct.

But Milton drew the line of liberty at what he calls 'neighbouring differences, or rather indifferences.' The Arminian controversy had loosened the bonds with which the newly liberated churches of the Reformation had made haste to bind themselves again, and weakened that authority of confessions, which had replaced the older but not more intolerant authority of the universal church. Other controversies which raged during the first half of the seventeenth century, — those between Catholics and Protestants, between prelatists and presbyterians, between Socinians and Trinitarians, between latitudinarians, puritans, and sacramentalists, — all tended to weaken theological exclusiveness. This slackening, however, was no more than partial. Roger Williams, indeed, the Welsh founder of Rhode Island, preached, as early as 1631, the principles of an unlimited toleration, extending to Catholics, Jews, and even infidels. Milton stopped a long way short of this. He did not mean "tolerated popery and open superstition, which, as it extirpates all religious and civil supremacies, so itself should be extirpate, provided first that all charitable and compassionate means be used to win and regain the weak and the misled: that also which is impious or evil absolutely either against faith or manners no law can possibly permit that intends not to unlaw itself."

Locke, writing five and forty years later, somewhat widened these limitations. His question was not merely whether there should be free expression of opinion, but whether there should furthermore be freedom of worship and of religious union. He answered both questions affirmatively, — not on the semi-sceptical grounds of Jeremy Taylor, which is also one of the grounds taken by Mr. Mill, that we cannot be sure that our own opinion is the true one, — but on the strength of his definition of the province of the civil magistrate. Locke held that the magistrate's whole jurisdiction reached only to civil concernments, and that "all civil power, right, and dominion, is bounded to that only care of promoting these things; and that it neither can nor ought in any manner to be extended to the saving of souls. This chiefly because the power of the civil magistrate consists only in outward force, while true and saving religion consists in the inward persuasion of the mind, without which nothing can be acceptable to God, and such is the nature of the understanding that it cannot be compelled to the belief of anything by outward force. . . . It is only light and evidence that can work a change in men's opinions; and that light can in no manner proceed from corporal sufferings, or any other outward penalties." "I may grow rich by an art that I take not delight in; I may be cured of some disease by remedies that I have not faith in; but I cannot be saved by a religion that I distrust and a ritual that I abhor." (*First Letter concerning Toleration.*) And much more in the same excellent vein. But Locke fixed limits to toleration. 1. No opinions contrary to human society, or to those moral rules which are necessary to the preservation of civil society, are to be tolerated by the magistrate. Thus, to take examples from our own day, a conservative minister would think himself right on this principle in suppressing the Land and Labour League, a Catholic minister in dissolving the Education League, and any minister in making mere member-ship of the Mormon sect a penal offence. 2. No tolerance ought to be extended to "those who attribute unto the faithful, religious, and orthodox, that is in plain terms unto themselves, any peculiar privilege or power above other mortals, in civil concernments; or who upon pretence of religion do challenge any manner of authority over such as are not associated with them in their ecclesiastical communion." As I have seldom heard of any sect, except the Friends, who did not challenge as much authority as it could possibly get over persons not associated with it, this would amount to a universal proscrip-tion of religion; but Locke's principle might at any rate be invoked against Ultramontanism in some circumstances. 3. Those are not at all to be tolerated who deny the being of God. The taking away of God, *though but even in thought*, dissolves all society; and promises, covenants, and oaths, which are the bonds of human society, have no hold on such. Thus the police ought to close Mr. Bradlaugh's Hall of Science, and perhaps on some occasions the Positivist School.

Locke's principles depended on a distinction between civil concernments, which he tries to define, and all other concernments. Warburton's arguments on the alliance between church and state turned on the same point, as did the once famous Bangorian controversy. This distinction would fit into Mr. Mill's cardinal position, which consists in a distinction between the things that only affect the doer or thinker of them, and the things that affect other persons as well. Locke's attempt to divide civil affairs from affairs of salvation was satisfactory enough for the comparatively narrow object with which he opened his discussion. Mr. Mill's account of civil affairs is both wider and more definite; naturally so, as he had to maintain the cause of toleration in a much more complex set of social conditions, and amid a far greater diversity of speculative energy, than any one dreamed of in Locke's time. Mr. Mill limits the province of the civil magistrate to the repression of acts that directly and immediately injure others than the doer of them. So long as acts, including the expression of opinions, are purely self-regarding, it seems to him expedient in the long run that they should not be interfered with by the magistrate. He goes much further than this. Self-regarding acts should not be interfered with by the magistrate; not only self-regarding acts, but all opinions whatever, should, moreover, be as little interfered with as possible by public opinion, except in the way of vigorous argumentation and earnest persuasion in a contrary direction; the silent but most impressive solicitation of virtuous example; the wise and careful upbringing of the young, so that when they enter life they may be most nobly fitted to choose the right opinions and obey the right motives.

The considerations by which he supports this rigorous confinement of external interference on the part of government, or the unorganized members of the community whose opinion is called public opinion, to cases of self-protection, are these, some of which have been already stated: —

1. By interfering to suppress opinions or experiments in living, you may resist truths and improvements in a greater or less degree.
2. Constant discussion is the only certain means of preserving the freshness of truth in men's minds, and the vitality of its influence upon their conduct and motives.
3. Individuality is one of the most valuable elements of well-

being, and you can only be sure of making the most of individuality if you have an atmosphere of freedom, encouraging free development and expansion.

4. Habitual resort to repressive means of influencing conduct tends more than anything else to discredit and frustrate the better means, such as education, good example, and the like. (*Liberty*, 148.)

The principle which he deduces from these considerations is — "that the sole end for which mankind are warranted, individually or collectively, in interfering with the liberty of action of any of their number is self-protection; the only purpose for which power can be rightfully exercised over any member of a civilised community, is to prevent harm to others. His own good, either physical or moral, is not a sufficient warrant. He cannot be rightfully compelled to do or forbear because it will make him happier, because in the opinion of others to do so would be wise, or even right. These are good reasons for remonstrating with him, or reasoning with him, or persuading him, or entreating him, but not for compelling him, or visiting him with any evil in case he do otherwise. To justify that the conduct from which it is desired to deter him must be calculated to produce evil to others." (*Liberty*, 22.)

Two disputable points in the above doctrine are likely at once to reveal themselves to the least critical eye. First, that doctrine would seem to check the free expression of disapproval; one of the most wholesome and indispensable duties which anybody with interest in serious questions has to perform, and the non-performance of which would remove the most proper and natural penalty from frivolous or perverse opinions and obnoxious conduct. Mr. Mill deals with this difficulty as follows: — "We have a right in various ways to act upon our unfavourable opinion of any one, not to the oppression of his individuality, but in the exercise of ours. We are not bound, for example, to seek his society; we have a right to avoid it (though not to parade the avoidance), for we have a right to choose the society most acceptable to us. We have a right, and it may be our duty, to caution others against him, if we think his example or conversation likely to have a pernicious effect on those with whom he associates. We may give others a preference over him in optional good offices, except those which tend to his improvement. In these various modes a person may suffer very severe penalties at the hands of others for faults which directly concern only himself; but he suffers these penalties only in so far as they are the natural, and as it were the spontaneous, consequences of the faults themselves, not because they are purposely inflicted on him for the sake of punishment." (*Liberty*, 139.) This appears to be a satisfactory way of meeting the objection. For though the penalties of disapproval may be just the same, whether deliberately inflicted, or naturally and spontaneously falling on the object of such disapproval, yet there is a very intelligible difference between the two processes in their effect on the two parties concerned. A person imbued with Mr. Mill's principle would feel the responsibility of censorship much more seriously; would reflect more carefully and candidly about the conduct or opinion of which he thought ill; would be more on his guard against pharisaic censoriousness and that desire to be ever judging one another, which Milton well called the stronghold of our hypocrisy. The disapproval of such a person would have an austere colour, a gravity, a self-respecting reserve, which could never belong to an equal degree of disapproval in a person who had started from the officious principle, that if we are sure we are right, it is straightway our business to make the person whom we think wrong smart for his error. And in the same way such disapproval would be much more impressive to the person whom it affected. If it was justified, he would be like a froward child who is always less effectively reformed — if reformable at all — by angry chidings and passionate punishments, than by the sight of a cool and austere displeasure which lets him persist in his frowardness is he chooses.

The second weak point in the doctrine lies in the extreme vagueness of the terms, protective and self-regarding. The practical difficulty begins with the definition of these terms. Can any opinion or any serious part of conduct be looked upon as truly and exclusively self-regarding? This central ingredient in the discussion seems insufficiently laboured in the essay on Liberty. Yet it is here more than anywhere else that controversy is needed to clear up what is in just as much need of elucidation, whatever view we may take of the inherent virtue of freedom — whether we look on freedom as a mere negation, or as one of the most powerful positive conditions of attaining the highest kind of human excellence.

We may best estimate the worth and the significance of the doctrine of liberty by considering the line of thought and observation which led to it. To begin with, it is in Mr. Mill's hands something quite different from the same doctrine as preached by the French revolutionary school; indeed one might even call it reactionary in respect of the French theory of a hundred years back. It reposes on no principle of abstract right, but like all the rest of its author's opinions, on principles of utility and experience. Dr. Arnold used to divide reformers into two classes, popular and liberal; the first he defined as seekers of liberty, the second as seekers of improvement; the first were the goats, and the second were the sheep. Mr. Mill's doctrine denied the mutual exclusiveness of the two parts of this classification, for it made improvement the end and the test, but it proclaimed liberty to be the means. Every thinker now perceives that the strongest and most durable influences in every western society lead in the direction of democracy, and tend with more or less rapidity to throw the control of social organization into the hands of numerical majorities. There are many people who believe that if you only make the ruling body big enough, it is sure to be either very wise itself, or very eager to choose wise leaders. Mr. Mill, as any one who is familiar with his writings is well aware, did not hold this opinion. He had no more partiality for mob rule than De Maistre or Goethe or Mr. Carlyle. He saw its evils more clearly than any of these eminent men, because he had a more scientific eye, and because he had had the invaluable training of a political administrator on a large scale and in a most responsible post. But he did not content himself with seeing these evils, and he wasted no energy in passionate denunciation of them, which he knew must prove futile. Guizot said of De Tocqueville that he was an aristocrat who accepted his defeat. Mr. Mill was too penetrated by popular sympathies to be an aristocrat in De Tocqueville's sense, but he, likewise, was full of ideas and hopes which the unchecked or undirected course of democracy would defeat without chance of reparation. This fact he accepted, and from this he started. Mr. Carlyle, and one or two rhetorical imitators, poured malediction on the many-headed populace, and with a rather pitiful impatience insisted that the only hope for men lay in their finding and obeying a strong man, a king, a hero, a dictator. How he was to be found, neither the master nor his still angrier and more impatient mimics could ever tell us. The scream of this whole school is a mockery.

Now Mr. Mill's doctrine laid down the main condition of finding your hero; namely, that all ways should be left open to him, because no man, nor majority of men, could possibly tell by which of these ways their deliverers were from time to time destined to present themselves. Wits have caricatured all this by asking us whether by encouraging the tares to grow you give the wheat a better chance. This is as misleading as such metaphors usually are. The doctrine of liberty rests on a faith drawn from the observation of human progress, that though we know wheat to be serviceable and tares to be worthless, yet there are in the great seed-plot of human nature a thousand rudimentary germs, not wheat and not tares, of whose properties we have not had a fair opportunity of assuring ourselves. If you are too eager to pluck up the tares, you are very likely to pluck up with them these untried possibilities of human excellence, and you are, moreover, very likely to injure the growing wheat as well. The demonstration of this lies in the recorded experience of mankind.

Nor is this all. Mr. Mill's doctrine does not lend the least countenance to the cardinal opinion of some writers in the last century, that the only need of human character and of social institutions is to be let alone. He never said that we were to leave the ground uncultivated to bring up whatever might chance to grow. On the contrary, the ground was to be cultivated with the utmost care and knowledge, with a view to prevent the growth of tares — but cultivated in a certain manner. You may take the method of the Inquisition, of the more cruel of the Puritans, of De Maistre, of Mr. Carlyle; or you may take Mr. Mill's method of cultivation. According to the doctrine of Liberty, we are to devote ourselves to prevention, as the surest and most wholesome mode of extirpation. Persuade, argue, cherish virtuous example; bring up the young in habits of right opinion and right motive; shape your social arrangements so as to stimulate the best parts of character. By these means you will gain all the advantages that could possible have come of heroes and legislative dragooning, as well as a great many more which neither heroes nor legislative dragooning could ever have secured.

It is well with men, Mr. Mill said moreover, in proportion as they respect truth. Now they at once prove and strengthen their respect for truth by having an open mind to all its possibilities, while at the same time they hold firmly to their own proved convictions, until they hear better evidence to the contrary. There is no anarchy, nor uncertainty, nor paralysing air of provisionalness in such a frame of mind. So far is it from being fatal to loyalty or reverence, that it is an indispensable part of the groundwork of the only loyalty that a wise ruler or teacher would care to inspire — the loyalty springing from a rational conviction that in a field open to all comers he is the best man they can find. Only on condition of liberty without limit is the ablest and most helpful of "heroes" sure to be found; and only on condition of liberty without limit are his followers sure to worthy of him. You must have authority, and yet must have obedience. The noblest and deepest and most beneficient kind of authority is that which rests on an obedience that is rational, deliberate, and spontaneous.

The same futile impatience which animates the political utterances of Mr. Carlyle and his more weak-voiced imitators, takes another form in men of a different training or temperament. They insist that if the majority has the means of preventing vice by law, it is folly and weakness not to resort to those means. The superficial attractiveness of such a doctrine is obvious. Criminal lawyers and passionate philanthropists treat is as self-evident. The doctrine of liberty implies a broader and a more patient view. It says: — "Even if you could be sure that what you take for vice is so — and the history of persecution shows how careful you should be in this preliminary point — even then it is an undoubted and, indeed, a necessary tendency of this facile repressive legislation to make those who resort to it, neglect the more effective, humane, and durable kinds of preventive legislation. You pass a law (if you can) putting down drunkenness; there is a neatness in such a method very attractive to fervid and impatient natures. Would you not have done better to leave that law unpassed, and apply yourselves sedulously instead to the improvement of the dwellings of the more drunken class, to the provision of amusements that might compete with the ale-house, to the extension and elevation of instruction, and so on? You may say that this should be done, and yet the other should not be left undone; but, as matter of fact and history, the doing of the one has always gone with the neglect of the other, and ascetic law-making in the interests of virtue, has never been accompanied either by law-making or any other kinds of activity for making virtue easier and more attractive. It is the recognition how little punishment can do, that leaves men free to see how much social prevention can do." I believe, then, that what seems to the criminal lawyers and passionate philanthropists self-evident, is in truth an illusion, springing from a very shallow kind of impatience, heated in some of them by the addition of a cynical contempt for human nature and the worth of human existence.

If people believe that the book of social or moral knowledge is now completed, that we have turned over the last page and heard the last word, much of the foundation of Mr. Mill's doctrine would disappear. But those who hold this can hardly have much to congratulate themselves upon. If it were so, and if governments were to accept the principle that the only limits to the enforcement of the moral standard of the majority are the narrow expediencies of each special case, without reference to any deep and comprehensive principle covering all the largest social considerations, why then the society to which we ought to look with most admiration and envy is the Eastern Empire during the ninth and tenth centuries, when the Byzantine system of a thorough subordination of the spiritual power had fully consolidated itself.

Mr. Stephen's recent examination of Mr. Mill's doctrine does not seem to contribute much to its rectification. Many passages in that examination read as if the author had not by any means grasped the principle which he repudiates in so operose a manner. The dialectic has an imposing air of strictness and cogency, yet it continually lands you in the fallacy of Irrelevancy. Mr. Stephen labours certain propositions which Mr. Mill never denied, such as that society ought to have a moral standard and ought to act upon it. He proves the contradictory of assertions which his adversary never made, as when he cites judicial instances which imply the recognition of morality by the law. He wishes to prove that social coercion would in many cases tend to make men virtuous. He does so by proving that the absence of coercion does not tend in such cases to make men virtuous. Of course the latter proposition is no more equivalent to the former, than the demonstration of the inefficacy of one way of treating disease is equal to a demonstration of the efficacy of some other way. A short glance at some of Mr. Stephen's propositions will be a convenient mode of setting Mr. Mill's doctrine in a clearer light.

1. "Before he affirmed that in Western Europe and America the compulsion of adults for their own good is unjustifiable, Mr. Mill ought to have proved that there are among us no considerable differences in point of wisdom, or that if there are, the wiser part of the community does not wish for the welfare of the less wise" (p. 25). Why so? Mr. Mill's very proposition is that though there is a wiser part, and though the wiser part may wish well to the less wise, *yet* even then the disadvantages of having a wise course forced upon the members of civilised societies exceed the disadvantages of following an unwise course freely. Mr. Stephen's allegation of the points which Mr. Mill should have proved, rests on the assumption of the very matter at issue — namely, whether freedom is not in itself so valuable an element in social life (in civilised communities), that for the sake of it we should be content to let the unwiser part have their own way in what concerns themselves only.

2. "Look at our own time and country, and mention any single great change which has been effected by mere discussion. Can a single case be mentioned in which the passions of men were interested where the change was not carried by fear — that is to say ultimately by the fear of revolution?" It may be said, parenthetically, first, that it was free discussion which converted the force, and brought it over to the side of the change; say Free Trade, or the Reform of Parliament, or the Irish Land Act. And secondly, that there is all the difference between the fear of a revolution and a revolution actual, and this is a powerful argument in favour of the unlimited discussion which Mr. Mill vindicates, and of the social system that favours it. But, apart from this, have these great changes been made by force in the sphere which Mr. Mill set apart from the operation of force? Was the imposition of the corn-duties a purely self-regarding act? Did the duties hurt nobody but the imposers? Was the exclusion of householders under ten pounds rental from the electoral body a self-regarding act? If not, Mr. Stephen is only beating the air by this talk about force being the *ultima ratio*. It is an organic part of Mr. Mill's doctrine that the whole social force may be exerted in matters which concern others than the doers. Then, Mr. Stephen retorts, "the principle cannot be applied to the very cases in which it is most

needed — cases where men happen to be living under a political or social system with the principles or with the working of which they are not satisfied, and in which they may fight out their differences, the conqueror determining the matter in dispute according to his own will" (p. 22). Is this in the least degree true? Take the most memorable of these cases, the first French Revolution. Will Mr. Stephen seriously contend that the principle of leaving self-regarding acts alone could not have been applied to any parts of that transaction? Hardly so, if he reflects that the most monstrous acts of the Revolution were exactly due to the neglect of this very truth, that there is a province of thought and action — the self-regarding, namely — which ought to be free from social or legislative interference. It was precisely because the Jacobins, headed by Robespierre and Saint Just, borrowed the principles of Hobbes and Rousseau, as Mr. Stephen does; it was precisely because they rode roughshod over such a principle as Mr. Mill's, interfered alike with self-regarding conviction and self-regarding act, and adopted Mr. Stephen's formula of the *á priori* expediency of identifying the law-maker and the moralist, that the worst exploits and most fantastic aspirations which are associated with the French Revolution stained and perverted the movement. To say therefore that Mr. Mill's principle is incapable of application in the cases where it is most needed, or that "it assumes the existence of an ideal state of things in which every one has precisely the position which he ought to hold," is either to forget the most tremendous event in modern history, or else to show that you have never fully considered what Mr. Mill's principle is.

3. "If the object aimed at is good, if the compulsion employed such as to attain it, and *if the good obtained overbalances the inconvenience of the compulsion, I do not understand how upon utilitarian principles the compulsion can be bad.* I may add that this way of stating the case shows that Mr. Mill's simple principle is really a paradox. It can be justified only by showing as a fact that, self-protection apart, no good object can be attained by any compulsion which is not in itself a greater evil than the absence of the object which the compulsion obtains" (p. 50). The words in italics are introduced in a way, and have a significance, which show that, strange as it may appear, Mr. Stephen failed from beginning to end of his criticism to see that the very aim and object of Mr.

Mill's essay is to show on utilitarian principles that compulsion in a definite class of cases, the self-regarding parts of conduct namely, and in societies of a certain degree of development, is always bad. Mr. Stephen's third proviso in the above quotation could never be complied with in self-regarding acts, according to his adversary's doctrine, and that it could never be complied with, was the central object of Mr. Mill's reasoning. He did show, or thought he had shown, that "as a fact," the good obtained in self-regarding acts could not overbalance the general inconvenience of the compulsion. I do not see that Mr. Stephen has anywhere directly confronted this position in the only manner proper to confute it, namely, by an enumeration, first, of the advantages of compulsion in self-regarding acts, second, of its disadvantages, followed by an attempt to strike the balance between the sum of the advantages and the sum of the disadvantages. The last three lines of the above quotation involved a similar misunderstanding. What Mr. Mill had to show was, not that any good object attained by compulsion was "in itself" a greater evil than the absence of the object procured by the compulsion, but something quite different, namely this; that though compulsion may procure objects which are good, yet the general consequences of the compulsion more than counterbalance the special good. Thus, to take a well-known illustration; sobriety might perhaps be procured by some form of coercive legislation, but the evil inherent in such legislation, its enervating effect on character, its replacement of self-control, self-respect, and the rest, by a protective paternal will from without, would more than counterbalance the advantages of sobriety so gained. This may be a mistake. Mr. Mill may or may not prove his case. But where is the sense of calling such a position a paradox?

Hence Mr. Stephen's third and favourite test of the utility of coercion, — that it should not be employed at too great an expense — is a mere *ignoratio elenchi* as against Mr. Mill, who held that in all self-regarding matters it was necessarily employed at too great an expense. This position Mr. Mill defended on strictly utilitarian principles, which have been already stated [see above, p. 275]. Mr. Stephen has missed one of the cardinal points in the whole contention, that "it is of importance not only what men do, but also what manner of men they are that do it" (*Liberty*, 106). It is its robust and bracing influence on character which makes wise men prize freedom, and strive for the enlargement of its province. "They are not skilful considerers of human things," wrote Milton, "who imagine to remove sin by removing the matter of sin. Though ye take from a covetous man his treasure, he has yet one jewel left, ye cannot bereave him of his covetousness. Banish all objects of lust, shut up all youth into the severest discipline that can be exercised in any hermitage, ye cannot make them chaste that came not thither so. Suppose we could expel sin by this means; look how much we thus expel of sin, so much we expel of virtue. And were I the chooser, a dram of well-doing should be preferred before many times as much the forcible hindrance of evil-doing. For God sure esteems the growth and completing of one virtuous person more than the restraint of ten vicious."

The same omission to recognise that the positive quality of liberty is the essence of the doctrine which Mr. Stephen has hastily taken upon himself to disprove, is seen in such statements as that "Discussions about liberty are in truth discussions about a negation. Attempts to solve the problems of government and society by such discussions are like attempts to discover the nature of light and heat by inquiries into darkness and cold" (p. 181). This, by the way, is not so felicitous as Mr. Stephen's illustrations sometimes are, for assuredly he would be a very wretched kind of investigator who thought he could discover the laws of heat without reference to the conditions of cold, or the laws of light without reference to the conditions of darkness. But is it true that liberty is a negation? You may certainly say, if you choose, that freedom from import duties is a negation, but even then I am not aware that the comparative advantages of free trade and protection are incapable of being profitably discussed. Mr. Mill, however, held that liberty was much more than a negation; and that there is plenty of evidence in the various departments of the history of civilisation that freedom exerts a number of positively progressive influences. It was Mr. Stephen's business to refute this, if he could. That he has failed to do so, further than by a number of blunt assertions and reassertions to the contrary, is a proof either that he was not able to refute the most essential part of Mr. Mill's doctrine, or else that he did not perceive in what its essential part consisted. Metaphors about wasps in a garden, and imaginary dialogues with the waters of a stagnant marsh, and the like, really do not help us.

Mr. Stephen had to prove two things. First he had to show that freedom from interference in the expression of opinion and in purely self-regarding acts, is not a good thing in its general consequences. Most people, he says, cannot be improved by free discussion. "I confine myself to saying that the utmost conceivable liberty would not in the least degree tend to improve them." But he should not have confined himself to saying this. He should have tried to demonstrate it, which I cannot see that he does. Second, Mr. Stephen had to show that though liberty cannot improve people, compulsion or restraint can. Instead of this, he takes for granted that because liberty would not improve people, therefore compulsion must. An assumption that begs the whole question at issue.

Mr. Carlyle, more tersely than Mr. Stephen, has boldly said, in one of the Latter Day Pamphlets, that most people are fools. Mr. Mill himself in the book which has occasioned the present controversy has said something of the same sort. The essay on Liberty is in fact one of the most aristocratic books ever written (I do not mean British aristocratic, 'with the politest and gracefullest kind of woman to wife'). It is not Mr. Carlyle, but Mr. Mill, who speaks of "that miscellaneous collection of a few wise and many foolish individuals, called the public" (Liberty, 40). "No government by a democracy or a numerous aristocracy ever did or could rise above mediocrity, except in so far as the sovereign Many have let themselves be guided by the counsel and influence of the more highly gifted and instructed One or Few. The initiation of all wise or noble things comes and must come from individuals; generally at first from some one individual" (p. 119). "On any matter not self-evident, there are ninety-nine persons totally incapable of judging of it, for one who is capable" (p. 30). In the face of passages like these it is rather absurd to say that "the great defect of Mr. Mill's later writings is that he has formed too favourable an estimate of human nature" (Stephen, 43); and it is particularly absurd in a writer who, two hundred pages further on in the very same book (p. 244), assures us that it would be easy to show from Mr. Mill's later works, "what a low opinion he has of mankind at large." Which of the two contradictory assertions that he has made does Mr. Stephen elect to stand by?

But now mark the use which Mr. Mill makes of his proposition that ninety-nine men are incapable of judging a matter not self-evident, and only one man capable. For this reason, he argues, leave the utmost possible freedom of thought, expression, discussion, to the whole hundred, because no other terms can you be quite sure that the judgment of the hundredth man, the one judgment you want, will be forthcoming or will have a change of making itself effectively heard over the incapable judgments? Mr. Stephen says otherwise. He declares it to be an idle dream "to say that one man in a thousand really exercises much individual choice as to his religious or moral principles, and I doubt whether it is not an exaggeration to say that one man in a million is capable of making any very material addition to what is already known or plausibly conjectured on these matters" (p. 73). *Argal*, beware of accepting any nonsensical principle of liberty which shall leave this millionth man the best possible opening for making his material addition; by the whole spirit of your legislation, public opinion, and social sentiment, habitually discourage, freeze, browbeat, all that eccentricity which would be sure to strike all the rest of the million in the one man and his material addition. If Mr. Stephen's book does not mean this, it means nothing, and his contention with Mr. Mill's doctrine of liberty is only a joust of very cumbrous logomachy.

We can thus understand how Mr. Stephen comes to accuse Mr. Mill of worshipping mere variety and "confounding the proposition that variety is good with the proposition that goodness is various" (p. 47). Mr. Mill deliberately held that variety is good on the ground that it is the essential condition of the appearance and growth of those new ideas, new practices, new sentiments, some of which must contain the germs of all future improvements in the arts of existence. It shows an incapacity to understand the essence of the doctrine, to deal with it by such statements as that it involves "a worship of mere variety." It plainly does no such thing. Mr. Mill prizes variety, not at all as mere variety, but because it furnishes most chances of new forms of good presenting themselves and acquiring a permanent place. He prized that eccentricity which Mr. Stephen so heartily dislikes, because he perceived that all new truth and new ways of living, must from the nature of things always appear eccentric to persons accustomed to old opinions and old ways of living; because he saw that most of the personages to whom mankind owes its chief steps in moral and spiritual advance were looked upon by contemporaries as eccentrics, and very often cruelly ill treated by them (on Mr.

Stephen's principles) for eccentricity, which was in truth the very deliverance of humanity from error or imperfection. Not all novelties are improvements, but all improvements are novel, and you can only, therefore, be sure of improvements by giving eccentricity a fair hearing, and free room for as much active manifestation as does no near, positive, recognisable, harm to other people.

Mr. Stephen, however, has a very qualified faith in improvement. He seems to think that the only change in the world is the constant multiplication of the total number of its inhabitants. One of the most extraordinary pieces in his book is a very strained passage (pp. 177–8) after the manner of Mr. Carlyle — only not every one can bend the bow of the great Ulysses — to the effect that the world is like a sort of Stilton cheese, filled with so many millions of indomitable cheese-mites. Apart from the lofty poetic quality and delicate picturesqueness of the trope, it carries its author too far. If men are cheese-mites, I do not see why, for example, able lawyers should strain every nerve, writing articles, reading papers, urging politicians, stimulating ministers, merely in order that a puny group of these cheese-mites, say as many as you could press up on a thumb-nail — to sustain the nobility of the image — may have their laws done up into a code. Mr. Carlyle was much more consistent. He told men they were shadows, and he pursued with loud bursts of not always musical laughter, Political Economy, and Bentham, and parliamentary Reform, and everything else that has made the England of to-day a better place for men or mites to live in than it was half a century ago. Mr. Stephen, to do him justice, gives us very little of this kind of talk. It would be the stultification of his own special ability if he did so. For law, equally with freedom, is only interesting and only worth a serious man's attention in the way of reform, in so far as the progress and the improvement which Mr. Stephen burlesques in the above passage are substantive realities. But his conception of the possibilities of improvement is a narrow one. He draws hard and fast lines in respect of each of the greater interests of men, and anything beyond them he brands as eccentric and chimerical. Mr. Stephen some years ago hurt the feelings of old fashioned metaphysicians by delineating the case of an imaginary world in which two straight lines should be universally supposed to include a space. It is a matter of regret that he has not an equally courageous and powerful imagination in the region of morals. If he had, he would have less trouble in sympathizing with the idea that the limits of human improvement, though they exist in every direction, have as yet not only not been reached, but are not even viable. And if he had appreciated this idea he would have seen deeper into Mr. Mill's principle than to detect, in one of the conditions attending it, nothing beyond a worship of mere variety.

And after all, even if it were so, is he warranted in taking for granted that worship of variety is less creditable or in any way more singular than worship of unity? Whatever the value of progress may be, says Mr. Stephen, "unity in religious belief would further it" (p. 63). But we really cannot be expected to take Mr. Stephen's authority for this. Such a proposition is one part of the great question at issue. I am not aware that the Byzantine empire, where there eventually existed a more complete unity of belief than has ever existed in any other part of Christendom, was the scene of any remarkable furtherance of progress in consequence. Or take the great theocracies, ancient Egypt, Islam under the Caliphs, India under Buddhists or Brahmins. What element of progress did this unity give? Is not unity of religious belief the very note of stationary societies? It is no doubt true that unity in religious belief as in other things will slowly draw nearer, as the result of the gradual acceptance by an increasing number of men of common methods of observing and interpreting experience. As Mr. Mill says — "As mankind improve, the number of doctrines which are not longer disputed or doubted will be constantly on the increase; and the well-being of mankind may almost be measured by the number and gravity of the truths which have reached the point of not being contested" (*Liberty*, 79). But all the consequences of this quasi-unity may not prove to be beneficial, or favourable to progress, not is it at all clear, as Mr. Stephen takes for granted, that unity of religious belief would further progress, unless you replaced the discussions to which such unity had put an end, by some other equally dividing subject of equal interest to an equal number of people. In Mr. Stephen's opinion it would be impossible ever to find any other such subject, for he lays down the proposition which, I confess, strikes me as truly extravagant that "If we were all of one mind, and that upon reasonable grounds, about the nature of men, and their relation to the world or worlds in which they live, [this is equivalent to previous expressions about "the attainment of religious truth"], we should be able *at once and with but little difficulty* to solve all the great moral and political questions which at present distract and divide the world" (p. 62).

4. A good deal of rather bustling ponderosity is devoted to proving that the actual laws in many points do assume the existence of a standard of moral good and evil, and that this proceeding is diametrically opposed to Mr. Mill's fundamental principles (p. 153, etc.). To this one would say, first, that the actual existence of laws of any given kind is wholly irrelevant to Mr. Mill's contention, which is, that it would be better if laws of such a kind did not exist. Second, Mr. Mill never says, nor is it at all essential to his doctrine to hold, that a government ought not to have "a standard or moral good and evil, which the public at large have an interest in maintaining and in many cases enforcing." He only set apart a certain class of cases to which the right or duty of enforcement of the current standard does not extend — the self-regarding cases. Mr. Stephen would not have been any wider of the mark if he had devoted an equal number of pages to demonstrating against Mr. Mill that not only society, but an individual, ought to have a standard of good and evil, which he is to maintain through good report and ill report. Mr. Mill no more denied this of a government than he denied it of an individual. All he said was — "It is a mistake to enforce your standard on me, if my non-recognition of it does no harm to any one but myself. Clearly there is a number of matters — lying, unchastity, and so forth — in which there is no attempt to enforce the recognised standard of good and evil. I extend this class of neglected breaches of the current laws of morals, so as to include all self-regarding matters whatever." Consequently, the statement that the assumption of a standard of moral good and evil which the public at large have an interest in many cases in enforcing, is diametrically opposed to Mr. Mill's fundamental principle, involves a misunderstanding of that principle; and such a statement ignores the plain fact that this principle does emphatically recognise the right of the state to enforce that part of its moral code which touches such acts as are not self-regarding.

A similar neglect to master the real position taken by Mr. Mill is shown in Mr. Stephens's remarks about Pilate, and his parallel of the case of a British officer confronted by a revolutionary teacher in India. "If it is said that Pilate ought to have respected the principle of religious liberty as propounded by Mr. Mill, the answer is that if he had done so, he would have run the risk of setting the whole province in a blaze" (Stephen, 94, etc.). Then in such a case Mr. Mill expressly lays down the limitation proper to the matter, in a passage to which Mr. Stephen appears not to have paid attention. "No one pretends," says Mr. Mill, "that actions should be as free as opinions. On the contrary, even opinions lose their immunity when the circumstances in which they are expressed are such as to constitute a positive instigation to some mischievous act. An opinion that corn-dealers are starvers of the poor, or that private property is robbery, ought to be unmolested when simply circulated through the press, but may justly incur punishment when delivered orally to an excited mob assembled before the house of a corn-dealer, or when handed about among the same mob in the form of a placard. Acts of whatever kind, which, without justifiable cause, do harm to others, may be, and in the more important cases absolutely require to be, controlled by the unfavourable sentiment, and when needful, by the active interference of mankind" (*Liberty*, 100–1).

5. Let us take a concrete case with which Mr. Stephen furnishes us.

> "A set of young noblemen of great fortune and hereditary influence, the representatives of ancient names, the natural leaders of the society of large districts, pass their whole time and employ all their means in gross debauchery. Such people are far more injurious to society than common pickpockets, but Mr. Mill says that if any one having the opportunity of making them ashamed of themselves uses it in order to coerce them into decency, he sins against liberty, unless their example does assignable harm to specific people. It might be right to say, 'You the Duke of A. by extravagantly keeping four mistresses, set an example which induced your friend F. to elope with Mrs. G. and you are a great blackguard for your pains, and all the more because you are a duke.' It could never be right to say, 'You, the Duke of A. are scandalously immoral and ought to be made to smart for it, though the law cannot touch you.' (p. 131).

But these two forms of remonstrance by no means exhaust the matter. An advocate of Mr. Mill's principle might say to the debauched duke one of three things: (*a*) 'Your grace ought to be made to smart, only it is not worth while for the sake of making a poor creature like you smart, to invoke a principle which would endanger really fruitful experiments in living.' (*b*) 'We are much indebted to you for destroying your influence and character. Society will be more than compensated for the loss of your social services by the admirable deterrent effect which so hideous a spectacle as your grace, so conspicuous as your high station makes you, will exert over other dukes and men, in spite of your friend F., who imitates you. You are the Helot among dukes.' (*c*) 'My duke, codifiers and others would like to make you smart by law. We less peremptory heads perceive that you do smart. You smart by being the poor gross creature you are.' Any of these rebukes would lie in the mouths of those who accepted Mr. Mill's principle, while the single rebuke which Mr. Stephen has imputed to such persons is the least adequate of the four, and is certainly not the rebuke to be found in the Essay on Liberty. (see *Liberty*, 136, 139, &c.)

Take another case put by Mr. Stephen: —

"A number of persons form themselves into an association for the purpose of countenancing each other in the practice of seducing women, and giving the widest possible extension to the theory that adultery is a good thing. They carry out their objects by organizing a system for the publication and circulation of lascivious novels and pamphlets calculated to inflame the passions of the young and inexperienced. The law of England would treat this as a crime. It would call such books obscene libels, and a combination for such a purpose a conspiracy. Mr. Mill would not only regard this as wrong, but he would regard it as an act of persecution if the newspapers were to excite public indignation against the parties concerned by language going one step beyond the calmest discussion of such an experiment in living." (p. 124)

I venture to propound two questions to Mr. Stephen. Is the practice of seducing women a self-regarding practice? And is the *circulation* of pamphlets calculated to inflame the passions of the young an act that hurts nobody but the circulator? The answer to these questions shows the illustration to be utterly pointless. It shows the assertion that on Mr. Mill's principles

police interference would be wrong and public anger would be
of the nature of persecution, to be prodigious piece of
misrepresentation. There was in the last century a famous case
exactly in point, that of Wilkes and the Franciscans of
Medmenham Abbey. These debauchees were as gross and
scandalous a set of profligates as ever banded together. But
they conformed to the conditions laid down in the doctrine of
liberty, and no one thought of interfering with them. The law
in this respect was conformable to Mr. Mill's principle. The
exception to this non-interference shows the true side of this
principle, and confirms the popular acceptance of it, under the
circumstances described in Mr. Stephen's imaginary and, for
the purposes of the discussion, quite inapposite case. Wilkes
printed at his private press a few copies of the *Essay on
Woman*, a ribald poem. The government contrived by
corrupting a compositor to obtain a copy of it, it was ordered
that Wilkes should be prosecuted for publishing a blasphemous
libel, and he was convicted by the Court of King's Bench. This
conviction has always been held a miscarriage of law, because
there was no real publication. Mr. Mill's doctrine condemns
the prosecution of Wilkes for the Essay on Woman, as all
public opinion since has condemned it. A man has a right to
keep poisons in his closet, it has been finely said, though he has
no right publicly to distribute them for cordials — which is
exactly Mr. Mill's position. Does Mr. Stephen hold that Wilkes
was justifiably punished for this improperly imputed crime? If
not, where is the force of his illustration?

6. At the bottom of all Mr. Stephen's argumentation lies a
fundamental reluctance to admit that there are such things as
self-regarding acts at all. This reluctance implies a perfectly
tenable proposition, a proposition which has been maintained
by nearly all religious bodies in the world's history in their non-
latitudinarian stages. Comte denied the existence of such a
division among acts, and made care of health, cleanliness,
sobriety, and the rest, into social obligations.[1] Mr. Stephen
does not exactly deny either the possibility or the expediency of
recognising the distinction between acts that affect only the
doer and acts that affect the rest of society; But if he does not
deny this, neither does he admit it, nor treat admission of it as

---

[1]   In the matter of health Mr. Mill professed the same opinion. See his
   Auguste Comte and Positivism, p. 147.

all important to the controversy. Yet that, I submit, ought to
have been the field of his discussion on Mr. Mill's doctrine, for
it is from that that the other differences really spring. In default
of this larger principle, he is constantly obliged to fall back on
illustrations of the consequences which might, and very
probably would, happen to other people from conduct that
seems fairly definable as self-regarding. There is one objection
obviously to be made to these illustrations. The connection
between the act and its influence on others is so remote, using
the word in a legal sense, though quite certain, distinct, and
traceable, that you can only take the act out of the self-
regarding category, by a process which virtually denies the
existence of any such category. You must set a limit to this
"indirect and at a distance argument," as Locke called a similar
plea, and the setting of this limit is the natural supplement to
Mr. Mill's 'simple procedure.' Set it where you will, it must, to
be a limit at all, come a long way short of Mr. Stephen's notion
of self-protection.

In fact Mr. Stephen has failed to state in a definite and
intelligible way his conception of the analysis of conduct on
which the whole doctrine of Liberty rests. To some persons
that analysis as performed by Mr. Mill seems metaphysical and
arbitrary. To distinguish the self-regarding from the other parts
of conduct strikes them not only as unscientific, but as morally
and socially mischievous. They insist that there is a social as
well as a personal element in every human act, though in very
different proportions, while there is no gain, they contend, and
there may be much harm, in trying to mark off actions in which
the personal element decisively preponderates, from actions of
another sort. Mr. Mill did so distinguish actions, nor was his
distinction either metaphysical or arbitrary in its source. As a
matter of observation, and for the practical purposes of
morality, there are kinds of action whose consequences do not
go beyond the doer of them. No doubt, you may say that by
engaging in these kinds in any given moment, the doer is
neglecting the actions in which the social element preponderates, and therefore even acts that seem purely self-regarding
have indirect and negative consequences to the rest of the
world. But to allow considerations of this sort to prevent us
from using a common-sense classification of acts by the
proportion of personal element in them, is as unreasonable as if
we allowed the doctrine of the conservation of physical force,

or the evolution of one mode of force into another, to prevent us from classifying the affections of matter independently as light, heat, motion, and the rest. The division between self-regarding acts and others, then, rests on observation of their actual consequences. And why was Mr. Mill so anxious to erect self-regarding acts into a distant and important class, so important as to be carefully and diligently secured by a special principle of liberty? Because observation of the recorded experience of mankind teaches us that the recognition of this independent provision is essential to the richest expansion of human faculty. To narrow or to repudiate such a province, and to insist exclusively on the social bearing of each part of conduct, is to limit the play of motives, and to thwart the doctrine — which Mr. Stephen at any rate is not likely to disown — that "mankind obtain a greater sum of happiness when each pursues his own, under the rules and conditions required by the rest, than when each makes the good of the rest his only object." To narrow or to repudiate such a province is to tighten the power of the majority over the minority, and to augment the authority of whatever sacerdotal or legislative body may represent the majority. Whether the lawmakers are laymen in parliament, or priests of humanity exercising the spiritual power, it matters not. Mr. Stephen and Comte rest their respective aspirations on a common principle — the assertion of the social element in every part of conduct. If Comte had lived to read the essay on Liberty he would have attacked it on the same side, by denying the possibility of saying of any part of conduct that it is self-regarding. Only he would have denied it boldly, while Mr. Stephen denies it in a timorous manner — not unnatural, perhaps, in one who holds that self is the centre of all things, and that we have no motives that are not self-regarding.

7. We may now notice one or two of Mr. Stephen's *obiter dicta*.

(*a*) "No rational man can doubt that Christianity, taken as a whole and speaking broadly, has been a blessing to men" (p. 89). Personally I am of Mr. Stephen's opinion that Christianity has been a blessing to men, but I should think twice before feeling myself entitled on the strength of this conviction to deny the title of "rational man" to such persons as the learned and laborious Gibbon, the shrewd, versatile, humane Voltaire, the scientific D'Alembert, the philosophic

Condorcet. But would these eminent men have doubted what
Mr. Stephen says no rational man can doubt, if they had seen
the Revolution? Condorcet, at any rate, saw the Revolution,
and it did not shake his conviction, and men like James Mill
and Mr. Grote came after the Revolution, and both of them
doubted, or went beyond doubting, the beneficence of
Christianity. Mr. Stephen makes too much play with his
rational man, and reasonable people. The phrase does not
really come to much more than the majority of the males of a
generation, engaged in the pleasing exercise of "that hide-
bound humour which they call their judgment."

(b) "There are innumerable propositions on which a man
may have a rational assurance that he is right, whether others
are or are not at liberty to contradict him. Every proposition of
which we are assured by our own senses falls under this head"
(p. 37). Were not men assured by their own senses that the
earth is a plain, and that the sun revolves round the earth? It
may be said that before Copernicus they had a rational
assurance that they were right in this. The belief was not
correct, but it was a rational assurance. Precisely; and people
would have lived to this day with their erroneous rational
assurance uncorrected, unless Copernicus had been at liberty to
contradict them.

(c) "The cry for liberty in short is a general condemnation of
the past." Not condemnation at all, in any accurate or serious
sense. In buying a new coat I do not condemn the old one; on
the contrary, I look to it with gratitude for helpful service,
though it is now worn out or has become too scanty for me. We
do not believe that the principle of all things is water, or that
number is the principle of matter; but the rejection of such
notions is not equivalent to a condemnation of Thales and
Pythagoras. On the contrary, we are thoroughly appreciative
of the services rendered by them and their now worn-out
speculations in first setting the human intelligence to work in a
certain direction. The catholic church has contributed
immensely to the progress of civilisation; to believe that it has
now become retrogressive and obscurantist is not to condemn
its past, but its present. Many of the forces of the past are now
spent, but to hold this is a very different thing from saying that
they were never forces, or that as forces they did no good, and
a very different thing from condemning them — unless Mr.
Stephen insists on using condemnation in the same arbitrary

and unprecedented senses which he assigns to coercion. Mr. Stephen lacks historical perspective; he does not practise the historic method; we see no flexibility in his premises or his conclusions, not any reference of them to specific social stages. He is one of those absolute thinkers who bring to the problems of society the methods of geometry. The cry for liberty, he says, "has shattered to pieces most of the old forms in which discipline was a recognised and admitted good' (p. 175), — as if this were really the one cause, and as if the old forms had not been previously disorganized by internal decrepitude, the result of their association with one or two great groups of ideas which had been slowly robbed of their vitality by a large number of various forces.

(d) "If Mr. Mill's view of liberty had always been adopted and acted on to its full extent — if it had been the view of the first Christians or of the first Mahommedans — every one can see that there would have been no such thing as organized Christianity or Mahommedanism in the world" (p. 17). To this one might reply by asking how we know that there might not have been something far better in their stead. We know what we get by effective intolerance, but we cannot ever know what possible benefactions we lose by it.

(e) "Concede the first principle, that unfeigned belief in the Roman Catholic creed is indispensably necessary to salvation, or the first principle, that the whole Roman Catholic system is a pernicious falsehood and fraud, and it will be found impossible to stop short of the practical conclusions of the Inquisition and the Terror. Every real argument against their practical conclusions is an argument to show either that we cannot be sure as to the conditions of salvation, or that the Roman Catholic religion has redeeming points about it." Unless we agree to limit the meaning of "real" arguments to such as would convince the author of these assertions, such a statement is wholly inadequate. You may belief that the Roman Catholic religion is a pernicious falsehood and fraud, and that it has no redeeming point about it, and still stop short of the Terror, and not only of the Terror but of any coercive interference whatever, in consequence of this consideration, namely that falsehoods and frauds in religion are not to be extirpated by massacre or any penalties of that kind. Why is not that a real argument?

Nor is this the only possible restraining consideration. I may be convinced that I could stamp out the given form of pernicious belief by persecution, but yet may be of opinion that for various reasons — such as the effect of persecution on the character of the persecutor, the colour and bias given to my own true creed by associating it with cruelty to a false one, and so forth — for these reasons the evils incident to violent repression would counterbalance the evils incident to the tolerance of a faith without a single redeeming point. Why is not that also a real argument? Mr. Stephen asks any one who doubts his position to try to frame an argument which could have been addressed with any chance of success to Philip II. against the persecution of the Protestants, or to Robespierre against the persecution of Catholicism. Well, the two arguments I have just offered might well have been addressed alike to Philip II. and to Robespierre. The fact that they would have had no chance of success, which I admit, is just what explains the abhorrence with which the world regards their names. They are arguments resting on a balance of expediencies, as shown through the experience of mankind. But Robespierre was proof against such arguments. He believed with Rousseau and Mr. Stephen in the duty of putting down vice and error coercively. He shared Mr. Stephen's enthusiasm "for a powerful and energetic minority, sufficiently vigorous to impose their will on their neighbours, having made up their minds as to what is true," and so forth. Well, according to the doctrine of liberty, this energetic way of violently imposing your will on other people, by guillotine or act of parliament, is as futile as it is hateful, and not only a crime but a mistake. Like the boisterous pæns of literary men in honour of coercive energy, eagerness to resort to drastic remedies is the outcome of mere unscientific impatience.

EDITOR

BLACKWOODS EDINBURGH MAGAZINE
Vol. 114, September 1873
[Herbert Cowell]

Liberty, Equality, Fraternity[1]: Mr John Stuart Mill

A Calcutta newspaper recently assured its readers that there was no truth in the report that the sudden death of Mr. Mill had been occasioned by a perusal of Mr Stephen's book, and his consequent remorse for having inundated society with principles and theories which stood refuted and denounced before the world. The writer altogether underrates the impenetrable armour of self-confidence and disdain which sustain and befit an advanced philosopher. There is no faith which equals in intensity that of a true Aryan philosopher in the emanations of his own brain, and in the principles which he has himself disclosed or enforced; and to judge from the later writings and the public actions of Mr Mill, there was no trace in his mind of self-distrust or hesitation as to the truth even of the wildest of the doctrines which he has bequeathed to mankind.

There is something utterly unaccountable in the overweening confidence of philosophers in themselves, and in the fervent devotion with which their utterances are invariably received by a select circle of admirers. A candid view even of the famous productions of Mr Mill leads to the belief that the questions which he actually solves are very few; that the difficulties he starts are often greater than those which he removes; and that the real use of such efforts of intellect is not that they attain by themselves to absolute truth, but that they are contributions to our social science, to be used with caution, not with enthusiasm. However active and vigorous an intellect may be, it never wanders very far from the domain of personal experience, at all events with any chance of accurate investigation; in other words, a man's generalisations will be largely

---

[1] Liberty, Equality, Fraternity. By J. F. Stephen, Esq., Q.C. London, Smith, Elder & Co. 1873.

determined by his own habits, surroundings, and associations. The world will never improve without philosophers; we owe them at all times a tribute of respect. Practical men have been described as men who are content to practise the blunders of their predecessors. But when the theories which are to correct our blunders take the whole range of human conduct and life within their scope, and attack the very foundations of social life, a rash assent to them is mischievous in the last degree. Language is often so inadequate, that it is difficult to tell what view of society is really present to the author's mind. We are promised in time an autobiography of Mr Mill. Such a book will doubtless be useful; for the conclusions at which he arrived ought to be studied by the light of his antecedents and surroundings, and of their own intrinsic worth, and not merely by the light of the particular arguments which he has selected to enforce them. In reading Mr Mill's works on 'Liberty,' and 'The Subjection of Women,' it ought always to be borne in mind that his life was one in which intellectual tastes and sympathies predominated over all others; and that, as his dedication of the former work shows, his own experience of the institution which he wishes to transform was of an exceptional nature. From a marriage experience, of which "great thoughts," learned leisure, and no children, are the predominant characteristics, the consequent theories are sure to betray limited acquaintance with married life, and a cramped and narrow view of its real conditions. Accordingly, one book applies to a society where all have disciplined tastes and correct judgments; the other applies where education and artificial life are supposed to have destroyed the natural divisions of the sexes, and the wide separation in their several functions and duties.

We have the writings of two distinguished men before us, and we propose to offer a few observations upon them and their authors. Mr Fitzjames Stephen is the author of 'Liberty, Equality, and Fraternity,' a book which is written to examine and to denounce the doctrines which are usually denoted by that war-cry of Republican politics. He has stepped aside from active professional and political life to encounter theories which he believes to be absurd and impracticable. And he has this claim to be heard, that he is a man of wide experience, versed in the affairs of men, civil and political. An active professional career peculiarly fitted to give a man insight into human conduct and society, was interrupted during the chief part of Lord Mayo's short but famous viceroyalty by official life in India, which he signalised by considerable legislative achievements, constituting by themselves a vast imperial code, and almost forming an epoch in the history of that empire. And when we compare, for instance, the extravagant and excited proceedings of Mr Mill in reference to the Jamaica insurrection, with the grave and statesmanlike minute of Lord Napier (attributed to Mr Stephen) or the analogous case of the suppression of the *Kooka* outbreak, we are decidedly in favour of the man whose philosophy proves equal to emergencies. The public career of one man is marked by strong sense and successful achievement; that of the other, although covered with fame, was, nevertheless, whenever he touched the world of action, signalised by serious failures, over which his friends must mourn, and which were fresh in the minds of men at the last general election. The three years which elapsed from Mr Mill's triumphant return by the Westminster constituency, and the "lessons" which he told the electors were conveyed thereby, down to his rejection by the same constituency, are not the least valuable portion of his career. The extravagances of conduct, which we will not now dilate upon, throw light upon the character of the theories which he preached and upon the career by which they were evolved.

In reading Mr Stephen's book and the works of Mr Mill which it is devoted to refute, it is as well to bear in mind the total dissimilarity of their respective careers. The worshipper of the regulated law of force is the man who has successfully struggled with life and taken part in the almost despotic government of a great empire. The advocate of liberty, in the sense of every man rebelling against the society of which he is a part, and of every woman rebelling against the man whom she is sworn to obey, is a man whose speculations have been pursued away from the haunts of men and active life, whose brief contact with the world of action produced a short career checkered by defeat and embittered by failures. Mr Mill began public life with sanctioning the Jamaica insurrection; he ended it by presiding over one of the worst exhibitions of class hatred and animosity that Exeter Hall has witnessed. And in his writings during this short but eventful period, he presents his ideal panorama of human society as a scene of one vast Jamaica revolt, in which all sense of duty and subordination is merged in the divine right of every man and woman to do as he pleases. In this dissolving view of anarchy and confusion, everyone, man and woman alike, is free "to develop his individuality," whatever that barbarous phrase may mean; and without stopping to inquire to what portentous consequences such freedom may lead, the result is assumed to constitute the grand *finale* of civilisation.

We venture to say with regard to these evanescent theories of society, its constitution and rights, that they will never gain a lasting hold on the minds of the great mass of English society. The commonplace middle-class liberalism which dates from Tom Paine's rights of man, and ends with Mill's rights of women, is now symmetrical and complete. It is at once the child and the patron of that extraordinary form of civilisation which we have developed, which neither feels nor excites enthusiasm, which is without faith or even capacity for happiness, the scene of a tumultuous activity and bustling energy which begins and ends with doing and getting. The view of it presented by Mr Matthew Arnold is worth recalling when we are considering how far theories of unbounded licence are applicable. "Consider these people," he says — "their way of life, their habits, their manners, the very ones of their voice: look at them attentively; observe the literature they read, the things that give them pleasure, the words which come forth out of their mouths, the thoughts which make the furniture of their minds; — would any amount of wealth be worth having with the condition that one was to become just like these people by having it?" Under such a system we have produced a population which is steeped in poverty and ignorance, and which largely combines wealth with uncouthness and vulgarity, while we have lost the power of keeping the peace in our streets, or of teaching religion in our schools. The right to do as he pleases is dear to the true British Philistine; but rights are mostly relative and conventional, and form a shifting foundation for large social theories. The vaunted Radicalism of the present day is founded upon the rights of man; Toryism regards the duties of citizens, it is the religion of political and social duty. And it is from the consideration of duties, which are far more easily defined and ascertained than rights, that rules of conduct may be usefully deduced; and rules of conduct are, or ought to be, the ultimate object of all philosophical theories upon the constitution of society and its internal relations.

Mr Mill's subject is social liberty, — that is, to define the limits of the power which society has a right to exercise over the individual. He inveighs against the tyranny of political rulers, and the tyranny of majorities. He admits that all that makes existence valuable depends upon the enforcement of restraints upon the actions of other people. But he complains that the rules of conduct which are tacitly framed to provide those restraints are enforced by custom, and not by sound reason. They are determined, he says, by the likings and dislikings of society, its prejudices or superstitions. The yoke of opinion in England sits heavily on the individual, though that of law is lighter than anywhere in Europe. The intolerance of society is never cured except when it is removed by indifference, and that is also an evil. He then goes on to assert that one very simple principle ought to govern absolutely the dealings of society with the individual in the way of compulsion and control, — viz., that self-protection is the sole end for which mankind are warranted individually or collectively in interfering with the liberty of action of any of their number. In other words, every one is so absolutely entitled to do as he pleases, no matter what his pleasure may be, that so long as he does not injure others, he must be free from all social restraint. The standard of manners, morality, and mutual obligation which may prevail, is to be utterly disregarded. The individual has a sacred right to be independent of it; society injures him if it endeavours to enforce it. This is the doctrine, and it is not surprising that Mr Mill falls an easy victim to his critic. It justifies the orgies of Wilkes, and vindicates the existence of the Hell-fire Club. It is the cry of revolt and rebellion; the question is, whether it is against unlawful authority or against clear social obligation and in violation of reciprocal duties. "To please yourself and hurt nobody else" is the religion of the future, the sum total of mankind's rights and duties — the simple principle which is to save society.

This is no misrepresentation; it is a view solemnly stated and enforced, and a large portion of Mr Stephen's book is devoted to refute it. Mr Mill's treatise on Liberty teems with passages in support of it. Mormonism is defended as an "experiment in living" to which every man has a right to resort; and an indignant outburst is reserved for the "language of downright persecution which breaks out from the press of this country whenever it feels called upon to notice the remarkable phenomenon of Mormonism."

It is denied that society has any right to coerce or suppress opinion; and the examples of Socrates, Jesus Christ, and Marcus Aurelius, are adduced in support of that view. And the same doctrine is extended to "experiments in living." "As it is useful that while mankind are imperfect there should be different opinions, so is it that there should be different experiments of living; that free scope should be given to varieties of character short of injury to others; and that the worth of different modes of life should be proved practically when any one thinks fit to try them."

This freedom to do as one likes is surely a very despicable thing when regarded as the end and final aim of human existence. Free room in which to develop, not one's "individuality," but one's best self, by the light of all that is best and greatest, is an indispensable condition of human improvement, a necessary means to a desirable end. But that implies a great deal more than freedom — viz., a constraining sense of duty, which is a binding fetter on liberty as Mr. Mill understands it. Liberty, according to Mr Mill, is so sacred and divine, that he even shrinks from saying that pimps and gambling-house keepers ought to be punished and repressed; apparently on the ground that the police represent tyrannical power, while these worthies represent the principle of freedom. He rides off, it is true, on the moral anomaly of allowing the principal to whom those worthies pander to go free while the accessories are punished; but if would not have been difficult, if that were the real ground of objection, to find a distinction between the exemption of private vices from State control, and the free establishment of trades and callings to minister to and support those vices. Criminal law cannot repress immorality; but it can — but for Mr Mill's principle of liberty — prevent men from trading on the vices of others, and thereby acquiring a direct interest in promoting and encouraging them.

Freedom to do as one likes, independently even of social control, is, even on Mr Mill's own showing, liable to so many exceptions, that probably, if the exceptions were all gathered together and deducted from the apparent universality of the principle, it would leave so little vitality and meaning in it as to form the strongest condemnation out of the author's own mouth of the reckless way in which a most injurious doctrine has been authoritatively preached to the world. The real idea with which the treatise was written was probably to protect against men being regarded with disfavour or incurring odium by reason of avowing an unpopular religious belief or absence of belief. And in hoisting the flag of liberty high enough to secure immunity to professions which shock existing sentiments, he has enunciated a principle which, without check and exceptions sufficient to destroy its force and meaning, is equivalent to reckless and undisciplined licence of thought, word, and deed.

Assuming the simple principle that the sole fitting restraint on my liberty to do as I please, springs from the right of others to protect themselves, there are three exceptions propounded to the right to possess this almost unlimited freedom. In the first place, age is a ground of exception, and children are not free to do as they please, apparently from the infirmity of their powers, and want of discretion; an exception which covers these hostile positions — that restraint is good; that education is a subordination of the will as a means to purify and strengthen it; and that the capacity to make a good use of freedom is the measure of the right to possess it. Then, again, all backward states of society are exempted from the application of this principle. Thirdly, Mr Mill in terms admits that capacity for freedom depends on the capacity to be guided to improvement by conviction or persuasion. The three rival principles to that of unlimited freedom are thus established out of his own mouth; and then what does the original doctrine, so startling and unjustifiable, amount to? A most dangerous principle is started, and then pared away by wide-reaching exceptions and distinctions; but there are many people who are ready enough to justify eccentricity of deed and expression by this 'simple principle,' who purposely disregard the exceptions. Again, the whole of the section of the treatise on Liberty which deals with the limits to the authority of society over the individual, resolves itself into very little. The freedom of the individual is insisted upon, but the restraints which society may impose are very numerous; pity and dislike may be manifested, but anger and resentment are forbidden. But surely all this is a question of degree. Once admit that society has jurisdiction over the language and conduct of individuals, and may pity or dislike those who depart from its standard, and then in every case society must judge according to the circumstances, and not by any preconceived rule, what amount of authority it will exercise, or of censure it will impose. It is all very well to say that "purely personal conduct" is not to be interfered with; but purely personal conduct is nowhere defined, and is at all points interwoven with the feelings of others, sufficiently to give society a handle against it. So also in another passage it is said, that "to extend the bounds of what may be called moral police, until it encroaches on the most unquestionable legitimate liberty of the individual, is one of the most universal of all human propensities," and of course is an unwarrantable propensity. But "unquestionable legitimate liberty' is again nowhere defined; it is left to be gathered from the whole book, and amounts to this: the right to please myself, provided I hurt nobody else, limited by checks and exceptions, which may be overlooked, or which may at pleasure be expanded, so as to cut down the right to an extent which renders it not worth asserting.

The whole treatise appears to us utterly indefensible. Its principal object is, no doubt, to assert the right to profess religious belief or disbelief freed from all social or moral hindrances, and to denounce as tyranny indirect interference with conscience. These hindrances are, in our opinion, not by any means an unmixed evil. If I want to strike at universal social sentiment, I ought to be prepared to stand the consequences, and to be armed at all points. Mr Mill says that any man, however defenceless, may strike the blow; society injures him, and deprives itself of the priceless boon of originality, if it interposes the shield of anger or even conscientious disapproval. The tyranny of custom, and the power of society to enforce obedience to its recognised standards, are denounced as the death of all true originality. And in arguing out this wild doctrine, principles are laid down, not with regard to society as it is, good, bad, and indifferent, inextricably mixed together; but with reference to individuals who are honestly seeking their own improvement by the best light available to them, who are of an age to judge for themselves, who are in a society not too backward to possess sufficient light, and who are "capable of being guided to improvement by conviction or persuasion." Did any society ever exist, all classes and individuals of which satisfy these conditions? If not, it is useless, and worse than useless, to preach the doctrine that eccentricity is a merit, and insubordination a virtue; that each may please himself so long as he hurts no one else. Such a doctrine, having regard to the existing state of society, is licentious and wicked; and no amount of checks and exceptions to its application, even to the extent of rendering it a nullity, except amongst the wise and virtuous, will serve to redeem it, especially when the author, by his reference to Mormonism, and certain degraded callings, shows that he does not always himself bear his own important limitations in mind. Mr Stephen, in his new book, accuses Mr Mill of taking far too high an estimate of human nature. This is quite true, when Mr Mill is engaged in scanning the application of his own theories, and estimating their results. But when he is discussing society as it is, existing men and women, the reverse is the truth; for his later writings show a growing misanthropy, and a disposition, without any sufficient excuse or justification, to impute to both sexes alike the evils and demoralisation of slavery.

Now, in our point of view (we are not Radicals, philosophical or otherwise), rights, as such, are very difficult to define, and altogether unsafe to dogmatise about, and deduce principles from, which are to form the foundation of society. Especially a right to rebel, woman against man, man against society, is a doctrine which we ought to think over once, twice, thrice, before we adopt it, unless we have a Jamaica insurrection to justify, or a crusade to encourage. Society is founded on a graduated force which runs from one end of it to the other. We cannot get rid of the actual force which exists; that depends upon the nature of individuals, but law can define and control it. Liberty is not a mere negation of another's power; it is an assertion of authority, of the right to compel the observance of other people's duties to ourselves. It requires as much limitation and careful definition as power; especially in a country where power is extremely difficult to exercise. Otherwise liberty becomes a name for unbridled licence and for the tyranny of the individual, as disgusting and intolerable as any other form of tyranny, especially when exercised in a crowded country, and in defiance of its best judgment and highest ideals. A man can no more say to a civilised community of which he is part, "I will have my own life to myself," than he can say, "I will have my own cubic feet of air to myself;" and it ought not to be preached to him that he can have it, and ought to have it, in order to exhibit originality. The feelings and rights and wishes of others meet us at every corner, and along every path of social life. Society has a right to enforce attention to customs which express its standard of morals and manners, and no one is at liberty to disregard them unless from a sense of duty which is paramount to them; an exception which assuredly does not cover eccentric attempts to develop individuality.

Rights are so difficult to define that it is far better to dogmatise from duties. When we fall back on our conscious-ness it is difficult to say that we have any abstract and absolute rights; they exist relatively to time, place, and circumstance, and seem generally to be the result of other people's duties towards us. We have duties to God; but we have no rights as against Him — not even the right to live. The right even to live is not absolute against our fellow-creatures; we may forfeit it on Mr Mill's 'simple principle,' by violating society's right to protect itself, or our duty to go on a forlorn-hope may be paramount to our right to live. The main lines of duty, on the other hand, are obvious and eternal; and our notion of liberty is associated with the idea of a sound balance struck, having regard to time, place, and circumstance, between the duty we owe to society, and the duties society owes to us. Man's will, or the power which he has of giving effect to it, is, or ought to be fettered by the duties which he owes to others and to his own best self. Of personal liberty a wise man never allows himself more than this; but of social and political liberty he cannot possess more than is consistent with the enforcement of social and public duties. The amount of individual restraint necessary to that enforcement will differ according to circumstances, and no possible rule, simple or otherwise, can be laid down which will uniformly apply to it. Mr Mill says that the test is — what is necessary to self-protection; but he has never proved it by argument or illustration, and has provided so many exceptions that it ceases to be operative. We all admit that society has no right to persecute an individual for his religious belief, notwithstanding that Dr Johnson has argued that persecution is a test through which truth should pass. And then it is argued by Mr Mill that neither should society disapprove an individual's religious belief — disapproval may be very injurious, and it rests on the same principle as persecution; society may be stifling that which is true, or preventing the refutation of error. But surely it is question of degree. Society may not arm itself with the weapon of persecution; but, if not of disapproval, it will be at the mercy of individuals, and cannot protect itself against flippancy, wilful indecorum, or ignorant self-assertion. Turn the question round and look at it as one of duty and not of right. Our duty to abstain from expression of religious belief or disbelief — offensive, or it may be blasphemous, in the eyes of society — and, on the other hand, to avow it, is bounded by the sincerity and strength of our convictions and consequent obligation to others. Society, on the other hand, is bound to listen when that sincerity is tested. It may not apply the test of persecution, but may it not resort to any other? May it not disapprove a Wilkes or a Bradlaugh, or does its obligation to listen deprive it of all right to criticise or disapprove? The difficulty of departing from the standard belief or manners of the day is the measure of the power of society against the average individual. It is, we believe, a wholesome check on eccentricity and spurious originality, but is powerless against real force of character. The uniformity of society may be a bad sign, and may, as Mr. Mill says, denote absence of originality; but the way to cure it is to promote culture and thought, and so to increase real originality, not to foster a vulgar imitation of it. To use Mr Stephen's simile, to expect of a common place member of society originality, and vigour of thought and character, because he is free to please himself, is as wise as "to say to the water of a stagnant marsh, 'Why in the world do you not run into the sea? You are perfectly free. There is not a single hydraulic work within a mile of you. There are no pumps to suck you up, no defined channel down which you are compelled to run, no harsh banks and no mounds to confine you to any particular course, no dams and no floodgates; and yet there you lie, putrefying and breeding fever, frogs, and gnats, just as if you were a mere slave.' The water might probably answer, if it knew how, 'If you want me to turn mills and carry boats, you must dig proper channels and provide proper water-works for me.' "

The other branch of this subject of liberty involves the relations between the sexes. Bearing in mind Mr Stephen's protest in reference to this discussion, "not exactly on the score of decency, but of unpleasantness in the direction of inde-corum," it is impossible to discuss it freely, not is it a subject which Mr Mill was justified in following into so much detail. That there is much to be corrected in those relations may be

admitted; but to denounce as vicious the principle of due
subordination which regulates them, which is admitted to have
been of universal operation, generally satisfactory in its results,
and in accordance with what the world has regarded as the
intention of nature and the ordinance of God, is to draw a bill
of indictment against God and nature which the evidence does
not support, and is only required by the exigencies of a creed
which holds out equality among mankind as its one article of
faith, and the "development of individuality" as its one idea of
duty. A man must be terribly enamoured of his own intellectual
processes before he abstains from verifying his conclusions by
reference to what he admits to be universal experience,
universal instinct, universal acceptance as the intention of
nature and the ordinance of God. The apology for this
overweening confidence, which brings these visionary philosophers into constant disrepute, is, that "we call everything
instinct which we find in ourselves, and for which we cannot
trace any reasonable foundation;" and again, "this degrading
worship of instinct will give way before a sound psychology,
laying bare the real root of much that is bowed down to as the
intention of nature and the ordinance of God."

So much rhodomontade is talked in these days about the
equality of the sexes and their equal rights, that we are forced
back upon first principles to a degree which is required by no
other subject of public discussion. Mr Mill's contribution to its
solution is contained in these *dicta*: First, justice requires it.
Second, the absence of equality in this particular case is
exceptional — "an isolated fact in modern social institutions."
Third, "the nature of women is an eminently artificial thing,
the result of forced repression in some directions, unnatural
stimulation in others." Mr Stephen completely demolishes the
value of this contribution to our social science, by showing that
that doctrine of equality rests upon an unsound view of history,
an unsound view of morals, and a grotesquely distorted view of
facts.

The whole theory of equality between the sexes rests upon
the notion that absolute equality between individuals is the law
of life, and that the position which women occupy is a violation
of it, produced by an artificial system of tyranny which has no
reasonable warrant. Universal experience may be appealed to
as showing that there are no two men or two women who are
exactly equal to one another in natural or acquired advantages;

and that, therefore, the proposition that all men and all women are on a footing of absolute equality is an impossible one. Mr Mill's account of the existing inequality between the sexes is that from the "very earliest twilight of human society every woman was found in a state of bondage to some man;" and that law converted a physical fact into a legal right. Others, and we think Mr Mill also, are accustomed to refer to the varying position according to women in different stages of history, as the test of the current degree of civilisation. And Mr Mill, in drawing a picture of perfect marriage, describes the relation of men and women as one of reciprocal superiority in powers and attainments. From this he deduces the doctrine of absolute equality: we, on the contrary, infer that where nature, physical strength, and functions alone are considered, woman, as a matter of fact, is inferior to man; and that in proportion as education proceeds, that basis of inequality supports a relationship which ought to be, and generally is, one of reciprocal superiority in powers and attainments. The inequality remains through all stages; the division between men and women as classes can never be lost sight of, and the reciprocal superiority will generally be found in totally different spheres of action.

In what we have to say upon this subject we shall confine ourselves exclusively to the law of the marriage relation, which it is proposed wholly to revolutionise. As a general principle we accept the platitudes as satisfactory, that whatever tends to raise women in thought, in knowledge, in independence, and nobility of nature and aims, is of incalculable service to both sexes alike. The fortunes of the two divisions of the human race are so closely intertwined, that whatever deteriorates or impedes the full development of the feminine nature and character, inevitably reacts upon and deteriorates men. And if civilisation can only reach completion by the harmonious co-operation and development of both sexes, the new creed of revolt — the new duty of women to rebel against their place in creation, and to aim at masculine virtues, and abandon feminine ones — is the vulgarest and most pernicious doctrine of the spurious middle-class liberalism of the day. The whole teaching of the 'subjection of women' is to proclaim a general insurrection of women against men, of wives against husbands; to inculcate what Mr Stephen correctly describes as "a base, unworthy, mutinous disposition, utterly subversive of all that is most worth having in life."

In respect of the first subject, the grievances to be removed are inferiority of education, disadvantages in procuring employment compared with men, inequality as regards the franchise; all of which, if they are grievances, can be removed without introducing the preposterous notion that there is no radical inequality between the sexes, and that their general relations in all the affairs of life, even in marriage, are those of absolute equality. And in respect of the second, the grievance is that there is not equality before the law, that husbands and wives are not "partners" with equal authority and equal rights. The wife is legally subordinate to her husband, which means tyranny on the one side, slavery on the other, with the whole train of evil results which flow from the *status* of slavery. It is a degradation to a woman to assign to her a place in the family in which her will is subordinate to her husband's.

With regard to the institution of marriage, Christianity and modern society have for centuries decided in favour of monogamy — indissolubility, except for very grave and urgent reasons — and the exemption of the details of family government from control by law and law courts, and the consequent vesting of authority in the husband. Under this system marriage is the basis of an association which may last for a considerable time, and which, including children, servants, and dependants, may be numerous. It is, while it lasts, a distinct unit of society; in external dealings it must have its representative; privacy requires that its internal affairs should be withdrawn from the cognisance and control of courts of justice. This withdrawal necessitates the substitution of some internal government; and accordingly, the law provides that all internal authority and external responsibility should rest with the husband; and it defines the extent of that authority, — first, as regards the wife; second, as regards the children under age; thirdly, as regard servants.

The only questions that we are here concerned with is as between the husband and wife, first, whether that authority is to be inoperative as regards her, as inconsistent with her rights and liberties; secondly, whether she is to be admitted to an equal division of power with him over the household, for the purpose not of exercising it by delegation and consent

— for that can be and constantly is done now — but of exercising it, if so minded, in opposition to his wishes.

Taking the latter question first, Mr Mill's view of the exigencies of the position is, in his own words — "One person must have the sole control. But it does not follow that this should always be the same person. The natural arrangement is a division of powers between the two; each being absolute in the executive branch of their own department, and any change of system and principle requiring the consent of both. The division neither can be nor should be pre-established by the law, since it must depend on individual capacities and suitabilities. If the two persons chose, they might pre-appoint it by the marriage contract." This does not commend itself to us as a ripe and sound philosophy. John Jones and Emily Smith, when about to contract a marriage, are very little qualified to draw up a legislative code by the which the future family is to be governed, and power apportioned. The law of the land ought to do that for them. In ninety-nine cases out of a hundred, they are mostly concerned with their external relations, how a livelihood is to be won and expenses met. They are apt to believe that their internal relations will be harmonious and successful, provided that those more pressing matters which concern the outer world can be satisfactorily dealt with. But suppose the code is duly drawn up and unforeseen difficulties arise. These can only be provided for by consent, and therefore, in case of difference, there is no one person who has the sole control. It is obvious that the plan is too ridiculous to be worth a moment's thought. Where marriage is happy and its affairs are harmoniously conducted, it is admitted, both by Mr Mill and Mr Stephen, and is obvious, that the question of control does not arise. But assume a state of things which requires the interposition of control, and an absence of agreement as to which of the two should exercise control, there arises a dead-lock in family affairs, — say a question whether a servant should be dismissed, a governess engaged, a daughter sent to school, an establishment reduced, particular details of family life or discipline followed or disregarded, or any case where there is irremovable antagonism of will. Reasonable people will of course settle the difficulty, for they are a law to themselves. But if the antagonism remains, which is to give way? Is the wife to have the legal right to set her husband at defiance? If not, the principle of obedience is admitted. If she is to have such right the household is reduced to anarchy, or the purposes of the marriage contract are at an end.

The existing law would solve the difficulty by saying that the husband's voice shall prevail and the wife's shall succumb. Mr Mill replies that that establishes a school of tyranny and a school of slavery, and that unless the good sense of mankind mitigated the injustice of law, "society would be a hell upon earth." "A family," he says, "is often, as regards its chief, a school of wilfulness, overbearingness, unbounded self-indulgence, and a double-dyed and idealised selfishness, of which sacrifice itself is only a particular form: . . . what better is to be looked for under the existing form of the institution?" But he offers and can offer no other solution of the difficulty, — viz., how are the internal affairs of a household to be administered? He nowhere proposes the alternative that the interference of a court of justice should be invoked in every case of domestic confusion. If he did, he would cover his system with reproach.

Nor does he propose that when John Jones and Emily Smith are drawing up their domestic code, they should frame a clause referring either disputes or the making of new provisions to arbitration. He well knew that family life under the surveillance of law courts, or arbitrators would be scouted as absurd. Yet such surveillance is the necessary consequence of equal rights and powers, or the marriage must be dissoluble at will. Family life would be intolerable if law neither regulated it nor provided for its regulation except by a council of two, exercising power, without a casting vote in case of difference. And therefore the plan of raising up an *imperium in imperio*, or rather two conflicting jurisdictions — a second captain of half the ship, instead of a first lieutenant of the whole — is open to the objection that it will solve no existing difficulties. And further, it will entirely alter the existing constitution of the family; it provides for the occurrence of entanglements, and does not provide for their solution; and in place of the correlative duties of protection and obedience sanctioned by love, it offers a relationship of equality sanctioned by law courts. The conditions of permanent existence are lost sight of in the vain attempt to escape from that reasonable subordination, which, far more than equality, is the universal law of life.

Then, with regard to the personal relation of husband and wife, apart from the question of the government of the family, the fact is that, as Mr Stephen points out, all co-operation implies command and obedience. If two people join together to stitch an old shoe, one must have the power to decide in case of difference. If life-long engagements are made, the law must vest the power to decide, and it can only do so by converting the 'physical fact' into a legal right. Mr Mill's discussions and principles point to dissoluble unions, facility of divorce, a degradation of the marriage tie, and the weakening of authority in every household. He admits that the existing principle of subordination is so modified in practice that is works well. He admits that the principle is in accordance with recognised 'physical fact.' His own treatise ignores the 'physical fact,' and defines no other principle.

With regard to the extent of the husband's power, it is practically limited by the necessity for its exercise. Cruelty is a ground for separation, and marks the legal boundary of marital authority. But morals and manners and opinion step in to limit its exercise, to a degree suited to the station in life and tone of society in which the family is placed; in other words, its exercise is limited by that very social restraint which (it is part of Mr Mill's own case) is strong enough to forbid freedom of opinion, to stunt originality, and to check "experiments in living." This social restraint is generally in full operation; for it is admitted that under ordinary circumstances the husband's power cannot be exercised unreasonably. If the social restraint is inoperative, a low standard of manners and morals is implied, and then what remedy would Mr Mill's system work? If the husband is a savage, and the wife a slave, they will remain so as long as they live together, quite independently of marital authority. Bill Sykes did not require the legal authority of a husband to enable him to tyrannise over Nancy. It would be a mere mockery to give the wife a legal title to complete independence and equal power, if she is personally unable to assert them. The husband's authority is essential to the permanence of marriage and the government of a household. If the wife is competent, she will not merely obtain virtual independence, but will exercise by delegation nearly the whole of the authority; if she is incompetent, it is useless for the law to give her what will be of no use to herself or the family.

Then with regard to the extent of the wife's submission: it is said, but few wives or husbands will recognise the accuracy of the description, that under existing circumstances, marriage is

the relationship of tyrant and slave. We have been introduced
to the description of a family demoralised by the "double-dyed
and idealised selfishness' which results from the disastrous
nature of the marriage union; now we must contemplate the
equally disastrous effects of that tie upon the unfortunate
persons who have been rash enough to contract it. "A wife is
completely assimilated to a slave, and is denied any lot in life
but that of being the personal body-servant of a despot." Some
sense of exaggeration appears to have suggested itself to Mr
Mill's mind and apparently some recollection of cases from
which we might infer that the tyranny complained of was not
always on the same side of the house. Englishwomen, as a rule,
are not quite so despicable as their champion describes them;
nor is the position assigned to them in married life quite
inconsistent with the development of other faults than those
congenial to the *status* of slavery. "I know,' he says, "that there
is another side to the question. I grant that the wife, if she
cannot effectually resist, can at last retaliate, . . . using what
may be called the power of the scold or the shrewish sanction."
And upon this he observes that the power which a wife obtains
in a family, which he apparently traces entirely to her scolding
propensities, is no compensation for the loss of freedom which
she has undergone. Her power often gives her what she has no
right to, but does not enable her to assert her own rights.

This condition of slavery tempered by scolding is, according
to Mr Mill, by no means redeemed by conjugal affection; for,
he exclaims, intense attachments have before now existed
between master and slave. "Men, except the most brutish,
desire to have in the women most nearly connected with them
not a forced slave but a willing one, not a slave merely but a
favourite. They do not want solely the obedience of women,
they want their sentiments." "It is part of the irony of life," he
proceeds, "that the strongest feelings of devoted gratitude of
which human nature seems to be susceptible are called forth in
human beings towards those who having the power entirely to
crush their earthly existence voluntarily refrain from exercising
that power."

There is another idea which Mr Mill propounds, which
strikes at the very root of life-long unions, and points to
dissoluble marriage and facility of divorce — in short, to
Mohammedan or Mormonite arrangements. We reluctantly
reproduce a passage which is tainted with "unpleasantness in

the direction of indecorum," and shows that Mr Mill's indictment is against human nature and Christian marriage, and not merely against society and its constitution: "Hardly any slave," he says, "except one immediately attached to the master's person, is a slave at all hours and all minutes; in general he has, like a soldier, his fixed task; and when it is done, and when he is off duty, he disposes, within certain limits, of his own time, and has a family life into which the master rarely intrudes. But it cannot be so with the wife. Above all, a female slave has in Christian countries an admitted right to refuse to her master the last familiarity; not so the wife. However brutal the tyrant she may unfortunately be chained to, though she may know that he hates her, though it may be his daily pleasure to torture her, and though she may feel it impossible not to loathe him, he can claim from her and enforce the lowest degradation of a human being — that of being made the instrument of an animal function contrary to her inclination." We decline to enter into this discussion, except to say that separation will generally precede a state of things which literally answers such a description. Impediments to divorce, of course, may be in individual cases productive of unhappiness. But the Christian theory of indissoluble marriage involves some unhappy unions, from which Mohammedan contracts and Mormonite *liaisons* provide an easy escape.

The avowed and inevitable result to which Mr Mill's argument leads is, that the identity of husband and wife, which is the theory of canon and common law, should be replaced by a partnership contract, under which both should be equal and independent. That identity he refuses to distinguish from slavery tempered by scolding and profaned by peculiar degradation. Man and wife should both be perfectly free agents, competent to contract each with the other, each with the outside world, and liable to all the responsibilities which they severally undertake. It is one vital objection to this plan that it renders family government impossible; next, that it involves the surveillance of law courts over family life, for the sanction of the husband's authority being withdrawn, no other sanction is provided; thirdly, that the separate rights and responsibilities of "man and wife limited" will open the door to endless frauds upon third parties; and, lastly, that the relationship being one of contract, and not that of *status* defined by law and sanctioned by religion, must be dissoluble at will.

Our case is that, abolish the tenet of the wife's submission, and you provide no cure for unhappy marriages; while there is no argument in favour of the wife's independence which does not also point in favour of facile divorces and temporary unions. It is absurd to suppose that any man will undertake life-long liabilities which he is to be unable to control or regulate — will constitute a woman his agent, without power to limit or control her agency — will place her in command of his household without the right of ultimate decision in case of difference. Or if the wife is to be separately responsible for all that she does, it is absurd to suppose that the marriage relation is to continue while the wife is free to enter, in spite of his disapproval, into engagements, consisting with those of wife, mother, and mistress of the household, and generally to "develop her individuality" at the expense of her duties to her husband and children, and in a manner utterly disapproved by him. Mr Stephen has conclusively shown how entirely in the woman's favour is the condition of indissolubility introduced. She has life-long rights as against her husband, immunity from all civil responsibility, whilst she devotes herself to what is in truth the real female occupation, and which frequently absorbs all her time and energies; and in return for the right to life-long protection and support she owes the correlative duty of submission.

The true character and extent of this submission form the gist of the whole subject. Mr Mill's view or representation of it is exaggerated. The law recognises the wife's place in the family, and though it frees her from external responsibility, and merges her existence in that of her husband, it secures her a position of authority and independence within the household. Contrast her position with that of her grown-up daughter. The latter is no doubt *sui juris*; but the former has gained position and rights relative to her husband, which, so far from regarding as slavery, she considers as the reward of her life, and a source of emulation for her daughter. It is of far more importance that the submission of which we speak should be the duty of the wife than of a servant or a grown-up daughter. The wife is trusted with large powers, has permanent rights and authority, and is too absolutely identified with her husband to render her wilful disloyalty and disobedience anything short of the subversion of the household.

So far from the submission required being identical with slavery, it is only of that kind which is consistent with equal position in the eyes of society, identity of interest, the wife's right to use the husband's authority in the family, and generally to represent him in all matters connected with the household. It is of that kind which is required by loyal co-operation, and the faithful blending of lives and dispositions by common aims and mutual assistance. It does not prevent the due 'development' of the wife's 'individuality', but does prevent such development from being inconsistent with the discharge of conjugal duty. It emancipates the wife from outside responsibility, and gives her relatively to her husband the full rewards of life. And if in any point law falls short in according to her her just rewards, it can be amended without touching the vial principle of wife-like obedience and submission.

There may be, and probably is, in many classes, an undue neglect of female education, an altogether indefensible fostering of the notion that boys are infinitely, and in all respects, superior to girls, and a general encouragement to the notion that men may be selfish and tyrannical, and that wives should be helpless or even abject. But this is a matter of defective education, and can be altered without revolutionising the institution of marriage. At the present time, the tone of men with regard to women is a sure sign of their own degree of education, or of the capacities and acquirements of their own female relations.

Mr Mill takes the extravagant instance of the "vilest malefactor" who has some wretched woman tied to him, "against whom he can commit any atrocity except killing her, and if tolerably cautious, can do even that without much danger of incurring the legal penalty." Of course, if a vile malefactor, or any other brute, consorts with a fellow-creature, the result will be oppression and cruelty. But how will it be altered by giving the woman legal independence? A man cannot kill his wife in the exercise of marital authority, nor will her legal independence give her any security. If the law cannot protect life, much less will it protect her independence and equality.

Besides, of what avail is it to argue against an institution of universal interest from the conduct of savages to whom it was never meant to apply, or at least in whose favour it was never introduced? It is useless to revolutionise the institution of marriage on their account, for, according to Mr Mill's own theories, "probably the great majority of married people live in a spirit of a just law of equality," — *i.e.*, are perfectly happy with the existing relationship, and the only evil which requires a remedy so violent is the sentimental dislike of subjection, fostered by a pernicious teaching and an unripe philosophy. That sentimental dislike we characterise as "a base, unworthy, mutinous disposition, subversive of all that is most worth having in life." If a woman is really stronger in character and mental power than her husband, she ought, according to Mr Mill, to absorb the chief authority in the family for the interests of the family, and as her own right. Our answer is that she will do so now under existing circumstances, but that such superiority will be, and ought to be, toned down by reference to the principle of her official subordination and duty of submission. That this is degrading, or cutting her off from aspiring to the first place, is absurd. If the lieutenant is a better seaman than the captain, he will absorb more moral authority in the ship; but it will render all the more incumbent upon him the duties of loyal fidelity and subordination. If the leader of the House of Commons is a man of greater natural powers and capacity than a Premier in the House of Lords, he will practically supersede the authority of his chief; but it would denote "a base, unworthy, and mutinous disposition" if he were on that account to throw off the duty of subordination, and would render co-operation impossible.

In short, Christianity and good sense have solved the difficulties of sexual relationship by establishing monogamy, indissolubility of marriage, and the subordination of the wife to the husband, so far at least as is necessary to preserve the objects of marriage and the loyal cooperation of husband and wife. Under such a system those happy marriages are rendered possible which Mr Mill describes with so much force and eloquence. And no instance is brought in his works of which it can be said that it tends to condemn the system. Marriage is of all subjects and institutions the most serious one to tamper with. And while Mr Mill denounces the existing form of the institution in the strongest terms, and calls upon the whole female sex to revolt against it as unworthy, and to the lowest degree degrading, he proposes no other form which the institution should or could take, which is not on the face of it absurd, and which it is impossible should ever coexist with permanence of duration and unity and completeness of association. The duty of wife-like obedience will last as long as the Christian religion prevails, and can never be subverted until we are content to remedy the evils of our social system by a recourse to the practices of Mohammedans and Mormonites.

THE QUARTERLY REVIEW
Vol. 135, 1873
[John Wilson]

1. *Liberty, Equality, Fraternity.* By James Fitzjames Stephen,
   Q.C. London, 1873
2. *Old-Fashioned Ethics and Common-Sense Metaphysics,
   with some of their Applications.* By William Thomas
   Thornton, Author of a Treatise 'On Labour.' London,
   1873.
3. *Enigmas of Life.* by W. R. Greg. Fourth edition. London,
   1873.
4. *John Stuart Mill: Notices of his Life and Work.* Reprinted
   from the 'Examiner'. London, 1873.

'Liberty, Equality, and Fraternity, all over again! it's enough to
make one sick!' Such was the exclamation of a most liberal-
natured old gentleman, within our hearing and memory, when
the same stale watchwords of Parisian revolutionism again
resounded in 1848, which, in his youth, had frighted our isle
from its propriety in 1792–3. 'It is probable,' said Malthus,
'that if the world were to last for any number of thousand
years, systems of equality would be among those errors which,
like the tunes of a barrel-organ, will never cease to return at
certain intervals.'[1]

It is noticeable albeit negative tribute to the influence of the
writings of the late John Stuart Mill, that the authors of the
three remarkable works before us have the one point in
common, that they each take a position of more or less
pronounced antagonism towards one or other of the most
prominent doctrines — metaphysical, political, or economical
— of that eminent thinker. Mr. Fitzjames Stephen's 'Liberty,
Equality, Fraternity' is, from beginning to end, a series of
assaults upon all the main positions of the late Mr. Mill on
every relation, normal or abnormal, of men, women, and
communities. What is singular is that he espouses Mill's

[1] 'Essay on Population,' book iii. c. 3.

utilitarian principle, while combating almost all Mill's deductions from it. Mr. Thornton, on the other hand, boldly sets up an anti-utilitarian standard, and not content with challenging Mr. Mill then living, and an intimate friend of his, as an antagonist, enters the lists for a free and gentle passage of arms with Huxley, Darwin, and Tyndall, and even evokes, to do ghostly battle with, the sceptical spirit of David Hume. Mr. Greg takes exception to Mill's economical teaching on the Malthusian Population principle — maintained by him, as the essential foundation of all sound economical doctrine that can be addressed, in their own interest, to the working classes.

We believe that we shall best bring out what we have to say on the most important topics of the three recent publications above cited, by reviewing them in their character of critiques of the leading doctrines of Mill — of the moral and social philosophy of his tractates on 'Liberty' and 'Utilitarianism' — and of the rigid Malthusianism which conspicuously characterised his 'Principles of Political Economy.' We are the rather led to this, because the 'Notices of his Life and Work,' reprinted in pamphlet form from the 'Examiner,' offer a sort of challenge to all who, like ourselves, while admiring his intellectual achievements, consider his doctrines, so far as a permanent bias and direction was impressed on them by his early training and associations, anything rather than fitted to afford safe guidance, whether in morals or politics. We would speak with all respect of the late Mr. Mill personally. A man who had the moral courage to declare spontaneously, in mature life, his change of opinion from the conventionally popular to the conventionally unpopular side on such a question as the Ballot, by that one act honourably distinguished himself from the herd of vulgar politicians. Such an avowal could be prompted by no party tactic. It could have been made from no other motive than fidelity to honest conviction. The same thing may be said of Mill's strenuous and persistent advocacy of what has been styled the system of 'proportional representation.'[2] The tribute of respect fairly due to such instances of independent thought and action may be accorded irrespectively of coincident or

---

[2]   Mr. Bright has stigmatised the application of the principle in question to the School Board elections as 'the miserable sectarian expedient of the cumulative vote.' We are led to infer that the party he seeks to propitiate has found it inconveniently just in its working.

conflicting opinions on the several matters in question. It is the distinction of *having* an opinion and acting on it, which is becoming a rare phenomenon in politics. What may well be thought the worst evil of democracy is that its constituent masses *think in herds*, and expect their delegates to let, or affect to let the herd think for them.

The first political schooling of Mr. Mill was 'after the most straitest sect' Benthamite — that is, was received in a school systematically adverse to all powers that be, and confident in the creation of powers hereafter *to be* by philosophical fiat. He indeed made vigorous efforts in his manhood, for which he deserved all credit, to shake himself free from the sectarian narrowness of the school of his youth. But it may be doubted how far his second school — that of the old India House — was precisely the best fitted to correct, in the degree desirable for an English political thinker or actor, the tendencies to philosophical absolutism acquired in his first school — that of Queen's Square Place. His published views of the Irish Land question in particular seem to us a sort of cross between Jeremy Bentham and Tippoo Sahib.

There are curious points of parallelism, as well as of contrast, between the late Mr. Mill and his most uncompromising critic, Mr. Fitzjames Stephen. They have in common fearless freedom of speculation, apt to shock readers not used to it. The former in his youth sat, as we have said, at the feet of Bentham, and studied under the stern rule of his father, the elder Mill. The latter we should conjecture to have been nursed in the creed of Calvin, or 'the patent Christianity of Clapham Common.'[3] The manhood of both would seem to have had enough to do to shake off so much of the doctrinal teaching of youth as no longer fitted its maturer moral and intellectual frame. But to have outgrown Benthamism, as to have outgrown Calvinism, was not to have purged the soul of all tincture from those doctrinal sources. The indelible impression that what is, is wrong, in law, politics, or ethics, was the stamp set by Benthamism, aggravated by the anti-aristocratism of Mill senior, on the ductile mind of the younger Mill. The ultra-Protestant logic, which, wherever it sees not an Infallible, sees only an impostor, is the trait left by Calvinism, or something like it, in that of Fitzjames Stephen. But the differences of

[3] Sydney Smith.

mental temper between author and critic are not less conspicuous. With all his speculative daring, there was a sort of gentleness and even a sort of timidity in the temper of the younger Mill, which showed themselves in maturer years in attempts to reconcile differences between conflicting social creeds, and to seek allies amongst all enlisted in any way in the ranks of social progress. But Mr. Fitzjames Stephen seems to prefer enemies to allies at any time; and to be disposed at the outset, though he qualifies his sweeping sentences in the sequel, to quarrel with progress altogether, and regard Liberty as a moral and political nonentity. Mr. Mill, so far as his levelling zeal would let him, especially in his later years, combined the *suaviter in modo* with the *fortiter in re*, while Mr. Stephen would seem to have taken as his motto *fortiter in re, fortissime in modo*. His bark, indeed is often worse than his bite. The one may be said to have been almost all his life the recluse student, even at his bureaucratic desk in the City solitudes of the old India House, and notwithstanding the subsequent uncharacteristic episode of his election for Westminster. The latter alternates the *rôles* of the trenchant journalist and the vigorous advocate. If we might venture further into the forbidden fields of personal criticism, we might find further points of contrast between the 'feminine philosopher,' as Mill has been termed, with special reference to his fervid vindication of female equality, and his vigorous forensic critic, who takes little pains to disguise from the fairer half of the species his full sense of that masculine superiority, mental and physical, which Law must recognise, in order that Law may regulate.

Looking dispassionately at Mr. Fitzjames Stephen's critique of Mill's book on 'Liberty,' we are reminded of the quarrel about the colour and material of two different sides of one shield. The disputed object was looked at by either disputant from opposite points of view. Mr. Stephen rests his case on the actual course of things in this fighting and working world. Mr. Mill contemplated an ideal, for the better realisation of which he looked to the future. If the faculties and perceptions of each could have been combined in one — that with which each was accomplished completing that which was in each lacking — a more comprehensive political philosophy might certainly have been formed from the combination than can easily be extracted from either of the two separately. Mr. Mill's ideal of individual liberty, subjected to no restraint, even from public opinion, but such as society may find necessary for its self-protection, would have been all the better for correction by Mr. Stephen's knowledge from experience of what sort of thing human society really is; while the rough assertion by the latter of ordinary ways of acting and thinking might have been advantageously tempered and qualified by reference to some standard more elevated. Where Mr. Stephen does good service is in bringing hard facts into broad and clear view. We entirely agree with him in his fundamental position, that 'Power precedes liberty. Liberty, from the very nature of things, is dependent upon power; and it is only under the protection of a powerful, well-organised, and intelligent Government, that any liberty can exist at all.'

'Compulsion in its most formidable shape and on the most extensive scale — the compulsion of *war* — is one of the principles which lie at the root of national existence. It determines whether nations are to be, and what they are to be. It decides what men shall believe, how they shall live, in what mould their religion, law, morals, and the whole tone of their lives, shall be cast. It is the *ratio ultima*, not only of kings, but of human society in all its shapes. It determines precisely, for one thing, how much and how little individual liberty is to be left to exist at any specific place or time.'

In another page Mr. Fitzjames Stephen says, with equal truth:—

'War and conquest determine all the great questions of politics, and exercise a nearly decisive influence in many cases upon religion and morals. We are what we are because Holland and England, in the sixteenth century, defeated Spain, and because Gustavus Adolphus, and others, successfully resisted the Empire in Northern Germany. Popular prejudice and true political insight agree in feeling and thinking that the moral and religious issues decided at Sadowa and Sedan were more important than the political issues. Here, then, we have compulsion on a gigantic scale producing vast and durable political, moral, and religious effects. Can its good and evil, its right and wrong, be measured by the single simple principle that it is good when required for purposes of self-protection, otherwise not?'

'The question,' concludes Mr. Stephen, 'how large ought

the province of liberty to be is really identical with this: in what respects must men influence each other if they want to attain the objects of life, and in what respects must they leave each other uninfluenced?'

Undoubtedly that is the question. Mr. Stephen's objects of life are the actual objects of the work-day world. Mr. Mill's objects of life were always projected into the future — often the far future. His main object was to elevate the life of the generality to higher condition; and his doctrine of 'Liberty' was to forbear from social discouragement of whatsoever 'experiments in living' individuals might choose to try — how eccentric soever such experiments might generally appear to be. With this object in view, he recommended society to restrain itself from putting down, *even by the force of opinion*, any 'experiment in living' which should not take the shape of overt acts of war with legal authority. 'That so few now dare to be eccentric,' he said, 'makes the chief danger of the time.' In these days of the International, the Commune, Spanish and Irish Federalism, lack of eccentricity, at least in politics, is not perhaps the malady with which the World, whether Old or New, feels itself most afflicted.

'It is the opinions men entertain and the feelings they cherish,' said Mr. Mill, 'respecting those who disown the beliefs they deem important, which make this country not a place of mental freedom.' This country, then, is to be rendered a place of mental freedom by giving full freedom to eccentrics and fanatics to 'express' their eccentricity and fanaticism, while refusing to the sane and sober portion of society any corresponding freedom of bringing its condemnatory sentiments to bear upon such vagaries. Just see where society would be landed by 'Liberty' of this one-sided sort. Do not suppose eccentrics and fanatics are of a tolerant breed themselves; if they invoke tolerance, it is only for lack of power to persecute. Once concede unlimited right of insult to the beliefs the mass of society hold important, while refusing society all right of expressing its sense of such insults — a large step is made to giving the insulters in the end the upper hand. Under such conditions, it becomes a most unequal conflict between society on the one hand and its would-be subverters on the other —

'Si pugna est ubi tu pulsas, ego vapulo tantum.'

But what is most to be noted is that the very principle of individual liberty, professedly asserted, is violated by this unilateral mode of maintaining it. A minority is to be at liberty to insult all that a majority holds sacred. A majority is not to be at liberty to resent the insult by the equally free expression of condemnatory opinion on its part. What! is the majority not composed of individuals as well as the minority? Is the liberty of the many less entitled to exercise than that of the few? Then it would seem a new aristocracy of Liberty is to be installed amongst us, in which fanatics and monomaniacs are alone to have full swing for their thick-coming fancies, while the sane and sober must simply 'assist,' in the French sense of the word, *i.e.* stand up and say nothing. Upon what extraordinary hypothesis can such wondrous conclusions be founded? Upon the hypothesis apparently that whatever is is wrong, and that all things stable should be subverted.

The doctrine maintained in the late Mr. Mill's tractate on 'Liberty' was, in brief, that society ought in no case to permit itself to make any *deterrent* demonstrations, even although these should be unenforced by legal penalties, against anything any of its members might say, or write, or do — except for the single purpose of direct and immediate self-protection. This doctrine led him to some queer conclusions in particular cases. The *general* answer to it is well given as follows by Mr. Fitzjames Stephen: —

'Criminal legislation proper may be regarded as unimportant as an engine of prohibition in comparison with morals and the forms of morality sanctioned by theology. For one act from which one person is restrained by fear of the law of the land, many persons are restrained from innumerable acts by the fear of the disapprobation of their neighbours, which is the moral sanction; by the fear of punishment in a future state of existence, which is the religious sanction; or by the fear of their own disapprobation, which may be called the conscientious sanction, and may be regarded as a compound case of the other two. Now, in the innumerable majority of cases, disapprobation, or the moral sanction, has nothing whatever to do with self-protection. The religious sanction is, by its nature, independent of it.

'The morality of the vast mass of mankind is simply to do what they please up to the point at which custom puts a restraint upon them, arising from the fear of disapprobation. The custom of looking upon certain courses of conduct with aversion is the essence of morality, and the fact that this aversion may be felt by the very person whose conduct occasions it, and may be described as arising from the action of his own conscience, makes no difference which need be considered here. The important point is, that such disapprobation could never have become customary unless it had been imposed upon mankind at large by persons who themselves felt it with exceptional energy, and who were in a position which enabled them to make other people adopt their principles, and even their tastes and feelings.'

Mr. Mill himself furnished an instance of the extreme lengths to which he would have asserted his principle of individual liberty, by taking under his philosophic patronage a poor monomaniac convicted at Bodmin assizes in 1857 'for uttering and writing on a gate some offensive words concerning Christianity.' This conviction he cited as a more than ordinarily flagrant example of the infliction of legal penalties for the mere expression of opinion. Now, the counsel for the prosecution in the case in question (if we recollect right, the present Attorney-General), published a statement on the first appearance of Mr. Mill's book, that the man Pooley was not punished for the expression of opinion, but for the commission of a public nuisance by scrawling the most outrageous blasphemies on every gate-post and dead wall in his neighbourhood, with the presumptive intention of insulting public opinion and defying public decency. The counsel asked for a conviction on the ground of that offensive intention, and the judge charged the jury that on no other ground would they be justified in giving their verdict against the prisoner. Upon that ground a verdict of guilty was accordingly given, but the convict was soon after released from prison as of unsound mind. Now, here was an extreme, by Mr. Mill singled out as an exemplary, instance of that eccentricity in opinion and conduct which he regarded as highly to be encouraged in these days of tame and abject conformity.

There is, as it seems to us, a pervading contradiction in the late Mr. Mill's 'Liberty' doctrine — a contradiction honourable to his sincere consideration for individual liberty, if inconsistent with thorough-going adhesion to the formula of his old Gamaliel, Bentham. Prepossessed with that formula — 'greatest happiness of greatest number' — solicitous (if we may borrow the happy expression of Mr. Stephen) to see equal 'rations of happiness' served out to all the world and his wife — 'every one to count for one, no one for more than one,' Mr. Mill showed himself, nevertheless, fully alive to the importance and difficulty of preserving somehow something of individual force and freedom from the Argus eyes and Briareus hands of a 'tyrant majority'.

Shall we finally conclude with Mr. Fitzjames Stephen, that all 'discussions about Liberty are, in truth, discussions about a negation;' that all 'attempts to solve the problems of government and society by such discussion are like attempts to discover the nature of light and heat by inquiries into darkness and cold;' and, lastly, that 'enthusiasm about Liberty is altogether thrown away?' Enthusiasm about anything may, of course, be wrongly directed; but, surely, the sense of freedom is something more, by the common consent of mankind, than that of a negation. Liberty may not have been clearly traced to its true sources, or correctly defined in its indispensable conditions by Mr. Mill. But to a critic, whose forte should lie in discrimination more than Mr. Fitzjames Stephen's does, that would be no reason for regarding Liberty itself as a moral and social nonentity.

It may be admitted, indeed, that liberty is a matter of feeling rather than of specific fact; but we should not, therefore conclude it the less fit a subject of disquisition or enthusiasm. The sense of freedom is the sense of exemption from arbitrary authority; and what seems to us its source and indispensable condition is individual consciousness of actual or potential participation in the governing power of the community. The sense of such participation — actual, or, as we said, potential — is not necessarily dependent on any particular form of rule. There might be kept alive in feudal servitude itself, as Burke said, 'the spirit of an exalted freedom.' The humblest clansman of the proudest Highland chief felt himself and his claymore essential constituents of the military power of the head of his clan, and, in contributing to maintain that power, might have the full feeling of liberty — that is to say, of spontaneous unconstrained action. The actual possession, or facility of attainment, of the elective franchise, gives the humblest British subject or American citizen a sense of political power which would not fail to make itself felt on any adequate provocation. On the other hand, the subject of a ruler who has made himself absolute by grace of bayonet and bullet, or of a foreign sovereignty, like that of Russia in Poland, so long as the native despotism or the foreign domination lasts, cannot easily cheat himself into the notion that he himself has any share in the governing power, and cannot, therefore, have that contented sense of liberty which alone makes safe subjects. Such alone can be those who feel themselves partners, albeit sleeping partners, in the political firm. When England, wisely or unwisely, went to war with Russia in 1854, she did so on the impulse of her voting or unvoting millions who hated the Czar for his iron rule in Poland, and for his aid to Austria to maintain hers in Hungary. When the American North, wisely or unwisely, made war with the South, she did so on the like popular impulse. Those wars were wars of national feeling in both countries, and therefore their vicissitudes endangered the governing power in neither country. But when Napoleon the Third made his crusade in Mexico, he acted on no impulse but his own, and had no voluntary national force to fall back upon. Liberty must be *something*, however unregarded in imperial calculation of forces, for its presence or absence to make all the difference in the degree of persistency with which external enterprises can be carried out, in the teeth of reverses, or malcontent subjects made partakers in the benefits of national institutions, in spite of their too manifest disposition — *e.g.* in Ireland — to use them no otherwise than as weapons of hostility to the very power that imparts them.

On one subject Mr. Mill's memory is certainly entitled to all the honours which attended the funeral of that famous medieval Master-Singer, surnamed 'Frauenlob,' whom the grateful female subjects of his poetical panegyrics carried, it is said, to the grave with their own arms, rained tears over the tomb in which they laid him, and, it is added, poured so much wine also over it, that they flooded the church.

There are two questions about women's rights which are very distinct, but which have been a good deal confused by Mr. Mill and his female clients, who contend for those rights. The first, which never should have been any question at all, is whether the legal nullity of women, under the old Roman and the old feudal law, should be the legal doctrine of days of more advanced civilisation. That women have an equal right with men to recognition as persons, and to every civil right following on that recognition, is no longer likely to be disputed in any quarter. But another and larger question has been included in that of Women's Rights. That question is whether marriage involves, or does not involve, a subjection of Woman to Man, which is natural and necessary, not legal and artificial in its origin. Whether, in short, the proverb that when two ride on one horse one must ride behind, is, or is not, the best and briefest expression of the natural and irrepealable law of marriage.

If we were to state frankly what we believe firmly to be the real views of the sex represented as aggrieved in this matter, we should say that what they chiefly feel they have to complain of, is rather the prevailing deficiency than the prevailing excess of the sort of subjection which the conjugal relation draws after it. There are really too many women for whom the artificial circumstances of our times do not provide occupation of the sort most congenial to their sex. Whatever independent occupations the distinctive delicacy of female organisation affords women a prospect of following with success, ought to be, and will be, thrown open to them.[4] But here we are met on the threshold by the Darwinian principle of Natural Selection. The earliest, we believe, and ablest championess of 'the Rights of Women,' Mary Wollstonecraft, frankly admitted what Mr.

---

[4] How much the division of labour between men and women is matter of convention and usage — and therefore, it may be supposed, of the concurrent convenience of both parties — how little of law — we might cite many instances, and shall be content with one from the autobiography of Madame Schopenhauer, who was the wife of a Dantzic merchant, and who describes as follows the recollections of her youth of the female business-habits she found prevailing at Brussels just before the French Revolution of 1789.

'I was most of all surprised at the intimate knowledge the ladies had of the business transctions of the house; they seemed, indeed, better informed on these subjects than the nominal head of the firm; and in all conversations about their commercial affairs with Schopenhauer, I observed that the husbands generally sat by in silence. The wives of the first bankers usually spent the forenoon in the counting-house, richly dressed, and surrounded by their grown-up daughters, who discharged the duties of cashiers. There they sat, in a place somewhat apart, whence they could see all that passed; writing, dictating, casting accounts, receiving all strangers who came in, calucating the course of exchange, and counting out to them the cash they were to receive. Thus were things done fifty years ago; it struck me as being a strange arrangement, and one which I did not admire. Time and circumstances have greatly altered it since.'

Mill and his female followers have ignored or disputed — viz. a superiority in physical, involving a certain superiority of mental strength in men. This natural aristocracy of Man over Woman — of sexual strength over sexual weakness — this natural incapacity of woman to become the rival and competitor, however well fitted to be the partner and helpmate of Man, no legislative assertion of the equality of the sexes, an equality which does not exist, can alter. Women, as a body, perfectly well know this; as a body, women will never agitate for universal admission to equal and similar functions with the stronger sex, for which there is already scramble enough among that sex, and for which the nominal licence of the weaker to scramble with the stronger can never be more than the empty aspiration of stray philosophers, male or female, who understand neither sex.

Most women desire, a majority of women obtain, a partnership for life with some individual of the stronger sex. Now when a partnership comes to be formed for life, it is clear that the party, in whose special interest that lifelong duration is stipulated, must accept the terms on which alone a lifelong partnership can be agreed to by the party who has a less apparent, though not perhaps less real, interest in its formation. A committee or parliament of strong-minded women might draw up terms for marriage contracts, which should formally abolish the conjugal subjection, and vindicate the conjugal equality of women. The only consequence would be that men would be uncommonly shy of entering into female partnership for life on such conditions. Strong-minded females might rejoin, 'We do not want to form life partnerships.' We can only appeal to ladies less strong-minded, whether partnerships terminable at will would suit *their* taste.

'Marriage,' says Mr. Fitzjames Stephen, 'is one of the subjects with which it is absolutely necessary both for law and morals to deal in some way or other. All that I need consider in reference to the present purpose is the question whether the laws and moral rules which relate to it should regard it as a contract between equals, or as a contract between a stronger and a weaker person, involving subordination for certain purposes on the part of the weaker to the stronger. I say that a law which proceeded on the former and not the latter of these views would be founded on a totally false assumption, and would involve cruel injustice in the sense of extreme general inexpediency, especially to women. If the parties to a contract of marriage are treated as equals, it is impossible to avoid the inference that marriage, like other partnerships, may be dissolved at pleasure. The advocates of women's rights are exceedingly shy of stating this plainly. Mr. Mill says nothing about it in his book "On the Subjection of Women," though in one place he comes very near to saying so; but it is as clear an inference from his principles as anything can possibly be, nor has he ever disavowed it. If this were the law, it would make women the slaves of their husbands. A woman loses the qualities which make her attractive to men much earlier than men lose those which make them attractive to women. The tie between women and young children is generally far closer than the tie between them and their fathers. A woman who is no longer young, and who is the mother of children, would thus be absolutely in her husband's power, in nine cases out of ten, if he might put an end to the marriage when he pleased. This is one inequality in the position of the parties which must be recognised and provided for beforehand, if the contract is to be for their common good. A second inequality is this: when a man marries, it is generally because he feels himself established in life. He incurs, no doubt, a good deal of expense, but he does not in any degree impair his means of earning a living. When a woman married she practically renounces in all but the rarest cases the possibility of undertaking any profession but one, and the possibility of carrying on that one profession in the society of any man but one. Here is a second inequality. It would be easy to mention others of the deepest importance; but these are enough to show that to treat a contract of marriage as a contract between persons who are upon an equality in regard of strength, and power to protect their interest, is to treat it as being what it notoriously is not.'

Nine-tenths of thinking women would, we are convinced, acquiesce in Mr. Fitzjames Stephen's statement that the ties of marriage, as hitherto maintained in civilised communities, are essentially protective of female weakness against male reckless-ness, and that the freedom claimed for both sexes from the generally indissoluble obligation of those ties would be freedom for the stronger at the cruel cost of the weaker sex.

Turning to Mr. Thornton's volume on 'Old-Fashioned Ethics and Common-Sense Metaphysics,' we may begin with an anecdote of the late Mr. Mill's reception of it (the work was published shortly before his death), which we find given by the Editor of the 'Notices of his Life and Work.' 'We were speaking' says that gentleman, 'of Mr. Thornton's recently published Old-Fashioned Ethics and Common-Sense Metaphysics, when I remarked on Mr. Mill's wide divergence from most of the views contained in it.' 'Yes,' he replied, 'it is pleasant to find something on which to differ from Thornton.' This something, which it was pleasant to find on which to differ, was nothing less than the whole foundation and sanctions of religion and morals. But Mill had large philosophical tolerance where he had political or social sympathies. He was agreed with Mr. Thornton about peasant-proprietorship, and about that remarkable piece of statistics in its favour which we took occasion, in a former number, to reduce to its real value as fact — that 'the agriculture of' Guernsey and Jersey 'maintains, besides cultivators, non-agricultural populations, respectively, four or five times as dense as that of Britain!'

Mill, according to the Editor of the above-cited Notices, 'had no other creed, or dogma, or gospel, than Bentham's axiom, "the greatest happiness of the greatest number."' Mr. Thornton, with an acute perception which we find in many parts of his book, of the confusion introduced by large and loose phrases in moral discussions, observes as follows on the ambiguity of this Benthamic axiom, which, it seems, is to be the sole future gospel of the Gentiles:—

> 'The greatest happiness of the greatest number may mean either the largest total of happiness in which the largest number of those concerned can participate, or a still larger total, which, if some of the possible participants are excluded, would be divisible among the remainder. The largest aggregate of happiness attainable by any or by all concerned means the largest sum total absolutely, without reference to the number of participants. Writers on Utilitarianism seem to have sometimes the first, sometimes the second, of these totals in view, but more frequently the second than the first.'

It is a markworthy fact, which however we nowhere remember

to have seen remarked, that Bentham himself in his later years became distrustful of his own famous formula. 'In the later years of Bentham's life,' says his literary executor, the late Sir John Bowring, 'the phrase "greatest happiness of the greatest number" appeared, on a closer scrutiny, to be wanting in that clearness and correctness which had originally recommended it to his notice and adoption.' The following was the old man's quaint expression of tardy resipiscence on that point: —

'Be the community in question what it may, divide it into two unequal parts; call one of them the majority, the other the minority. Number of the majority suppose 2001, number of the minority 2000. Suppose, in the first place, the *stock of happiness* [what a conception of happiness as a stock, divisible by authority into *coupons*!]. Take now from every one of the 2000 his *share of happiness*, and divide it any how among the 2001; instead of augmentation, vast is the diminution you will find to be the result. At the outset, place your 4001 in a state of perfect equality in respect of the means, or say, instruments of happiness; every one of them in a state of equal liberty; every one independent of every other; every one of them possessing an equal portion of money or money's worth. In this state it is that you find them. Taking in hand now your 2000, reduce them to a state of slavery, and, no matter in what proportions of the slaves thus constituted, divide the whole number, with their property, among your 2001. The operation performed — of the happiness of what number will an augmentation be the result? The question answers itself.'[5]

That the old philosopher put the question to himself did credit to his candour. But what becomes of Benthamism, shorn of its shibboleth — its pet phrase, "greatest happiness of greatest number?"

Mill never shook himself free from the Benthamite chimera of *rationing out* happiness — from the fixed idea that the problem to be solved by 'social arrangements' is that of making the rations, so far as may be, equal. Arrange as you will, you will not arrange away human nature, of which inequality is, ever and everywhere, the most prominent and conspicuous character. That every one should be equal *in the eye of the law*

---

[5] Bentham's 'Deontology,' vol. i. p. 328.

was no discovery of Bentham. That legislation should seek to make every one equal *in condition* by agrarian or other devices, is a principle which may shatter to fragments an old social system, but can never permanently organise a new one.

To promote men's happiness, so far as 'social arrangements' of any kind can promote it, you must first of all consider what it was that brought men together — what it is that keeps them together in social union. Certainly not the philanthropic project of maximising felicity for some abstract and anonymous 'greatest number,' born or unborn. The men who first formed societies formed them that what they had conquered or acquired by their own right hands, whether in war or labour, might have such additional safeguard as social guarantees could give. At the present day, the far-western backwoodsman, without troubling himself about 'social arrangements,' which he has left many days' journeys behind, shoulders his rifle, and makes *that* guard the plot he has cleared and cultivated. The Californian Vigilance-Committee man, in the early lack of legal tribunals, took summary measures, in league with his immigrant neighbours who had acquired aught to lose, to string up, *sans autre forme de procès*, whatever practical philosophers came in their way, who showed themselves intent on equalising conditions, and making fresh distributions of rations of 'greatest happiness' amongst 'greatest numbers.' Those who first founded, and those who have since maintained the social order of communities, never asked, and do not now ask, philosophers to serve them out rations of happiness. They can manage that for themselves. What they ask is security of possession and production. Property even more than life (for in the last resort a man can make his hand guard his head) is that which societies were mainly formed to secure. Most assuredly no society on earth, not foredoomed to destruction, will let philosophers disorganise it under the delusion of reorganising it on some fantastic principle of socialist agrarian or trading association. 'Those countries are fortunate,' wrote Mr. Mill in his 'Advice to Land Reformers,' dating in the present year, '*or would be fortunate if decently governed*, in which, as in a great part of the East, the land has not been allowed to become the permanent property of individuals.' Strange! that those fortunate Eastern countries, which have had the State so many ages for sole landowner, are precisely the countries that never have been decently governed; and that the comparatively well-governed West gets farther and farther away from every remaining vestige of feudal limitations of permanent landed property! It is but just to Mr. Mill's memory to add that, notwithstanding the sweeping agrarian principles above enunciated, he admitted, in the same papers which we have just quoted, that the scheme of 'nationalisation of the land'[6] — in other words, a Ryotwarree settlement of millions of small cultivators with a gigantic and remorselessly exacting bureaucracy for sole landlord (and with collectors perhaps armed with thumbscrews to get the State its rents) — 'is altogether unsuited to the present time.' Alas! that England and America are not such 'fortunate countries' as Mr. Mill learned to fancy, and helped to administer at the old India House!

What strikes us most in Mr. Thornton's volume is his boldness in publishing it. Not that any one is afraid, in these days, of coming out with his Confession of Faith. It is the article most in vogue in the mental market, but upon one condition — your confession must have an air of novelty and heterodoxy. Any African, German, or British professorial magician, that now cries through the streets 'Who will exchange old lamps for new?' is sure of an audience more or less inclined for the proposed barter. Whatever, on the other hand, wears an over-orthodox aspect finds enlisted against it all that indolent prejudice which formerly would have been enlisted for it. In entitling his book 'Old-Fashioned Ethics and Common-sense Metaphysics,' Mr. Thornton has set himself — we cannot but suppose deliberately — to swim against the stream, and battle, as he does bravely, with a strong current of opinion. The great danger of our day is not, as Mr. Mill imagined, lack of taste for eccentricity, but rather excess of receptivity for paradox. The credulity of unbelief — 'credulosity,' as Mr. Thornton terms it, 'run mad' in stolidly systematic negation of primary truths — fundamental cognitions unsusceptible of evidence because self-evident — is the physico-metaphysic *tic* of the times. Consciousness is no proof of existence! experience no test of ethics. The cow hath run a-dry — let us go milk the bull!

---

[6] See an excellent paper against 'Nationalisation of the Land,' by Professor Fawcett, M.P., in the 'Fortnightly Review,' for December, 1872.

Via prima salutis
Quâ minime reris *Grantâ* pandetur ab urbe.

The Nemesis of Faith appears as distinctly in these days as in Berkeley's — irreligious philosophy performs on itself as complete a *reductio ad absurdum* — commits on itself as clear a logical suicide in the persons of the Nescient Philosophers of our time as in the 'Minute Philosophers' of his. Our professors of physical science in these days — who set up for metaphysicians — in arguing away all direct knowledge of their own existence, argue away all possibility of philosophising or doing anything else. No other conclusion ever was reached, or ever will be reached, by the pseudo-scientific teachers of what has happily been termed by Mr. St. George Mivart the Agnostic Philosophy, than that set forth in the famous parody of Byron in the 'Rejected Addressed' —

'Thinking is but an idle waste of thought,
And nought is everything, and everything is nought.'

As an additional example of the general fact which we have already noted, viz., that heterodoxy has become the popular article in the mental market, we find Mr. Greg prefacing his 'Enigmas of Life' with a sort of apology to 'the severer class of scientific reasoners,' by whom, he says, he is aware that 'it will be noted with disapproval that throughout this little book there runs an under-current of belief in two great doctrines, which yet I do not make the slightest attempt to prove. I have everywhere,' it will be said, '*assumed* the existence of a Creator and a continued life beyond the grave, though I give no reason for my faith in either!' If by 'the severer class of scientific reasoners' Mr. Greg means Positivists and Agnostics, he might have replied to both that, as they do not dogmatise Atheism, but only affirm that it is impossible for us to have any knowledge, on Positivist or purely scientific grounds, whether there is a God or not, he should consider it as superfluous, and scarcely civil, to seek to prove to them what they declare impossible to know.[7]

---

7   The Positivists, *ad exemplar* of the Founder of their queer faith, are fond of pronouncing impossible all investigations the pursuit of which passes the narrow limits of their own minds and methods. Comte, for example, taught dogmatically (as he taught everything, and therefore, to the orthodox Positivist, infallibly) that all research into the *chemical composition* of the celestial bodies was entirely beyond the reach of 'positive' science. But let us quote the *ipsissima verba* of this modern Revealer of the *Grand Etre* (viz. the abstract idea of Humanity, which is to dethrone all Deity, and silence all

Following the rule, with which we set out, of treating the
publications before us primarily as critiques of Mill, we shall

speculation about a 'Providence,' or a 'Universe'). In the 19th Lecture of his
'Course de Philosophie Positive,' Comte lays down, as follows, the *principe
fondamental* of what he calls Positive Astronomy.

'Toute recherche qui n'est point finalement réductible à de simples
observations visuelles nous est donc nécessairement interdite au sujet des
astres, qui sont ainsi de tous les êtres naturels ceux qui nous pouvons
connaître sous les rapports les moins variés. Nous concevons la possibilité
de déterminer leurs formes, leurs distances, leurs grandeurs et leurs
mouvemens; tandis que nous ne saurions jamais étudier par aucun moyen
leur composition chimique. . . . Ainsi, pour fixer les idées dans la célèbre
question des atmosphères des corps célestes, on pouvait certainement
concevoir, même avant la découverte des ingénieux moyens imaginés pour
leur exacte exploration, qu'une telle recherche nous présentait quelque
chose d'accessible, à cause des phénomènes lumineux plus ou moins
appréciables que ces atmosphères doivent evidemment produire; mais il est
tout aussi sensible (par la même considération) que nos connaissances, à
l'égard de ces enveloppes gazeuses, sont *nécessairement* bornées à celles de
leur existence, de leur étendue plus ou moins grande, et de leur vrai pouvoir
réfringent, sans que nous puissons nullement déterminer ni leur composition chimique, ni même leur densité,' &c.

It follows that it has been an astronomical heresy, amenable to the
Positivist Holy Inquisititon of the Future, to attempt, and attempt
successfully, the analysis of the solar spectrum; and the *chemical* results
arrived at by that analysis — and prophetic of more — would clearly be
punishable, if Positivism were the established faith (as it means to be, and
threatens to be as intolerant as arrogant ignorance, when it has climbed into
the chair of authority, always has been), on the same principle of an
infallible authority teaching *ex cathedrâ*, and enduring no contradiction, as
the Roman Inquisition applied so exemplarily in the case of Galileo.
Positivism, if faithful to its founder, can tolerate no discoveries which that
founder has pronounced beyond human power to make. 'Il faut concevoir
l'astronomie *positive*,' said Comte, in the lecture above cited; 'comme
consistant essentiellement dans l'étude *géométrique* et *mécanique* du petit
nombre de corps célestes qui composent le *monde* dont nous faisons partie.'
The idea of a *Universe* is to be discarded in future as unpositive, and all
investigation or discovery beyond the bounds of the solar system,
considered as more curious than useful.

The late Dr. Whewell called Comte 'a shallow pretender,' so far as all the
modern sciences, except astronomy, are concerned. We think we have
shown that astronomy was no exception to the narrow exclusiveness and
ignorant dogmatism of his intellectual temper on all subjects.

Mr. Fitzjames Stephen, as most of our readers are aware, drew on himself
a sharp attack from Mr. Frederic Harrison by an incidental notice of
Comte, in which he said, 'what the value of Comte's speculations on natural
science may have been I do not pretend to guess, but the writings of his
disciples give me a strong impression that his social and moral speculations
will not ultimately turn out to be of much real value.'

Here was more than enough to put the back up of any Positivist. Of 'the
value of Comte's speculations on natural science' perhaps we have given our
readers a sufficient specimen.

confine ourselves at present to the two important chapters of Mr. Greg's book, entitled respectively '*Malthus Notwithstanding*,' and '*Not-Survival of the Fittest*' in which he contests the foundation of the Population Theory of Malthus — whose doctrine Mr. Mill made a cardinal point and 'head-stone of the corner' of his whole economical teaching. 'J. S. Mill,' says Mr. Greg, 'dwells urgently on the necessity of workmen limiting their numbers, if they wish their wages to increase and their condition to improve. I wish to show that the object will be as effectually gained by *dispersion* as by *limitation*. It is not multiplication, but multiplication *on a restricted field*, on a given area, that lowers wages and brings privation. . . . . Mankind might multiply unchecked, if only they would disperse unchecked. That pressure of population on the means of subsistence, with all the misery it involves, which Malthus held to be not only *ultimately* but *perpetually* inevitable, is — at least in its severer form — mainly gratuitous and nearly always premature.'

The strange illusions and stern facts of the epoch, at which Malthus brought out the first edition of his famous Essay, gave it all the advantage of a *pièce de circonstance*, but may be considered in the same degree to have obstructed the philosophical comprehensiveness of his view of the subject, and impaired the completeness of the work. His main object was to dissipate the illusions of writers like Godwin, whose 'Political Justice' drew its inspiration (by the author's frank avowal) from such French originals as the '*Système de la Nature*.' In opposition to the frigidly audacious philosophy of that schools Malthus undertook to show that what stood in the way of the realisation of their Utopia was the natural order of things — not the artificial arrangements of society — and that a community that should have pulled down all distinctions of rank, and emancipated itself from all restraints on sexual intercourse, would soon find the iron bars of physical necessity interposing themselves against the lawless enjoyment of its newly achieved moral and social liberties.

Malthus was undeniably successful in showing that the restoration of no earthly Eden would follow from the establishment, of the Godwinian model, of social equality and sexual connection at will, which now figures under the *alias* of Free Love. He might have avoided all that was morally questionable in his Essay, and probably therefore all the odium of it, by placing in front of his battle the vindication of the nature of man as a religious, moral, and rational being. It was this that the Godwinian Utopists had ignored, in their philosophic repudiation of marriage and property. They should have been answered by showing that man, as a religious, moral, and rational being, could dispense with neither the one institution nor the other. It should have been shown that the attempt to keep men together in any form of association in which marriage and property should not be recognised as connecting links, must end, if made on any extensive scale, in disruption — from moral impossibilities of concord — even before it found itself confronted by those physical impossibilities of prolonged existence, marshalled against it by the population-theory of Malthus. It might have been added, but should not have been advanced as the head and front of the argument, that the Godwinian polity, or rather anarchy (for government of any kind was the *bête noire* of the Utopists of that epoch) — waiving all its moral impossibilities of cohesion — would be pulled up physically, as brute increase is, or that of men where found on a social level only just above brutes.

But Malthus was less successful, unless partially, and as it were by afterthought, in substituting for the 'Liberty, Equality, and Fraternity' doctrines of his day, the visionary character of which was sufficiently exposed in his 'Essay on Population,' a positive philosophy of his subject drawn from civilised human experience. So little, indeed, did he at first address himself to that wider aim, that in the first edition of his Essay (published in 1798) vice and misery only were pointed out as the 'positive checks' on the otherwise unlimited increase of population beyond the means of subsistence. Moral restraint, as a 'preventive check,' was an afterthought. 'Emeritus Professor Francis W. Newman,' as he rejoices to style himself, in a remarkable Essay on 'Malthusianism True and False,' published a year or two back in a monthly magazine, took note of the fact that the crude wording of the title-page in Malthus's first edition stood unchanged in his sixth — a stumbling-block to sober minds at the very threshold of the inquiry. It ran thus — 'An Essay on the Principle of Population, or a View of its Past and Present Effects on Human Happiness, with an Enquiry into our Prospects respecting the future Removal or Mitigation of the *Evils* which it occasions.' What would be thought of an Essay on the principle of *gravitation*, which should include an inquiry into the prospects of removing the evils which *it* occasions? Surely that it was a somewhat uncalled-for imputation on an innocent law of Nature. It is true that by that law a man is in danger of falling every instant he does not exert an effort, however unconscious, to preserve his equilibrium. But when he does fall, who ever thinks of charging the *evil* on the law of gravitation? Or what would be said of a theory which affirmed, in its very title-page, that 'the principle of alimentation' *occasioned* all the evils experienced, on the one hand, from over-eating, and on the other, from want of means of sufficient eating? Who ever thinks of speaking of any physical law as occasioning evils, avoidable by acting upon the knowledge (practical at least) of that law, which it was man's business, as a rational being, to acquire?

Cobbett, with that unique instinct of invective which dictated his choice of epithets, thought it superfluous to seek for any more damaging designation of the author of the 'Essay on Population' than '*Parson* Malthus.' The incongruity between his religious profession and his irreligious doctrine was thus indicated in a word. And, indeed, without any intention of personal aspersion or slur on professional ortho-doxy, a doctrine may well be seemed irreligious which fails so completely to bind facts together so as to illustrate their higher general and providential laws. Yet, as Mr. Newman observed, Malthus 'reverentially believed that the evils occasioned (as he perversely put it) by the principle of population were essential to human progress in virtue. Some one has attributed to him the saying that God intended this world, with all its trials, to be *a manufactory of mind.*' It is unfortunate that Malthus, with his excellent feelings and intentions, kept not in view more steadily, in the first scope of his Essay, the legitimate sovereignty which it belongs to Mind to exercise over Nature and Circumstance.

If by the 'principle of population' Malthus meant the physical instinct which impels the lower animals to propagate their kind without care of the future, there could be no question but that evil to man must be occasioned by the action of a principle so unhuman. With the Godwinians on one side of him preaching abolition of property and disuse of marriage, and the country-gentleman on the other perverting the administration of the Poor Laws to uproot in the minds of English peasants all idea of regarding themselves as responsible for supporting the children they brought into the world, Malthus might be excused for giving undue prominence to the animal and abnormal side of the question. And at the time of war and restricted intercourse with the world at large, at which he wrote, he might naturally view our population as pent within our 'tight little island;' and, proceeding on the assumption of unlimited and unchecked promptings to increase and multiply within so limited an area, might not less naturally, and indeed logically from such premises, arrive at the conclusion that the process of human multiplication must be brought up short by the impossibility of multiplying in an equal ratio the means of sustenance. Malthus's theory, in the manner of its first presentment, missed the final cause — the providential sense and design of the natural law of human increase. Nature is very uniform in her mode of dealing with man, whether individually or in masses. She makes him uneasy, in order that she may make him *keep moving*. It is an imperfect idea of the designs of Nature or Providence, that consigns to the background the intention to impel as well as to restrain — to restrain only in order to give full force to the onward impulse. Nature, indeed, will not make man a gratuitous present of the satisfaction of any of the wishes 'Nature's self inspires.' But she will always *sell* him that satisfaction *á prix fixe*. 'What would you have?' asked the great German poet.[8] 'What would you have? 'TAKE it, and *pay the price.*'

Malthus, in his later editions, tacitly admitted, by his extensions of his original theory, that it had not breadth enough to form a basis for a law of population applicable to a community in any degree civilised. Notwithstanding his efforts to enlarge it, the narrowness of his foundation still marred his work. He had, in fact, and most gratuitously, descended to the ground occupied by his opponents. He had presented the unchecked sexual impulse as identical with the 'principle of population.' So it is amongst brutes — so it might be amongst savages of the lowest grade, or Godwinian or Communist philosophers of the highest — but so it is not amongst men in any degree raised above the brutal or savage state, or the pseudo-philosophic state of retrogradation to savagery.

[8] Goethe.

What, after all, does the Malthusian assertion of the constant tendency of population to increase, so as to press perpetually on the means of subsistence, when stripped of the pomp of abstract phraseology, put in plain English, and reduced to conformity with plain facts, really amount to more than this — that the bringing of more mouths into the world creates a demand for more food to fill them? Mr. Greg justly remarks that *the necessity of exertion is all that Malthus's law indispensably implies and involves.* That necessity scarcely needed demonstration in three volumes octavo. But Malthus fancied he had demonstrated something more, and Malthus's economic sectaries have gone on fancying the same thing ever since, namely, that human increase, at all times, and whatever new fields for expansion and production are opened, is, and must be, pressing fatally and inexorably on the means of subsistence.

To make out his constant tendency of population to increase faster than food for its sustenance, Malthus had to assume unlimited propagation within a limited area. Upon what evidence did he assume either as a general fact? The process of *depopulation* form occult (apparently moral and physiological) causes is quite as frequent a phenomenon in human history as the process of over-population.[9] The world is in no proximate peril of being over-peopled.

---

[9] In addition to Mr. Greg's citations of instances ancient and modern, (for which we must refer our readers to his own pages) of depopulation apparently owing to moral rather than physical causes the following testimony of Polybius may be taken, as extracted in the last volume of Bishop Thirlwall's 'History of Greece.' It is not the least striking of those to be found in the world's history, nor, perhaps, the least noteworthy, with reference to some of the self-indulgent proclivities of our own times.

'We have the evidence of Polybius' (ii. 62), says Bishop Thirlwall, 'that in the period either immediately preceding or immediately subsequent to the establishment of the Roman government — a period which he describes as one of concord and comparative prosperity, when the wounds which had been inflicted on the peninsula were beginning to heal — even then the poulation was rapidly shrinking, through causes quite independent of any external agency, and intimately connected with the moral character and habits of the society itself. He is giving an example of a case in which it was unnecessary to consult an oracle. For instance, he observes, "in our times all Greece has been afflicted with a failure of offspring, in a word, with a scarcity of men, so that the cities have been left desolate and the land waste, though we have not been visited either with a series of wars, or with epidemic diseases. Would it not," he asks, "be absurd to send to inquire of the oracles by what means our numbers may be increased, and our cities

The true law of population for a being who 'looks before and after' must be a different law from that which constrains (and decimates) creatures that do neither. If Man is fated

'To tear his pleasures with rough strife
Thorough the iron bars of life.'

he is privileged to see the bars before him, and avoid, if he will dashing himself against them. He is not only capable of prevision of, but of provision for, the future necessities of his existence — not only capable of foreseeing the time when the produce of his native land must fail to feed himself and his offspring, but of calling in aid Art and Commerce to supply the shortcomings of Nature, and — when these have exhausted all their powers and resources within the limits of one locality — migrating to fresh fields and pastures new.

The British Islands and Germany, each in her own way, may boast to be an *officina gentium*, a nation-manufactory for both hemispheres. France, on the other hand, in recent times, has honoured Malthus by her remarkable abstinence from the British and German habit of having large families. What has been the consequence, or, at least, the accompaniment, of the Malthusian 'moral restraint' of France in this matter? That colonial enterprise, for which she was formerly eminent amongst nations, is in France at this day extinct; while the prolific races replenish the earth and subdue it. And, as regard war, the following passage may be forth quoting from a letter written a year or two ago from Metz by Mr. Samuel Capper, during his tour of charity at the close of the war of 1870-71: —

'Very striking was the remark of Madame the wife of the Mayor of Toul: "My countrymen are always talking of their revenge; to make successful war upon Germany we must

become more floushing, when the cause is manifest, the remedy rests with ourselves? For when men gave themselves up to ease, and comfort, and indolence, and would neither marry nor rear children born out of marriage, or at most only one or two, in order to leave these rich, and to bring them up in luxury, the evil soon spread, imperceptibly, but with rapid growth; for when there was only a child or two in a family for war or disease to carry off, the inevitable consequence was that houses were left desolate, and cities by degrees became like deserted hives. And there is no need to consult the gods about the mode of deliverance from this evil, for any man would tell us, that the first thing we have to do is to change our habits, or at all events to enact laws compelling parents to rear their children." ' — Thirlwell's 'History of Greece,' chap. lxvi.

have plenty of men. How many children have we in our families? *One* or *two*. A Saxon colonel quartered upon me told me he had five sons, and all in the army." '[10]

'The ordinary size of families in England and Wales' (we again cite Mr. Greg), 'judging by a comparison of the yearly marriages with the yearly births, is now about 4.15 children, and we may fairly assume that with us no artificial means, of abstinence or otherwise, are employed to prevent each marriage yielding its natural number of offspring.' What is the orthodox Malthusian limit to be fixed henceforth for the size of families? Mr. Mill did not say, though he would have had some such limit prescribed and enforced by public opinion, or by law, if necessary.[11]

It is worth noting that, whereas Malthus's Essay was written expressly for the discouragement of the 'Liberty, Equality, and Fraternity' enthusiasts of his own day, the staunchest Malthusians of later times have been writers so far in sympathy with the D'Holbach and Godwin school, that they have nourished an equal hatred with that school for all aristocracy, all priesthood, and all indissoluble conjugal relations. Mill, the elder (James), was full of what we should call the fanaticism of Malthusianism; to such a degree that he risked his own fairly-earned reputation with decent people, and involved in the like discreditable danger the youth of his son, by running a Malay muck against what he called the 'superstitions of the nursery' with regard to sexual relations, and giving the impulse to a sort of shameless propaganda of prescriptions for artificially checking population. We should not even have alluded to this grave offence against decency on the part of the elder and the younger Mill, had it not been forced upon our notice by recent events.

In an interesting conversation with Mr. John Stuart Mill, a few days before he left England, reported by the Editor of the 'Fortnightly Review' in his June number, it is mentioned that 'he (Mill) made remarks on the difference of the feeling of modern refusers of Christianity as compared with men like his father, impassioned deniers, who believed that if you only broke up the power of the priests and checked superstition, all

---

[10]   'Times,' April 6, 1871.

[11]   'Principles of Political Economy,' Book II. c. xiii, § 2.

would go well; a dream from which they were partially
awakened by seeing that the French Revolution, which
overthrew the Church, still did not bring the millennium.'
somewhere in his writings — we cannot just now lay our finger
on the passage — Mill the younger has expressed his
apprehension that the new spiritual power of the press might
prove as perilous to the pure cause of truth as ever had been the
old spiritual power of the priesthood. We find in the 'Notices'
above cited of Mill's 'Life and Work' the following astonishing
sentence from the pen of Professor W. A. Hunter: — 'Mr. Mill
has never written once sentence to give the least encouragement
to Christianity.' All who have studied, as we will charitably
suppose this Professor has not, Mr. Mill's later writings, will
know what to think of this sweeping and strangely worded
assertion. Mill seemed to hold himself ready, almost as much
as Bunsen, to conform to some 'Church' or Christianity 'of the
Future.' His religion that was to be, like his other aspirations,
recked little of the past or present, and embraced, we should
say, a cloud for a goddess looming in some far futurity. But his
recognition of Christianity, as it flowed from its source, was
frank and frequent. In his 'Liberty' he says — 'I believe that the
sayings of Christ are irreconcilable with nothing which a
comprehensive morality requires; that everything which is
excellent in ethics may be brought within them.' In his
'Utilitarianism' he says — 'In the golden rule of Jesus of
Nazareth we read the complete spirit of the ethics of utility. To
do as you would be done by, and to love your neighbour as
yourself, constitute the ideal perfection of utilitarian morality.'
The teaching of Christ then fulfilled Mill's ideal of moral
perfection. His error was in supposing, as he apparently did,
that Christian belief might undergo, without fatal alteration, a
metamorphosis into a vague Religion of Humanity with Man
for its God. There is a homely proverb about giving a hungry
dog a piece of his own tail to eat, and it seems to us about as
hopeful to seek to satisfy man's heart-hunger for a religion by
telling him as Comte did, to fall down and worship himself and
Madame Clothilde de Vaux.

'Eh, bien! me disent-ils,' says the honest republican Edgar
Quinet, who has wonderful lucid intervals, 'adorez donc
l'Humanité. O loe curieux fétiche! Je l'ai vu de trop près.
M'agenouiller devant celui qui est à deux genoux devant toute
force triomphante! Ramper devant cette bête rampante aux

milliards de pieds! Ce n'est pas là ma foi. Que ferais-je de ce dieu-là? Ramenez-moi aux ibis et aux serpens à colliers du Nil.'[12]

---

12 'La Révolution,' vol. ii. p. 418.

THE CONTEMPORARY REVIEW
Vol. 36, 1879
[F. Max Müller]

On Freedom[1]

Not more than twenty years have passed since John Stuart Mill sent forth his plea for Liberty.[2]

If there is one among the leaders of thought in England who, by the elevation of his character and the calm composure of his mind, deserved the so often misplaced title of Serene Highness, it was, I think, John Stuart Mill.

But in his Essay "On Liberty," Mill for once becomes passionate. In presenting his Bill of Rights, in stepping forward as the champion of individual liberty, a new spirit seems to have taken possession of him. He speaks like a martyr, or the defender of martyrs. The individual human soul, with its unfathomable endowments, and its capacity of growing to something undreamt of in our philosophy, becomes in his eyes a sacred thing, and every encroachment on its world-wide domain is treated as sacrilege. Society, the arch-enemy of the rights of individuality, is represented like an evil spirit, whom it

[1] An Address delivered on the 20th October, before the Birmingham and Midland Institute.

[2] Mill tells us that his Essay "On Liberty" was planned and written down in 1854. It was in mounting the steps of the Capitol in January, 1855, that the thought first arose of coverting it into a volume, and it was not published till 1859. The author, who in his Autobiography speaks with exquisite modesty of all his literary performances, allows himself one single exception when speaking of his Essay "On Liberty." "None of my writings," he says, "have been either so carefully composed or so sedulousy corrected as this." Its final revision was to have been the work of the winter of 1858 to 1859 which he and his wife had arranged to pass in the South of Europe, a hope which was frustrated by his wife's death. "The 'Liberty,' " he writes, "is likely to survive longer than anything else that I have written (with the possible exception of the 'Logic'), because the conjunction of her mind with mine has rendered it a kind of philosophic text book of a single truth, which the changes progressively taking place in modern society tend to bring out into stronger relief: the importance, to man and society, of a large variety of character, and of giving full freedom to human nature to expand itself in innumerable and conflicting directions."

behoves every true man to resist with might and main, and whose demands, as they cannot be altogether ignored, must be reduced at all hazards to the lowest level.

I doubt whether any of the principles for which Mill pleaded so warmly and strenuously in his Essay "On Liberty" would at the present day be challenged or resisted, even by the most illiberal of philosophers, or the most conservative of politicians. Mill's demands sound very humble to *our* ears. They amount to no more than this, "that the individual is not accountable to society for his actions so far as they concern the interests of no person but himself, and that he may be subjected to social or legal punishments for such actions only as are prejudicial to the interests of others."

Is there any one here present who doubts the justice of that principle, or who would wish to reduce the freedom of the individual to a smaller measure? Whatever social tyranny may have existed twenty years ago, when it wrung that fiery protest from the lips of John Stuart Mill, can we imagine a state of society, not totally Utopian, in which the individual man need be less ashamed of his social fetters, in which he could more freely utter all his honest convictions, more boldly propound all his theories, more fearlessly agitate for their speedy realization; in which, in fact, each man can be so entirely himself as the society of England, such as it now is, such as generations of hard-thinking and hard-working Englishmen have made it, and left it as the most sacred inheritance to their sons and daughters?

Look through the whole of history, not excepting the brightest days of republican freedom at Athens and Rome, and I know you will not find one single period in which the measure of Liberty accorded to each individual was larger than it is at present, at least in England. And if you wish to realize the full blessings of the time in which we live, compare Mill's plea for Liberty with another written not much more than two hundred years ago, and by a thinker not inferior either in power or boldness to Mill himself. According to Hobbes, the only freedom which an individual in his ideal state has a right to claim is what he calls "freedom of thought,' and that freedom of thought consists in our being able to think what we like — so long as we keep it to ourselves. Surely, such freedom of thought existed even in the days of the Inquisition, and we should never call thought free, if it has to be kept a prisoner in solitary and silent confinement. By freedom of thought we mean freedom of speech, freedom of the press, freedom of action, whether individual or associated, and of that freedom the present generation, as compared with all former generations, the English nation, as compared with all other nations, enjoys, there can be no doubt, a good measure, pressed down, and shaken together, and sometimes running over.

It may be said that some dogmas still remain in politics, in religion, and in morality; but those who defend them claim no longer any infallibility, and those who attack them, however small their minority, need fear no violence, nay, may reckon on an impartial and even sympathetic hearing, as soon as people discover in their pleadings the true ring of honest conviction and the warmth inspired by an unselfish love of truth.

It has seemed strange therefore to many readers of Mill, particularly on the Continent, that this cry for Liberty, this demand for freedom for every individual to be what he is, and to develop all the germs of his nature, should have come from what is known as the freest of all countries, England. We might well understand such a cry of indignation if it had reached us from Russia; but why should English philosophers, of all others, have to protest against the tyranny of society? It is true, nevertheless, that in countries governed despotically, the individual, unless he is obnoxious to the Government, enjoys far greater freedom, or rather licence, than in a country like England, which governs itself. Russian society, for instance, is extremely indulgent. It tolerates in its rulers and statesmen a haughty defiance of the simplest rules of social propriety, and it seems amused rather than astonished or indignant at the vagaries, the frenzies, and outrages, of those who in brilliant drawing-rooms or lecture-rooms preach the doctrines of what is called Nihilism or Individualism,[3] — viz., "that society must be regenerated by a struggle for existence and the survival of the strongest, processes which Nature has sanctioned, and which have proved successful among wild animals." If there is a danger in these doctrines the Government is expected to see to it. It may place watchmen at the doors of every house and at the corner of every street, but it must not count on the better

---

[3] Herzen defined Nihilism as " the most perfect freedom from all settled concepts, from all inherited restraints and impediments which hamper the progress of the Occidental intellect with the historical drag tied to its foot."

classes coming forward to enrol themselves as special constables, or even on the co-operation of public opinion which in England would annihilate that kind of Nihilism with one glance of scorn and pity.

In a self-governed country like England, the resistance which society, if it likes, can oppose to the individual in the assertion of his rights, is far more compact and powerful than in Russia, or even in Germany. Even where it does not employ the arm of the law, society knows how to use that softer, but more crushing pressure, that calm, but Gorgon-like look which only the bravest and stoutest hearts know how to resist.

It is rather against that indirect repression which a well-organized society exercises, both through its male and female representatives, that Mill's demand for Liberty seems directed. He does not stand up for unlimited licence; on the contrary, he would have been the most strenuous defender of that balance of power between the weak and the strong on which all social life depends. But he resents those smaller penalties which society will always inflict on those who disturb its dignified peace and comfort: — avoidance, exclusion, a cold look, a stinging remark. Had Mill any right to complain of these social penalties? Would it not rather amount to an interference with individual liberty to wish to deprive any individual or any number of individuals of those weapons of self-defence? Those who themselves think and speak freely, have hardly a right to complain, if others claim the same privilege. Mill himself called the Conservative party the stupid party *par excellence*, and he took great pains to explain that it was so, not by accident, but by necessity. Need he wonder if those whom he whipped and scourged used their own whips and scourges against so merciless a critic?

Freethinkers, and I use that name as a title of honour for all who, like Mill, claim for every individual the fullest freedom in thought, word, or deed, compatible with the freedom of others, are apt to make one mistake. Conscious of their own honest intentions, they cannot bear to be mistrusted or slighted. They expect society to submit to their often very painful operations as a patient submits to the knife of the surgeon. That is not in human nature. The enemy of abuses is always abused by his enemies. Society will never yield one inch without resistance, and few reformers live long enough to receive the thanks of those whom they have reformed. Mill's unsolicited election to Parliament was a triumph not often shared by social reformers; it was as exceptional as Bright's admission to a seat in the Cabinet, or Stanley's appointment as Dean of Westminster. Such anomalies will happen in a country fortunately so full of anomalies as England; but, as a rule, a political reformer must not be angry if he passes through life without the title of Right Honourable; nor should a man, if he will always speak the truth, the whole truth, and nothing but the truth, be disappointed if he dies a martyr rather than a Bishop.

But granting even that in Mill's time there existed some traces of social tyranny, where are they now? Look at the newspapers and the journals. Is there any theory too wild, any reform too violent, to be openly defended.? Look at the drawing-rooms or the meetings of learned societies. Are not the most eccentric talkers the spoiled children of the fashionable world? When young lords begin to discuss the propriety of limiting the rights of inheritance, and young tutors are not afraid to propose curtailing the long vacation, surely we need not complain of the intolerance of English society.

Whenever I state these facts to my German and French and Italian friends, who from reading Mill's Essay "On Liberty" have derived the impression that, however large an amount of political liberty England may enjoy, it enjoys but little of intellectual freedom, they are generally willing to be converted so far as London, or other great cities, are concerned, But look at your Universities, they say, the nurseries of English thought! Can you compare their mediæval spirit, their monastic institutions, their scholastic philosophy, with the freshness and freedom of the Continental Universities? Strong as these prejudices about Oxford and Cambridge have always been, they have become still more intense since Professor Helmholtz, in an inaugural address which he delivered at his installation as Rector of the University of Berlin, lent the authority of his great name to these misconceptions. "The tutors," he says,[4] in the English Universities cannot deviate by a hair's-breadth from the dogmatic system of the English Church, without exposing themselves to the censure of their Archbishops and losing their

---

[4] Ueber die Akademische Freiheit der Deutschen Universitäten, Rede beim Antritt des Rectorats an der Friedrich-Wilhelms-Universität in Berlin, am 15 October 1877, gehalten von Dr. H. Helmholz.

pupils." In German Universities, on the contrary, we are told that the extreme conclusions of materialistic metaphysics, the boldest speculations within the sphere of Darwin's theory of evolution, may be propounded without let or hindrance, quite as much as the highest apotheosis of Papal infallibility.

Here the facts on which Professor Helmholtz relies are entirely wrong, and the writings of some of our most eminent tutors supply a more than sufficient refutation of his statements. Archbishops have no official position whatsoever in English Universities, and their censure of an Oxford tutor would be resented as impertinent by the whole University. Nor does the University, as such, exercise any such very strict control over the tutors, even when they lecture not to their own College only. Each Master of Arts at Oxford claims now the right to lecture (*venia docendi*), and I doubt whether they would ever submit to those restrictions which, in Germany, the Faculty imposes on every *Privat-docent*. *Privat-docents* in German Universities have been rejected by the Faculty for incompetence, and silenced for insubordination. I know of no such cases at Oxford during my residence of more than thirty years, nor can I think it likely that they should ever occur.

As to the extreme conclusions of materialistic metaphysics, there are Oxford tutors who have grappled with the systems of such giants as Hobbes, Locke, or Hume, and who are not likely to be frightened by Büchner and Vogt.

I know comparisons are odious, and I am the last man who would wish to draw comparisons between English and German Universities unfavourable to the latter. But with regard to freedom of thought, of speech, and action, Professor Helmholtz, if he would spend but a few weeks at Oxford, would find that we enjoy a fuller measure of freedom here than the Professors and *Privat-docents* in any Continental University. The publications of some of our professors and tutors ought at least to have convinced him that if there is less of brave words and turbulent talk in their writings, they display throughout a determination to speak the truth, which may be matched, but could not easily be excelled, by the leaders of thought in France, Germany, or Italy.

The real difference between English and Continental Universities is that the former govern themselves, the latter are governed. Self-government entails responsibilities, sometimes restraints and reticences. I may here be allowed to quote the words of another eminent Professor of the University of Berlin, Du Bois Reymond, who, in addressing his colleagues, ventured to tell them,[5] "We have still to learn from the English how the greatest independence of the individual is compatible with willing submission to salutary, though irksome, statutes." That is particularly true when the statues are self-imposed. In Germany, as Professor Helmholtz tells us himself, the last decision in almost all the more important affairs of the Universities rests with the Governments and he does not deny that in times of political and ecclesiastical tension, a most inconsiderate use has been made of that power. There are, besides, the less important matters, such as raising of salaries, leave of absence, scientific missions, even titles and decorations, all of which enable a clever Minister of Instruction to assert his personal influence among the less independent members of the University. In Oxford the University does not know the Ministry, nor the Ministry the University. The acts of the Government, be it Liberal or Conservative, are freely discussed, and often powerfully resisted by the academic constituencies, and the personal dislike of a Minister or Ministerial Councillor could as little injure a professor or tutor as his favour could add one penny to his salary.

But these are minor matters. What gives their own peculiar character to the English Universities is a sense of power and responsibility: power, because they are the most respected among the numerous corporations in the country; responsibility, because the higher education of the whole country has been committed to their charge. Their only master is public opinion as represented in Parliament, their only incentive their own sense of duty. There is no country in Europe where Universities hold so exalted a position, and where those who have the honour to belong to them may say with greater truth, *Noblesse oblige*.

I know the dangers of self-government, particularly where higher and more ideal interests are concerned, and there are probably few who wish for a real reform in schools and Universities who have not occasionally yielded to the desire for

---

[5] Ueber eine Akademie der Deutschen Sprache, p. 34. Another keen observer of English life, Dr. K. Hillebrand, in an article in the October number of the *Nineteenth Century*, remarks: "Nowhere is there greater individual liberty than in England, and nowhere do people renounce it more readily of their own accord."

a Dictator, of a Bismarck or a Falk. But such a desire springs only from a momentary weakness and despondency; and no one who knows the difference between being governed and governing oneself, would ever wish to descend from that higher though dangerous position to a lower one, however safe and comfortable it might seem. No one who has tasted freedom would ever wish to exchange it for anything else. Public opinion is sometimes a hard taskmaster, and majorities can be great tyrants to those who want to be honest to their own convictions. But in the struggle of all against all, each individual feels that he has his rightful place, and that he may exercise his rightful influence. If he is beaten, he is beaten in fair fight; if he conquers, he has no one else to thank. No doubt despotic Governments have often exercised the most beneficial patronage in encouraging and rewarding poets, artists, and men of science. But men of genius who have conquered the love and admiration of a whole nation are greater than those who have gained the favour of the most brilliant Courts; and we know how some of the fairest reputations have been wrecked on the patronage which they had to accept at the hands of powerful Ministers or ambitious Sovereigns.

But to return to Mill and his plea for Liberty. Though I can hardly believe that, were he still among us, he would claim a larger measure of freedom for the individual than is now accorded to every one of us in the society in which we move, yet the chief cause on which he founded his plea for Liberty, the chief evil which he thought could be remedied only if society would allow more elbow-room to individual genius, exists in the same degree as in his time — aye, even in a higher degree. The principle of Individuality has suffered more at present than perhaps at any former period of history. The world is becoming more and more gregarious, and what the French call our *nature moutonnière*, "our mutton-like nature," our tendency to leap where any bell-wether has leapt before, becomes more and more prevalent in politics, in religion, in art, and even in science. M. de Tocqueville expressed his surprise how much more Frenchmen of the present day resemble one another than did those of the last generation. The same remark, adds John Stuart Mill, might be made of England in a greater degree. "The modern *régime* of public opinion,' he writes, "is in an unorganized form what the Chinese educational and political systems are in an organized; and unless individuality shall be able successfully to assert itself against this yoke, Europe, notwithstanding its noble antecedents and its professed Christianity, will tend to become another China."

I fully agree with Mill in recognizing the dangers of uniformity, but I doubt whether what he calls the *régime* of public opinion is alone, or even chiefly, answerable for it. No doubt there are some people in whose eyes uniformity seems an advantage rather than a disadvantage. If all were equally strong, equally educated, equally honest, equally rich, equally tall, or equally small, society would seem to them to have reached the highest ideal. The same people admire an old French garden, with its clipped yew-trees, forming artificial walls and towers and pyramids, far more than the giant yews which, like large serpents, clasp the soil with their coiling roots, and overshadow with their dark green branches the white chalk cliffs of the Thames. But those French gardens, unless they are constantly clipped and prevented from growing, soon fall into decay. As in nature, so in society, uniformity means but too often stagnation, while variety is the surest sign of health and vigour. The deepest secret of nature is its love of continued novelty. Its tendency, if unrestrained, is towards constantly creating new varieties, which, if they fulfil their purpose, become fixed for a time, or, it may be, for ever; while others, after they have fulfilled their purpose, vanish to make room for new and stronger types.

The same is the secret of human society. It consists and lives in individuals, each being meant to be different from all the others, and to contribute his own peculiar share to the common wealth. As no tree is like any other tree, and no leaf on the same tree like any other leaf, no human being is exactly like any other human being, nor is it meant to be. It is in this endless, and to us inconceivable, variety of human souls that the deepest purpose of human life is to be realized; and the more society fulfils that purpose, the more it allows free scope for the development of every individual germ, the richer will be the harvest in no distant future. Such is the mystery of individuality that I do not wonder if even those philosophers who, like Mill, reduce the meaning of the word *sacred* to the very smallest compass, see in each individual soul something sacred, something to be revered, even where we cannot understand it, something to be protected against all vulgar violence.

Where I differ from Mill and his school is on the question as to the quarter from whence the epidemic of uniformity springs which threatens the free development of modern society. Mill points to the society in which we move; to those who are in front of us, to our contemporaries. I feel convinced that our real enemies are at our back, and that the heaviest chains which are fastened on us are those made, not by the present, but by past generations — by our ancestors, not by our contemporaries.

It is on this point, on the trammels of individual freedom with which we may almost be said to be born into the world, and on the means by which we may shake off these old chains, or at all events carry them more lightly and gracefully, that I wish to speak to you this evening.

You need not be afraid that I am going to enter upon the much discussed subject of heredity, whether in its physiological or psychological aspects. It is a favourite subject just now, and the most curious facts have been brought together of late to illustrate the working of what is called heredity. But the more we know of these facts, the less we seem able to comprehend the underlying principle. Inheritance is one of those numerous words which by their very simplicity and clearness are so apt to darken our counsel. If a father has blue eyes and the son has blue eyes, what can be clearer than that he inherited them? If the father stammers and the son stammers, who can doubt but that it came by inheritance? If the father is a musician and the son a musician, we say very glibly that the talent was inherited. But what does *inherited* mean? In no case does it mean what *inherited* usually means — something external, like money, collected by a father, and, after his death, secured by law to his son. Whatever else inherited may mean, it does not mean that. But unfortunately the word is there, it seems almost pedantic to challenge its meaning, and people are always grateful if an easy word saves them the trouble of hard thought.

Another apparent advantage of the theory of heredity is that it never fails. If the son has blue, and the father black eyes, all is right again, for either the mother, or the grandmother, or some historic or prehistoric ancestor, may have had blue eyes, and atavism, we know, will assert itself after hundreds and thousands of years.

Do not suppose that I deny the broad facts of what is called by the name of heredity. What I deny is that the name of heredity offers any scientific solution of a most difficult problem. It is a name, a metaphor, quite as bad as the old metaphor of *innate ideas*; for there is hardly a single point of similarity between the process by which a son may share the black eyes, the stammering, or the musical talent of his father, and that by which, after his father's death, the law secures to the son the possession of the pounds, shillings, and pence which his father held in the Funds.

But whatever the true meaning of heredity may be, certain it is that every individual comes into the world heavy-laden. Nowhere has the consciousness of the burden which rests on each generation as it enters on its journey through life found stronger expression than among the Buddhists. What other people call by various names, "fate or providence," "tradition or inheritance," "circumstances or environment," they call *Karman*, deed — what has been done, whether by ourselves or by others, the accumulated work of all who have come before us, the consequences of which we have to bear, both for good and for evil. Originally this *Karman* seems to have been conceived as personal, as the work which we ourselves have done in former existences. But, as personally we are not conscious of having done such work in former ages, that kind of *Karman*, too, might be said to be impersonal. To the question how *Karman* began, the accumulation of what forms the condition of all that exists at present, Buddhism has no answer to give, any more than any other system of religion or philosophy. The Buddhists say it began with *avidyâ*, and *avidyâ* means ignorance.[6] They are much more deeply interested in the question how *Karman* may be annihilated, how each man may free himself from the influence of *Karman*, and Nirvâna, the highest object of all their dreams, is often defined by Buddhist philosophers as "freedom from *Karman*."[7]

What the Buddhists call by the general name of *Karman*, comprehends all influences which the past exercises on the present, both physically and mentally.[8] It is not my object to

6 Spencer Hardy, "Manual of Buddhism," p. 391.

7 *Ibid.*, p. 39.

8 "As one generation dies and gives way to another, the heir of the consequences of all its virtues and its vices, the exact result of pre-existent causes, so each individual, in the long chain of life, inherits all, of good or evil, which all its predecessors have done or been; and takes up the struggle towards enlightenment precisely there where they left it." — Rhys Davids, *Buddhism*, p. 104.

examine or even to name all these influences, though I confess nothing is more interesting than to look upon the surface of our modern life as we look on a geological map, and to see the most ancient formations cropping out everywhere under our feet. Difficult as it is to colour a geological map of England, it would be still more difficult to find a sufficient variety of colours to mark the different ingredients of the intellectual surface of this island.

That all of us, whether we speak English or German, or French or Russian, are really speaking an ancient Oriental tongue, incredible as it would have sounded a hundred years ago, is now admitted by everybody. Though the various dialects now spoken in Europe have been separated many thousands of years from the Sanskrit, the ancient classical language of India, yet so unbroken is the bond that holds the West and East together than in many cases an intelligent Englishman might still guess the meaning of a Sanskrit word. How little difference is there between Sanskrit *sûnu* and English *son*, between Sanskrit *duhitar* and English *daughter*, between Sanskrit *vid*, to know, and English *to wit*, between Sanskrit *vaksh*, to grow, and English to wax! Think how we value a Saxon urn, or a Roman coin, or a Celtic weapon! how we dig for them, clean them, label them, and carefully deposit them in our museums! Yet what is their antiquity compared with the antiquity of such words as *son* or *daughter*, *father* and *mother*. There are no monuments older than those collected in the handy volumes which we call Dictionaries, and those who know how to interpret those English antiquities — as you may see them interpreted, for instance, in Grimm's Dictionary of the German, in Littré's Dictionary of the French, or in Professor Skeats' Etymological Dictionary of the English Language — will learn more of the real growth of the human mind than by studying many volumes on logic and psychology.

And as by our language we belong to the Aryan stratum, we belong through our letters to the Hamitic. We still write English in hieroglyphics; and in spite of all the vicissitudes through which the ancient hieroglyphics have passed in their journey from Egypt to Phœnicia, from Phœnicia to Greece, from Greece to Italy, and from Italy to England, when we write a capital F *ℱ*, when we draw the top line and the smaller line through the middle of the letter, we really draw the two horns of the cerastes, the horned serpent which the ancient Egyptians used for representing the sound of f. They write the name of the king whom the Greeks called *Cheops*, and they themselves *Chu-fu*, like this:[9]

chu
fu
u

Here the first sign, the sieve, is to be pronounced *chu*; the second, the horned serpent, *fu*, and the little bird, again, *u*. In the more cursive or Hieratic writing the horned serpent appears as ; in the later Demotic as and . The Phœnicians, who borrowed their letters from the Hieratic Egyptian, wrote and . The Greeks, who took their letters from the Phœnicians, wrote ⅂ . When the Greeks, instead of writing like the Phœnicians from right to left, began to write from left to right, they turned each letter, and as Ӿ became K, our k, so ⅂ , vau, became F, the Greek so-called Digamma, the Latin F.

The first letter in *Chu-fu*, too, still exists in our alphabet, and in the transverse line of our H we must recognize the last remnant of the lines which divide the sieve. The sieve appears in Hieratic as ∅ , in Phœnician as 日 , in ancient Greek as 日 , which occurs on an inscription found at Mycaneæ and elsewhere as the sign of the spiritus asper, while in Latin it is known to us as the letter H.[10] In the same manner the undulating line of our capital ℒ still recalls very strikingly the bent back of the crouching lion, which in the later hieroglyphic inscriptions represents the sound of L.

If thus in our language we are Aryan, in our letters Egyptian, we have only to look at our watches to see that we are Babylonian. Why is our hour divided into sixty minutes, our minutes into sixty seconds? Would not a division of the hour into ten, or fifty, or a hundred minutes have been more natural? We have sixty divisions on the dials of our watches simply because the Greek astronomer Hipparchus, who lived in the second century B.C., accepted the Babylonian system of reckoning time, that system being sexagesimal. The Babylonians knew the decimal system, but for practical purposes they counted by *sossi* and *sari*, the *sossos* representing 60, the *saros* 60×60, or 3600. From Hipparchus that system found its way

9   Bunsen, "Egypt," ii., pp. 77, 150.

10   Mémoire sur l'Origine Egyptienne de l'Alphabet Phénicien, par E. de Rougé, Paris, 1874.

into the works of Ptolemy, about 150 A.D., and thence it was carried down the stream of civilization, finding its last resting-place on the dial-plates of our clocks.

And why are there twenty shillings to our sovereign? Again the real reason lies in Babylon. The Greeks learnt from the Babylonians the art of dividing gold and silver for purpose of trade. It has been proved that the current gold piece of Western Asia was exactly the sixtieth part of a Babylonian *mná*, or *mina*. It was nearly equal to our sovereign. The difficult problem of the relative value of gold and silver in a bi-monetary currency had been solved to a certain extent in the ancient Mesopotamian kingdom, the proportion between gold and silver being fixed at 1 to 13⅓. The silver shekel current in Babylon was heavier than the gold shekel in the proportion of 13⅓ to 10, and had therefore the value of one-tenth of a gold shekel; and the half silver shekel, called by the Greeks a drachma, was worth one-twentieth of a gold shekel. The drachma, or half silver shekel, may therefore be looked upon as the most ancient type of our own silver shilling in its relation of one-twentieth of our gold sovereign.[11]

I shall mention only one more of the most essential tools of our mental life — namely, our *figures*, which we call Arabic, because we received them from the Arabs, but which the Arabs called Indian, because they received them from the Indians — in order to show you how this nineteenth century of ours is under the sway of centuries long past and forgotten; how we are what we are, not by ourselves, but by those who came before us, and how the intellectual ground on which we stand is made up of the detritus of thoughts which were first thought, not on these isles nor in Europe, but on the shores of the Oxus, the Nile, the Euphrates, and the Indus.

Now you may well ask *Quorsum hæc omnia?* — What has all this to do with freedom and with the free development of individuality? Because a man is born the heir of all the ages, can it be said that he is not free to grow and to expand, and to develop all the faculties of his mind? Are those who came before him, and who left him this goodly inheritance, to be called his enemies? Is that chain of tradition which connects him with the past really a galling fetter, and not rather the

---

11   See Brandis, "Das Münzwesen."

leading-strings without which he would never learn to walk straight?

Let us look at the matter more closely. No one would venture to say that every individual should begin life as a young savage, and be left to form his own language, and invent his own letters, numerals, and coins. On the contrary, if we comprehend all this and a great deal more, such as religion, morality, and secular knowledge, under the general name of *education*, even the most advanced defenders of individualism would hold that no child should enter society without submitting, or rather without being submitted, to education. Most of us would even go further, and make it criminal for parents or even for communities to allow children to grow up uneducated. The excuse of worthless parents that they are at liberty to do with their children as they like, has at last been blown to the winds. I still remember the time when pseudo-Liberals were not ashamed to say that, whatever other nations, such as the Germans, might do, England would never submit to compulsory education. That wicked sophistry, too, has at last been silenced, and among the principal advocates of compulsory education, and of the necessity of curtailing the freedom of savage parents of savage children, have been Mill and his friends, the apostles of liberty and individualism.[12] A new era may be said to date in the history of every nation from the day on which "compulsory education" becomes part of their statute-book; and I congratulate the most Liberal town in England on having proved itself the most inexorable tyrant in carrying out the principle of compulsory education.

But do not let us imagine that compulsory education is without its dangers. Like a powerful engine, it must be carefully watched, if it is not to produce, what all compulsion will produce, a slavish receptivity, and, what all machines do produce, monotonous uniformity.

We know that all education must in the beginning be purely dogmatic. Children are taught language, religion, morality, patriotism, and afterwards at school, history, literature, mathematics, and all the rest, long before they are able to

---

[12] "It is not almost a self-evident axiom, that the State should require and compel the education, up to a certain standard, of every human being who is born its citizen? Yet who is there that is not afraid to recognize and assert this truth? — *On Liberty*, p. 188.

question, to judge, or choose for themselves, and there is hardly anything that a child will not believe if it comes from those in whom the child believes.

Reading, writing, and arithmetic, no doubt, must be taught dogmatically, and they take up an enormous amount of time, particularly in English schools. English spelling is a national misfortune, and in the keen international race between all the countries of Europe, it handicaps the English child to a degree that seems incredible till we look at statistics. I know the difficulties of a Spelling Reform, I know what people mean when they call it impossible; but I also know that personal and national virtue consists in doing so-called impossible things, and that no nation has done, and has still to do, so many impossible things as the English.

But, granted that reading, writing, and arithmetic occupy nearly the whole school-time and absorb the best powers of the pupils, cannot something be done in play-hours? Is there not some work that can be turned into play, and some play that can be turned into work? Cannot the powers of observation be called out in a child while collecting flowers, or stones, or butterflies? Cannot his judgment be strengthened either in gymnastic exercises, or in measuring the area of a field, or the height of a tower? Might not all this be done without a view to examinations or payment by results, simply for the sake of filling the little dull minds with one sunbeam of joy, such sunbeams being more likely hereafter to call hidden precious germs into life than the deadening weight of such lessons as, for instance, that *th-ough* is though, *thr-ough* is through, *en-ough* is enough. A child who believes that will hereafter believe anything. Those who wish to see Natural Science introduced into elementary schools frighten schoolmasters by the very name of Natural Science. But surely every schoolmaster who is worth his salt should be able to teach children a love of Nature, a wondering of Nature, a curiosity to pry into the secrets of Nature, an acquisitiveness for some of the treasures of Nature, and all this acquired in the fresh air of the field and the forest, where, better than in frouzy lecture-rooms, the edge of the senses can be sharpened, the chest be widened, and that freedom of thought fostered which made England what it was even before the days of compulsory education.

But in addressing you here to-night it was my intention to speak of the higher rather than of elementary education.

All education, as it now exists in most countries in Europe, may be divided into three stages — *elementary*, *scholastic*, and *academical*; or call it *primary*, *secondary*, and *tertiary*.

Elementary education has at last been made compulsory in most civilized countries. Unfortunately, however, it seems impossible to include under compulsory education anything beyond the very elements of knowledge, — at least for the present; though, with proper management, I know from experience that a well-conducted elementary school can afford to provide instruction in extra subjects — such as natural science, modern languages, and political economy — and yet, with the present system of Government grants, be self-supporting.[13]

The next stage above the elementary is *scholastic* education, as it is supplied in grammar schools, whether public or private. According as the pupils are intended either to go on to a university, or to enter at once on leaving school on the practical work of life, these schools are divided into two classes. In the one class, which in Germany are called *Real-schulen*, less Latin is taught, and no Greek, but more of mathematics, modern languages, and physical science; in the other, called *Gymnasia* on the Continent, classics form the chief staple of instruction.

It is during this stage that education, whether at private or public schools, exercises its strongest levelling influence. Little attention can be paid at large schools to individual tastes or talents. In Germany, even more perhaps than in England, it is the chief object of a good and conscientious master to have his class as uniform as possible at the end of the year; and he receives far more credit from the official examiner if his whole class marches well and keeps pace together, than if he can parade a few brilliant and forward boys, followed by a number of straggling laggards.

And as to the character of the teaching at school, how can it be otherwise than authoritative or dogmatic? The Socratic method is very good if we can find the *viri Socratici* and leisure for discussion. But at school, which now may seem to be called almost in mockery σχολή, or leisure, the true method is, after all, that patronized by the great educators of the seventeenth and eighteenth centuries. Boys at school must turn their mind into a row of pigeon-holes, filling as many as they can with

---

[13] *Times*, January 25, 1879.

useful notes, and never forgetting how many are empty. There is an immense amount of positive knowledge to be acquired between the ages of ten and eighteen — rules of grammar, strings of vocables, dates, names of towns, rivers, and mountains, mathematical formulas, &c. All depends here on the receptive and retentive powers of the mind. The memory has to be strengthened, without being overtaxed, till it acts almost mechanically. Learning by heart, I believe, cannot be too strongly recommended during the years spent at school. There may have been too much of it when, as the Rev. H. C. Adams informs us in his "Wykehamica" (p. 357), boys used to say by heart 13,000 and 14,000 lines, when one repeated the whole of Virgil, nay, when another was able to say the whole of the English Bible by rote: — "Put him on where you would, he would go fluently on, as long as any one would listen."

No intellectual investment, I feel certain, bears such ample and such regular interest as gems of English, Latin, or Greek literature deposited in our memory during our childhood and youth, and taken up from time to time in the happy hours of our solitude.

One fault I have to find with most schools, both in England and on the Continent. Boys do not read enough of the Greek and Roman classics. The majority of our masters are scholars by profession, and they are apt to lay undue stress on what they call accurate and minute scholarship, and to neglect wide and cursory reading. I know the arguments for minute accuracy, but I also know the mischief that is done by an exclusive devotion to critical scholarship before we have acquired a real familiarity with the principal works of classical literature. The time spent in our schools in learning the rules of grammar and syntax, writing exercises, and composing verses, is too large. Look only at our Greek and Latin grammars, with all their rules and exceptions, and exceptions on exceptions? It is too heavy a weight for any boy to carry; and no wonder that when one of the thousand small rules which they have learnt by heart is really wanted, it is seldom forthcoming. The end of classical teaching at school should be to make our boys acquainted not only with the language, but with the literature and history, the ancient thought of the ancient world. Rules of grammar, syntax, or metre, are but means towards that end; they must never be mistaken for the end itself. A young man of eighteen, who has probably spent on an average ten years in learning

Greek and Latin, ought to be able to read any of the ordinary
Greek or Latin classics without much difficulty; nay, with a
certain amount of pleasure. He might have to consult his
dictionary now and then, or guess the meaning of certain
words; he might also feel doubtful sometimes whether certain
forms came from ἵημι, I send, or εἶμι, I got, or εἰμί, I am,
particularly if preceded by prepositions. In these matters the
best scholars are least inclined to be pharisaical; and whenever
I meet in the controversies of classical scholars the favourite
phrase, "Every schoolboy knows, or ought to know, this," I
generally say to myself, "No, he ought not." Anyhow, those
who wish to see the study of Greek or Latin retained in our
public schools ought to feel convinced that it will certainly not
be retained much longer, if it can be said with any truth that
young men who leave school at eighteen are in many cases
unable to read or to enjoy a classical text, unless they have seen
it before.

Classical teaching, and all purely scholastic teaching,
ought to be finished at school. When a young man goes to
University, unless he means to make scholarship his profession, he ought to be free to enter upon a new career. If he
has not learnt by that time so much of Greek and Latin as is
absolutely necessary in after-life for a lawyer, or a student of
physical science, or even a clergyman, either he or his school
is to blame. I do not mean to say that it would not be most
desirable for every one during his University career to attend
some lectures on classical literature, on ancient history,
philosophy, or art. What is to be deprecated is, that the
University should have to do the work which belongs
properly to the school.

The best colleges at Oxford and Cambridge have shown by
their matriculation examinations what the standard of classical
knowledge ought to be at eighteen or nineteen. That standard
can be reached by boys while still at school, as has been proved
both by the so-called local examinations, and by the examinations of schools held under the Delegates appointed by the
Universities. If, therefore, the University would reassert her old
right, and make the first examination, called at Oxford
Responsions, a general matriculation examination for
admission to the University, not only would the public schools
be stimulated to greater efforts, but the teaching of the
University might assume, from the very beginning, that

academic character which ought to distinguish it from mere schoolboy work.

Academic teaching ought to be not merely a continuation, but in one sense a correction of scholastic teaching. While at school instruction must be chiefly dogmatic, at University it is to be Socratic, for I find no better name for that method which is to set a man free from the burden of purely traditional knowledge; to make him feel that the words which he uses are often empty, that the concepts he employs are, for the most part, mere bundles picked up at random; that even where he knows facts, he does not know their evidence; and where he expresses opinions, they are mostly mere dogmas, adopted by him without examination.

But for the Universities, I should indeed fear that Mill's prophecies might come true, and that the intellect of Europe might drift into dreary monotony. The Universities always have been, and, unless they are diverted from their original purpose, always will be, the guardians of the freedom of thought, the protectors of individual spontaneity; and it was owing, I believe to Mill's ignorance of true academic teaching that he took so desponding a view of the generation growing up under his eyes.

When we leave school, our heads are naturally brimful of dogma, that is, of knowledge and opinions at second-hand. Such dead knowledge is extremely dangerous, unless it is sooner or later revived by the spirit of free inquiry. It does not matter whether our scholastic dogmas be true or false. The danger is the same. And why? Because to place either truth or error above the reach of argument is certain to weaken truth and to strengthen error. Secondly, because to hold as true on the authority of others anything which concerns us deeply, and which we could prove ourselves, produces feebleness, if not dishonesty. And, thirdly, because to feel unwilling or unable to meet objections by argument is generally the first step toward violence and persecution.

I do not think of religious dogmas only. They are generally the first to rouse inquiry, even during our schoolboy days, and they are by no means the most difficult to deal with. Dogma often rages where we least expect it. Among scientific men the theory of evolution is at present becoming, or has become, a dogma. What is the result? No objections are listened to, no difficulties recognized, and a man like Virchow, himself the strongest supporter of evolution, who has the moral courage to say that the descent of man from any ape whatever is, as yet, before the tribunal of scientific zoology, "not proven," is howled down in Germany in a manner worthy of Ephesians and Galatians. But at present I am thinking not so much of any special dogmas, but rather of that dogmatic state of mind which is the almost inevitable result of the teaching at school. I think of the whole intellect, what has been called the *intellectus sibi permissus*, and I maintain that it is the object of academic teaching to rouse that intellect out of its slumber by questions not less startling than when Galileo asked the world whether the sun was really moving and the earth stood still; or when Kant asked whether time and space were objects, or necessary forms of our sensuous intuition. Till our opinions have thus been tested, and stood the test, we can hardly call them our own.

How true this is with regard to religion has been boldly expressed by Bishop Beveridge.

"Being conscious to myself," he writes in his "Private Thoughts on Religion," "how great an ascendant Christianity holds over me beyond the rest, as being that religion whereinto I was born and baptized; that which the supreme authority has enjoined and my parents educated me in; that which every one I meet withal highly approves of, and which I myself have, by a long-continued profession, made almost natural to me: I am resolved to be more jealous and suspicious of this religion than of the rest, and be sure not to entertain it any longer without being convinced, by solid and substantial arguments, of the truth and certainty of it."

This is bold and manly language from a Bishop nearly two hundred years ago, and I certainly think that the time has come when some of the divinity lecturers at Oxford and Cambridge might well be employed in placing a knowledge of the sacred books of other religions within the reach of undergraduates. Many of the difficulties — most of them of our own making — with regard to the origin, the handing down, the later corruptions and misinterpretations of sacred texts, would find their natural solution, if it was shown how exactly the same difficulties arose and had to be dealt with by theologians of other creeds. If some — ay, if many — of the doctrines of Christianity were met with in other religions also, surely that would not affect their value, or diminish their truth; while nothing, I feel certain, would more effectually secure to the pure and simple teaching of Christ its true place in the historical development of the human mind than to place it side by side with the other religions of the world. In the series of translations of the "Sacred Books of the East," of which the first three volumes have just appeared,[14] I wished myself to include a new translation of the Old and New Testaments; and when that series is finished it will, I believe, be admitted that nowhere would these two books have had a grander setting, or have shone with a brighter light, than surrounded by the Veda, the Zendavesta, the Buddhist Tripitaka, and the Qur'än.

But as I said before, I was not thinking of religious dogmas only, or even chiefly, when I maintained that the character of academic teaching must be Socratic, not dogmatic. The evil of dogmatic teaching lies much deeper, and spreads much further.

Think only of language, the work of other people, not of ourselves, which we pick up at random in our race through life. Does not every word we use require careful examination and revision? It is not enough to say that language assists our thoughts or colours them, or possibly obscures them. No, we know now that language and thought are indivisible. It was not from poverty of expression that the Greek called reason and language by the same word, λόγος. It was because they knew, that, though we may distinguish between thought and speech, as we distinguish between body and soul, it is as impossible to tear the one by violence away from the other as it is to separate the concave side of a lens from its convex side. This is something to learn and to understand, for, if properly understood, it will supply the key to most of our intellectual puzzles, and serve as the safest thread through the whole labyrinth of philosophy.

"It is evident," as Hobbes remarks,[15] "that truth and falsity have no place but amongst such living creatures as use speech. For though some brute creatures, looking upon the image of a man in a glass, may be affected with it, as if it were the man himself, and for this reason fear it or fawn upon it in vain; yet

---

[14] "Sacred Books of the East," edited by M. M., vols. i., ii., iii.; Clarendon Press, Oxford, 1879.

[15] "Computation or Logic," t. iii., viii., p. 36.

they do not apprehend it as true or false, but only as like; and in this they are not deceived. Wherefore, as men owe all their true ratiocination to the right understanding of speech, so also they owe their errors to the misunderstanding of the same; and as all the ornaments of philosophy proceed only from man, so from man also is derived the ugly absurdity of false opinion. For speech has something in it like to a spider's web (as it was said of old of Solon's laws), for by contexture of words tender and delicate wits are ensnared or stopped, but strong wits break easily through them."

Let me illustrate my meaning by at least one instance.

Among the words which have proved spider's webs, ensnaring even the greatest intellects of the world from Aristotle down to Leibniz, the terms *genus*, *species*, and *individual* occupy a very prominent place. The opposition of Aristotle to Plato, of the Nominalists to the Realists, of Leibniz to Locke, of Herbart to Hegel, turns on the true meaning of these words. At school, of course, all we can do is to teach the received meaning of *genus* and *species*; and if a boy can trace these terms back to Aristotle's γένος and εἶδος, and show in what sense that philosopher used them, every examiner would be satisfied.

But the time comes when we have to act as our own examiners, and when we have to give an account to ourselves of such words as *genus* and *species*. Some people write, indeed, as if they had seen a *species* and a *genus* walking about in broad daylight; but a little consideration will show us that these words express subjective conceptions, and that, if the whole world were silent, there would never have been a thought of a *genus* or a *species*. There are languages in which we look in vain for corresponding words; and if we had been born in such a language, these terms and thoughts would not exist for us. They came to us, directly or indirectly, from Aristotle. But Aristotle did not invent them, he only defined them in his own way, so that, for instance, according to him, all living beings would constitute a *genus*, men a *species*, and Socrates an *individual*.

No one would say that Aristotle had not a perfect right to define these terms, if those who use them in his sense would only always remember that they are thinking the thoughts of Aristotle, and not their own. The true way to shake off the fetters of old words, and to learn to think our own thoughts, is to follow them up from century to century, to watch their development, and in the end to bring ourselves face to face with those who first found and framed both words and thoughts. If we do this with *genus* and *species*, we shall find that the words which Aristotle defined — viz., γένος and εἶδος — had originally a very different and far more useful application than that which he gave to them. Γένος, *genus*, meant generation, and comprehended such living beings only as were known to have a common origin, however they might differ in outward appearance, as, for instance, the spaniel and the bloodhound, or, according to Darwin, the ape and man. Εἶδος or species, on the contrary, meant appearance, and comprehended all such things as had the same form or appearance, whether they had a common origin or not, as if we were to speak of a species of four-footed, two-footed, horned, winged, or blue animals.

That two such concepts, as we have here explained, had a natural justification we may best learn from the fact that exactly the same thoughts found expression in Sanskrit. There, too, we find *gâti*, generation, used in the sense of *genus*, and opposed to *âkriti*, appearance, used in the sense of *species*.

So long as these two words or thoughts were used independently (much as we now speak of a genealogical as independent of a morphological classification) no harm could accrue. A family, for instance, might be called a γένος, the *gens* or clan was a γένος, the nation (gnatio) was a γένος, the whole human kith and kin was a γένος; in fact, all that was descended from common ancestors was a true γένος; There is no obscurity of thought in this.

On the other side, taking εἶδος or species in its original sense, one man might be said to be like another in his εἶδος or appearance. An ape, too, might quite truly be said to have the same εἶδος or species or appearance as a man, without any prejudice as to their common origin. People might also speak of different εἴδη or forms or classes of things, such as different kinds of metals, or tools, or armour, without committing themselves in the least to any opinion as to their common descent.

Often it would happen that things belonging to the same γένος, such as the white man and the negro, differed in their εἶδος or appearance; often also that things belonging to the same εἶδος, such as eatables, differed in their γένος, as, for instance, meat and vegetables.

All this is clear and simple. The confusion began when these two terms, instead of being co-ordinate, were subordinated to each other by the philosophers of Greece, so that what from one point of view was called a *genus*, might from another be called a species, and *vice versá*. Human beings, for instance, were now called a *species*, all living beings a *genus*, which may be true in logic, but is utterly false in what is older than logic — viz., language, thought, or fact. According to language, according to reason, and according to Nature, all human beings constitute a γένος, or generation, so long as they are supposed to have common ancestors; but with regard to all living beings we can only say that they form an εἶδος — that is, agree in certain appearances, until is has been proved that even Mr. Darwin was too modest in admitting at least four or five different ancestors for the whole animal world.[16]

In tracing the history of these two words, γένος and εἶδος, you may see passing before your eyes almost the whole panorama of philosophy, from Plato's ideas down to Hegel's *Idea*. The question of *genera*, their origin and subdivision, occupied chiefly the attention of natural philosophers, who, after long controversies about the origin and classification of *genera* and *species*, seem at last, thanks to the clear sight of Darwin, to have arrived at the old truth which was prefigured in language — namely, that Nature knows nothing but *genera*, or generations, to be traced back to a limited number of ancestors, and that the so-called *species* are only *genera*, whose genealogical descent is *as yet* more or less obscure.

But the question as to the nature of the εἶδος became a vital question in every system of philosophy. Granting, for instance, that women in every clime and country formed one species, it was soon asked what constituted a species? If all women shared a common form, what was that form? Where was it? So long as it was supposed that all women descended from Eve, the difficulty might be slurred over by the name of heredity. But the more thoughtful would ask even then how it was that, while all individual women came and went and vanished, the form in which they were cast remained the same?

Here you see how philosophical mythology springs up. The very question what εἶδος or species or form was, and where

---

16 Lectures on Mr. Darwin's "Philosophy of Language," *Fraser's Magazine*, June, 1873, p. 26

these things were kept, changed those words form predicates into subjects. Εἶδος was conceived as something independent and substantial, something within or above the individuals participating in it, something unchangeable and eternal. Soon there arose as many εἴδης or forms or types as there were general concepts. They were considered the only true realities of which the phenomenal world is only as a shadow that soon passeth away. Here we have, in fact, the origin of Plato's ideas, and of the various systems of idealism which followed his lead, while the opposite opinions that ideas have no independent existence, and that the one is nowhere found except in the many (τὸ ἓν παοὰ τὰ πολλά), was strenuously defended by Aristotle and his followers.[17]

The same red thread runs through the whole philosophy of the Middle Ages. Men were cited before councils and condemned as heretics because they declared that *animal, man,* or *woman* were mere names, and that they could not bring themselves to believe in an ideal animal, an ideal man, an ideal woman as the invisible, supernatural, or metaphysical types of the ordinary animal, the individual man, the single woman. Those philosophers, called *Nominalists,* in opposition to the *Realists,* declared that all general terms were *names only,* and that nothing could claim reality but the individual.

We cannot follow this controversy further, as it turns up again between Locke and Leibniz, between Herbart and Hegel. Suffice it to say that the knot, as it was tied by language, can be untied by the science of language alone, which teaches us that there is and can be no such thing as "a name only." That phrase ought to be banished from all works on philosophy. A name is and always has been the subjective side of our knowledge, but that subjective side is as impossible without an objective side as a key is without a lock. It is useless to ask which of the two is the more real, for they are real only by being, not two, but one. Realism is as one-sided as Nominalism. But there is a higher Nominalism, which might better be called the Science of Language, and which teaches us that, apart from sensuous perception, all human knowledge is by names and by names only, and that the object of names is always the general.

This is but one out of hundreds and thousands of cases to show how names and concepts which come to us by tradition

17   Prantl, "Geschichte der Logik," vol. i. p. 121.

must be submitted to very careful snuffing before they will yield a pure light. What I mean by academic teaching and academic study is exactly this process of snuffing, this changing of traditional words into living words, this tracing of modern thought back to ancient primitive thought, this living, as it were, once more, so far as it concerns us, the whole history of human thought ourselves, till we are as little afraid to differ from Plato or Aristotle as from Comte or Darwin.

Plato and Aristotle are, no doubt, great names; every schoolboy is awed by them, even thought he may have read very little of their writings. This, too, is a kind of dogmatism that requires correction. Now, at University, a young student might hear the following, by no means respectful, remarks about Aristotle, which I copy from one of the greatest English scholars and philosophers: — "There is nothing so absurd that the old philosophers, as Cicero saith, who was one of them, have not some of them maintained; and I believe that scarce anything can be more absurdly said in natural philosophy than that which now is called Aristotle's Metaphysics; or more repugnant to government than much of that he hath said in his Politics; nor more ignorantly than a great part of his Ethics." I am far from approving this judgment, but I think that the shock which a young scholar receives on seeing his idols so mercilessly broken is salutary. It throws him back on his own resources; it makes him honest to himself. If he thinks the criticism thus passed on Aristotle unfair, he will begin to read his works with new eyes. He will not only construe his words, but try to reconstruct in his own mind the thoughts so carefully elaborated by that ancient philosopher. He will judge of their truth without being swayed by the authority of a great name, and probably in the end value what is valuable in Aristotle, or Plato, or any other great philosopher far more highly and honestly than if he had never seen them trodden under foot.

But do not suppose that I look upon the Universities as purely iconoclastic, as chiefly intended to teach us how to break the idols of the schools. Far from it! But I do look upon them as meant to freshen the atmosphere which we breathe at school, and to shake our mind to its very roots, as a storm shakes the young oaks, not to throw them down, but to make them grasp all the more firmly the hard soil of fact and truth! "*Stand upright on thy feet*" ought to be written over the gate of every college, if the epidemic of uniformity and sequacity which Mill saw approaching from China, and which since his time has made such rapid progress Westward, is ever to be stayed.

Academic freedom is not without its dangers; but there are dangers which it is safer to face than to avoid. In Germany — as far as my own experience goes — students are often left too much to themselves, and it is only the cleverest among them, or those who are personally recommended, who receive from the professors that personal guidance and encouragement which should and could be easily extended to all.

There is too much time given in the German Universities to mere lecturing, and often in simply retailing to a class what each student might read in books often in a far more perfect form. Lectures are useful if they teach us how to teach ourselves; if they stimulate; if they excite sympathy and curiosity; if they give advice that springs from personal experience; if they warn against wrong roads; if, in fact, they have less the character of a show-window than of a workshop. Half an hour's conversation with a tutor or a professor often does more than a whole course of lectures in giving the right direction and the right spirit to a young man's studies. Here I may quote the words of Professor Helmholtz, in full agreement with him. "When I recall the memory of my own University life," he writes, "and the impression which a man like Johannes Müller, the professor of psychology, made on us, I must set the highest value on the personal intercourse with teachers from whom one learns how thought works on independent heads. Whoever has come in contact but once with one or several first-class men will find his intellectual standard changed for life."

In English Universities, on the contrary, there is too little of academic freedom. There is not only guidance, but far too much of constant personal control. It is often thought that English undergraduates could not be trusted with that amount of academic freedom which is granted to German students, and that most of them, if left to choose their own work, their own time, their own books, and their own teachers, would simply do nothing. This seems to me unfair and untrue. Most horses, if you take them to the water, will drink; and the best way to make them drink is to leave them alone. I have lived long enough in English and in German Universities to know that the intellectual fibre is as strong and sound in the English as in the German youth. But if you supply a man, who wishes to learn swimming, with bladders — nay, if you insist on his using them — he will use them, but he will probably never learn to swim. Take them away, on the contrary, and depend on it, after a few aimless strokes and a few painful gulps, he will use his arms and his legs, and he will swim. If young men do not learn to use their arms, their legs, their muscles, their senses, their brain, and their heart too, during the bright years of their University life, when are they to learn it? True, there are thousands who never learn it, and who float happily on through life buoyed up on mere bladders. The worst that can happen to them is that some day the bladders may burst, and they may be left stranded or drowned. But these are not the men whom England wants to fight her battles. It has often been pointed out of late that many of those who, during this century, have borne the brunt of the battle in the intellectual warfare in England, have not been trained at our Universities, while others who have been at Oxford and Cambridge, and have distinguished themselves in after-life, have openly declared that they attended hardly any lectures in college, or that they derived no benefit from them. What can be the ground of that? Not that there is less work done at Oxford than at Leipzig, but that the work is done in a different spirit. It is free in Germany; it has now become almost compulsory in England. Though an old professor myself, I like to attend, when I can, some of the professorial lectures in Germany; for it is a real pleasure to see hundreds of young faces listening to a teacher on the history of art, on modern history, on the science of language, or on philosophy, without any view to examinations, simply from love of the subject or of the teacher. No one who knows what the real joy of learning is, how it lightens all drudgery and draws away the mind from mean pursuits, can see without indignation that what ought to be the freest and happiest years in a man's life should often be spent between cramming and examinations.

And here I have at last mentioned the word, which to many friends of academic freedom, to many who dread the baneful increase of uniformity,may seem the cause of all mischief, the most powerful engine for intellectual levelling — *Examination*.

There is a strong feeling springing up everywhere against the tyranny of examinations, against the cramping and withering influence which they are supposed to exercise on the youth of England. I cannot join in that outcry. I well remember that the first letters which I ventured to address to the *Times*, in very imperfect English, were in favour of examinations. They were signed *La Carrière ouverte*, and were written long before the days of the Civil Service Commission! I well remember, too, that the first time I ventured to speak, or rather to stammer, in public, was in favour of examinations. That was in 1857, at Exeter, when the first experiment was made, under the auspices of Sir T. Acland, in establishing the Oxford and Cambridge Local Examinations. I have been an examiner myself for many years, I have watched the growth of that system in England from year to year, and in spite of all that has been said and written of late against examinations, I confess I do not see how it would be possible to abolish them, and return to the old system of appointment by patronage.

But though I have not lost my faith in examinations, I cannot conceal the fact that I am frightened by the manner in which they are conducted, and by the results which they produce. As you are interested yourselves at this Midland Institute, in the successful working of examinations, you will perhaps allow me in conclusion to add a few remarks on the safeguards necessary for the efficient working of examinations.

All examinations are a means to ascertain how pupils have been taught; they ought never to be allowed to become the end for which pupils are taught.

Teaching with a view to examinations lowers the teacher in the eyes of his pupils; learning with a view to examinations is apt to produce shallowness and dishonesty.

Whatever attractions learning possesses in itself, and whatever efforts were formerly made by boys at school from a sense of duty, all this is lost if they once imagine that the highest object of all learning is gaining marks in examinations.

In order to maintain the proper relation between teacher and pupil, all pupils should be made to look to their teachers as their natural examiners and fairest judges, and therefore in every examination the report of the teacher ought to carry the greatest weight. This is the principle followed abroad in all examinations of candidates at public schools; and even in their examination on leaving school, which gives them the right to enter the University, they know that their success depends far more on the work which they have done during the years at school, than on the work done on the few days of their examination. There are outside examiners appointed by Government to check the work done at schools and during the examinations; but the cases in which they have to modify or reverse the award of the master are extremely rare, and they are felt to reflect seriously on the competency or impartiality of the school authorities.

To leave examinations entirely to strangers reduces them to the level of lotteries, and fosters a cleverness in teachers and taught often akin to dishonesty. An examiner may find out what a candidate knows *not*, he can hardly ever find out all he knows; and even if he succeeds in finding out *how much* a candidate knows, he can never find out *how* he knows it. On these points the opinion of the masters who have watched their pupils for years is indispensable for the sake of the examiner, for the sake of the pupils, and for the sake of their teachers.

I know I shall be told that it would be impossible to trust the masters, and to be guided by their opinion, because they are interested parties. Now, first of all, there are far more honest men in the world than dishonest, and it does not answer to legislate as if all schoolmasters were rogues. It is enough that they should know that their reports would be scrutinized, to keep even the most reprobate of teachers from bearing false witness in favour of their pupils.

Secondly, I believe that unnecessary temptation is now being placed before all parties concerned in examinations. The proper reward for a good examination should be honour, not pounds, shillings, and pence. The mischief done by pecuniary rewards offered in the shape of scholarships and exhibitions at school and University, begins to be recognized very widely. To train a boy of twelve for a race against all England is generally to overtrain his faculties, and often to impair his usefulness in later life; but to make him feel that by his failure he will entail on his father the loss of a hundred a year, and on his teacher the loss of pupils, is simply cruel at that early age.

It is always said that these scholarships and exhibitions enable the sons of poor parents to enjoy the privilege of the best education in England, from which they would otherwise be debarred by the excessive costliness of our public schools. But even this argument, strong as it seems, can hardly stand, for I believe it could be shown that the majority of those who are successful in obtaining scholarships and exhibitions at school or at University are boys whose parents have been able to pay the highest price for their children's previous education. If all these prizes were abolished, and the funds thus set free used to lessen the price of education at school and in college, I believe that the sons of poor parents would be far more benefited than by the present system. It might also be desirable to lower the school-fees in the case of the sons of poor parents, who were doing well at school from year to year; and, in order to guard against favouritism, an examination, particularly *vivâ voce*, before all the masters of a school, possible even with some outside examiner, might be useful. But the present system bids fair to degenerate into mere horse-racing, and I shall not wonder if, sooner or later, the two-year olds entered for the race have to be watched by their trainer that they may not be overfed or drugged against the day of the race. It has come to this, that schools are bidding for clever boys in order to run them in the races, and in France, I read, that parents actually extort money from schools by threatening to take away the young racers that are likely to win the Derby.[18]

If we turn from the schools to the Universities we find here, too, the same complaints against over-examination. Now it seems to me that every University, in order to maintain its position, has a perfect right to demand two examinations, but no more: one for admission, the other for a degree. Various attempts have been made in Germany, in Russia, in France, and in England to change and improve the old academic tradition, but in the end the original, and, as it would seem, the natural system, has generally proved its wisdom and reasserted its right.

If a University surrenders the right of examining those who wish to be admitted, the tutors will often have to do the work of schoolmasters, and the professors can never know how high or how low they should aim in their public lectures. Besides this, it is almost inevitable, if the Universities surrender the right of a matriculation-examination, that they should lower, not only their own standard, but likewise the standard of public schools. Some Universities, on the contrary, like over-anxious mothers, have multiplied examinations so as to make quite sure, at the end of each term or each year that the pupils confided to them have done at least some work. This kind of forced labour may do some good to the incorrigibly idle, but it does the greatest harm to all the rest. If there is an examination at the end of each year, there can be no freedom left for any

---

[18] L. Noiré, "Pädagogisches Skizzenbuch," p. 157; "Todtes Wissen."

independent work. Both teachers and taught will be guided by the same pole-star — examinations; no deviation from the beaten track will be considered safe, and all the pleasure derived from work done for its own sake, and all the just pride and joy, which those only know who have ever ventured out by themsleves on the open sea of knowledge, must be lost.

We must not allow ourselves to be deceived by the brilliant show of examination papers.

It is certainly marvellous what an amount of knowledge candidates will produce before their examiners; but those who have been both examined and examiners know best how fleeting that knowledge is, and how different from that other knowledge which has been acquired slowly and quietly, for its own sake, for our own sake, without a thought as to whether it would ever pay at examinations or not. A candidate, after giving most glibly the dates and the titles of the principal works of Cobbett, Gibbon, Burke, Adam Smith, and David Hume, was asked whether he had ever seen any of their writings, and he had to answer, No. Another, who was asked which of the works of Pheidias he had seen, replied that he had only read the first two books. That is the kind of dishonest knowledge which is fostered by too frequent examinations. There are two kinds of knowledge, the one that enters into our very blood, the other which we carry about in our pockets. Those who read for examinations have generally their pockets cram full; those who work on quietly and have their whole heart in their work are often discouraged at the small amount of their knowledge, at the little life-blood they have made. But what they have learnt has really become their own, has invigorated their whole frame, and in the end they have often proved the strongest and happiest men in the battle of life.

Omniscience is at present the bane of all our knowledge. From the day he leaves school and enters the University a man ought to make up his mind that in many things he must remain either altogether ignorant, or be satisfied with knowledge at second-hand. Thus only can he clear the deck for action. And the sooner he finds out what his own work is to be, the more useful and delightful will be his life at University and later. There are few men who have a passion for all knowledge, there is hardly one who has not a hobby of his own. Those so-called hobbies ought to be utilized, and not, as they are now, discouraged, if we wish our Universities to produce more men like Faraday, Carlyle, Grote, or Darwin. I do not say that in an examination for a University degree of a minimum of what is now called general culture should not be insisted on; but in addition to that, far more freedom ought to be given to the examiner to let each candidate produce his own individual work. This is done to a far greater extent in Continental than in English Universities, and the examinations are therefore mostly confided to the members of the *Senatus Academicus*, consisting of the most experienced teachers, and the most eminent representatives of the different branches of knowledge in the University. Their object is not to find out how many marks each candidate may gain by answering a larger or smaller number of questions, and then to place them in order before the world like so many organ pipes. They want to find out whether a man, by the work he has done during his three or four years at University, has acquired that vigour of thought, that maturity of judgment, and that special knowledge, which fairly entitle him to an academic status, to a degree, with or without special honours. Such a degree confers no material advantages;[19] it does not entitle its holder to any employment in Church or State; it does not vouch even for his being a fit person to be made an Archbishop or Prime Minister. All this is left to the later struggle for life; and in that struggle it seems as if those who, after having surveyed the vast field of human knowledge, have settled on a few acres of their own and cultivated them as they were never cultivated before, who have worked hard and have tasted the true joy and happiness of hard work, who have gladly listened to others, but always depended on themselves, were, after all, the men whom great nations delighted to follow as their royal leaders in their onward march towards greater enlightenment, greater happiness, and greater freedom.

To sum up. No one can read Mill's Essay "On Liberty" at the present moment without feeling that even during the short period of the last twenty years the cause which he advocated so strongly and passionately, the cause of individual freedom, has made rapid progress, aye, has carried the day. In no country *may* a man be so entirely himself, so true to himself and yet loyal to society, as in England.

---

[19]   Mill' "On Liberty," p. 193.

But, although the enemy whose encroachments Mill feared most and resented most had been driven back and forced to keep within his own bounds, — though such names as Dissent and Nonconformity, which were formerly used in society as fatal darts, seem to have lost all the poison which they once contained, — Mill's principal fears have nevertheless not been belied, and the blight of uniformity which he saw approaching with its attendant evils of feebleness, indifference, and sequacity, has been spreading more widely than even in his days.

It has even been maintained that the very freedom which every individual now enjoys has been detrimental to the growth of individuality; that you must have an Inquisition if you want to see martyrs; that you must have despotism and tyranny to call forth heroes. The very measures which Mill and his friends advocated so warmly, compulsory education and competitive examinations, are pointed out as having chiefly contributed to produce that large array of pass-men, that dead level of uninteresting excellence, which is the *beau idéal* of a Chinese Mandarin, while it frightened and disheartened such men as Humboldt, Tocqueville, and John Stuart Mill.

There may be some truth in all this, but it is certainly not the whole truth. Education, as it has to be carried on, whether in elementary or in public schools, is no doubt a heavy weight which might well press down the most independent spirit; it is, in fact, neither more nor less than placing, in a systematized form, on the shoulders of every generation the ever-increasing mass of knowledge, experience, custom, and tradition that has been accumulated by former generations. We need not wonder, therefore, if in some schools all spring, all vigour, all joyousness of work is crushed out under that load of names and dates, of anomalous verbs and syntactic rules, of mathematical formulas and geometrical axioms, which boys are expected to bring up for competitive examinations.

But a remedy has been provided, and we are ourselves to blame if we do not avail ourselves of it to the fullest extent. Europe erected its Universities, and called them the homes of the Liberal Arts, and determined that between the slavery of the school and the routine of practical life every man should have at least three years of freedom. What Socrates and his great pupil Plato had done for the youth of Greece,[20] these new academies were to do for the youth of Italy, France, England, Spain, and Germany; and, though with varying success, they have done it. The mediæval and modern Universities have been from century to century the homes of free thought. Here the most eminent men have spent their lives, not merely in retailing traditional knowledge, as at school, but in extending the frontiers of science in all directions. Here, in close intercourse with their teachers, or under their immediate guidance, generation after generation of boys, fresh from school, have grown up into men during the three years of academic life. Here, for the first time, each man has been encouraged to dare to be himself, to follow his own tastes, to depend on his own judgment, to try the wings of his mind, and, lo, like young eagles, thrown out of their nest, they could fly. Here the old knowledge accumulated at school was tested, and new knowledge acquired straight from the fountain-head. Here knowledge ceased to be a mere burden, and became a power invigorating the whole mind, like snow which during winter lies cold and heavy on the meadows, but when it is touched by the sun of spring melts away, and fructifies the ground for a rich harvest.

That was the original purpose of the Universities; and the more they continue to fulfil that purpose the more will they secure to us that real freedom from tradition, from custom, from mere opinion and superstition, which can be gained by independent study only; the more will they foster that "human development in its richest diversity" which Mill, like Humboldt, considered as the highest object of all society.

Such academic teaching need not be confined to the old Universities. There is many a great University that sprang from smaller beginnings than your Midland Institute. Nor is it necessary, in order to secure the real benefits of academic teaching, to have all the paraphernalia of a University, its colleges and fellowships, its caps and gowns. What is really wanted are men who have done good work in their life, and who are willing to teach others how to work for themselves, how to think for themselves, how to judge for themselves. That is the true academic stage in every man's life, when he learns to

---

[20]   Zeller, "Ueber den wissenschaftlichen Unterricht bei den Griechen," 1878, p. 9.

work, not to please others, be they schoolmasters or examiners, but to please himself, when he works from sheer love of work, and for the highest of all purposes, the conquest of truth. Those only who have passed through that stage know the real blessing of work. To the world at large they may seem mere drudges — but the world does not know the triumphant joy with which the true mountaineer, high above clouds and mountain walls that once seemed unsurpassable, drinks in the fresh air of the High Alps, and away from the fumes, the dust, and the noises of the city, revels alone, in freedom of thought, in freedom of feeling, and in the freedom of the highest faith.

F. MAX MÜLLER

THE CONTEMPORARY REVIEW
Vol. 37, 1880
[J. T. Mackenzie]

Professor Max Müller on Mr. Mill and Liberty

Professor Max Müller is a noble and delightful writer, with a speciality in which he is unapproachable; but the topic of his article "On Freedom" (CONTEMPORARY REVIEW for November, 1879) is debateable ground for all intelligent people. As I think so much of it as related to Mr. Mill's essay "On Liberty" is in some points seriously misleading and mischievous, and in others hardly accurate, I venture to submit a few paragraphs upon it for the consideration of thoughtful readers. It will be observed that the main question for the moment is, not whether Mr. Mill was right either in his principles or in the application of them, but what he said and meant. Fortunately this is a matter in which we are not left to conjecture, for the book exists, is written in pellucid English, and is presented to us by Mill himself as "a kind of philosophic text-book" of a certain "truth." It would be rather strange if his meaning were not accessible, and yet no book of his has been less understood. This is partly because the sentiment of justice was exceedingly strong in Mill, and his "detachment" of mind very great; whereas in the majority of us the sentiment of justice is weak, and prejudice of routine or position strong; but no doubt the "passionate" manner in which Professor Max Müller truly says it is written, tends to arouse antagonism before reflection has had time to do its work; and, with all his caution, which is marked, Mill managed to offend a good many interests besides those of what he oddly and mistakenly called Calvinism, and those of the Permissive-Prohibitory Alliance. His use of the work Calvinism is an example of his desire to avoid giving unnecessary vexation to certain readers; he had a vague idea that Calvinism was, of all forms of orthodox Christianity, the one that had the fewest friends, and so he used that word for the purpose of "hedging" upon a much wider question than any that might lie in dispute between

Jonathan Edwards and John Wesley. However, in running through the Essay this point will recur, though my chief concern will be with his "Applications," direct and indirect; because from those alone his meaning might be extracted.

The first comment of the learned Professor which surprised me was that in his essay "On Liberty" "Mill *for once* becomes passionate." It is perfectly true that Mill does become passionate here, but as he is very much more passionate in his essay "On the Subjection of Women," the instance is not solitary, however Mr. Mill may "deserve the title of Serene Highness." This, however, is not important.

The passage in the Professor's article which most of all startled me was the following (p. 375): — "I can hardly believe that, were he [Mill] still among us, he would claim a larger measure of freedom for the individual than is now accorded to every one of us in the society in which we move." As I said before, we are not remitted to conjecture in this matter, for his words are in our possession. But his deeds are in our possession also, and we know that he deliberately risked his seat for Westminster by subscribing towards Mr. Bradlaugh's expenses in his candidature for Northampton. Charles Lever, in that much underrated book of his, "The Confessions of Paul Goslett," summed up the usual Foreign Office instructions to British agents sent abroad on political missions in some such words as these — "in short, you will do what you please, and take the consequences." It is also a well-known doctrine of certain jurists, that in the case of *mala prohibita*, as distinguished from *mala in se*, the citizen may be held guiltless if he disobeys the law, so long as he submits to the penalty — that being the choice offered to him, and accepted by him under a tacit political compact. But the "liberty" for which Mr. Mill contended was hardly the liberty to do what you please and take the consequences; and his words and his deeds leave us in no doubt as to what he would have said and done in the case of the infamous C. D. Acts (his opinion about *them* is specifically on record); in the case of the Mrs. Besant dead-lock; in the case of the latest Truelove prosecution; in the case of the attempts in America to put down Mormon polygyny by force — a subject upon which I shall quote his exact words, as an *à fortiori* instance. Neither the reader nor myself stands under any obligation to decide upon these matters in the abstract; the question before us is, what Mr. Mill wrote and meant.

And we must bear in mind that he was in the habit of choosing extreme cases for purposes of illustration; and that for the just and obvious reason that extreme cases are valuable for testing principles — *q.d.*, if the argument will take us as far as Z, then, *à multo fortiori*, it will take us to K or L. In "Liberty" Mr. Mill has referred to Mr. Truelove by name (chap. ii. on "Liberty of Thought and Discussion"), and though I am unable to say what Mr. Mill would have thought of the incriminated pamphlet, — for I have not seen it, and he was himself a very cautious and reticent propagandist, — yet we may be sure — "with less ado than a volume," as Milton phrases it — that he would have subscribed for Mr. Truelove as boldly as he did for Mr. Bradlaugh, and that his notion of the liberty of printing and publishing did not mean that a publisher was to be at "liberty" to issue any book he pleased on condition that he would pick oakum for six months and sleep on a plank with a block for a pillow. Neither, passing from legal to social penalties (though in practice they are but little distinguishable, because unjust social penalties generally *lead to* breaches of the law), did Mr. Mill, when he advocated freedom of discussion, mean that a Norman Macleod should have full "liberty" to express himself on the Sabbath question, provided he would submit to be hissed on the streets, and "cut" by troops of comrades. At least, to use Professor Max Müller's own pleasant phrase, "I can hardly believe" Mr. Mill would have written an impassioned "philosophical text-book" to no stronger purpose than that.

And there is one other momentous topic, as to which "I can hardly believe" the accomplished Professor has, in referring to Mill, followed the principle adopted by John Locke in another case — "An Essay towards the understanding of Saint Paul's Epistles *by consulting Saint Paul himself.*" Mill was a passionate and persistent advocate of National Education; it was one of the gravest points in the *credenda* and *agenda* of his school of thought. But when I have quoted, as I propose to do, his exact words upon that subject in "Liberty," I engage that the reader will "hardly believe" that the author would acquiesce in either the law or the practice as it stands. Both are dead in the teeth of his express words.

It will be unnecessary to quote Mr. Mill's vehement condemnation of "picketing," and generally of the policy of the Trades' Unions; but, whether he was right or wrong on any of these points, and some others, we shall find, I think, that the sentence I have quoted above from the article (beginning "I can hardly believe") is, as I have called it, mischievous and misleading — that is to say, if Mr. Mill's opinions in one of his chief works are worthy of discussion. Equally wide of the mark, though more difficult to dispute, is the following (pp. 369-70): —

> "I doubt whether any of the principles for which Mill pleaded so warmly and strenuously in his essay 'On Liberty' would at the present day be challenged or resisted, even by the most illiberal of philosophers or the most conservative of politicians. Mill's demands sound very humble to *our* ears. They amount to no more than this: 'that the individual is not accountable to society for his actions so far as they concern the interests of no person but himself, and that he may be subjected to social or legal punishments for such actions only as are prejudicial to the interests of others.' "

Deeply as I have the honour of admiring a large part of Professor Max Müller's article, I am unable to follow the meaning, or, should I say, to get at the weight or significance of what the Professor alleges as his primary point of disagreement with Mill. He admits that "the principle of individuality" is in danger; but doubts whether what Mill calls "the *régime* of public opinion is chiefly answerable for it." The learned Professor shifts the burden to what the Buddhists call *Karman*: "Our real enemies are at our back: the heaviest chains fastened on us are those made by our ancestors, not our contemporaries." I have looked very carefully at this, but I cannot see how it alters the problem. It looks like saying our real enemies are not our present opinions, but the past opinions which have helped to create the present opinions; or something of that sort; for I find myself puzzled in trying to reduce the proposition to any form whatever which shall not resemble an identical proposition. The "*régime* of public opinion" says that the bride shall cut the cake with her own hand at the wedding breakfast. Very good. I read Mr. McLennan, or Mr. Tylor, or Sir John Lubbock, and I am told (and fully believe) that this is a survival from the time when the woman was bound to be the wife of the whole tribe for a certain number of days before the husband could appropriate her. I can certainly conceive that if this fact were published broadcast throughout the land, it would so disgust brides and bridegrooms that the custom would be dropped, because it would then become marked. But the case is hardly in point. I presume that when Sir Robert Peel "in his place" took a sovereign out of his waistcoat pocket, and, meditatively twirling it round, asked the House that immortal question, "What is a pound?" Professor Max Müller might have murmured "Babylon;" but it does not seem to lead up to much; and since nobody contends that the sovereign and the shilling are creatures of the Pure Reason, one ground for keeping them or kicking them out is as good as another.

However, there are no doubt cases in which the very best thing to be done to break the back of a powerful tradition, social or other, would be to relate the history of it, and show how it came to be here. But how this stands related to the questions debated in Mr. Mill's "Liberty" is not clear to me. We must have ancestors; and we shall be ancestors to those who follow us. Inevitably we have received something from the past; inevitably we shall pass something on. But it will still remain true that "the *régime* of public opinion" is the enemy of "individuality" and free growth — and all the weapons forged by Mill must be as good as ever, if good; and as much wanted, if wanted. The reader may judge for himself, looking carefully at the article, whether I have or have not reason to feel puzzled by the proposed shifting of the ground.

Towards the close of the article there are two paragraphs which are very noticeable, repeating, as they do, what is, in my opinion, misleading and mischievous — that is to say, if Mr. Mill's opinions are of any value to us:—

"To sum up. No one can read Mill's essay "On Liberty" at the present moment without feeling that even during the short period of the last twenty years the cause which he advocated so strongly and passionately, the cause of individual freedom, has made rapid progress, aye, has carried the day. In no country *may* a man be so entirely himself, so true to himself and yet loyal to society, as in England.

"But, although the enemy whose encroachments Mill feared most and resented most has been driven back and forced to keep within his own bounds, though such names as Dissent and Nonconformity, which were formerly used in society as fatal darts, seem to have lost all the poison which they once contained, Mill's principal fears have nevertheless not been belied, and the blight of uniformity which he saw approaching with its attendant evils of feebleness, indifference, and sequacity, has been spreading more widely than ever in his days."

Here, indeed, there is a plain issue. "No one can read Mill's essay 'On Liberty' without feeling that even during the short period of the last twenty years the cause which he advocated so strongly and passionately, the cause of individual freedom, has made rapid progress, aye, has carried the day." Now, if this means merely freedom to do as you like and take the consequences, I have nothing to say; but that it not what Mill meant. I have read Mr. Mill's "Liberty," and I hold that during the last twenty years "the cause which he advocated" has had a mixed history, but that on the whole it is a great deal worse off than it was twenty years ago. There is scarcely one of the shackles to which Mill referred by name that has been removed; while several of the old weapons against freedom have been hunted up and loaded, ready to go off in case of need. Some causes of opprobrium have been removed, for example, by the Secular Oaths Bill; but, speaking broadly, whatever legal freedom of discussion and action has gained, has been gained by compromise or a fluke. The opening of museums, picture galleries, &c., on Sunday (which he advocates in strong terms, but as to which I hesitate greatly), will probably be carried before long; but, on the whole, the power of society over the individual, whether by law or otherwise, has been immensely fortified. Mr. Max Müller looks at these things from the summits of "the mountains of Rasselas," or some such place, with that splendid and capacious brain of his full of Sanskrit. If he will read more newspapers, and read them minutely, he will receive a very different impression from that which now possesses him. Judges, magistrates, barristers, and officials of various kinds have taken to putting on the legal screw in ways which were not dreamt of in the days when Mr. Mill wrote his Essay. I could quote from memory a score of instances within the last few months — instances, I mean, in which official administrators of one kind or the other have used the law as a screw to compel not only judicially formulated compliance, but compliance far beyond that limit. It is one of the vilest forms of persecution, and it is a growing one. The specific cases are passed over in silence, or half silence, because no one likes to touch pitch; but that is what the administrators count upon. In those serene academic groves in which Professor Max Müller walks with his *viri Socratici*, he misses all this; but if he were a journalist, a shop-keeper, a city clerk, or some other hard-worked poor man or woman of precarious income, but holding heresies, he would quickly find where the shoe pinches. I think Sir Fitzjames Stephen took a much more accurate view of the situation in his "Liberty, Equality, and Fraternity," and it is very different from the one before me — in fact, the direct opposite, if my memory serves me. And there was a characteristic paper of his in this REVIEW, in which he warned us of the existence of certain ancient blunderbusses of statute law, which might be made to go off some day in a manner sufficiently unfavourable to the liberty of which we are told we have so much. "In no country *may* a man be so entirely himself, so true to himself, and yet loyal to society, as in England," says Professor Max Müller. The proposition is a cheap one, and true; but it is liable to the retort, "Yes, this country is better than others, but bad is the best; and the liberty you cite is, for too many people, liberty to starve or to conform." The following passage from Mr. Mill's "Liberty," is as true now as when he wrote it, and events seem to promise that it will acquire additional rather than diminished force:—

> "Unhappily there is no security in the state of the public mind, that the suspension of the worst forms of legal persecution, which has lasted for about the space of a generation, will continue. In this age the quiet surface of routine is as often ruffled by attempts to resuscitate past evils as to introduce new benefits. . . . Where there is the strong permanent leaven of intolerance in the feelings of a people, which at all times abides in the middle classes of this country, it needs but little to provoke them into actively persecuting those whom they have never ceased to think proper objects of persecution. For it is this — it is the opinion men entertain, and the feelings they cherish, respecting those who disown the beliefs they deem important, which makes this country not a place of mental freedom. For a long time past the chief mischief of the legal

penalties is that they strengthen the social stigma. It is that stigma which is really effective, and so effective is it, that the profession of opinions which are under the ban of society is much less common in England, than is in many other countries the avowal of those which incur risk of judicial punishment. In respect of all persons but those whose pecuniary circumstances make then independent of the good-will of others, opinion . . . is as efficacious as law, men might as well be imprisoned as excluded from the means of earning their bread. Those whose bread is secured, and who desire no favours of men in power, or from bodies of men, or from the public, have nothing to fear from the open avowal of any opinions but to be ill thought of and ill spoken of, and this it ought not to require a very heroic mould to enable them to bear. There is no room for any appeal *ad misericordiam* in behalf of such persons. But though we do not now inflict so much evil on those who think differently from us, as it was formerly our custom to do, it may be that we do ourselves as much evil as ever by our treatment of them."

In all this, and indeed in much more and on the whole, it must be borne in mind that Mr. Mill did not say all he meant or anything near it. He wrote with a halter round his neck, and knew it. I do not mean that he temporized or fenced, but I do mean that his policy was to introduce the thin end of the wedge, because he thought that was the only way of gaining any advantage for the cause he had at heart, namely, absolute freedom of discussion and of conduct — including, of course, the liberty to make fresh experiments of living — in all particulars in which specific injury to others could not be made out upon purely secular principles. It would be rude to say that his treatment of the difficulty which arises in his path from the fact of Christianity being the law-established religion of this country, and the indirect effect of the Blasphemy Law, the Test Acts, and similar things, existing or passed away but still surviving as influences, — I say it would be rude to affirm that his treatment of that difficulty and some others was tiresome and weak, but it was a failure. His beating about the bush in this matter is a startling comment on his own text, Personally, I think the whole argument of the book breaks down for want of the Theistic premiss. If no theory of morals can be created by

the "practical Reason,"[1] without the postulate of a Divine
Providence in some shape, much less can we arrive without that
postulate at the stringent conclusions involved in the plea for
"Liberty." Unless I believe that I am taken care of in every
perilous act of conscience by a Power higher than my own;
unless I can, in resisting unjust force, fall back upon Divine
sympathy, in the full confidence that the final result is no
business of mine, but that its goodness, or, as Mr. Sidgwick
would say, its "felicific" character, is insured whatever becomes
of *me*, the back of my moral energy is inevitably broken. In
comparing Mr. Mill's treatment of the question of "Liberty"
with Sir Fitzjames Stephen's criticism of that treatment, I
should say that the latter has a considerable advantage — for
his "God" scarcely deserves the name — practically he trundles
the ideal of providence off the platform. And he then, quite
consistently, discusses the question of freedom as if human
beings were vermin, with no horizons and no guaranteed
hopes. The outcome is somewhat brutal, and the "gentle
reader" feels rather as if he has been kicked than argued with;
but it is impossible, in my opinion, to deny the inconsequence
of Mr. Mill's position. If the theory of liberty is condemned for
ever to move in this circle, "Society must not ignore Individuality because Individuality is sacred — Individuality must not
ignore Society because Society is sacred" (which is what Mr.
Mill is reduced to), then we can do nothing but live from hand
to mouth as cases arise. Hence the inevitable weakness of much
of his argument, and the difficulty which nearly every friend of
his book is placed in: since it looks all but ridiculous for any
one to stand forward and say, "I agree in the main with these
conclusions, and with most of the special arguments employed

---

1   See the concluding paragraphs of Mr. Sidgwick's "Methods of Ethics,"
comparing the first and second editions: — "It is, one may say, a matter of
life and death to the Practical Reason that this premiss" (*i.e.*, Theism, or an
equivalent) "should be somehow obtained. And I cannot fall back on the
resource of thinking myself under a moral necessity to regard all my duties
as if they were commandments of God, although not entitled to hold
speculatively that any such Supreme Being really exists . . . . It seems plain
that in proportion as man has lived in the exercise of the Practical Reason —
as he believed — and feels as an actual force the desire to do what is right
and reasonable as such, his demand for this premiss will be intense and
imperious. Thus we are not surprised to find Socrates — the type for all
ages of the man in whom this desire is predominant — declaring with simple
conviction that if the Rulers of the Universe do not prefer the just man to
the unjust, it is better to die than to live'

to support them, but still I think there is no force in them, unless you first supply a point of leverage which the author ignores."

From all this the reader will have gathered, or will at least be prepared to hear, that there are careful readers of the "Liberty," who hold that it has rarely been understood, and rarely attacked as it should be by those who dislike it. I have mentioned both points because they cannot well be separated, though the first is the one now immediately before us.

Professor Max Müller, quoting the sentence which he gives as representing Mill's "demands," remarks that "they sound very humble to *our* ears." The sentence he quotes is merely the very wide generalization that "the individual should only be subjected to legal or social penalties for such actions as are prejudicial to the interests of others." This, as it stands, is indeed "very humble;" and while, on the one hand Mill would never have written a book, much less a "passionate" one, to support so obvious a proposition; on the other, it is incredible that twenty years should have made much difference as to the need for such an appeal as he did really intend and did really write. The truth is that the above passage is, by itself, barren and futile — because every act that a human being can perform affects the interests of others, and may be prejudicial to them. The question to which Mill bends all his strength is a subsequent one. If all our acts affect others (for instance, a Saxon eats more than an Italian, the successful lover ousts the unsuccessful), any one of our acts may prejudice others. Where to draw the line, — that is the question. Now Mill's general principles, as a Utilitarian, tied him down to a necessity for a great deal of remote and wire-drawn reasoning about consequences, but he betrays all along a tendency to fall back upon the simplest issue he can find; in fact, upon what a few troglodytes would call the dictates of plain justice. It is quite true that I can neither eat nor drink, nor take a house, nor succeed in business, nor fail in business, nor preach, nor teach, without the risk of harm to some one. Suppose — to take the teaching and preaching — suppose I preached some fond father's daughter into a nunnery. The father might say, "You have, in my opinion, injured my daughter, and you have certainly injured me, because you have hurt my feelings, deprived me of her society, and disgraced the well-known Protestantism of our family." And he might go on to say, "Unless

the law gives me a remedy, I will have your blood for this." I
have put a fair illustrative case, and one which has abundantly
numerous parallels in everyday life. But where is the answer to
such a father's demand? There is none ready to hand if we
simply take the sentence quoted by the Professor as our guide
to Mill's doctrine. The act of preaching a daughter into a
nunnery is clearly not a "self-regarding" act. Might society
justly punish the preacher? Let us not deceive ourselves. A
lately deceased clergyman urged from the pulpit that any
Anglican priest practising Confession (I believe that was it)
should be punished with death.[2] Now there are tens of
thousands of pious English men and women who would
support some such suggestion, and we are frequently having
outbreaks of brutality which spring from a similar root. But the
line drawn by Mr. Mill — in accordance with natural justice —
is this, that the individual is not fairly punishable, either by law
or otherwise, for acts which — though they may actually hurt
others — *need not hurt them unless they like*. The offending
preacher might and would, obviously, reply to the angry father
— "Your daughter could have resisted my arguments if she had
chosen, and it is with your choice or submission that you are
hurt. How have I wronged you? I did not interfere with your
freedom of action or with hers. You were fully at liberty to do
your best to keep her out of a nunnery, and if you did do so,
and failed, what is that to me, or how am I responsible to any
human tribunal for your sufferings?"

Here, however, are some of Mr. Mill's own words, from the
Essay, and I call special attention to the passages in italics: —

"The only freedom which deserves the name, is that of
pursuing our own good in our own way, *so long as we do
not attempt to deprive others of theirs or impede their efforts
to obtain it*. Mankind are greater gainers by suffering each
other to live as seems good to themselves than by compelling
each to live as seems good to the rest . . .

"Though this doctrine is anything but new, and to some
persons may have the air of a truism, there is no doctrine
which stands more directly opposed to the general tendency
of existing opinions and practice. . . .

---

[2] He afterwards expressed, and publicly, his grief for having made this
proposal.

"There is in the world at large an increasing inclination to stretch unduly the powers of society over the individual both by the force of opinion and even by that of legislation; and as the tendency of all the changes taking place in the world is to strengthen society and diminish the power of the individual, this encroachment is not one of the evils which tend spontaneously to disappear, but, on the contrary, to grow more and more formidable. *The disposition of mankind, whether as rulers or as fellow-citizens, to impose their own opinions and inclinations as a rule of conduct on others, is so energetically supported by some of the best and by some of the worst feelings incident to human nature, that it is hardly ever kept under restraint by anything but want of power; and as the power is not declining, but growing, unless a strong barrier of moral conviction can be raised against the mischief, we must expect in the present circumstances of the world, to see it increase.*"

It was this "strong barrier of moral conviction" that Mill wanted to see built up; but down to this time not a stone has been placed upon the foundation he raised. Rich agnosticism or atheism does not care, and penniless conscience is too weak, to help in the erection. But let us hear Mill again: —

"The acts of an individual may be hurtful to others, or wanting in due consideration for their welfare, without going to the length of violating any of their constitutional rights. The offender may then be justly punished by opinion, though not by law. As soon as any part of a person's conduct affects prejudicially the interests of others, society has jurisdiction over it, and the question whether the general welfare will or will not be promoted by interfering with it, becomes open to discussion. *But there is no room for entertaining any such question when a person's conduct affects the interests of no persons beside himself, or needs not affect them unless they like (all the persons concerned being of full age, and the ordinary amount of understanding). In all such cases, there should he perfect freedom, legal and social, to do the action and stand the consequences.*"

If this is not plain language, what are dictionaries for? And yet scarcely anybody, except Sir Fitzjames Stephen, seems to have understood it. Why, the words contain the germ of a social revolution; there is not a corner of life into which they do not pierce; and yet Professor Max Müller can write like this: —

> "Whatever social tyranny may have existed twenty years ago, when it wrung that fiery protest from the lips of John Stuart Mill, can we imagine a state of society, not totally Utopian, in which the individual man need be less ashamed of his social fetters, in which he could more freely utter all his honest convictions, more boldly propound all his theories, more fearlessly agitate for their speedy realization? . . .
>
> "Granting even that in Mill's time there existed some traces of social tyranny, where are they now? Look at the newspapers and the journals. Is there any theory too wild, any reform too violent, to be openly defended?"

If I had simply heard these words, I should certainly not have believed my ears. Of course the words "not totally Utopian" may be made to carry off nearly anything; otherwise I should have said the passage was ironical. Let Mr. Max Müller try his fortune in the open as a heterodox journalist, preacher, or lecturer, and he will speedily be undeceived, however moderate he may be in his new "theories," or however careful in the use of language.

I have already presented in Mr. Mill's own language the principle of the essay "On Liberty," namely, that in matters in which the conduct of A need not hurt B or C unless they like, there should be perfect freedom, legal and social, to do the act and stand the consequences. But, of course, this does not justify the infliction by society of penal "consequences" (outside of the action of the law I mean, for we now speak of social freedom) such as would be justly applicable to conduct which was *intended* by A to be injurious to C and D, or which must inevitably and beyond dispute be so to them or others. I invite special attention to this point, for it is of the very essence of the case, and it is constantly overlooked. It will be observed that by this hypothesis the ground taken up by A is open ground. He may be wrong: B and C and all the rest my think him so, and they are entitled to exhibit their view of the matter both to A and among themselves. Of course, too, as no one is bound to take any one else as a friend or acquaintance, C and D are entitled to avoid B; but, adds Mr. Mill, with his usual delicacy of conscience, "not to parade the avoidance" — which would be inflicting an injury. B acquires or retains his freedom at the cost of taking all the natural consequences of his act; *the general constitution of the society being supposed to remain as it was before he did it* — for, by the supposition, he is only doing what he is entitled to do. This is the principle, and to a kindly, self-disciplined spirit, not to say to a just man, it is very plain and easy. There is, of course, no intentional shortcoming in what Professor Max Müller has to say upon this subject; but, considering the immense brutality of the masses in all ranks of society, and the very hard times which "freedom's battle" has always had, it seems dangerous to touch so lightly the question of merely social penalties. "Had Mill any right to complain of these social penalties?" No, certainly not, if proportion were kept; nor did he — all he contends for is that new opinion should have a fair hearing, and new conduct fair handling. This, assuredly, does not include the right of twenty millions of people to put down a handful of heretics or insurgent persons by indirectly starving them or breaking their hearts or hopes; unless — *unless* Sir Fitzjames Stephen's view of the question be the right one. If it be, there is an end. Kill them all; the devil will know his own; and we must take care of our own hides.

It is in the chapter entitled "Applications" that Mill most freely discloses his drift. In the chapter preceding that, however, he has some very indignant words about the treatment which the Mormons seemed likely to receive. It will be observed that he assumed (of course he did) that the women, and the others concerned, were free agents: and that he utters a protest — which so well known a man might have spared — against their peculiar institution: —

"I cannot refrain from adding to these examples of the little account commonly made of human liberty, the language of downright persecution which breaks out from the press of this country whenever it feels called on to notice the remarkable phenomenon of Mormonism. . . .

"The article of the Mormonite doctrine, which is the chief provocative to the antipathy which thus breaks through the ordinary restraints of religious tolerance, is its sanction of polygamy; which, though permitted to Mahomedans, and Hindoos, and Chinese, seems to excite unquenchable animosity when practised by persons who speak English, and profess to be a kind of Christians. No one has a deeper disapprobation than I have of this Mormon institution; both for other reasons, and because, far from being in any way countenanced by the principle of liberty, it is a direct infraction of that principle, being a mere riveting of the chains of one half of the community, and an emancipation of the other from reciprocity of obligation towards them. Still, it must be remembered that this relation is as much voluntary on the part of the woman concerned in it, and who may be deemed the sufferer by it, as is the case with any other form of the marriage institution. . . .

"I am not aware that any community has a right to force another to be civilized. So long as the sufferers by the bad law do not invoke assistance from other communities, I cannot admit that persons entirely unconnected with them ought to step in and require that a condition of things with which all who are directly interested appear to be satisfied, should be put an end to because it is a scandal to persons some thousand of miles distant, who have no part of concern in it. Let them send missionaries, if they please, to preach against it; and let them by any fair means (of which silencing the teachers is not one), oppose the progress of similar doctrines among their own people.

It has been already pointed out by me that Mill evidently selects his illustrations with a desire to use them as *à fortiori* cases, and this must be remembered in reading the above quotation. It should also be borne in mind in reading his indigant criticism of the Prohibitory Liquor Law movement. This may be summed up in the Bishop of Peterborough's declaration that he would consider a free people who drank in a more hopeful way than an enslaved people who kept sober. There is no invasion of human liberty which the theory of this movement would not justify: — that is Mr. Mill's declared opinion, and it is powerfully argued. But let it be again understood that my business now is not to support or to contest his opinions, but to help to make it a little clearer what they really were, so far as they are expressed in the essay "On Liberty."

Mr. Mill, as we have seen, and as was well-known, was a very earnest advocate for national education. What his precise opinions of Mr. Forster's measure were is not within my knowledge. We may be certain that he would have been ready

to submit to a considerable amount of theoretical inconsistency
or inconvenience, if it appeared to be the condition of a great
beenfit. But we may be certain also that he would have found
much to quarrel with, both as to principle and as to
administration, in the new law, and that we have not yet
approached his ideal of popular culture, so far as it was to be
matter of State compulsion. The following passages, from a
discussion which I greatly abbreviate, will show in his own
words, what that ideal was: —

"Were the duty of enforcing universal education once
admitted, there would be an end to the difficulties about
what the State should teach, and how it should teach, which
now convert the subject into a mere battlefield for sects and
parties. If the Government would make up its mind to
require for every child a good education, it might save itself
the trouble of providing one. It might leave to parents to
obtain the education where and how they pleased, and
content itself with helping to pay the school-frees of the
poorer classes of children, and defraying the entire school
expenses of those who have no one else to pay for them. The
objections which are urged with reason against State
education do not apply to the enforcement of education by
the State, but to the State's taking upon itself to direct that
education; which is a totally different thing. That the whole
or any large part of the education of the people should be in
State hands, I go as far as any one in deprecating. A general
State education is a mere contrivance for moulding people to
be exactly like one another, and as *the mould in which it
casts them is that which pleases the predominant power in
the Government*, whether this be a monarch, a priesthood,
an aristocracy, or *the majority of the existing generation*; in
proportion as it is efficient and successful, it establishes a
despotism over the mind, leading by natural tendency to one
over the body. If the country contains a sufficient number of
persons qualified to provide education under Government
auspices, the same persons would be able and willing to give
an equally good education on the voluntary principle.

"The instrument for enforcing the law could be no other
than public examinations extending to all children, and
beginning at an early age. To prevent the State from
exercising, through these arrangements, an improper

influence over opinion, the knowledge required for passing an examination (beyond the merely instrumental parts of knowledge, such as languages and their use) should, even in the higher classes of examinations, be confined to facts and positive science exclusively. The examinations on religion, politics, or other disputed topics, should not turn on the truth or falsehood of opinions, but on the matter of fact that such an opinion is held, on such grounds, by such authors, or schools, or churches."

This is so plain as to require no comment, but it will be noticed that the words which I have put in italics would have the effect of classifying as State education the education provided by the School Boards, in spite of the elective machinery applying to those bodies.

Whoever has read the essay "On the Subjection of Women" knows, notwithstanding the extreme caution with which it is written, how strong were Mill's opinions on the anomalies of English law in the matter of marriage. Two of the reforms which he advocated in that essay have been effected since his death. But though he sometimes carries the *suppressio veri* to a length which almost approaches the *suggestio falsi*,[3] it is clear that no object was nearer to his heart than the obtaining of greater freedom of voluntary separation for the married, and that one of his chief motives for urging liberty of remunerative vocation for women was, that if they had it they would be capable of more independent action in all that relates to men. Towards the close of the essay "On Liberty," he proceeds very quietly to discuss the subject of freedom to make or dissolve contracts, and leads up to his main point by introducing the topic of slavery. The reader does not require to think twice in order to see his hand. Any contract in which a man absolutely parts with his freedom is void in morals; and, by parity of reason, he goes on to argue that no contract in which the will is *indefinitely* bound should be permanent. He makes the final transition by quoting a dictum from Wilhelm von Humboldt: —

"The principle of freedom cannot require that a man should be free not to be free. It is not freedom to be allowed to

---

[3] See, however, Mr. John Morley's "Critical Miscellanies," second series, p. 272.

alienate his freedom. These reasons, the force of which is so conspicuous in this peculiar case, are evidently of far wider application: yet a limit is everywhere set to them by the necessities of life, which continually require that we should consent to this and the other limitation of it. The principle, however, which demands uncontrolled freedom of action in all that concerns only the agents themselves, requires that those who have become bound to one another, in things which concern no third party, should be able to release one another from the engagement; and, even without such voluntary release, there are perhaps no contracts or engagements except those that relate to money or money's worth, of which one can venture to say that there ought to be no liberty whatever of retraction. Baron Wilhelm von Humboldt, in the excellent essay from which I have already quoted, states it as his conviction that engagements which involve personal relations or services, should never be legally binding beyond a limited duration of time; and that the most important of these engagements, marriage, having the peculiarity that its objects are frustrated unless the feelings of both parties are in harmony with it, should require nothing more than the declared will of either party to dissolve it."

Mr. Mill does not appear to have been aware that Paley had expressed the same opinion of the contract *quâ* contact ("Moral and Political Philosophy." book iii., part 3, chap. vii.), but he proceeds to lay down obvious limitations to the principle, or rather what he would call necessary additions to it. For example, he remarks that there may be claims to be satisfied, with regard to children and otherwise, which must affect the *moral* freedom of either one or both of the parties to disregard the past and enact a mere naked dissolution of the contract. But he adds that the interest of the contracting parties is the main thing, and that though he has made these qualifications, they are rather necessary in order to formal completeness of discussion than for any practical reason. As I am expressing no opinion on the main questions, here or elsewhere in this paper, I may without offence add that it is a little curious that a man like Mr. Mill should have overlooked the consideration that in homes where there is miserable discord children are sure to be infinitely more injured than benefited by the society of the parents. However, the general conclusion he arrives at is that nothing can require the fulfilment of the contract "at all costs to the *reluctant* party." The italics are mine, but the force of the dictum lies in that adjective. We may conjecture that if Mr. Mill were now living and were to address himself to this subject generally, he would first of all demand that with regard to the one ground on which English law now *dissolves* the contract, the wife should be placed (as she is in Scotland) upon a footing of entire equality with the husband; secondly, that there should be liberty for the spouses to dissolve the contract by mutual agreement, under proper guarantees; and, thirdly, he would maintain that the one injury which is held in England to dissolve the contract (from the husband's side) is not in itself necessarily the worst or most fatal, and that therefore the list of causes for which one of the spouses may by compulsion get freed should be made wider. But he was, as I have remarked, a very cautious and reticent propagandist, and it is only by close watching and *reading particular passages in the light of general propositions which are locally a long way off from them*, that you get at his whole meaning. One thing, meanwhile, is clear, that Mr. Mill's "demands" in relation to this subject are not met by the state of the law and custom in England — which, on one great point, is far behind that of Scotland.

On the subject of the tendency to what Mr. Mill called Chinese uniformity, and indirect repression of individuality by the unconscious squeezing power of commonplace multitudes, there appears to be no important difference between him and Professor Max Müller. The danger is admitted — or rather the disaster is upon us like a foreseen inundation. The essay "On Liberty" is worth reading over again, if only for the sake of its prophetic passages. *If* Mr. Mill's opinions on these matters are of much value, I cannot conceive anything more mischievous in its way than even to suggest that the demands he made in the name of freedom have been even remotely complied with since he uttered them. It is not only a delusion, but to my mind an unaccountable one. I repeat that even that greater freedom of discussion of which we hear is, where it is at all real, a freedom of fluke and compromise, enjoyed on sufferance only, with persecution in the background; a freedom which involves semi-cynical winking all round; which keeps the word of promise to the ear, and breaks it to the hope.

It is not a little remarkable that Mr. Mills' "Liberty" should be so little understood in its ultimate bearings and claims, when no longer ago than 1873 Sir Fitzjames Stephen, in his book entitled "Liberty, Equality, and Fraternity," examined it with care, produced its propositions to their necessary consequences, and proved, I think successfully, in however harsh a way, that Mr. Mill's premises will not bear the weight he puts upon them.

But there is something more remarkable still. Sir Fitzjames Stephen expressly excludes all "transcendental or mystical" methods of handling the questions discussed, whether in the search for premises or otherwise. And he is right in that policy. But the curious thing is what I am now about to call attention to. There is a well-known and much beloved writer on religion, whose books are used as moral and spiritual tonics by thousands of good and thoughtful people. You take him from the shelf, as you might Milton, or Wordsworth, or any other pure strong soul whose wing of trust in God and man never flags, and you find there is no mood so low that he cannot lift you up from it; none so feeble that he cannot help you to strength. I mean Channing, who, in spite of his quasi-rationalistic classification as a Biblical critic, was admittedly a transcendentalist. Now, there is extant by Channing an essay, entitled "Remarks on the Formation of Associations to Accomplish Objects by Organized Masses of Society" — and of all essays in the world, this essay, by that gentlest of fair souls, most resembles Mr. Mill's "Liberty." Of course it is quite out of the latitude of Sir Fitzjames Stephen. It talks freely and solemnly of the reverence due to the individual soul, and maintains, in the strongest possible language, that the tendency of modern thought and action is to invert the natural or divine order of things. Society is for man, not man for society — that is the sum. "Resistance of the pressure [of society] is our only safeguard; and it is essential to virtue. . . . No man should part with his individuality. . . . *Inward* power is the end: a power which is to triumph over and control the influence of society. . . . There is no moral worth in being swept away by a crowd even towards the best objects. . . . The good, as well as the bad, may injure us, . . . through that intolerance which is a common infirmity of all good men. . . . The influences of society at present tend strongly to excess, and especially menace that individuality of character for which they can yield no adequate compensation. . . . *The propensity in our fellow-*

creatures which we have most to dread is . . . the propensity to rule, . . . to make themselves standards for other minds."

If would be difficult to frame a stronger expression of opinion than the last, and coming from a man so gentle it is very striking. The above sentences have been gathered at random from only a few pages. The general upshot of the essay is that all associations for the exercise of power over individuals should be jealously watched, and, even if their objects be good, should stand condemned if they endanger personal freedom and aim at promoting even virtue by the imposition of artificial yokes. When we remember the very numerous passages in which Channing, even in dealing with moral questions on which civilized opinion now tends to unanimity, has exhibited a similar jealousy on behalf of freedom, we may well wonder how it is that in the discussions aroused by Mr. Mill's essay, Channing's was overlooked. It is interesting to notice how he differs in the application of his principles. In spite of his passionate abhorrence of slavery, it is easy to see that he would have condemned the Civil War in America, and said, "Let us, the North, clear our own souls, but let our brethren in the South secede if they will, and act upon their own responsibility." It seems certain that he would have supported the Permissive Prohibitory Bill. But these remarks are only collateral. The main point is that Channing, who deserved the title of "Serene Highness' even more than Mill, should have been overlooked in these discussions.

Whether we agree with Mill or not in the "demands" he makes in the essay "On Liberty," I repeat that it is of the utmost consequence to shut out the idea that what he demanded has been granted. In spite of the criticism to which he has been subjected since his death, every fresh reading of his books impresses the mind anew with his moral and intellectual greatness. Quite apart from its main threads of argument (with much of which I disagree), the essay "On the Subjection of Women" contains, perhaps, more acute criticism of human nature in general than any modern book of only equal size. It is of the highest moment that we should know what such a man thought. And as his was the last voice raised for "Liberty" in this country, it cannot be well to put that essay of twenty years ago aside as a dead thing, when it is certain that were he living now he would repeat it all with added emphasis and passion more vehemently kindled.

If ever there was a time at which it behoved the friends of
freedom in this country to keep alive and well re-echoed every
worthy voice in its favour, that time is the present. For six years
out of the twenty spoken of by Professor Max Müller we have
been under the hoofs of the Tories. Now the regimen of
Toryism always was, and in the nature of things must be,
unfavourable to liberty, and the evolution of what has been
called Jingoism is only one illustration out of a thousand of the
degradation which the popular sentiment has undergone. What
the vulgar soul everywhere loves and cherishes is the sense of
power; he will cheerfully part with a portion of his own liberty
if he can only enjoy the feeling of trampling upon others. That
is the moral, or part of the moral, or our political and social
history for about one-third of the time during which we are
told the cause of freedom has been flourishing. The hoisting of
the Tory flag should be taken as a warning that the spirit of
absolutism will do the worst it can, and that a period of cynical
indifference is about to commence. Now that people have got
into their heads the idea that their pockets have suffered
through the policy they have cheered on, they begin to overhaul
the past; otherwise, the political outlook is not very hopeful.
There is little sign of a changed spirit in the people — of a
renovated political life.

A curious side-light happens to be thrown upon some of my
comments in the foregoing pages by the outcry which has
followed the proposal to make the next census include a
column for "denominational returns," as they are called. One
of the grounds on which this is objected to is that the result
would lead to more or less direct persecution. It is one thing for
Thompson, the tradesman, to be under the rose a freethinker
or a Gallio, and for Johnson and Wilson to wink and keep
silence — it is another thing for Thompson to write himself
down a sceptic or a Secularist in a column that is public. The
chances are that he will rather resort to some subterfuge; for, if
he tells the plain truth, he will lose the custom of Johnson or
the goodwill of Wilson. So much for "freedom." In a street of a
thousand adult inhabitants there will probably be eight
hundred who seldom, if ever, enter a place of worship, and
perhaps five hundred who are more or less deliberately
secularistic Gallios. But there is scarcely a man among them
who will dare to write himself down what he really is, for he
knows he will suffer for it — certainly in social position, and all

but certainly in pocket. This is not fancy; it is hard fact. Sir Fitzjames Stephen and a good many others would probably maintain that it is a desirable state of things; but it is hardly the kind of freedom that Mill wanted.

There is one more point which I cannot pass over. I have called the C. D. Acts "infamous," and they are. Now, if the Government printers had refused to give out the MS. of the Acts and Schedules to their men; if the compositors had struck rather than set up anything so utterly filthy and detestable; if policemen and surgeons had refused to exercise their powers, and had barbed their refusal with scorn and execration; if magistrates had come down from the bench rather than adjudicate in any case coming before them under the Acts; if there had been a general insurrection and refusal to pay taxes on the part of English men so long as the Acts stood upon the statute-book; and if English women had gone into sackcloth and kept it till the law was repealed — then there would be reason to believe that the spirit of liberty was not lying in a swoon of drunken luxury in the English people. But so long as, while a few helpless men and women break their hearts in silence, the majority suck their cowardly thumbs, and Commissions and Committees sit with stony faces to inquire into "the working of" these dastardly laws, let us not talk of liberty. For heaven's sake — if we believe in a heaven — let us learn to face our shame, and let us *not* ask, with placid brows, what outrages on liberty Mr. Mill would find to complain of if he were now among us.

JAMES T. MACKENZIE.

THE NINETEENTH CENTURY
Vol. 13, March 1883
[Leslie Stephen]

The Suppression of Poisonous Opinions

Mr. Froude, in his *Life of Carlyle*, incidentally sets forth a theory of toleration. Cromwell, he tells us, held Romanism to be 'morally poisonous;' therefore Cromwell did not tolerate. We have decided that it is no longer poisonous; therefore we do tolerate. Cromwell's intolerance implied an intense 'hatred of evil in its concrete form;' our tolerance need not imply any deficiency in that respect, but merely a difference of opinion as to facts. Upon this showing, then, we are justified in extirpating, by fire and sword, any doctrine if only we are sincerely convinced that it is 'morally poisonous.' I do not take this as a full account either of Carlyle's theory, or of Mr. Froude's. I quote it merely as a pointed statement of a doctrine which in some ways would appear to follow more directly from the utilitarianism which Carlyle detested. The argument is simple. A 'poisonous opinion' is one which causes a balance of evil. The existence of such opinions is admitted. Nor, again, is it denied that under certain conditions an opinion may be suppressed by persecution. The persecution, then, of a poisonous opinion must do some good, and must produce a balance of good if the evil effects of the opinion suppressed exceed the various evils due to the persecution. But that which causes a balance of good is right according to utilitarians; and therefore persecution may sometimes be right. If you have to suppress a trifling error at the cost of much suffering, you are acting wrongly, as it would be wrong to cure a scratch by cutting off a finger. But it may be right to suppress a poisonous opinion when the evil of the opinion is measured by the corruption of a whole social order, and the evil of the persecution by the death, say of twelve apostles. In such a case it is expedient, and therefore right, that one man or a dozen should perish for the good of the people.

Mill attacked the applicability, though not the first principle, of this reasoning in the most forcible part of his *Liberty*. He argues in substance that the collateral evils due to persecution are always, or almost always, excessive. He could not, as a utilitarian, deduce toleration from some absolute *à priori* principle. But by pointing out evil consequences generally overlooked, he could strengthen the general presumption against its utility in any particular case. His utilitarian opponents may still dispute the sufficiency of his reasoning. They urge, in substance, that the presumption is not strong enough to justify an absolute rule. Granting that there is a presumption against persecution generally, and that all the evils pointed out by Mill should be taken into account, yet, they say, it is still a question of expediency. We must be guided in each particular case by a careful balance of the good and evil, and must admit this general presumption only for what it is worth: as a guiding rule in doubtful cases, or where we do not know enough to balance consequences satisfactorily, but not as possessing sufficient authority to override a clear conclusion in the opposite sense. Practically, we may assume, the difference comes to very little. Mill's opponents might often be as tolerant as himself. He says, indeed, that toleration is the universal rule; yet even he might admit that, as in other moral problems, a casuist might devise circumstances under which it would cease to be absolute. On the other hand, his opponents, though holding in theory that each case has to be judged on its merits, would, in fact, agree that no case ever occurs at the present time in which the balance is not in favour of toleration. The discussion, therefore, has less practical application than one might at first sight suppose. One man says, 'Toleration is always right, but at times this, like other moral rules, may be suspended.' The other, 'It is not a question of right or wrong, but of expediency: but, on the other hand, in almost every conceivable case, toleration is clearly expedient.' It is only, therefore, as illustrating an interesting ethical problem — interesting, that is to people capable of feeling an interest in such gratuitous logic-chopping — that I would consider the problem.

I remark, therefore, in the first place, that one argument of considerable importance scarcely receives sufficient emphasis from Mill. The objection taken by the ordinary common sense of mankind to persecution is very often that the doctrines expressed are false. Toleration, beyond all doubt, has been advanced by scepticism. It is clearly both inexpedient and wrong to burn people for not professing belief in mischievous lies or even in harmless errors. Mill extends the argument to cases where power and truth are on the same side; but he scarcely brings out what may be called the specifically moral objection. I may hold that Romanism is false and even 'poisonous.' I may still admit that a sincere Romanist is not only justified in believing — for, so far as his belief is logical, he cannot help believing — but also that he is morally bound to avow his belief. He is in the position of a man who is sincerely convinced that a food which I hold to be poisonous is wholesome, or, rather, an indispensable medicine. If he thinks so, it is clearly his duty to let his opinion be known. A man holds that prussic acid will cure when it really kills. He is mistaken, but surely he is bound to impart so important a truth to his fellows. So long, indeed, as men held that it was not only foolish but wicked to hold other religious opinions than their own, this argument did not apply. But I need not argue that sincere errors are in themselves innocent. The most virtuous of men will be a Calvinist in Scotland, a Catholic in Spain, and a Mohammedan in Turkey. And so far as this possibility is admitted, and as the contrary conviction spreads — namely that the leaders of heresies are generally virtuous, because it requires virtue to uphold an unpopular opinion — the dilemma becomes pressing. The persecutor, as a rule, is punishing the virtuous for virtuous conduct, and, moreover, for conduct which he admits to be virtuous. For this is not one of those cases with which casuists sometimes puzzle themselves. The fact that a man thinks himself acting rightly, or is wicked on principle, is not a sufficient defence against legal punishment. If a man is a Thug, the government is not the less bound to hang him because he thinks murder right. A thief must be punished, though he objects to property in general; and a man who deserts his wife, though he disapproves of marriage. A man is in such cases punished for an action which the ruler holds to be immoral. But the persecutor has to punish a man precisely for discharging a duty admitted even by the persecutor to be a duty, and a duty of the highest obligation. If the duty of truthfulness be admitted, I am bound not to express belief in a creed which I hold to be false. If benevolence be a duty, I am bound to tell my neighbour how he can avoid hell-fire. The dilemma thus brought about — the necessity of crushing conscience by law — will be admitted to be an evil, though it may be an inevitable evil. The social tie carries with it the necessity of sometimes forcing particular people to do that which both they and we admit to be wrong. But the scandal so caused is one main cause of the abhorrence felt for the persecutor, and the sympathy for his victims. The ordinary statement of the impolicy of making men martyrs testifies to the general force of the impression. And it must, in fact, be taken into account upon any method of calculation, in so far, at least, as the revulsion of feeling excited by persecution tells against the efficacy of the method adopted. The persecutor, that is, must clearly remember that by burning a man for his honesty, he is inevitably exciting the disgust of all who care for honesty, even though they do not prize it more than orthodoxy. It must be in all cases a great, even if a necessary, evil, that the law should outrage the conscience of its subjects. And whatever conclusion may be reached, it is desirable to consider how far and on what principles the acceptance of this dilemma can be regarded as unavoidable.

The utilitarian can, of course, give a consistent reply. The ultimate criterion, he says, of virtue is utility. Sincerity is a virtue because it is obviously useful to mankind. That men should be able to trust each other is a first condition of the mutual assistance upon which happiness depends. But here is a case in which we — that is, the rulers — are convinced that sincerity does harm. We shall be illogical if we allow the general rule derived from particular cases to govern us in the case where it plainly does not apply. We admit all the evils alleged: the suffering of a sincere man because of his sincerity, the encouragement to hypocrisy, the demoralisation of those whose lips are closed; but, after admitting all this, we still see so clearly the mischief which will follow from the spread of the opinions we question, that we pronounce it to exceed all the other admitted mischief, and are therefore still bound to persecute. Turn it and twist it as you will, the question still comes to this: Which way does the balance of happiness incline? Is it better that virtuous Romanists should go to the stake and Romanism be so stamped out, or that so poisonous an opinion be allowed to spread? We fully admit all the evils which you have noted, and willingly put them in the balance; but we must weigh them against the evils which will follow from the toleration, and our action must be determined by a final comparison.

Undoubtedly the argument has great apparent strength. It fixes the issues which are generally taken: and when helped by the assumption that belief in a creed may determine a man's happiness for all eternity, and that men or some body of men may possess infallibility, it makes a very imposing show. Nor do I wish to dispute the fundamental principle; that is, the principle that utility is in some sense to be the final criterion of morality. I think, however, that here, as in other cases, a thoroughgoing application of that criterion will lead us to a different conclusion from that which results from a first inspection. And, in order to show this, I must try to point out certain tacit assumptions made in the application of this principle to the facts. Granting that we must test persecution by its effects upon human happiness, I must add that we cannot fairly measure these effects without looking a little more closely into the conditions under which they are necessarily applied. The argument starts from the generalisation of something like a truism. The alleged fact is simply this, that pain, threatened or inflicted, will stop a man's mouth. It can hardly convert him, but it will prevent him from converting others. I do not dispute the statement: I feel, for my part, that, so far as I am able to form an opinion as to my own conduct, there is no creed which I would not avow or renounce rather than be burnt alive. I think that I might probably prefer distant damnation to immediate martyrdom. Many men, happily for the race, have been more heroic; but burning stopped even their mouths, and so far suppressed their influence. We have, however, to modify this statement before we can apply it to any serious purpose. We have to show, that is, that we not only suppress the individual but eradicate the opinion from society; and this raises two questions. There is a difficulty in catching the opinion which is to be suppressed, and there is a difficulty about arranging the machinery through which the necessary force is to be supplied. When we examine the conditions of success in the enterprise, it may turn out that it is impossible in many cases, and possible in any case only at the cost of evils which would more than counterbalance any possible benefit. Only by such an investigation can we really measure the total effect of persecution, and it will, I think, appear to be still more far-reaching and disastrous than is implied even by Mill's cogent reasoning.

Mill, in fact, conducts the argument as though he made an assumption (for I will not say that he actually made it) which appears to me at least to be curiously unreal. His reasoning would be sometimes more to the purpose if we could suppose an opinion to be a sort of definite object, a tangible thing like the germ of a disease, existing in a particular mind, as the germ in a particular body, and therefore capable of being laid hold of and suppressed by burning the person to whom it belongs, as the germ is suppressed by being dipped in boiling water. This corresponds to what one may call the 'happy thought' doctrine of scientific discovery. Popular writers used sometimes to tell the story of Newton's great discovery as though Newton one day saw an apple fall, and exclaimed 'Ah! an apple is a kind of moon!' This remark had occurred to no one else, and might never have struck anybody again. If, therefore, you had caught Newton on the spot and stamped him out, the discovery of gravitation might have been permanently suppressed. Mill would, of course, have perceived the absurdity of such a statement as clearly as any one; yet he seems to make a very similar assumption in his *Liberty*. It is, he is arguing, a 'piece of idle sentimentality' that truth has any intrinsic power of prevailing against persecution. 'The real advantage which truth has consists in this, that when an opinion is true it may be extinguished once, twice, or many times, but in the course of ages there will generally be found persons to rediscover it'; and when, he adds it is rediscovered in a propitious age, it may 'make such head' as to resist later attempts at suppression. Surely this is a most inadequate account of the strength of truth. The advantage dependent upon a chance of rediscovery is equally possessed by error; old superstitions are just as much given to reappearance as old truths. Every one who has examined stupid lads knows very well that the blunders which they make are just as uniform as the truths which they perceive. Given minds at a certain stage, and exposed to certain external conditions, we can predict the illusions which will be generated. So to quote the familiar instances: the mass of mankind still believes that the sun goes round the earth, and is convinced that a moving body will stop of itself, independently of external resistance. The advantage of truth is surely put in the other fact, that it can, as Mill says, 'make head.' It gathers strength by existing; it gathers strength, that is, because it can be verified and tested, and every fresh test confirms the belief, and it gathers strength again in so far as it becomes part of a general system of truths, each of which confirms, elucidates, and corroborates the others, and which together form the organised mass of accepted knowledge which we call science. So far as we are possessed of anything that can be called scientific knowledge, we have not to deal with a list of separate assertions, each of which has to be judged upon its own merits, and each of which may stand or fall independently of all the others: but with a system of interdependent truths, some of which are supported by irresistible weight of evidence, whilst the remainder are so inextricably intertwined with the central core of truth that they cannot be separately rejected. To talk, therefore, of suppressing an opinion as if it were not part of a single growth, but a separable item in a chaotic aggregate of distinguishable theories, is to overlook the most essential condition of bringing any influence to bear upon opinion generally.

Consider, first, the case of any scientific theory. Newton's great achievement was supposed to lead to questionable theological inferences; as, indeed, whatever may be the logical inferences, there can be no doubt that it was fatal to the mythological imagery in which the earth appeared as the centre of the universe. Suppose, then, that it has been decided that the opinion was poisonous, and that anybody who maintained that the earth went round the sun should be burnt! Had such a system been carried out, what must have happened? If we suppose it to be compatible with the continued progress of astronomical and physical inquiries, this particular conclusion might still be ostensibly conceded. Kepler's discoveries, and all the astronomical observations assumed by Newton, might have been allowed to be promulgated, as affording convenient means of calculation, and Newton's physical theories might have been let pass as interesting surmises in speculation, or admitted as applicable to other cases. It might still be asserted that, so far as the solar system was concerned, the doctrines possessed no 'objective truth.' Something of the kind was, I believe, actually attempted; it needs, however, no argument to show that such a persecution would be childish, and would be virtually giving over the key of the position to the antagonist with some feeble ostensible stipulation that he should not openly occupy one dependent outwork. The truth would not have been suppressed, but the open avowal of the truth. The only other alternative, would have been to suppress physical theories and astronomical observation altogether, in order to avoid the deduction of the offensive corollary. In such a case, then, the only choice, by the very nature of the case, is not between permitting or suppressing 'an opinion,' but between permitting or suppressing scientific inquiry in general. There are, no doubt, bigots and stupid people enough to be ready to suppress speculation at large; but they would find it hard to induce people to suppress things of obvious utility; they cannot suppress the study of astronomy for purposes of navigation, and yet when the truth has been acquired for this end its application to others follows by a spontaneous and irresistible process. The victory is won, and the only question is whether the conqueror shall march in openly or in a mask.

This familiar example may illustrate the extreme difficulty of catching, isolating, and suppressing so subtle an essence as an opinion. Stop all thought, and of course you can annihilate the particular doctrine which it generates. But the price to pay is a heavy one, and clearly not to be measured by the particular sets of consequences which result from the specified dogma. The same principle is everywhere operative. The greatest shock lately received by the conservative theologians has been due to the spread of Darwinian theories. How, granting that rulers and priests had at their disposal any amount of persecuting power, would they have proposed to suppress those theories? They object to the belief that men have grown out of monkeys. Would they, then, allow men to hold that the horse and ass have a common ancestor? or to question the permanency of genera and species of plants? Would they prohibit Mr. Darwin's investigations into the various breeds of pigeons, or object to his exposition of the way in which a multiplication of cats might be unfavourable to the fertilisation of clover? The principle shows itself in the most trifling cases; once established there, it spread by inevitable contagion to others; the conclusion is obvious to all men, whether tacitly insinuated or openly drawn. To suppress it you must get rid of the primitive germ. When once it has begun to spread, no political nets or traps can catch so subtle an element. It would be as idle to attempt to guard against it, as to say that smallpox may rage as it pleases everywhere else, but you will keep it out of Pall Mall by a cordon of policemen to stop people with an actual eruption. The philosophy of a people is the central core of thought, which is affected by every change taking place on the remotest confines of the organism. It is sensitive to every change in every department of inquiry. Every new principle discovered anywhere has to find its place in the central truths; and unless you are prepared to superintend and therefore to stifle thought in general, you may as well let it alone altogether. Superintendence means stifling. That is not the less true, even if the doctrine suppressed be erroneous. Assuming that Darwinianism is wrong, or as far as you please from being absolutely true, yet its spread proves conclusively that it represents a necessary stage of progress. We may have to pass beyond it; but in any case we have to pass through it. It represents that attitude of mind and method of combining observations which is required under existing conditions. It may enable us to rise to a point from which we shall see its inadequacy. But even its antagonists admit the necessity of working provisionally, at least, from this assumption, and seeing what can be made of it; and would admit, therefore, that a forcible suppression, if so wild an hypothesis can be entertained, would be equivalent to the suppression not of this or that theory, but of thought.

The conclusion is, briefly, that, so far as scientific opinion is concerned, you have to choose between tolerating error and suppressing all intellectual activity. If this be admitted in the case of what we call 'scientific' knowledge, the dilemma presents itself everywhere. We are becoming daily more fully aware of the unity of knowledge; of the impossibility of preserving, isolating, and impounding particular bits of truth, or protecting orthodoxy by the most elaborate quarantine.It is idle to speak of a separation between the spheres of science and theology, as though the contents of the two were entirely separate. There is, doubtless, much misconception as to the nature of the relation; false inferences are frequently made by hasty thinkers; but the difference, whatever it may be, is not such as divides two independent series of observations, but such that every important change in one region has a necessary and immediate reaction on the other. If we accept the principle of evolution — whether we take the Darwinian version or any other as our guide — as applied to the history of human belief, we more and more realise the undeniable facts that the history must be considered as a whole; that the evolution, however it takes place, has to follow certain lines defined by the successive stages of intellectual development; that it consists of a series of gradual approximations, each involving positive errors, or at least provisional assumptions accepted for the moment as definitive truths; and that every widely spread belief, whether accurate or erroneous, has its place in the process, as representing at least the illusions which necessarily present themselves to minds at a given pint of the ascending scale. The whole process may be, and, of course, frequently has been, arrested. But, if it is to take place at all, it is impossible to proscribe particular conclusions beforehand. The conclusions forbidden may, of course, be such as would never have been reached, even if not forbidden. In that case the persecution would be useless. But if they are such as would commend themselves to masses of men but for the prohibition, it follows that they are necessary 'moments' in the evolution of thought, and therefore can only be suppressed by suppressing that evolution.

The vagueness of the argument stated in these general terms is no bar to its value in considering more special cases. It suggests, in the first place, an extension of one of Mill's arguments which has been most frequently criticised. He tries to prove this advantage of persecution by a rather exaggerated estimate of the value of contradiction. 'Even admitted truths,' he says, 'are apt to lose their interest for us unless stimulated by collision with the contradictory error.' It is, of course, obvious to reply that we believe in Euclid or in the ordinary principles of conduct, though nobody ever denies that two sides of a triangle are greater than the third, or doubts that water quenches thirst. An opinion, I should say, gains vividness rather from constant application to conduct than from habitual opposition. But, as far as Mill's argument has to do with toleration, it seems to be cogent, and to derive its strength from the principle I am defending. Many opinions, if ever entertained, would doubtless die out by inherent weakness. It would be idle to punish men for maintaining that two and two make five, because the opinion would never survive a practical application. The prohibition of a palpably absurd theory would be a waste of force, and might possibly suggest to a few eccentric people that there must, after all, be something to say for the absurdity, and therefore, if for no other reason, it is undesirable. But it was, of course, not of such opinions that

Mill was thinking. The only opinions which any one would seriously desire to frustrate are plausible opinions; opinions, that is, which would flourish but for persecution; and every persecutor justifies himself by showing, to his own satisfaction, that his intervention is needed. He rejects the argument by which Gamaliel defended the first plea for toleration. He holds that opinions, though coming from God, require human defence. He thinks that even the devil's creed would flourish but for a stake, and this assumption is the sole justification of the stake. That is to say, persecution is always defended, and can only be defended, on the ground that the persecuted opinion is highly plausible, and the same plausibility of an opinion is a strong presumption that is an essential part of the whole evolution. Even if it be wrong, it must represent the way in which a large number of people will think, if they think at all. It corresponds to one aspect, though an incomplete or illusory aspect, of the facts. If there be no reason there must be some general cause of the error; a cause which, in the supposed case, must be the prevalence of some erroneous or imperfect belief in the minds of many people. The predisposing cause will presumably remain even if this expression of opinion be silenced. And, in all such cases, the effect of suppression will be prejudicial to the vigour even of the true belief. The causes, whatever they be, which obstruct its acceptance will operate in a covert form. Real examination becomes impossible when the side which is not convicted is not allowed to have its reasons for doubt tested; and we reach the dilemma just stated. That is to say, if thought is not suppressed, the error will find its way to the surface through some subterranean channels; whilst, if thought is suppressed, the truth and all speculative truth will of course be enfeebled with the general enfeeblement of the intellect. To remedy a morbid growth, you have applied a ligature which can only succeed by arresting circulation and bringing on the mortification of the limb. To treat intellectual error in this fashion must always be to fall into the practice of quackery, and suppress a symptom instead of attacking the source of the evil.

The assertion is, apparently at least, opposed to another doctrine in which Mill agrees with some of his antagonists. He says, as we have seen, that a belief in the natural prevalence of truth is a piece of idle sentimentality: it is a 'pleasant falsehood' to say that truth always triumphs; 'history teems with instances

of successful persecution;' and he confirms this by such cases as
the failure of the Reformers in Spain, Italy, and Flanders, and
of the various attempts which preceded Luther's successful
revolt. Arguments beginning 'all history shows' are, I will
venture to say, always sophistical. The most superficial
knowledge is sufficient to show that, in this case at least, the
conclusion is not demonstrated. To prove that persecution
'succeeded' in suppressing truth, you must prove that without
persecution truth would have prevailed. The argument from
the Reformation must surely in Mill be an *argumentum ad
hominem*. He did not hold that Luther or Knox or the Lollards
preached the whole truth; hardly, even, that they were nearer
the truth than Ignatius or St. Bernard. And the point is
important. For when it is said that the Reformation was
suppressed in Italy and Spain by persecution, we ask at once
whether there is the slightest reason to suppose that, if those
countries had been as free as England at the present day, they
would have become Protestant? Protestantism had its day of
vitality, and in some places it is still vigorous; but with all the
liberty of conscience of modern Italy, the most enthusiastic
Protestant scarcely expects its conversion before the
millennium. If, when there is a fair field and no favour,
Protestant stands still, why should we suppose that it would
once have advanced? Macaulay, in a famous article, insisted
upon the singular arrest of the Protestant impulse. The
boundaries between Protestantism are still drawn upon the
lines fixed by the first great convulsion. It is at least as plausible
to attribute this to the internal decay of Protestantism as to the
external barriers raised by persecution. In the seventeenth
century philosophical intellects had already passed beyond the
temporary compromise which satisfied Luther and his contemporaries. Protestantism, so far as it meant a speculative
movement, was not the name of a single principle or a coherent
system of opinion, but of a mass of inconsistent theories
approximating more or less consciously to pure deism or
'naturalism.' Victories over Romanism were not really won by
the creed of Calvin and Knox, but by the doctrines of Hobbes
and Spinoza. Otherwise, we may well believe the Protestant
creed would have spread more rapidly instead of ceasing to
spread at all precisely when persecution became less vigorous.
When we look more closely at the facts, the assumption really
made shows its true nature. Persecution might strike down any

nascent Protestantism in Spain; but it can hardly be said that it created the very zeal which it manifested. If no persecution had been possible, the enthusiasm of Loyola and his successors might (even if I may not say, would) have burnt all the more brightly. And if the orthodox had been forbidden to strike a foul blow, they might have been equally successful when confined to legitimate methods. The reasoning, in fact, is simple. Protestantism died out when persecution flourished. But persecution flourished when zeal was intense. It is impossible, then, to argue that the extinction of heresy was due to the special fact of the persecution in order to account for the fact that it did not spread in the regions where faith was strongest. In any case, if we assume, as we must assume, that the old faith was congenial to a vast number of minds, we might be sure that it would triumph where it had the most numerous and zealous followers. Under the conditions of the times, that triumph of course implied persecution; but it is an inversion of all logic to put this collateral effect as the cause of the very state of mind which alone could make it possible. So, again, Protestantism died out in France (which Mill does not mention) and survived in England; and in England, says Mill, the death of Elizabeth or the life of Mary would 'most likely' have caused its extirpation. Possibly, for it is difficult to argue 'might have beens.' But it is equally possible that the English indifference which made the country pliable in the hands of its rulers would have prevented any effective persecution, and the ineffectual persecution have led only to a more thoroughgoing revolution when the Puritan party had accumulated a greater stock of grievances. If, again, Protestantism had been really congenial to the French people, is it not at least probable that it would have gathered sufficient strength in the seventeenth century — whatever the disadvantages under which it actually laboured — to make a subsequent revival of vigorous per-secution impossible? The ultimate condition of success lay, partly at any rate, in the complex conditions, other than the direct action of rulers, which predisposed one society to the Catholic and others to the Protestant doctrine; and if we are not entitled to assume that this was the ultimate and determining condition of the final division, we are certainly not entitled to seek for it in the persecution which is, in any land, a product of a spiritual force capable of acting in countless other ways.

Once more we come across that 'happy thought' doctrine which was natural to the old method of writing history. Catholics were once content to trace the English Reformation to the wickedness of Henry the Eighth or Elizabeth; Protestants to the sudden inspiration of this or that reformer. Without attempting to argue the general question of the importance of great religious leaders, this as least is evident, that the appropriate medium is as necessary as the immediate stimulus. There were bad men before Henry the Eighth, and daring thinkers and reformers before Luther. The Church could resist plunder or reform whilst it possessed sufficient vital force; and the ultimate condition of that force was that its creeds and its worship satisfied the strongest religious aspirations of mankind. Luther himself at an earlier period would have been a St. Bernard. Its weakness and the success of assailants, good or bad, was due, as no one will now deny, to the morbid condition into which it had fallen, from causes which could only be fully set forth by the profoundest and most painstaking investigation. If this be granted, it follows that Protestantism, whether a wholesome or a pernicious movement, meant the operation of certain widely-spread and deeply-seated causes rendering some catastrophe inevitable. To apply an effective remedy it would have been necessary to remove the causes, to restore the old institutions in working order, and to renew the vitality of the faiths upon which its vigour essentially depended. So far as the opponents of reform relied upon persecution they were driving the disease inwards instead of applying an effectual remedy. Such observations — too commonplace to be worth more than a brief indication — must be indicated in order to justify the obvious limitations to Mill's estimate of the efficacy of persecution. In the first place, it is not proved that it was properly 'efficacious' at all; that is, that the limits of the creeds would not have been approximately the same had no persecution been allowed. Secondly, if efficacious, it was efficacious at a cost at which the immediate suffering of the martyrs is an absurdly inadequate measure. In Spain, Protestantism was stamped out when it might have died a natural death, at the price of general intellectual atrophy. Had the persecutors known that the system from which persecution resulted was also a system under which their country should decline from the highest to the most insignificant position, their zeal might have been cooled. In France, again, if Protestantism was suppressed by the State, Catholics of to-day may reckon the cost. Thought, being (upon that hypothesis) forced into a different mode of expressing dissent, has not only brought about the triumph of unbelief, but the production of a type of infidelity not only speculatively hostile to Catholicism, but animated by a bitter hatred which even the most anti-Catholic of reasoners may regret. I am unable to decide the problem whether it is worth while to save a few souls at the moment with the result of ultimately driving a whole nation to perdition; but it is one which even those who rely upon the hell-fire argument may consider worth notice. And if, in England, we have escaped some of these mischiefs, we may ask how much good we have done by an ineffectual persecution of Catholics in Ireland — a point upon which it is needless to insist, because every one admits the folly of ineffectual persecution.

The facts so considered seem to fit best with the doctrine which I am advocating. Persecution may be effective at the cost of strangling all intellectual advance; it may be successful for a time in enforcing hypocrisy, or, in other words, taking the surest means of producing a dry-rot of the system defended; or, finally, it may be ineffectual in securing its avowed object, but singularly efficacious in producing bitter antipathy and accumulating undying ill-will between hostile sections of society. When, therefore, the argument is stated as though all the evils to be put in the balance against persecution were the pain of the immediate sufferers and the terror of sympathisers, I should say that the merest outside of the case has really been touched. Once other consideration is enough for this part of the question. Persecution may discourage unbelief; but it cannot be maintained that it has the least direct tendency to increase belief. Positively it must fail, whatever it may do negatively. The decay of a religion means a decline of 'vital faith' — of a vivid realisation of the formulæ verbally accepted. That is the true danger in the eyes of believers; and, if it be widely spread, no burning of heretics can tend to diminish it. People do not believe more vigorously because believers in a different creed are burnt. They only become more cowardly in all their opinions; and some other remedy of a totally different nature can alone be efficacious. You can prevent people from worshipping another God, but you cannot make them more zealous about their own. And perhaps a lukewarm believer is more likely to be damned, certainly he is not less likely to be mischievous, than a vigorous heretic.

To complete the argument, however, or rather the outline of the argument, it would be necessary to follow out another set of considerations. Granting that you can suppress your heresy by persecution enough, we have to ask how you can get persecution enough. Persecution which does not suppress is a folly as well as a crime. To irritate without injuring is mischievous upon all hypotheses. In that case, if not in others, even cynics allow that the blood of the martyrs is the seed of the Church. The danger of advertising your opponent is pretty well understood by this time; and popular riots, or a petty bit of municipal despotism, is the very thing desirable for the Salvation Army. It is agreed, then, that the weapon is one to be used solely on condition that it is applied with sufficient stringency. Now, if we ask further how this is to obtained, and especially if we ask that question in the light of the preceding inquiry, we shall arrive at a conclusion difficult to state in adequate terms. It may be possible to stamp out what we may call a particular opinion. The experiment at least has often been tried, though I do not know that it has often succeeded. When it was criminal to speak of a king's vices, the opinion entertained about particular kings was hardly more flattering, though flatterers alone could speak openly, than it is now. But to suppress so vague and penetrating a thing as a new religious opinion is a very different and a very serious matter. The change may not be the less efficacious because it is not overt. Nothing, for example, could be easier than to advocate the most infidel opinions in the language of perfect orthodoxy. The belief in God is generally taken to be a cardinal article of faith. But the words may be made to cover any state of mind. Spinoza and Hobbes both professed to believe in a God who, to their opponents, is no God at all. The quaint identification of 'deist' with 'atheist,' by orthodox writers, is an illustration of the possible divergence of meaning under unity of phrase. One set of theologians hold to the conception of a Being who will help a pious leader to win a battle if a proper request be made. Another set, equally sincere and devout, regard any such doctrine as presumptuous and profane. Briefly, what is common to all who use the word, is a substance known only by attributes which are susceptible of indefinite variation. And what is true of this is true of all articles of faith. I will be a

believer in any theological dogma to-morrow, if you will agree
that I shall define the words precisely as I please; nor do I think
that I should often have to strain them beyond very respectable
precedents in order to cover downright positivism. How is this
difficulty to be met? how is a nominal belief in Christianity to
be guarded from melting away without any change of
phraseology into some vague pantheism or agnosticism, or, in
the other direction, to a degrading anthropomorphism? A mere
chain of words is too easily borne to be cared for by anybody.
You may crush a downright Tom Paine; but how are you to
restrain your wily latitudinarian, who will swallow any
formula as if he liked it? Obviously, the only reply can be that
you must give discretionary powers to your Inquisition. It must
be empowered to judge of tendencies as well as of definite
opinions; to cross-examine the freethinker, and bring his
heresy to open light; to fashion new tests when the old ones
break down, and to resist the very first approaches of the
insidious enemy who would rationalise and extenuate. And,
further, as I have said, the same authority must lay his grasp,
not only on theologians and philosophers, but upon every
department of thought by which they are influenced; that is to
say, upon speculation in general. Without this the substance
may all slip away, and leave you with nothing but an empty
shell of merely formal assertion. The task is of course
practicable in proportion to the rarity of intellectual activity.In
ages when speculation was only possible for a rare philosopher
here and there, it might be easy to make the place too hot to
hold him, even if he escaped open collision with authority. But
in any social state approaching at all to the present, the
magnitude of the task is obvious beyond all need of
explanation.

This suggests a final conclusion. No serious politician
assumes off-hand that a law will execute itself. It may be true
that drunkenness and heresy would expire together if every
drunkard and heretic could be hanged. But before proposing a
law founded upon that opinion, the legislator has to ask, not
only whether it would be effective if applied, but whether it
could be applied. What are the conditions of efficiency of law
itself? Opponents of toleration seem to pass over this as
irrelevant. If heretics were bearable, heresy would die out.
Suppose that granted, how does it apply? The question as to
the possibility of carrying out a law is as important as any other

question about it. The Legislature is omnipotent in the sense that whatever it declares to be a law is a law; for that is the meaning of a law; but it is as far as possible from omnipotence in the sense of being able to impose any rule in practice. For anything to be effective persecution, you require your Inquisition — a body endowed with such authority as to be able not merely to proscribe a given dogma, but all the various disguises which it may assume; and to suppress the very germs of the doctrines by which the whole of a creed may be sapped without ostensible assaults upon its specific statements; to silence, not only the conscious heretic, but the most dangerous reasoner who is unintentionally furthering heretical opinions; to extend its dominion over the whole field of intellectual activity, and so stamp out, not this or that objectionable statement, but to arrest those changes in the very constituent principles of reasoning, which, if they occur, bring with them the necessity of correlative changes in particular opinions, and which can only be hindered from occurring by arresting the development of thought itself. When faith in the supernatural is decaying, it is idle to enforce internal homage to this or that idol. The special symptom is the result of a constitutional change which such measures have no tendency to remedy. How, then, is an administrative machinery equal to such purposes to be contrived, or the necessary force supplied for its effective working? Obviously it implies such an all-embracing and penetrating despotism as can hardly be paralleled in history; a blind spirit of loyalty which will accept and carry out the decisions of the political rulers, and that in the face of the various influences which, by the hypothesis, are bringing about an intellectual change, and presumably affecting the rulers as well as their subjects. And even so much can only be reached by limiting or asphyxiating the intellectual progress, with all which it implies. The argument, it must be added, applies to the case of erroneous, as well as of sound, opinions. That is to say, it is in all cases idle to attack the error unless you can remove the predisposing cause. I may hold, as in fact I do hold, that what is called the religious reaction of recent times involves the growth of many fallacies, and that it is far more superficial than is generally asserted. But, whatever its origin, it has its causes. So far as they are not to be found in the purely intellectual sphere, they must be sought in social conditions, or in the existence of certain emotional needs not yet provided for by the newer philosophy. To try to suppress such movements forcibly, if any such enterprise could be seriously proposed, would be idiotic. However strong our conviction of intellectual error, we must be content to have error as long as we have fools. For folly, education in the widest sense is the sole, though singularly imperfect, remedy; and education in that sense means the stimulation of all kinds of intellectual energy. The other causes can only be removed by thorough social reforms, and the fuller elaboration of a satisfactory philosophy. Persecution, were such a thing really conceivable, could at most drive the mischief to take other forms, and would remove one of the most potent stimulants to the more satisfactory variety of regenerating activity.

[April 1883]

(CONCLUDED.)

My reply to the question, Why do you not extirpate poisonous opinions by force? is briefly the old one — Because I object to quack remedies: to remedies in this case which can at most secure a negative result at the cost of arresting the patient's growth. When I come to the strictly ethical problem, Is persecution wicked, and, if so, why? I must answer rather more fully. All that I have said is a simple repetition of familiar and obvious arguments. Not only must Mill, whom I have criticised in particular points, have recognised all the alleged evils in a general way, but I am certain that others less favourable to toleration would admit them in any given case. If, that is, a systematic attack upon any opinion, or upon general freedom of thought, were proposed, every one would admit the futility of a partial persecution, and the impossibility of an effectual one. It is only the form into which the general argument is cast, that perplexes the general theory. It is so plain that a special utterance may be stopped by a sufficient penalty; and again, it seems so easy to assume that a dogma is a kind of entity with a particular and definable set of consequences adhering to it, that reasoners overlook the unreality which intrudes in the course of their generalisations. They neglect what according to me is an essential part of the case — all the secondary implications, that is, of an effectual persecution; the necessity of arresting a mental phase as well as a particular error, and of altering the whole political and social organisation in order to provide an effectual censorship. If these necessities are more or less recognised, they are thrust out of the argument by a simple device. The impossibility of organising an effectual persecution now is admitted; but then it is said that this is a proof of modern effeminacy — sentimentalism, or anarchy, or some other objectionable peculiarity. This is virtually to say that, though toleration must be admitted as a transitional phase, it implies a weakness, not strength; and, in brief, that the advocate of persecution would prefer a totally different social state, namely, such a one as combines all the requisites for an adequate regulation of opinion. Persecution is wrong, here and now, for you and me, because our teeth are drawn, and we can only mumble without biting; but we will hope that our teeth may grow again. The admission, in whatever terms it may be made, is perhaps enough for us. Virtually it is an admission that persecution cannot be justified unless certain conditions are realised which are not now realisable; and this admission is not less important because made in terms calculated to extenuate the importance and the permanence of these conditions. From my point of view, on the other hand, the circumstances thus treated as removable and trifling accidents, are really of the very essence of the case, and it is only by taking them into account that we can give a satisfactory theory of toleration. Toleration presupposes a certain stage of development, moral and intellectual. In the ruder social order, toleration is out of the question for familiar reasons. The rudimentary Church and State are so identified that the kingly power has the spiritual sanctity, and the priest can wield the secular arm. Heresy is a kind of rebellion, and the gods cannot be renounced without an attack upon political authority. Intellectual activity is confined to a small class, and opinions change by an imperceptible and unconscious process. Wherever such a condition is actually in existence, controversy can only be carried on by the sword. A change of faith is not caused by argument, but is part of the process by which a more powerful race conquers or extirpates its neighbours. The higher belief has a better chance, perhaps, so far as it is characteristic of a superior race, but owes little to its logical or philosophical merits. And, in such a state of things, toleration is hardly to be called a virtue, because it is an impossibility. If the equilibrium between sects, as between races, depends upon the sword, the propagator or the defender of the faith must use the sword as the essential condition of his success. If individuals perceive that toleration is desirable, they perceive also that it can only be achieved through an elevation of the whole race to a higher social condition. It remains as an unattainable ideal, dimly foreshadowed in some higher minds.

In the more advanced stage, with which we have to do, the state of things is altered. Church and State are no longer identified; a society has a political apparatus discharging one set of functions, and an ecclesiastical apparatus (or more than one) which discharges another set. Some such distinction exists as a plain matter of fact. There remains, indeed, the perplexed controversy as to its ultimate nature, and the degree in which it can be maintained. The priest is a different person from the ruler, and each individual is governed in part of his conduct by a reference to the political order, and in other parts by a reference to the spiritual order. On the other hand it is urged, and indeed it is undeniable, that the distinction is not a complete separation. Every spiritual rule has its secular aspect, and every secular rule its spiritual. Each power has an influence over the whole sphere of conduct, and it is idle to draw a line between theory and practice, inasmuch as all theory affects practice, and all practice is based upon theory. How are the conflicting claims of two powers to be reconciled when each affects the whole sphere of thought and conduct, without making one absolutely dependent upon the other?

This opens a wide field of controversy, upon which I must touch only so far as the doctrine of toleration is concerned. How are we to reconcile any such doctrine with the admission that the State must enforce certain kinds of conduct, that it must decide (unless it is to be absolutely dependent upon the Church, or, in other words, unless the Church is itself a State) what kinds of conduct it will enforce; and therefore that it may have to forbid practices commended by the Church, or to punish men, indirectly at least, for religious opinions — that is, to persecute? We may argue against the expediency in particular cases; but how can we lay down a general principle?

Before answering, I must begin by one or two preliminary considerations. The existence of any society whatever clearly presupposes an agreement to obey certain elementary rules, and therefore the existence of a certain desire for order and respect for constituted authority. Every society also contains antisocial elements, and must impose penalties upon antisocial conduct. It can, of course, deal with a small part only of such conduct. It can punish murder, but not ill-will. And further, though it cannot punish all immorality, it may punish no conduct which is not immoral. The criminal law covers only a part of the field of the moral law, and may nowhere extend beyond it. The efficacy, again, of all State action depends upon the existence of the organic instincts which have been evolved in its growth. Churches, like all other forms of association, depend upon the existence of similar instincts or sentiments, some of which are identical with those upon which the State is also founded, whilst others are not directly related to any particular form of political organisation. Many different churches may arise, corresponding to differences of belief upon questions of the highest importance, of which the members may yet be capable of uniting for political purposes, and of membership of the same State. Agnostics, Protestants, and Catholics may agree to hang murderers and enforce contracts, though they go to different churches, and some of them to no church at all; or hold the most contradictory opinions about the universe at large. The possibility, within some undefined limits, is proved by experience; but can we define the limits or deny the contrary possibility? May not a Church be so constituted that membership is inconsistent with membership of the State? If a creed says 'Steal,' must not believers go to prison? If so, and if the State be the sole judge on such points, do we not come back to persecution?

I reply, first, that the difficulty is in one way exaggerated, and in the way which greatly affects the argument. Respect, for example, for human life or for property represents different manifestations of that essential instinct which is essential to all social development. Unless murderers and thieves were condemned and punished, there could be no society, but only a barbarous chaos. These are fundamental points which are and must be settled before the problem of toleration can even be raised. The ethical sentiment which condemns such crimes must exist in order that priests and policemen may exist. It is not a product, but a precedent condition, of their activity. The remark is needed because it is opposed to a common set of theories and phrases. Theologians of one class are given to assert that morality is the creation of a certain set of dogmas. which have somehow dropped out of the skies. The prejudice against theft, for example, is due to the belief, itself due to revelation — that is, to a communication from without — that thieves will have their portion in the lake of fire. So long as this theory, or one derived from it, holds its ground, we are liable to the assumption that all morality is dependent upon specific beliefs about facts, of which we may or may not be ignorant, and has therefore something essentially arbitrary about it. It is a natural consequence that religion may change in such a way as to involve a reversal of the moral law, and therefore a total incompatibility between the demands of the religion and the most essential conditions of social life. I hold, though I cannot here attempt to justify the principle, that this represents a complete inversion of cause and effect; that morality springs simply from the felt need of human beings living in society; that religious beliefs spring from and reflect the prevalent moral sentiment instead of producing it as an independent cause; that a belief that murderers will be damned is the effect and not the cause of our objection to murder. There is doubtless an intimate connection between the two beliefs. In the intellectual stage at which hell seems a reasonable hypothesis, we cannot express our objection to murder without speaking in terms of hell-fire. But the hell is created by that objection when present to minds at a certain stage; and not a doctrine communicated from without and generating the objection. From this it follows that the religious belief which springs from the moral sentiments (amongst other conditions) cannot as a rule be in conflict with them, or with the corollaries deduced from them by the legislator. In other words, agreement between the State and the Church as to a very wide sphere of conduct must be the rule, because the sentiment upon which their vitality depends springs from a common root, and depends upon general conditions independent of special beliefs and forms of government. In spite of these considerations, the difficulty may undoubtedly occur. A religion may command criminal practices, and even practices inconsistent with the very existence of the society. Nihilists and communists may order men to steal or slay. Are they to be permitted to attack the State because they attack it in the name of religion? The answer, of course, is plain. Criminals must be punished, whatever their principle. The fact that a god commands an action does not make it moral. There are very immoral gods going about whose followers must be punished for obeying their orders.

Belief in his gods is no excuse for the criminal. It only shows that his moral ideas are confused. If the god has no better principles than a receiver of stolen goods, his authority gives no better justification for the act. The punishment does not transgress the principle that none but immoral acts should be punished, unless we regard morality as a mere name for actions commanded by invisible beings. Nor, leaving this for the moment, is this properly a case of persecution. Toleration implies that a man is to be allowed to profess and maintain any principles that he pleases; not that he should be allowed in all cases to act upon his principles, especially to act upon them to the injury of others. No limitation whatever need be put upon this principle in the case supposed. I, for one, am fully prepared to listen to any arguments for the propriety of theft or murder, or, if it be possible, of immorality in the abstract. No doctrine, however well established, should be protected from discussion. The reasons have been already assigned. If, as a matter of fact, any appreciable number of persons is inclined to advocate murder on principle, I should wish them to state their opinions openly and fearlessly, because I should think that the shortest way of exploding the principle and of ascertaining the true causes of such a perversion of moral sentiment. Such a state of things implies the existence of evils which cannot be really cured till their cause is known, and the shortest way to discover the cause is to give a hearing to the alleged reasons. Of course, this may lead to very difficult points of casuistry. We cannot always draw the line between theory and practice. An attack upon the evils of landed property, delivered in a certain place and time, may mean — shoot this particular landlord. In all such cases, it can only be said that the issue is one of fact. It is most desirable that the principles upon which property in land can be defended should be thoroughly discussed. It is most undesirable that any landlord should be assassinated. Whether a particular speech is really a part of the general discussion, or an act in furtherance of a murderous conspiracy, is a question to be decided by the evidence in the case. Sometimes it may be almost impossible to draw the line; I only urge that it should he drawn in conformity with the general rule. The propriety of every law should be arguable; but whilst it is the law, it must be enforced.

This brings us to a further difficulty. Who, it is asked, is to decide these cases? The State is to punish acts which are inconsistent with its existence or immoral. But if the State is to decide, its decision is ultimate; and it may decide, for example, as Cromwell decided, that the Mass was an immoral ceremony, and therefore as much to be suppressed as an act of theft. Simply to traverse the statement of fact would be insufficient. If we merely deny the immorality of the Mass, we say that Cromwell was mistaken in his facts, not that his conduct was immoral in itself. He was mistaken, as he would have been mistaken had he supposed that the congregation was collected to begin a political rising, when it simply came together for a religious ceremonial. The objection (if we may fairly judge Cromwell by a modern standard, which need not be here considered) is obviously different. It assumes that the suppression of the Mass was an act done in restraint of opinion. Nobody alleged that the Mass had any other ill consequences than its tendency to encourage the spread of a religion. A simple act of idolatry is not of itself injurious to my neighbour. I am not injured because, you being a fool, do an act of folly which is nothing but an open avowal of your folly. The intention of the persecutor was to restrain the spread of an opinion by terror; and just so far as that was the intention, it was an act of intolerance. It is easy to put different cases. If, for example, a creed commanded human sacrifices, it might be (I should say that it would be) right to suppress an antisocial practice. The murder would not be justified because of the invisible accomplice, though he were called a god. The action should therefore be punished, though we ought not to punish the promulgation of an argument in favour of the practice, nor to punish other harmless practices dictated by the same creed. But in the case of the Mass, the conduct would be admittedly harmless in every other respect than in its supposed effect upon opinion. The bare act of eating a wafer with certain ceremonies only became punishable because the actor attached to it, and encouraged others to attach to it, a particular religious significance. Restraint of opinion, or of its free utterance, by terror is the essence of persecution, and all conduct intended to achieve that purpose is immoral. The principle is entirely consistent with the admission that a legislator must decide for himself whether or not that is the real tendency of his legislation. There is no appeal from the Legislature, and therefore it must decide in the last resort. But it does not follow that a court from which there is no appeal follows no rules in fact, nor that all its decisions are morally right. In laying down such a principle, or any other first principle, we are not proposing a rule which can be enforced by any external authority. It belongs to a sphere which is antecedent to all legislation. We say simply that a legislator will accept it so far as he legislates upon sound principles. Nor is it asserted that the principle is always free from ambiguity in its applications. Granting that persecution is wrong, it may still be a fair question whether this or that law implies persecution. There may be irreconcilable differences of opinion. The legislator may declare that a particular kind of conduct is immoral, or, in other words, that the practice is irreconcilable with the essential conditions of social welfare. The priest may assert that it is commanded by his deity, and moreover that it is really moral in the same sense in which the legislator declares it to be immoral. Who is to decide? The principle of toleration does not of itself answer that question. It only lays down certain conditions for conducting the argument. It decides that the immorality must consist in something else than the evil tendency of any general doctrine. A man must not be punished for openly avowing any principles whatever. Any defence of the proposed rule is irrelevant unless it contains an allegation that the punishment is inflicted for something else than a defence of opinion. And further, if agreement be still impossible, the principle does not say who is to give the decision; it only lays down a condition as to the mode of obtaining the decision. In the last resort, we may say, the question must be fought out, but it must be fought out with fair weapons. The statesman, so long as he is seriously convinced, must uphold the law, but he must allow its policy and justice to be freely discussed. No statement can be made as to the result. The statesman appeals directly to one class of motives; the priest to others not identical, though not disparate. The ultimate success of one or the other will depend upon the constitution of the society, and the strength of all the various forces by which authority is supported and balanced. Toleration only ensures fair play, and implies the existence of conditions necessary for securing a possibility of ultimate agreement. The relevant issues are defined, though the question of fact remains for discussion. Even where brute force has the most unrestricted play, and rule is most decidedly based upon sheer terror, all power ultimately rests upon the belief and sentiments of the society. The advantage of toleration is to exclude that kind of coercion which tries to restrain opinion by sheer terror, and therefore by considerations plainly irrelevant to the truth of the opinions.

This leads to what are really the most difficult problems at the present day. No moral principle, I should say, and certainly not the principle of toleration, can lay down a distinct external criterion of right and wrong applicable at once to all concrete cases. No test, by the nature of the case, can be given which will decide at once whether a particular rule does or does not transgress the principle of toleration. This is especially true in the questions where the question of toleration is mixed up with the other question as to the proper limits of State interference. A great deal has been said, and very little has been decided, as to the latter problem. We may argue the propriety of the State undertaking the management of railways or interfering between labourers and capitalists, without considering the principle of toleration in the sense in which I have taken it. But when we come to such controversies as that about the Established Church or the national systems of education, the problem becomes more intricate. The briefest glance must suffice to show the bearing of my principles upon such problems. An Established Church was clearly open to objection on the ground of intolerance, so long as it was virtually and avowedly an organisation for propagating a faith. When it was supported on the ground that its doctrines were true, and dissent was regarded as criminal because heretical, persecution was accepted in principle and carried into practice. At the present day its advocates have abandoned this ground. All that can be said is that the State confers certain privileges upon, and assigns certain revenues to, persons who will discharge certain functions and accept certain tests. Dissenters, therefore, are excluded from the privileges on account of their faith. But it may be urged that the functions discharged by the Church are useful to the people in general, even to unbelievers, and that in the opinion of unbelievers themselves. And, again, it is argued that the formularies of the Church are maintained not as true but simply as expressing the opinions of the majority. There is no direct persecution, for any one may dissent as much as he pleases, and (unless he is Mr. Foote) attack any doctrines whatever. The existence of such an institution must of course act to some extent as a bribe, if not as a threat; but implies so little of direct intolerance that it is frequently defended expressly and sincerely on the ground that it is favourable to freedom of thought. To argue all the issues here suggested would require a treatise. I should certainly hold that so long as an Establishment exists, the free play of opinion is trammelled, in spite of some plausible arguments to the contrary. But I certainly hold also that it is impossible to condemn an Establishment purely and simply on the ground of toleration, without doing violence to fair argument. All that can be said is that questions of toleration are here involved, along with many other questions possibly of more importance in this particular case, and I am not prepared to cut the knot by any unqualified assertion. And this is equally true of national education. It does not necessarily imply any intolerance whatever. Not only may it be possible or easy in many cases to solve the problem by giving an education which all sects approve, and to leave the religious education to each sect; but there is another consideration. Toleration implies that each man must have a right to say what he pleases. It does not imply a right both to impress his own doctrines upon other people and to exclude the influence of other teachers. If I take the child of a Protestant and bring him up as a Catholic, or *vice versâ*, I am guilty undoubtedly of a gross act of tyranny. But I am not necessarily more intolerant than if I decided that a slave was to be educated by the State instead of by his master. The moral question falls under a different head. The Legislature in such a case is altering the relation between parents and children. It is handing over to others the authority over the children hitherto possessed by their parents. This is a very grave and, beyond narrow limits, a most objectionable proceeding, but it is not objectionable as intolerant. It is simply changing one kind of influence for another. The parent's right to his own opinions and their utterance is not the same as his right to instil them into other minds; the tyranny implied is the tyranny of limiting his power over his children; and that limitation, upon other ground, may be most oppressive. But if the child was sent to a school where he was allowed to hear all opinions, and his parents had access to him amongst others, he would clearly be freer to form his own creed, and, so far, there would be more room for the free play of opinion. To give the rule over him exclusively to his parents is so far to sanction private intolerance, though for other reasons this may be fully justifiable. The question of intolerance is raised at a different point. If, for example, one creed should be favoured at the expense of others, if all the schools of a country should be Protestant whilst some of the people were Catholic, we should clearly have a case of limiting opinion by force; and so, if any uniform creed were prescribed by the State, all dissenters might complain of persecution. It may further be urged that some such result is a natural result of a State system. I do not argue the question, which I only notice to show how the simple doctrine of toleration may be mixed up with other problems, here, for example, with the enormously important question of the proper limits of parental authority, which render impossible any off-hand decision. The principle of toleration may be simple; the importance of so organising society that it may be carried out without exceptions is enormous; but it is not the sole principle of conduct, and in a complex condition of society, full of fragments of institutions which have more or less deviated from their original functions, we must sometimes be content with an imperfect application, and permit it to be overridden by other principles which spring from the same root of social utility, and cannot be brought into harmony with it without changes which, for the moment, are impracticable.

How far, then, does the principle, thus understood, differ from the simple doctrine of expediency, and therefore exclude the admission that we have in every case to decide by the calculation of consequences? The final reply to this question will sum up what I have to say by indicating what I take to be the weakness or inadequacy of the simple utilitarian doctrine. I entirely agree with Mill that conduct is proved to be immoral by proving it to be mischievous, or, in other words, productive of a balance of misery. But I hold that his neglect of the conditions of social development deprives his argument of the necessary coherency. For the reasons already set forth, I say that toleration becomes possible and desirable at a certain stage of progress. If this condition be overlooked or insufficiently recognised, we fall into two errors. The advocate of toleration tries to prove that persecution is bad, irrespectively of this condition, and therefore that it was bad at the earliest as well as the latest stages. Since this is not true, and therefore cannot be proved, his argument seems to break down; and so we find that the arguments from history are indiscriminately joined, and that the advocates of persecution argue as if precedents drawn from primitive social stages were applicable without modification to the latest. They frequently try to defend this explicitly by assuming that human nature is always the same, and inferring that, if people once argued with the fist, we must always use that controversial weapon. That human nature always attains certain fundamental properties may be fully granted; but if this inference be sound, civilisation, which consists in great measure in learning to limit the sphere of brute force, must be an illusory phenomenon. From my point of view, on the other hand, the recognition that society does in fact grow is an essential point of the case. When we have to deal with the later stages, Mill's argument fails of cogency just so far as he treats its essential characteristics as though they were mere accidents. So, as we have seen, he says, virtually, that persecution may be effective in suppressing an opinion; and passes lightly over the consideration of the real meaning of this 'may be.' It 'may be' efficient if it is so vigorous as to choke thought as well as to excise particular results of thought, and if therefore a political organisation exists which becomes altogether impossible as society advances beyond a certain stage. But when we restore the condition thus imperfectly indicated to its proper place in the argument, Mill's arguments, cogently stated already, acquire fresh cogency. At that stage toleration becomes an essential condition of development, and therefore it becomes at the same time an essential condition of promoting happiness. Given such a social organisation as exists at present, the only kind of persecution which is possible is that which is condemned by every one as ineffectual. To persecute without suppressing, to stimulate hypocrisy without encouraging faith, is clearly to produce suffering without compensating advantage. Persecution is an anachronism and becomes a blunder, and upon this showing it is so palpably impolitic and therefore immoral that even a theoretical advocate of persecution admits that it is wicked under the conditions. The chief point of difference is that he does not recognise the necessity of the conditions, or fancies that he implicitly gets rid of them by saying that he dislikes them.

This suggests one further explanation. You assume, it is said, that progress is a blessing. We prefer the mediæval, or the pagan or the savage state of society, and deny that progress deserves the admiration lavished upon it by professors of claptrap. I make no such assumption, whatever my private opinion; I simply allege the fact of progress as showing historically what is the genesis of toleration, and therefore the conditions under which it has become essential. But whether progress be a good or a bad thing, whether men are happier or less happy than monkeys, the argument is unaffected. Perhaps a child is happier than a man; but a man does not therefore become happier by adopting childish modes of life. When society is at a given stage, you cannot restore the previous stage, nor can you adopt the old methods. The modes by which society progresses determine a certain organisation, and when that exists it becomes an essential part of the problem. It is still possible to be intolerant; but it is not possible to restore the conditions under which intolerance could be carried out as a principle, and therefore you can only tease and hamper and irritate without gaining any proportional advantage, if any advantage whatever. Even if there be a period at which it is still possible to arrest progress, you do not ensure a maintenance of the existing stage, but rather ensure actual decay. The choice is not between advancing and standing still, but between growing and rotting; and the bitterest denouncers of progress may think it less objectionable than actual decline. We have fortunately advanced beyond that period; and may therefore say that, given the existing order, toleration is not merely conducive on the average, but is unconditionally and necessarily conducive to happiness. I do not of course deny that in this, as in all moral principles, there may not be found, here and there, exceptional cases which may amuse a casuist; but they can be only such rare cases as might cause doubt to one thoroughly convinced of the essential importance of a complete permeation of society by tolerant principles. Something, indeed, remains to be done, perhaps much, before the principle can be thoroughly carried. There is a region of difficulties or anomalies not yet cleared up. Toleration, in fact, as I have understood it, is a necessary correlative to a respect for truthfulness. So far as we can lay it down as an absolute principle that every man should be thoroughly trustworthy and therefore truthful, we are bound to respect every manifestation of truthfulness. In many cases a man's opinions are really determined by his character, and possibly by bad characteristics. He holds a certain creed because it flatters him as a cowardly or sensual or selfish animal. In that case it is hard, but it is right, to distinguish between our disapproval of the passions, and our disapproval of the open avowal of the doctrines which spring from them. The virtue of truthfulness was naturally recognised in particular cases before the virtue of toleration. It was obviously necessary to social welfare that men should be able to trust each other, and, therefore, that in all private relations a man's word should be as good as his bond. The theory was virtually limited by the understanding that there were certain opinions which could not be uttered without endangering the social order. If an avowal of disbelief in the gods necessarily meant disloyalty, the heretic was punishable upon that ground, whatever might be thought of his virtue. The conflict began as soon as a respect for such sincerity was outraged by a punishment still held to be necessary. It is solved when society is organised in such a way that this necessity is removed; when, therefore, the outrage is not compensated even apparently, and the suppression of free utterance is seen to be in itself an inappropriate mode of meeting the difficulty. It is clenched by the spread of a general conviction that the only safe basis for any theory is the encouragement of its full discussion from every point of view. By a strange inconsistency, toleration is still sometimes denounced even by acute reasoners as a product of absolute scepticism. It may spring from scepticism as to the particular doctrines enforced; but it is certainly inseparable from the conviction, the reverse of sceptical, that truth is attainable, and only attainable, by the free play of intelligence. Toleration, it is said, is opposed to the 'principle of authority;' as if there could be a principle of authority in the abstract! To say that we are to accept authority in the abstract is to say that we are to believe anything that anybody tells us: that is, to believe direct contradictions. It is in fact opposed to any authority which does not rest upon the only possible ground of rational authority — the gradual agreement of inquirers free from all irrelevant bias, and therefore from the bias of sheer terror of the evils inflicted by persons of different opinion.

The principle, I have said, is not yet fully developed. Intolerance of the crudest kind is discredited, and has come to be regarded as wicked. It is admittedly wrong to burn any man because he does not think as I think. But there are the cases already noticed, in which, though heretical opinion is not punishable as such, it carries with it certain disqualifications or is marked by a certain stigma in consequence of institutions not exclusively designed for that purpose. Such anomalies may be gradually removed, but they cannot be adequately discussed under the simple heading of tolerance. We are, in regard to them, in the same position as our ancestors in regard to the primary questions of toleration. The concrete facts are still so ravelled that we have (if I may say so) to make a practical abstraction before we can apply the abstract theory. And, besides this, further corollaries may be suggested. It is a recognised duty not to punish people for expressing opinion; but it is not a recognised duty to let our opinions be known. The utterance of our creed is taken to be a right, not a duty. And yet there is a great deal to be said for objecting to passive as well as active reticence. If every man thought it a duty to profess his creed openly, he would be doing a service not only by helping to remove the stigma which clings to unpopular creeds, but very frequently by making the discovery that his opinions, when articulately uttered, were absurd, and the ground upon which they are formed ludicrously inadequate. A man often excuses himself for bigotry because he locks it up in his own breast instead of openly avowing it. Brought into daylight, he might see its folly and recognise the absurdity of the principle which makes it a duty to be dogmatic about propositions which we are palpably unable to understand or appreciate. If, however, the right of holding one's tongue be still considered as sacred, though it seems to be justified only by the remnant of the bigotry directed against free speech, there is an application of the principle in the sphere of politics which requires explicit notice. The doctrine of toleration requires a positive as well as a negative statement. It is not only wrong to burn a man on account of his creed, but it is right to encourage the open avowal and defence of every opinion sincerely maintained. Every man who says frankly and fully what he thinks is so far doing a public service. We should be grateful to him for attacking most unsparingly our most cherished opinions. I do not say that we should be grateful to him for attacking them by unfair means. Proselytism of all varieties is to my mind a detestable phenomenon; for proselytism means, as I understand it, the attempt to influence opinion in an underhand way, by appeals to the passions which obscure reason or by mere personal authority. The only way in which one human being can properly attempt to influence another is the encouraging him to think for himself instead of endeavouring to instil ready-made doctrines into his mind. Every sane person of course should respect the authority of more competent inquirers than himself, and not less in philosophical or religious than in scientific questions. But he should learn to respect because the authority is competent, not because it is that of some one whom he respects for reasons which have nothing to do with such competence.

The ultimate ground for any belief should be understood to be the fact that it can stand the freest possible discussion from every possible point of view. And, for this reason, I confess that I am quite unable to accept the excuses put forward in the case of the recent sentences for blasphemous libel. So far as the offenders were brutal or indecent in their language, or obtruded insults upon 'unwilling ears and eyes,' I of course admit that they were acting wrongly, and may have been obnoxious to the strongest possible language of moral reprobation. But it seems impossible to reconcile the infliction of a severe punishment with the theory that the manner alone was punishable and the matter perfectly justifiable. If I sincerely hold that a man is right in expressing his opinions and attacking my own so long as he does it decently; and further that he is not only exercising a right but discharging a duty in attacking what he holds to be a mischievous error, I find it very hard to say that he ought to be punished merely for the manner. Of course, an insult to any creed uttered in such a time and place as to provoke a breach of the peace should be restrained like any other provocation of the kind; and the measure of the appropriate punishment depends upon the tendency to produce the specific result. But, in this case, it is clear that the evil is simply the injury to the feelings of believers. Now, it is in the first place clear that a man may say things in all seriousness which hurt my feelings all the more because they are decently expressed. If I am seriously persuaded that Mahomet was a vile impostor, I can hardly convey my opinion to a Mahommedan in an agreeable way; and yet Christians will admit that it may be my duty to convey it, in proper time and place. It is very difficult, to say the least, to distinguish between the intrinsic offensiveness of certain opinions and the accidental aggravation in the mode of utterance, and difficult, therefore, to punish the offence without punishing the legitimate utterance. And hence, in the next place, it seems that the offensiveness of manner belongs to that kind of immorality which can best be suppressed by public opinion. A man who is brutal in language injures his own cause by his mode of advocacy, and that injury is the proper penalty for his offence. Brutal abuse is common enough in political controversy, and when it is not a provocation to violence it is rightly left to its own inevitable consequences. Nobody has done more service to Mr. Gladstone than some of his virulent denouncers.

If, in short, we really and sincerely held that the utterance of all opinions, orthodox or the reverse, was not only permissible but desirable; and wished to restrain only that kind of utterance which is needlessly offensive — whether offensive to Christians or infidels, Protestants or Catholics — we should, I imagine, be forced to the conclusion that criminal laws should not be called into play to punish people for outrages upon good taste, but only for directly inciting to violence. The fact that an opinion is offensive to a majority is so far a reason for leaving it to public opinion, which in most cases is perfectly capable of taking care of itself; and we are certainly not impartial or really tolerant till we are equally anxious to punish one of the majority for insulting the minority. But I am straying too far from the general question; and only wish to point out that a hearty acceptance of the principle of toleration, and a genuine recognition of the fact that a man is entitled to more than mere impunity when he attacks an established creed, would lead to some practical consequences not yet recognised.

LESLIE STEPHEN